THE CHICKASAWS

The Civilization of the American Indian Series

THE
CHICKASAWS

By
ARRELL M. GIBSON

Norman and London
University of Oklahoma Press

By Arrell M. Gibson

The Kickapoos: Lords of the Middle Border (Norman, 1963)
The Life and Death of Colonel Albert Jennings Fountain (Norman, 1965)
Fort Smith: Little Gibraltar on the Arkansas (with Edwin C. Bearss) (Norman, 1969)
The Chickasaws (Norman, 1971)
Wilderness Bonanza: The Tri-State District of Missouri, Kansas, and Oklahoma (Norman, 1972)
(Editor) *Frontier Historian: The Life and Work of Edward Everett Dale.*
The Oklahoma Story (Norman, 1978)
Oklahoma: A History of Five Centuries (Second Edition, Norman, 1981)
The Santa Fe and Taos Colonies: Age of the Muses, 1900–1942 (Norman, 1983)
The History of Oklahoma (Norman, 1984)

Library of Congress Catalog Card Number: 76–145499
ISBN: 0–8061–1042–2

The Chickasaws is Volume 109 in The Civilization of the American Indian Series.

8   9   10   11   12   13   14   15   16   17   18   19   20   21   22

DEDICATORY

Sam Gibson

Brother mine and mankind
   Artist, raconteur
Blithe spirit and simple trust
   Living in a rush
Missing naught, tasting all
   Strong in Life, bravest at Death's door
His legacy—paintings, humor, kindness, serenity

ACKNOWLEDGMENTS

This Chickasaw Nation narrative is possible largely because of the kindness and interest of many persons. Special recognition and gratitude are extended to Mrs. Laura Harrell, Mississippi State Archives; Mrs. Frank Owsley, Tennessee State Library and Archives; Miss Opal Carr, Mrs. Eunice Edmunds, Lee Carter, and Vynola Newkumet, University of Oklahoma Library; Mrs. Marie Keene and the late and beloved Hope Holway, Gilcrease Museum Library; Alice Timmons and Jack Haley, Western History Collections, University of Oklahoma Library; and Mrs. Rella Looney and Miss Muriel H. Wright, Oklahoma Historical Society. Appreciation is expressed to Shirley Black for research and editorial assistance, and Larna Stiffler and Linda Thomas for typing the manuscript. And I am indebted to Professor Duane Roller and the University of Oklahoma Faculty Research Committee, Boyce Timmons, Director of the University of Oklahoma Duke Indian History Project, and Professor Keever Greer, Director of the Stovall Museum at the University of Oklahoma for grants and other research assistance. A special word of recognition and appreciation must go to Mrs. June Witt, who managed a busy schedule for me and so capably assumed many duties which provided me precious research and writing time. Likewise, gratitude is expressed to the American Philosophical Society for a grant which financed much of the research in this work.

ARRELL M. GIBSON

Norman, Oklahoma

CONTENTS

ILLUSTRATIONS

MAPS

THE CHICKASAWS

CHAPTER ONE

CHICKASAW ETHNOHISTORY: A RECONSTRUCTION

BY the beginning of the nineteenth century, the Chickasaw Nation was in the throes of a comprehensive metamorphosis from the natural state to a general acceptance and application of the ways of Western civilization. One can better appreciate the drastic alterations which occurred in tribal social, economic, and spiritual life by first taking a look at the Chickasaws in their natural milieu. Two broad classes of sources make it possible to produce a generally satisfying reconstruction of this tribe's way of life in nature. One is the extensive body of reports by archaeologists and anthropologists. Their investigations yield professional and critically derived information which illuminates early Chickasaw life and practice. The writings of European agents and traders who resided in the Chickasaw Nation during the eighteenth century comprise another rich source. These men were, in a sense, on-the-spot witnesses to Chickasaw natural ways. Perceptive ones like James Adair not only appreciated their natural ways and went to great length to record them, but also detected the ferment of change which European innovations were bringing to Chickasaw life. Adair expressed nostalgic regret at the emerging disintegration of Chickasaw old ways: "We know by long observation, that, from the time our traders settled among them, they are every year more corrupt in their morals," not only in long-practiced taboos, but in many "religious customs of their forefathers."[1]

A synthesis of these reports and writings reveals that the Chickasaw tribe was a component of a vast ethnological province

---

[1] James Adair, *The History of the American Indians* (edited and with an introduction by Samuel C. Williams), 17.

3

bounded by the Ohio River on the north, the Gulf of Mexico on the south, and the Mississippi River on the west. Their early neighbors included the Choctaws, Natchez, Creeks, and Cherokees. Most Chickasaw lifeways resembled those of their neighbors. John R. Swanton, principal investigator of the Chickasaws and other southeastern tribes, has concluded that the material culture of these tribes was similar and that only a "few . . . local peculiarities" existed.[2]

The Chickasaws' closest cultural affinity was the Choctaws. Some authorities hold that at one time the Chickasaws were an integral part of the Choctaw tribe. The Choctaw-Chickasaw language, except for mild dialectal differences, is the same.[3] Their language, the Muskhogean, was described as "very agreeable to the ear, courteous, gentle and musical; the letter R is not sounded in one word of their language; the women in particular so fine and musical, as to represent the singing of birds; and when heard and not seen, one might imagine it to be the prattling of young children. The men's speech is indeed more strong and sonorous, but not harsh and in no instance guttural and I believe the letter R is not used to express any word in any language of the [Muskhogean] confederacy."[4]

The Chickasaw population ranged between an estimated thirty-five hundred and forty-five hundred, making it a relatively small Indian community when compared to the populous Choctaws who numbered perhaps over twenty thousand on the eve of European contact. The Chickasaws' strong warrior tradition and propensity for war had curious effects on the tribe's demographic composition. Population losses in combat were replaced by adoption of captives, absorption of small tribes residing on the periphery of the Chickasaw homeland, and, in one case, the reception of a remnant of the formerly populous and powerful Natchez after their near annihilation by a French army in 1730.[5]

---

2 John R. Swanton, "Social and Religious Beliefs and Usages of the Chickasaw Indians," *B.A.E. 44 Ann. Rept.* 173.

3 Interview with Muriel H. Wright, Oklahoma City, Oklahoma, July 18,1968.

4 William Bartram, *Travels Through North and South Carolina, Georgia, East and West Florida,* 517.

5 John R. Swanton, *The Indian Tribes of North America,* B.A.E. *Bulletin 145,* 179.

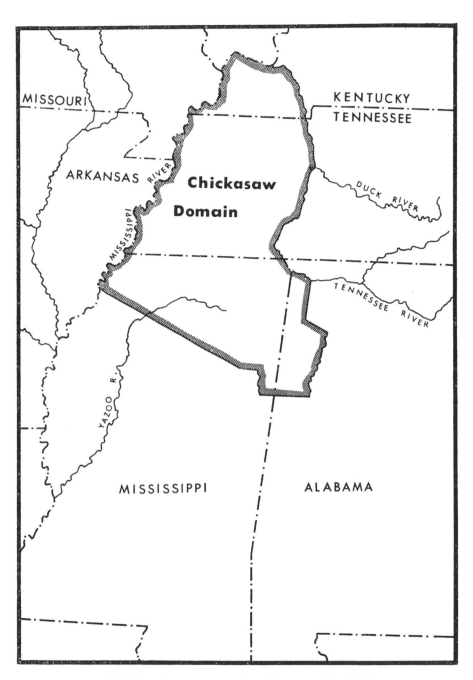

ANCIENT CHICKASAW DOMAIN

The early Chickasaw domain extended from the Tennessee-Cumberland divide north to the Ohio River and west to the Mississippi River, astride western Kentucky and Tennessee and northern Alabama and Mississippi. Chickasaws used most of this vast province as a hunting range. Their first settlements east of the Mississippi River, according to tribal legend, were situated near the Tennessee River in Madison County, Alabama, at the original Chickasaw Old Fields. In later times the tribe relocated Chickasaw Old Fields in northeastern Mississippi near the headwaters of the Tombigbee River where their settlements remained concentrated until the federal government removed the tribe to Indian Territory during the 1830's.[6]

Near the close of the seventeenth century, the Chickasaws occupied seven towns in the forests and upland prairies of the Tombigbee watershed. The tribal capital was at Chukafalaya, called Long Town by the British and Old Pontotoc by early American settlers. During the 1750's Chukafalaya contained over two hundred households. Akia, situated on a commanding ridge near Plymouth, was the principal military town. Its fortifications guarded approaches to the other Chickasaw towns. The Chickasaws were an expansive and restless people, and while the tribe as a whole maintained permanent residence in the Tombigbee watershed during the late prehistoric and most of the historic period, Chickasaw bands ranged eastward nearly to the Atlantic and west to the edge of the Great Plains. Their settlement patterns were determined by relations with other tribes and the Europeans. During periods of relative peace, they scattered across their country in small villages, at times into northwestern Alabama. At least two Chickasaw bands established semipermanent villages on the Savannah River in South Carolina and Georgia. In time of war, either with the other tribes or the French, the Chickasaws made their settlements more compact. The Chickasaw depredation range extended south to the Gulf of Mexico, up the Arkansas and Red River valleys in the trans-Mississippi region, and north of the Ohio River.[7]

[6] Robert S. Cotterill, *The Southern Indians: The Story of the Civilized Tribes Before Removal*, 7.

[7] John R. Swanton, *The Indians of the Southeastern United States*, B.A.E. Bulletin 137, 117.

One observer, in characterizing the southeastern tribes, called the Chickasaws the "Spartans" of the lower Mississippi valley, for "martial virtue, and not riches" was their only "standard for preferment." Chickasaw men were hunters and fighters first and agriculturalists only on occasion. Their women and Indian slaves performed the menial tasks of clearing land, caring for crops, and gathering firewood. Early visitors described Chickasaw warriors as "tall, well-built people," with reddish brown skin, raven black hair, and large, dark eyes, their actions exhibiting a superior and independent air. The women and older men wore their hair long. The warrior hairstyle was to shave the sides of the head, leaving a roach or crest which the wearer soaked with bear grease. Both men and women plucked all hair from their faces and bodies with tweezers made in early times of clam shells and later of wire. Chickasaw warriors painted their faces for ceremonies and war, the color and design indicating their clan association. They wore ear and nose ornaments and decorated their heads and shoulders with eagle feathers and a mantle of white swan feathers, the ultimate badge sought by every warrior.

James Adair, long-time trader among the Chickasaws and their chief advocate, was struck by the warriors' strength and endurance. He described them as exceedingly swift of foot: "In a long chase they will stretch away, through the rough woods, by the bare track, for two or three hundred miles, in pursuit of a flying enemy, with the continued speed, and eagerness, of a staunch pack of blood hounds, till they shed blood." Bernard Romans, an early visitor to the Tombigbee towns, was not as complimentary of the Chickasaws as was Adair. While granting that they were excellent hunters, expert swimmers, and fierce warriors, and were well made and powerful, Romans claimed that the Chickasaw warriors also were haughty, insolent, lazy, cruel, "filthy in their discourse," and "corrupt in their morals."[8]

Europeans described Chickasaw women as "beautiful ànd clean." They gave much attention to their appearance, "never

[8] Jean-Bernard Bossu, *Travels in the Interior of North America, 1751–1762* (translated and edited by Seymour Feiler), 172; Bartram, *Travels*, 481; and Adair, *History of the American Indians*, 5; Paul Weer, *Preliminary Notes on the Muskhogean Family*, 272; also see Bernard Romans, *A Concise Natural History of East and West Florida.*

forgetting to anoint, and tie up their hair, except in time of mourning," and bathed daily except during periods of menstrual seclusion. The basic male garment was the breechcloth; in the heat of summer their only clothing with a shirt of dressed deerskin. Long shaggy garments of panther, deer, bear, beaver, and otter skins, the fleshy side out, warmed them in winter. Hunters wore deerskin boots reaching to the thigh to protect against brambles and thorny thickets. Chickasaw women wore dresses made from skins sewed together with fishbone needles and deer sinews. In winter they wrapped themselves in buffalo-calf skins "with wintery shagged wool inward." After English traders brought cloth to the Chickasaw towns, native women made a loose petticoat, fastened with leather belt and brass buckle, which reached "only to their hams, in order to shew their exquisitely fine proportioned limbs." The women made shoes for their families from skins of deer, bear, and elk, carefully tanned and smoked to prevent hardening.[9]

The Chickasaw living mode was simple and steeped in nature. Their life cycle, institutions, and activities were expressed, to some degree, in religious terms. Chickasaw religion explained, interpreted, and provided answers for the mystifying aspects of life processes—birth, puberty, marriage, and death—and natural phenomena. Their methods for relating themselves to nature and one another were crystallized in set patterns or practices. All things in the Chickasaw universe had natural and religious overtones. Like other Indian tribes in the native state, the Chickasaws had no written language. Thus the tribal elders transmitted traditions, customs, lore, and accumulated knowledge to the young orally and by example.[10]

This tribe's immersal in nature was demonstrated by their method for calculating time, which was based largely on lunar cycles. The first appearance of every new moon was a time of tribal observance and rejoicing. An early observer noted that on this occasion "they always repeat some joyful sounds, and stretch out their hands towards her." The Chickasaw year began at the

[9] Adair, *History of the American Indians*, 6–7; and Bossu, *Travels*, 172.
[10] John R. Swanton, "Aboriginal Culture of the Southeast," B.A.E. *42 Ann. Rept.*, 358.

first new moon of the vernal equinox. They divided the year into the four natural seasons, applying to each a descriptive designation: for autumn, "Fall of the Leaf." Chickasaw elders were the keepers of time and tribal lore generally. They numbered years by units of lunar months and seasons and commonly used "winters" to designate a span of years. The Chickasaws constructed primitive calendars consisting of knots on cords or thongs and notched sticks. Tribal leaders distributed these among headmen of the different towns to number the winters, moons, sleeps, days in travel, and the appointed time for a tribal council or for a campaign against the enemy. As each day passed, holders of the common calendar loosened a knot or cut a notch.[11]

The substance of Chickasaw religion was contained in their deity concept, creation epic, migration legend, and eschatology. Over all the Chickasaw natural and social universe was a supreme being—Ababinili—a composite force consisting of the Four Beloved Things Above, which were the Sun, Clouds, Clear Sky, and He that Lives in the Clear Sky. This composite force made all men out of the dust of mother earth. Its earthly agents performed various creative and service functions useful to the Chickasaws. The crawfish brought up earth from the bottom of the "universal watery waste" and formed the earth. Other creatures produced light, darkness, mountains, and forests. That part of the composite force closest to the Chickasaws was the Sun, the great holy fire above. It was represented in each town by a sacred fire. Guardian priests watched over this fire and dispensed coals for household fires. This had the effect of bringing the composite force into each home.[12]

---

[11] Adair, *History of the American Indians*, 78–81.

[12] Charles C. Jones, *The History of Georgia*, I, 383–85; Frank G. Speck, "Some Outlines of Aboriginal Culture in the Southeastern United States," *American Anthropologist*, n.s., Vol. IX (April–June, 1907), 294; and Swanton, *Indians of the Southeastern United States*, 776. Additions to Chickasaw religious beliefs, demonstrating the influence and impact of Western culture, include a latter-day account of the destruction of the world by a flood. Water covered all the earth. Some Chickasaws made rafts to save themselves. Creatures, like large white beavers, cut the thongs that bound the rafts. All drowned except one family and a pair each of all animals. After the flood a raven appeared with a part of an ear of corn. The Great Spirit told the Chickasaws to plant it. Eventually the earth would be destroyed by fire, its ruin presaged by a rain of blood and oil. Henry R. Schoolcraft, *Historical and Statistical Information Respecting the History, Condition and Prospects of the Indian Tribes of the United States*, Part I, 310.

In addition to the supreme composite force, the Chickasaw pantheon contained several lesser deities, the Hottuk Ishtohoollo and Hottuk Ookproose. The Hottuk Ishtohoollo were good spirits who inhabited the higher regions. The Hottuk Ookproose were evil spirits residing in the dark regions of the West. The Chickasaws also believed that certain supernatural beings resided in their immediate environment. These included Lofas and Iyaganashas. Lofas were giants, ten feet tall, who carried off women, beat men, and vexed the Chickasaws by driving deer away, hiding game from hunters, and causing personal disasters. Iyaganashas were little people, three feet tall, who helped the Chickasaws. They trained Indian doctors, transmitting to them their special curative powers, and taught hunters how to pursue and catch deer and other game. Chickasaws also believed in witches who took on various forms in nature. Like the Lofas, witches caused personal misfortune and illness.[13]

A basic part of the Chickasaw religious corpus was the tribe's migration legend. Each generation was instructed by tribal elders in the long and difficult search for the homeland ordained for the tribe by their deities. This search began at some remote prehistoric time when the Chickasaws resided in the land of the setting sun. Their guide was an oracular pole, carried on each day's march by the tribe's holy men. At night, as the tribe rested from its march through the wilderness, the priests placed the pole upright in the ground. During the night, stirred by mystical forces, the pole moved about. The direction it had assumed at each dawn served as a compass to guide the day's march. Almost without fail it commanded that they move toward the rising sun. Eventually the Chickasaws crossed the Mississippi River. Their sacred pole continued to direct them eastward until they arrived at another river, the Tennessee, where they camped. Next morning the pole was as erect as the holy men had placed it the night before. With great rejoicing the Chickasaws cleared the land, planted corn, and built settlements which became Chickasaw Old Fields. The holy men kept a vigil over the sacred pole, and,

---

[13] Adair, *History of the American Indians*, 38; and Swanton, *Social and Religious Beliefs and Usages of the Chickasaw Indians*, B.A.E. *44 Ann. Rept.*, 249–50.

after a time, it leaned westward. The Chickasaws answered its command, abandoning their towns on the Tennessee River and marching in the direction whence they came. In the Tombigbee highlands of northeastern Mississippi the pole again assumed a perpendicular position. The tribe set to work and restored Chickasaw Old Fields.[14]

Chickasaw eschatology included a belief in an existence after death and implied a judgment and consignment by the celestial composite force to a life of joy in the sky or a life of torment in the Chickasaw hell. Their mortuary practice and mourning formula were essential steps in preparing the departed for the journey to the judgment. When a person died, the family dug a grave inside his house. They washed the corpse, anointed the head with oil, painted the face red, and dressed him in his best clothes. His gun, ammunition, pipe, tobacco, and a supply of corn were buried with him. The body was placed in a sitting position facing west "for otherwise it was thought that the soul would lose its way." The mourning formula included extinguishing the fire in his house, removing all ashes, and starting a new fire. The formal mourning period lasted twelve moons for about two hours a day. The widow or widower wept over the grave just before sunup and sundown for a month. Women played an important role in the extended obsequies as mourners. Those skillful at lamentation wailed. Warriors shot arrows near the grave to keep off evil spirits. Relatives commonly slept over the grave to "awaken the memory of their dead with their cries" and if "killed by an enemy, this helped to irritate and set on fire such revengeful tempers to retaliate blood for blood." The Chickasaws believed that the ghosts of those slain in battle haunted the dwellings of the living until revenged. In the Chickasaw eschatology, souls of the dead trav-

---

[14] Swanton, "Social and Religious Beliefs and Usages of the Chickasaw Indians, *B.A.E. 44 Ann. Rept.*, 174–79. A version of the Chickasaw migration epic, which corroborates the claim that at one time the Chickasaws and Choctaws were one tribe, tells how two brothers, Chacta and Chicsa, led their respective clans or Iksas from the West, following a sacred pole. Just after the tribe crossed the Mississippi River, the two leaders reconnoitered the country. Chicsa moved first, followed ten days later by Chacta. A heavy snow covered Chicsa's trail, and the brothers were separated. Chicsa selected a homeland on the Tombigbee. Chacta led his people to the south. Harry Warren, "Chickasaw Traditions, Customs, etc.," *Publications of the Mississippi Historical Society*, Vol. VIII (1904), 543–45.

eled west to the judgment. Those who had been good ascended to the sky world to live with the Great Composite Force. Evil ones were consigned to the western quarter of the Chickasaw universe, "from which came witchcraft."[15]

The Chickasaws observed ceremonies, taboos, and sacrifices as religious exercises to placate and win the favor of the composite force and lesser deities. Their diagnosis of illness and healing practices were steeped with spiritual overtones. They explained natural phenomena in a celestial context. Most tribal legends, transmitted by priests and elders, were conspicuously religious in theme. The Chickasaw social system, based on clans and totemic associations, as well as tribal institutions, were suffused with divine ordinance.

The worldly intermediaries between the Chickasaws and their deities were two Beloved Holy Men, the Hopaye, one chosen from each of the two great divisions of the tribe. Lesser priests assisted the Hopaye in performing their sacred duties. These included presiding at tribal ceremonies, principally the busk festival and the picofa ritual; supervising observance of the holy ordinances of the Great Composite Force; and advising tribal leaders on questions of great moment.[16]

The busk festival was observed each year at the beginning of the first new moon when the green corn was ripe. The Hopaye and their attendants extinguished the old sacred fire, removed the

[15] WPA Historical Research Project, Source Material for Mississippi History: Pontotoc County, Vol. LVIII, Part I (1936–38), unpublished manuscript, unpaged; Swanton, *Indians of the Southeastern United States*, 776; Swanton, "Social and Religious Beliefs and Usages of the Chickasaw Indians," B.A.E. 44 Ann. Rept., 247; and Swanton, "Aboriginal Culture," B.A.E. 42 Ann. Rept., 710. An altered Chickasaw eschatology was presented in the middle of the nineteenth century by a tribal informant who claimed that the Chickasaws "believe in a great spirit, that they were created by him, but they do not believe in any punishment after death; they believe that the spirit will leave the body as soon as they die, and that it will assume the shape of the body, and move about among the Chickasaws in great joy." When a Chickasaw dies, "they put the finest clothing they have on him. Also all their jewelry, beads, etc.: this, they say, is to make a good appearance as soon as they die. The sick are frequently dressed before they die. They believe that the spirits of all the Chickasaws will go back to Mississippi, and join the spirits of those that have died there: and then all the spirits will return to the west before the world is destroyed by fire." Schoolcraft, *Historical and Statistical Information*, Part I, 310.

[16] Frank G. Speck, "Notes on Chickasaw Ethnology and Folk-Lore," *Journal of American Folk-Lore*, Vol. XX (January–March, 1907), 51.

ashes, and struck a new sanctified fire. On this primitive altar the priests offered a bit of tobacco, button snakeroot, and several ears of new corn to the fresh flames. After a two-day fast, the people drank an emetic of boiled cusseena, button snakeroot, or red root. This caused them to vomit, the purpose being to purge all evil from their bodies. Following purification, they feasted on roasting ears.[17]

Tribal leaders used this four-day observance to conduct all manner of national business. The Hopaye prepared and blessed the medicine to protect the people's health in the year ahead. Warriors who had distinguished themselves were recognized and awarded the white swan mantle. A general pardon was declared for all criminals except those accused of murder. The Hopaye and clan elders admonished parents to maintain honor in their households and instructed youth in tribal traditions and lore. Ball games and dancing provided a lighter side of this otherwise serious observance. The Chickasaw green corn festival was deity-ordained for national "renewal and perpetuation of health."[18]

A paraspiritual class in Chickasaw society, partaking of the great spiritual powers of the Hopaye, were the Aliktce—the healers. Their religious connection was derived from the Chickasaw belief that sickness was due to the invasion of the body by an animal spirit. It was the function of the healers to know the secret ways to exorcise the illness-bearing spirit and transfer it to another animal.[19]

Thus the Aliktce had to have the talent to blend their power over the spirit world with the accumulated Chickasaw *materia medica*. To be worthy of their office and to be effective as healers, the Aliktce had to be pure. This was accomplished by enclosing the candidates in "a hot house for four days, to live on amber, strong drink made of tobacco and water." Next, the preceptors brought them out, fed them corn gruel, and returned them to the hot house for four additional days after which they were "suffered to come out emaciated." Then, they were required "for twelve

[17] Adair, *History of the American Indians*, 105–17.

[18] Swanton, *Indians of the Southeastern United States*, 775.

[19] Speck, "Some Outlines of Aboriginal Culture," *American Anthropologist*, n.s., Vol. IX (April–June, 1907), 292.

moons [to] abstain from women, meat, fat, and strong drink."
Finally they were accredited healers.[20]

Helped by the Iyaganashas, the Aliktce learned to mix spiritual
formulas with secret knowledge of Chickasaw pharmacopoeia:
spice wood, ginseng, and cottonwood, sarsaparilla, huckleberry,
red willow, black locust, and button snakeroots, skunk tree bark,
mistletoe, yarrow, common dock, crushed melon seeds, ends of
cedar limbs, elder, mint, and cusseena, as well as various herbs
and berries. With these they compounded potions, teas, poultices,
emetics, and drenches. Their preparations, administered inter-
nally, treated toothache, stomach disorders, snakebite, headache,
dysentery and constipation, back and leg ache, cramps, fever,
swelling, the itch, and eye trouble. They had remedies for female
disorders and miscarriage preventives. Their incantation-treat-
ment formula required a gourd rattle, healing songs, and special
terpsichorean routines to deal with particular spirits. To exorcise
a disease-carrying spirit, they commonly danced

> three times round the sick person, contrary to the course of the
> sun. . . . Then they invoke the raven, and mimic his croaking
> voice. . . . They also place a basin of cold water with some pebbles
> in it on the ground near the patient; then they invoke the fish,
> because of its cool element, to cool the heat of the fever. Again
> they invoke the eagle; . . . they solicit him, as he soars in the
> heavens, to bring down refreshing things for their sick and not to
> delay them, as he can dart down upon the wing quick as a flash
> of lightning.[21]

The martial tradition of the Chickasaws required the healers to
spend much of their time treating battle casualties. Often the
Aliktce diagnosed a wounded warrior as "witch shot." After bathing the patient with a prepared solution, the Aliktce would "suck
and bite the skin, beginning at his forehead, and extending on the
face, neck and trunk to the navel, professing in that this way they
can suck out the witch ball."[22]

[20] Percy L. Rainwater, "Indian Missions and Missionaries," *Journal of Mississippi History*, Vol. XXVIII (February, 1966), 25.

[21] Adair, *History of the American Indians*, 181–82.

[22] Rainwater, "Indian Missions," *Journal of Mississippi History*, Vol. XXVIII
(February, 1966), 25.

The Picofa ceremony was an extended Chickasaw healing fast presided over by the Aliktce for the purpose of giving special treatment to one seriously ill. The Aliktce spent three days with the patient administering their emetics and potions. On the third day the patient's clan, both men and women, gathered near his dwelling by a sacred fire. They danced and sang to drums. The women wore dried terrapin-shell rattles containing a few pebbles below the knee. The dance leader wore the feather or skin of the animal "believed to be responsible for the patient's trouble. This is to strengthen the medicine." The repertory included the turkey, duck, bear, buffalo, rabbit, snake, and eagle dance, and were "propitiatory . . . performed as prayers to the various animal deities and totems for the relief of the afflicted person." At dawn the Aliktce declared that the spirit had migrated from the patient to one of the dance subjects, and the attending clan feasted.[23]

Chickasaws did their own doctoring, too. Women used home remedies for treating common ailments in their households. They had secret herbs to thwart pregnancy and wore beaded strands of buffalo hair on their legs for ornaments "as well as a preservative against miscarriages, hard labor, and other evils."[24] Chickasaw warriors wore personal charms and carried small medicine bundles to counter certain spirits, draw on supernatural power, and receive good fortune. Common items in the warrior medicine bundle were consecrated pieces of bone and small exotic stones. Bundles sometimes included a "shadow fighting knife," for use in "spiritual encounters," which might be interred "with the dead to help him in fighting off enemies on his way to the world of spirits."[25]

As additional safeguards against arousing the displeasure of the many forces in their spiritual universe, the Chickasaws observed certain taboos and sacrifices. Taboos were observed as spiritual ordinances to guard against personal pollution. An impure person was unworthy of deity favors and was thus unprotected against

---

[23] Speck, "Notes on Chickasaw Ethnology," *Journal of American Folk-Lore*, Vol. XX (January–March, 1907), 54–55; and Schoolcraft, *Historical and Statistical Information*, Part I, 310.

[24] Adair, *History of the American Indians*, 178.

[25] James H. Howard, "Some Chickasaw Fetishes," *Florida Anthropologist*, Vol. XII (March, 1959), 47–55.

invasion by evil spirits which brought misfortune, illness, and even death. The principal taboos were associated with food and women. "They reckon all those animals to be unclean, that are either carnivorous, or live on nasty food; as hogs, wolves, panthers, foxes, cats, mice, rats. And if we except the bear, they deem all beast of prey unhallowed, and polluted food. . . . They abhor moles so exceedingly, that they will not allow their children even to touch them for fear of hurting their eyesight." They believed that spirits in nature had the power to transfer to humans the qualities of the animals they consumed. Thus,

> he who feeds on venison, is according to their physical system, swifter and more sagacious than the man who lives on the flesh of the clumsy bear . . . . This is the reason . . . their greatest chieftains observed a constant rule in their diet, and seldom ate of any animal of gross quality, or heavy motion of body, fancying it conveyed a dullness through the whole system, and disabled them from exerting themselves with proper vigour in their martial, civil, and religious duties.[26]

The most stringent and elaborate tribal taboos were associated with the female. The Chickasaws held the mysteries of her cycles and processes in great awe. She was required to separate herself each month, the lunar retreat, in a menstrual hut near her household. She also had to reside in her menstrual hut in isolation from her family and the tribe at childbirth and for a postnatal period of two months. During both times, touching food others consumed was regarded as contaminating. Indeed, a woman's very presence made her husband shunned as a risk on the hunt or warpath. At the end of her period she could return to her household, but only after she had bathed and observed the purification formula. Tribal sickness, misfortune, defeat, or other disasters could be blamed on non-observance of these taboos. Thus her quarantine, if violated, ranked in weight of offense with "breach of marriage law, and murder [which] they esteem the most capital crimes."[27]

[26] Adair, *History of the American Indians*, 139–40.
[27] Speck, "Notes on Chickasaw Ethnology, *Journal of American Folk-Lore*, Vol. XX (January–March, 1907), 57; and Adair, *History of the American Indians*, 130–31.

The Chickasaws used simple sacrifices to pacify and win the favor of their ubiquitous deities and to sanctify things and persons. These sacrifices included fasts and warrior ordeal. The Hopaye performed the official public sacrifices, such as consigning tobacco, button snakeroot, and green corn to the Great Composite Force in the rekindled holy fire. Personal sacrifices also were observed to win the favor of certain deities. Hunters cut a choice piece of flesh from the first deer slain on both the summer and winter hunt, offering it "as a thanksgiving for . . . health and for former success hunting" and petitioning the deities to continue their "divine care and goodness." The women customarily threw a small piece of meat into the fire before each meal, believing "to draw omens from it. They firmly believe such a method to be a great means of producing temporal good things, and of averting those that are evil."[28]

In their primitive state the Chickasaws found satisfying identity and meaning for themselves through personal and public observance of divine ordinances. They also exploited their religion to explain the physical universe and its wondrous workings. They placed seasons, animals, plants, and all other natural items in a non-materialistic, spiritual context. Conspicuous natural phenomena—lightning, thunder, and storms—were conceived to be the Great Composite Force expressing anger or displeasure.[29]

These explanations crystallized into myths and tales. Successive generations of tribal elders preserved and transmitted them. The regular presentation of these myths provided spiritual instruction as well as entertainment and storytelling. Elaborate requirements surrounded their telling. Some could be told in particular seasons. The workings of natural phenomena were accounted for in such tales as "How day and night were divided," "Why the opossum has no hair on his tail," "The origin of corn," and "How the Chickasaws got tobacco." Some Chickasaw myths lauded warriors and stressed the Chickasaw martial tradition, and others explained supernatural themes—"Visit to the world of the dead." Encounters with nature, especially with animals, and conversion to another life form, such as "The man who became a

[28] Adair, *History of the American Indians*, 121–24.
[29] *Ibid.*, 68.

snake," were popular story subjects. Social themes—"The un-faithful wife"—and human caricatures—"The wicked mother-in-law"—also appeared in their myths.[30]

The pervasive Chickasaw religion even colored tribal recreation and entertainment. Their music (made by singing and instruments), dances, and games served spiritual as well as social and recreational purposes. The principal instruments were pot and log drums, hand rattles, terrapin-shell knee rattles, and flutes. Chickasaw games included toli and chunkey, played only by the men, and akabatle where men and women opposed each other. Ceremony and pageantry, which preceded the contests, provided spiritual overtones. The Hopaye blessing was followed by singing and dancing. Toli, chunkey, and akabatle were played on prepared courts. Toli resembled lacrosse, but in toli each player used two rackets. The ball was made from a scraped deerskin stuffed with deer hair and sewed with deer sinew. The court was about five hundred feet long with a goal at each end. Chunkey was played with a rounded stone "kept with the strictest religious care, and from one generation to another and . . . exempted from being buried with the dead." Chunkey stones "belong to the town where they are used and are carefully preserved." As the stone was rolled across the court, warriors cast lances at it, the winner being the one to place his lance closest to the stone when it came to rest. In akabatle, men and women gathered about a single pole placed in the center of the court. The object of the game was to strike an effigy atop the pole with a ball. Great feasts for the players and the spectators followed the games.[31]

Religion also saturated Chickasaw social organization and institutions. The tribe was divided into two grand divisions or moieties—Imosaktca and Intcukwalipa. The Imosaktca had precedence over the Intcukwalipa, which meant that the High Minko, the nation's principal chief, came from that division of the tribe. Each moiety was divided into clans or gentes, groups of blood-related families. The number of clans in both moieties has

[30] John R. Swanton, *Myths and Tales of the Southeastern Indians*, B.A.E. Bulletin 88.

[31] Adair, *History of the American Indians*, 428–32; Swanton, *Indians of the Southeastern United States*, 775; and Swanton "Aboriginal Culture of the Southeast," B.A.E. 42 Ann. Rept., 706.

varied in Chickasaw history from seven to fifteen. They included the Minko—Chief, Shawi—Raccoon, Koishto—Panther, Spani—Spanish, Nani—Fish, and Hashona—Skunk gentes. Each clan or gens claimed a mythical origin and traced its genealogy to a common animal ancestor, a totem which served as patron saint or special guardian for clan members. Chickasaw clans were exogamic in that members were required to marry outside their clan and matrilineal in that descent was traced through the female line. Moiety and gens protocol included specific assignment by rank to each clan's location in the tribal town or encampment. For identity, the Imosaktca group painted across and above the cheek bones, the Intcukwalipa below the cheek bones. The principal clan in each moiety provided the Hopaye. His spiritual aides were selected from the lesser clans.[32]

A Chickasaw family was formed when a suitor from one clan wed the maid of his choice in another clan. He declared his matrimonial intentions by sending her a small present, perhaps a trinket or fine deerskin garment. Her acceptance meant engagement. The simple marriage ceremony was described thus: the groom takes "a choice ear of corn, and divides it in two before witnesses, gives her one half in her hand, and keeps the other half to himself; or otherwise he gives her a deer's foot, as an emblem of the readiness with which she ought to serve him; in return, she presents him with some cakes of bread, thereby declaring her domestic care and gratitude. . . . When this short ceremony is ended they may go to bed like an honest couple."[33]

Monogamy prevailed but polygamy was permitted. Commonly a man with plural wives had chosen a woman with several sisters, and he wed the lot. The advantage of this type of arrangement was that he needed to maintain only one household. Otherwise the polygamist established separate residences and visited his women on a circuit. A European writer observed that the Chickasaws in their natural state "were fond of variety, that they ridicule the white people as a tribe of narrow-hearted, and dull constitutioned animals, for having only one wife at a time; and

---

[32] Speck, "Notes on Chickasaw Ethnology," *Journal of American Folk-Lore,* Vol. XX (January–March, 1907), 51; and Swanton, *Social and Religious Beliefs and Usages of the Chickasaw Indians,* B.A.E. 44 *Ann. Rept.,* 196.

[33] Adair, *History of the American Indians,* 146.

being bound to live with and support her, though numberless circumstances might require a contrary conduct." Also he found that the Chickasaws permitted a form of companionate marriage. A young warrior "strikes up one of those matches for a few moons, which they term Toopsa Tawa, 'a make haste marriage,' because it wants the usual ceremonies, and duration of their other kind of marriages."[34]

A Chickasaw widow faced the ordeal of remaining single for four years, closely watched by her husband's clan to make certain that she did not falter. She had to remain inside her house in unkempt clothing and disheveled hair. Only her late husband's sisters and brothers could suspend this stringent law. A sister, by arranging a marriage between the widow and her brother, or he, by lying with the widow one night or by taking her as his wife, freed her from the penalties of widowhood. A widower had to endure about the same restrictions, though for only four months. Chickasaw law permitted both separation and divorce and defined adultery as a serious offense. The man seldom suffered punishment except that administered by his wife's clan or an irate husband. The woman could be whipped, her hair shorn, and her face disfigured. An adulterous couple able to elude tribal authorities until the next busk festival was assured a pardon during the propitiation ceremony. To promote harmonious domestic relations, the Chickasaws practiced son-in-law and mother-in-law avoidance.[35]

Chickasaw child-rearing practices reflected the tribe's matrifocal system and martial tradition. Male children were placed on panther skins, in the hopes that "the communicative principle" of the skins would convey qualities they desired the man-child to have—strength, cunning, smelling, and a prodigious spring. "They reckon such a bed is the first rudiments of war. But it is worthy of notice, they change the regimen in nurturing their young females; these they lay on the skins of fawns, or buffalo calves, because they are shy and timorous."[36]

Chickasaw mothers were reported to have followed the Choc-

[34] *Ibid.*, 145–46.
[35] Swanton, *Indians of the Southeastern United States*, 704–705.
[36] Adair, *History of the American Indians*, 452.

taw practice of flattening their infants' foreheads with a block of wood covered with buckskin or a bag of sand fastened to the head, but they abandoned this custom in the late prehistoric period. Children were related to the mother's household and clan, not the father's. Women had authority only over the girls. A disobedient son was sent to the oldest uncle of the mother's gens. For punishment, the elder might simply scold the youth, impose a small penance, appeal to his "feelings of honor or shame," or pour cold water on him. One punishment situation arose when an old uncle charged his nephew with being "more effeminate than became a warrior and with acting contrary to their old religious rites and customs." For this he was lashed with a whip of plaited grass. Mischievous or thievish children might be scratched on the back with dried snake's teeth.[37]

There was a precise division of responsibility by sex in the instruction of children. Women were responsible for the proper upbringing of girls. Boys between the ages of twelve and fifteen, the "age of proper discrimination," were assigned to village elders "who instructed them in all necessary knowledge, and desired qualifications to constitute them successful hunters and accomplished warriors": the arts of swimming, jumping, running, wrestling, and use of weapons. Their warrior ordeal included plunging into water at the coldest season and eating special herbs to increase their strength.[38]

The primitive Chickasaw government, an extension of the clan system, was particularistic. The clans and towns were self-governing and confederated in a single political unit—the tribe—for purposes of promoting the general welfare and protecting common interests. Officials in the tribal government, both local and national, held their positions because of clan status. Each clan was governed by a council of elders and a clan Minko or chief, sometimes called Capitani, selected by the clan council. At the top of the Chickasaw political hierarchy was the High Minko, a principal chief selected from the ranking clan of the Imosaktca moiety of the tribe. Assisting the High Minko was the Tishu

37 *Ibid.*, 163–64; H. B. Cushman, *History of the Choctaw, Chickasaw, and Natchez Indians*, 488–89; and Bossu, *Travels*, 171.
38 Swanton, *Indians of the Southeastern United States*, 715–16.

Minko, the national council speaker and principal deputy and adviser. The national council, composed of clan chiefs and certain other esteemed and wise elders, shared the function of tribal government at the national level. This group met on the call of the High Minko at the advice of his Tishu Minko, who sent runners to all towns summoning clan representatives to the national capital at Chukafalaya, site of the national council house. The Chickasaw national council was less a law-making body and more a consultative and policy-forming group for particular issues and situations of tribal concern.[39]

The weight of political authority rested lightly on Chickasaw citizens. A European observer commented that they were "governed by the plain and honest law of nature, their whole constitution breathes nothing but liberty." They "have no words to express despotic power, arbitrary kings, oppressed, or obedient subjects," and "they have exquisite pleasure in pursuing their own natural dictates."[40]

But with all the latitude of freedom enjoyed by Chickasaws in their natural state, they were reported to have taken their responsibilities and duties of citizenship seriously. "When any national affair is in debate, you may hear every father of a family speaking in his house on the subject, with rapid, bold language, and the utmost freedom that a people can use." And "they are equal—the only precedence any gain is by superior virtue, oratory, or prowess; and they esteem themselves bound to live and die in defence of their country. A warrior will accept no hire for performing virtuous and heroic actions. . . . The head-men reward the worthy with titles of honour, according to their merit in speaking, or the number of enemies scalps they bring home. Their hearts are fully satisfied, if they have revenged blood, enobled themselves by war actions, given cheerfulness to their mourning country, and fired the breasts of the youth with a spirit of emulation to guard the beloved people from danger, and revenge the wrongs of their country."[41]

[39] Speck, "Notes on Chickasaw Ethnology," *Journal of American Folk-Lore,* Vol. XX (January–March, 1907), 52–54; Adair, *History of the American Indians,* 460; and Schoolcraft, *Historical and Statistical Information,* Part I, 311.
[40] Adair, *History of the American Indians,* 406–407, 459.
[41] *Ibid.,* 406.

The Chickasaws' "plain and honest law of nature" was a direct and viable corpus juris. A basic precept was that the tribal domain was held in common ownership, a sacred gift from the Great Composite Force and thus inalienable. There was no private land ownership in the Chickasaw natural system. Each town had its common fields, and local citizens were required to work together in sowing and cultivating the crops at these public farms. They stored the yield in public granaries for issue in time of need. Private land use was permitted: families selected and farmed small plots of their own for household subsistence. The local council of elders served as an arbitration court, settling disputes arising out of private land use. Chickasaw citizens were required to assist in erecting public buildings, such as council houses and religious shrines, and in preparing ceremonial grounds, ball courts, and town defenses.[42]

Proscribed actions in Chickasaw law included homicide, theft, blasphemy, and adultery. The tribe practiced a mixed system of private and public punishment for law violation. The clan council of elders passed judgment on most crimes. Since retaliation and vengeance pervaded their legal customs, more often than not the council simply served as a detached tribunal to see that the aggrieved or his family did their duty in exacting proper retribution. In cases of theft, the local clan council supervised the punishment of the offender by public whipping.[43]

In homicide cases, where private action was a public duty, the relatives of the victim had a holy mandate to seek out and kill the slayer. If he could not be found, his brother could be substituted as a sort of sacrifice to the law of retaliation. This ended the matter. Adair claimed that Chickasaws would "go a thousand miles, for the purpose of revenge . . . to satisfy the supposed craving ghosts of their deceased relations."[44]

Crimes of blasphemy reflected a respect for religious ordinance

[42] Swanton, "Social and Religious Beliefs and Usages of the Chickasaw Indians," B.A.E. *44 Ann. Rept.*, 216.

[43] Cushman, *History of the Choctaw, Chickasaw, and Natchez Indians*, 495; and Speck, "Notes on Chickasaw Ethnology," *Journal of American Folk-Lore*, Vol. XX (January–March, 1907), 52–54.

[44] Adair, *History of the American Indians*, 157–58; and Swanton, "Social and Religious Beliefs and Usages of the Chickasaw Indians," B.A.E. *44 Ann. Rept.*, 217.

as well as the very practical consideration of sanitation. Chicka-saw citizens were expected to be clean in their homes and persons. Regular bathing was a religious and civil duty even in the coldest months. When the ground was covered with snow, Adair watched them leave their warm houses at dawn "singing their usual sacred notes" and plunge into the river. They returned home "rejoicing as they run for having so well performed their religious duty, and thus purged away the impurities of the pre-ceding day by ablution." Those careless of personal and house-hold cleanliness could expect to have their legs and arms raked with dried snake's teeth.[45]

Adair rated another form of blasphemy—nonobservance of the requirement that females isolate themselves during menstrual periods—as a crime ranking in seriousness with homicide and adultery. He wrote that "should any of the Indian women violate this law of purity, they would be censured, and suffer for any sudden sickness, or death that might happen among the people, as the necessary effect of the divine anger for their polluting sin, contrary to their old traditional law of female purity."[46]

Adulterers could expect both public and private punishment. In earlier times both parties were forced to run naked through the village exposed to the taunts and whips of righteous citizens. By Adair's time, the mid-eighteenth century, the male party to the act suffered only such private physical violence as the out-raged husband could inflict. The woman could expect a beating from her husband, facial disfigurement and hair cropping, and banishment from her household. Adair asked the Chickasaws "the reason of the inequality in their marriage law, in punishing the weaker passive party, and exempting the stronger, contrary to reason and justice." He was told "it had been so a considerable time—because their land being a continual seat of war, and the lurking enemy forever pelting them without, and the women decoying them within, if they put such old cross laws of marriage in force, all their beloved brisk warriors would soon be spoiled, and their habitations turned to a wild waste."[47]

---

[45] Adair, *History of the American Indians*, 126–27.
[46] *Ibid.*, 130.
[47] *Ibid.*, 150–53; Bossu, *Travels*, 172; and Romans, *Natural History*, 64.

In their natural state the Chickasaws derived sustenance, shelter, clothing, and other simple needs from nature's bounty by hunting and gathering, agriculture, some trade with other tribes, and plunder from their ubiquitous wars. Next to being a fighting man, the Chickasaw was a hunter. He mixed his invocation of spirit power and supernatural approval for success on the game trails with the familiar nature crafts of tracking, trapping, and using decoys and calls. The most extended seasonal hunt occurred in the autumn. If successful, Chickasaw hunters turned most of their skins and smoked meat over to their households, although customarily they used a portion of the meat for feasts and as food gifts to old people in the village. Chickasaw youths hunted wild turkeys and other small game near the villages as a part of their training.[48]

The basic natural food items in the Chickasaw economy were the deer and bear and, in earlier times, the bison. Of these, the deer was the most esteemed. Its flesh was eaten fresh or dried and smoked for winter's use. Its skin served as the principal material for clothing. Antler tips often were used as arrow points, and dried deer sinew and entrails were twisted and used for bow strings and as thread for sewing and weaving fishnets. Indian women used deer brains for softening and tanning skins. The bear ranked next in usefulness. Chickasaw wives fashioned heavy winter robes and bed coverings from bearskins. The tough hide was made into strong moccasins and hunting boots, and dried bear gut was a favorite with the warriors as bowstring material. They pierced bear claws for ornaments and necklaces. An important item derived from the bear was oil. Women took the slabs of fat from the bear's carcass, rendered it over fires "into clear well-tasted oil, mixing plenty of sassafras and wild cinnamon with it over the fire, which keeps sweet from one winter to another, in large earthen jars, covered in the ground." This easily digestible oil had a wide use in cooking and was popular as a "nutritive to hair" and as a body rub for common complaints.[49]

At certain seasons, fish was a popular food item. The Chickasaws compounded fish drugs from devil's shoestring, the buckeye,

---

[48] Swanton, *Indians of the Southeastern United States*, 312–20.
[49] *Ibid.*; and Adair, *History of the American Indians*, 446.

and crushed green walnut hulls which they cast into deep holes in the rivers and creeks near their villages. When catfish, drum, perch, bass, and suckers surfaced, they caught them by hand, speared them, or retrieved them with arrows fitted with a special barb and a hand line. Chickasaw fishermen also placed creels and nets on the edge of deep holes and on the river's riffles to trap fish.[50]

In season, Chickasaw women and children gathered wild onions, grapes, plums, persimmons, mulberries, strawberries, and blackberries, as well as walnuts, chestnuts, pecans, acorns, and hickory nuts. They dried plums and grapes into primitive prunes and raisins and pressed dried persimmons into bricks or cakes. Boiled sassafras roots made a popular tea. Chickasaws gathered salt from local licks and springs and robbed bee trees for honey, used as sweetening for the Indian household. They felled the bee tree and placed comb and liquid in a sewed deerskin container.[51]

Agriculture matched hunting in importance in the Chickasaw economy. Their public farms and household gardens were situated near the villages on meadow and prairie plots and cleared tracts in the timber. They cleared forest patches by deadening trees. Workmen cut a ring through the tree bark with notched stone axes and burned the dead trees, saplings, and undergrowth. Corn was the principal food crop. Between the grain hills in the corn patches, Chickasaw farmers planted melons, pumpkins, sunflowers, beans, peas, and tobacco. The women served green corn as roasting ears and processed ripe corn into porridge, grits, gruel, hominy, and meal for bread. They crushed the corn with a long-handled pestle in a mortar made from a chunk of hollowed hickory.[52]

The Chickasaws were inventive in adapting the many items in nature to meet their clothing, aesthetic, household, ceremonial, and shelter needs. Their primitive crafts included fashioning local clays into pottery vessels for cooking and for storing food and water. They spun thread and yarn for textiles out of the inner bark of mulberry trees and animal fur. They converted eagle,

[50] Swanton, *Indians of the Southeastern United States*, 265–67.
[51] *Ibid.*, 300.
[52] Adair, *History of the American Indians*, 435–36.

hawk, and swan feathers into elegant decorative pieces, notably the warrior's mantle. They colored textiles and finely tanned deerskins with an eye-catching yellow dye derived from sassafras roots and red, yellow, and black dyes from sumac. Walnut hulls yielded a rich, dark dye used to color baskets and to mix with bear's oil to anoint their hair.

The thick forests of the Chickasaws' Tombigbee homeland yielded many products useful in their crafts. Large logs were hollowed by fire, the charred insides scraped with clam shells or sharpened stones and fashioned as river boats. From pines they took material for framing their houses and made pitch torches to illuminate the night. Cane was another important plant in Chickasaw crafts. They wove cane baskets and mats, used woven cane for house siding, constructed cane fish traps, sieves, and fences, and made blowguns from hollowed cane pieces. The hickory tree had a number of uses in the Chickasaw economy. Besides using the nuts for food, they split hickory logs into strong resilient withes and wove house walls and heavy containers. Hickory was an important firewood, its bark was used to cover shelters, and craftsmen, respecting its strength, used it to make arrow shafts and bows. White hickory ranked with black locust as the favorite bow wood. Red hickory was used for making the pestle and mortar sets for grinding grain.[53]

A Chickasaw town consisted of several compounds or households. Each household contained a winter house, summer house, corn storage building, and menstrual hut. Some Chickasaw towns were reported to have numbered over two hundred households. In addition, each village had a log palisade fort, council, ceremonial and ball grounds, and a ceremonial rotunda and council house for the conduct of religious exercises and local government. The Chickasaw winter house was circular, about twenty-five feet in diameter, with an earthen floor excavated three feet below the surface. It was framed with pine logs and straight slender poles lashed with bark or thongs. Walls and roof were covered with woven hickory, oak, or cane withes. Chickasaw craftsmen covered the walls inside and out with a thick plaster made from clay and dry grass; thatched the roof with long dry grass; and white-

[53] Swanton, *Indians of the Southeastern United States*, 571–82.

washed the walls inside and out with a substance made from decayed oyster shells, coarse chalk, or white clay.

The Chickasaw summer house was rectangular, with reported dimensions of twelve by twenty-two feet, partitioned into two rooms with porches attached. Walls of this seasonal structure were ventilated by small orifices in the woven mat wall coverings. The gabled roof was covered with bark or grass thatch. An early visitor to the Chickasaw towns wrote: "When they build the whole town, and frequently . . . neighboring towns, [they] assist one another. . . . In one day they build, daub with their tough mortar mixed with dry grass, and thoroughly finish a good commodious house." He rated their homes "clean, neat, dwelling houses, whitewashed within and without." Home interiors included beds constructed around the walls on elevated frames of strong poles on short posts, and covered with mats and skins. Other household furnishings included small wooden seats or stools, wooden and ceramic dishes, wooden ladles and spoons, and bison-horn and shell scoops. Each household had sanitation facilities essential for group living, including pits for disposal of garbage and other wastes.[54]

Chickasaw economic life was enriched by commerce with other tribes. Chickasaws counted quantity by tens, the number of their fingers. Chickasaw traders exchanged deerskins, Indian slaves, and bear's oil sealed in clay urns with merchants from other tribes for special materials required in the construction of war implements; for conch shells, used as ceremonial chalices; and for pearls and sheet copper for making ornaments.[55]

There was a precise division of labor in the Chickasaw economic universe. Women did most of the menial work, cultivating fields and fetching firewood and water, as well as the customary household tasks. Prizing the Indian slaves captured in their tribe's many wars, Chickasaw women could be expected to urge their men to more fury, more raids, and more slaves, which changed their status from laborers to overseers of slave laborers. To pre-

[54] Adair, *History of the American Indians*, 443, 449; and Jessie Jennings, "Chickasaw and Earlier Indian Cultures of Northeast Mississippi," *Journal of Mississippi History*, Vol. III (July, 1941), 155–86.

[55] Speck, "Outlines of Aboriginal Culture," *American Anthropologist*, n.s., Vol. IX (April–June, 1907), 293.

vent escape from Chickasaw bondage, they mutilated the slaves' feet by cutting nerves or sinews just above the instep. Thus they could labor but could not flee.[56]

Chickasaw warriors labored on the public farms and other civil works, constructed houses, and made tools and implements of war. They spent most of their time on the game trail and warpath or resting from their exertions and watching their women and slaves toil. European traders condemned the warriors as slothful. They charged that a Chickasaw male bestirred himself only "when the devil is at his arse."[57]

But it was universally acknowledged that "they are the readiest, and quickest of all people in going to shed blood." The most scrupulous and elaborate preparations were made for a strike against the enemy. The only occasions of total war, involving the entire tribe, were defensive operations to protect their homeland from invasion. Offensive wars were conducted by small squads of warriors, generally formed from particular clans and seldom numbering over fifty men. An essential preliminary to making war was achieving sanctification to assure support of the deities. To accomplish this, the warriors joining the campaign leader fasted for three days and nights, regularly purging themselves with draughts of button snakeroot drink. During the fast, each warrior attended to his individual medicine bundle and inspected his bow, arrows, lance, warclub, and tomahawk. The clan war leader was required to undergo a more arduous fast and purification process because he and his "beloved waiter" carried into battle the clan medicine bundle, the "holy ark" described as a small box of charms and sacred pieces in which resided the latent medicine power of the clan.[58]

As the end of the fast approached, the warriors received their holy charge. A

> celebrated old chief or noted old warrior, with the war pipe in his hand . . . delivered a speech to the war-going company, in which

[56] Almon W. Lauber, *Indian Slavery in Colonial Times Within the Present Limits of the United States*, 40–41.

[57] Adair, *History of the American Indians*, 448; and Swanton, "Social and Religious Beliefs and Usages of the Chickasaw Indians," B.A.E. *44 Ann. Rept.*, 228–29.

[58] Adair, *History of the American Indians*, 448.

he rehearsed his own exploits, not in the spirit of self-adulation but as an honest exhortation to them to emulate his deeds of heroic valor; then encouraged them to go in trusting confidence; to be great in manly courage and strong in heart; to be watchful, keen in sight, and fleet in foot; to be attentive in ear and unfailing in endurance; to be cunning as the fox, sleepless as the wolf, and agile as the panther.

Propitiatory dances by the war party members concluded the preparation. They departed with great ceremony, and they returned with great ceremony, brandishing the scalps of slain enemies and displaying their captives and plunder.[59]

John R. Swanton, a distinguished scholar who intensively studied the lifeways of the tribes comprising the lower Mississippi ethnological province, concluded that the "material culture of all the southeastern tribes was . . . much alike." His studies show that the same could be said for the region's non-material culture. Thus the primitive Chickasaw lifeways were quite similar to those of their neighbors. But the Chickasaws in their natural state did have one unique quality which loomed conspicuously and which distinguished them from neighboring tribes—they were unconquerable. Their preoccupation with the warpath generated a vigorous and galvanizing pride. Time and again Chickasaw warriors crushed native armies raised from the more populous tribes on their borders. And they inflicted such regular and humiliating defeats on invading French columns that French administrators in Louisiana abandoned their determined attempt to force the Chickasaws to serve that nation's purpose. The holy charge to Chickasaw warriors, a continuum of pride transmitted by tribal elders through a chain of many generations, sustained the Chickasaw uniqueness. The startling decline of the Chickasaws, completed in less than fifty years, can be accounted for in part by the fact that the elder generation, which should have been transmitting age-old tribal values, became enraptured by insidious European ways and things. This broke the chain, the continuum of pride, and set in motion a progressive deterioration which made these proud and unconquered people of old easy marks for every form of exploitation.

[59] Cushman, *History of the Choctaw, Chickasaw, and Natchez Indians*, 492.

CHAPTER TWO

THE PROVINCE OF CHICAZA

IN 1540 the Chickasaws were first exposed to the force which would disturb and eventually destroy their old ways. The year before, a Spanish force headed by Hernando de Soto landed at Tampa to search for the fabled land of Cale. During December, 1540, De Soto's column reached the upper waters of the Tombigbee River. He set his men to work constructing rafts, and on December 17, they began the crossing. Chickasaw warriors attempted to check the strange invaders with volleys of arrows and managed to hold them up for three days, but the Spaniards persevered and finally reached the west bank. De Soto's chroniclers called this land the Province of Chicaza. They described the province as thickly populated, noting that the Chickasaws cultivated much of their fertile land and produced "plenty of maize"— enough to carry the Spaniards and their horse and hog herds "through the [winter] season." De Soto's men captured a number of hostages from the curious tribesmen and through them expressed De Soto's demand to see the Chickasaw chiefs. The chiefs came with attendants bearing skins, shawls, food, and other gifts for the Spaniards.[1]

De Soto required the Chickasaw chiefs to provide his men and livestock with shelter and subsistence for the winter. As the days passed, Chickasaw shyness faded, and there developed an uneasy but increasingly regular contact between the Indians and Spaniards. On one occasion Chickasaw chiefs urged the Spaniards to join them in a campaign on a neighboring tribe, the Chakchiumas. De Soto furnished thirty cavalry and eighty infantry. The Chak-

---

[1] Edward G. Bourne (ed.), *Narratives of the Career of Hernando De Soto*, I, 100–108.

chiumas, perhaps expecting the raid, had set fire to their village and fled ahead of the Chickasaw-Spanish force.[2]

By early March, 1541, De Soto was ready to resume the march. He called in the Chickasaw chiefs and demanded that they supply two hundred warriors to carry his column's baggage. Tired of the visitors and wearied by their incessant demands and impositions, the Chickasaws regarded De Soto's levy as an insult to tribal honor. It fired them to action. On the night of March 4, warriors slipped past sentries into the Spanish compound. Several Chickasaws carried hot coals in small clay pots. They ignited the crude barracks, and soon the Spanish camp was enveloped in flames. "The confusion and rout was so great that each man fled by the way that first opened to him, there being none to oppose the Indians. . . . The town lay in cinders." Chickasaw bowmen shot the fleeing soldiers, horses, and hogs. Twelve Spaniards and fifty-seven horses died. Only one hundred swine remained. Great quantities of military gear, clothing, and weapons burned in the holocaust.[3]

The surviving Spaniards, many of them naked, took refuge in a small village a league away. They covered their bodies with woven mats, collected food, and made preparations to evacuate Chicaza. On a forge, using bellows of bearskins, they retempered their swords, made lances, and fashioned new saddles. In mid-March the Chickasaws struck the Spaniards again, but this time they were vigilant and drove the Indians away. By April 26, 1541, the Spaniards had completed their preparations, and De Soto led his column out of the Province of Chicaza.[4]

The Spaniards' four months' residence among the Chickasaws had exposed these Indians only slightly to European ways and things. There followed nearly one hundred fifty years of no direct contact. Through intertribal trade and war the Chickasaws heard of their former acquaintances, the Spanish, as well as of new-

[2] *Final Report of the United States De Soto Expedition Commission*, 76 Cong., 1 sess., *House Doc. No. 71*, 1939, 214–15.

[3] Bourne, *Hernando De Soto*, I, 100–108.

[4] *Final Report of the De Soto Expedition*, 76 Cong., 1 sess., *House Doc. No. 71*, 1939, 226; Bourne, *Hernando De Soto*, I, 100–108, II 22; John R. Swanton, *Early History of the Creek Indians and Their Neighbors*, B.A.E. *Bulletin 73*, 414–15; and John R. Swanton, "De Soto's Line of March from the Viewpoint of an Ethnologist," *Proceedings of the Mississippi Valley Historical Association*, Vol. V (1911–12), 147–57.

comers called the French and the English, who traded, settled, and conquered ever closer to their domain. The French, from their stations in Canada and the Northwest, were the first Europeans to resume contact with the Chickasaws. In 1673 the Joliet-Marquette party passed the Chickasaw domain on its Mississippi River reconnaissance. Nine years later a second French party of fifty-five Frenchmen and Indians, headed by Robert Cavalier de la Salle, passed down the Mississippi en route to the Gulf. On February 24, 1682, La Salle camped on Chickasaw Bluffs, an extended line of headlands marking the western border of the Chickasaw domain. Pierre Prudhomme, the expedition armorer, lost his way while hunting in the thick forests near Chickasaw Bluffs. La Salle's men erected a stockade on the bluffs, Fort Prudhomme, as storage for expedition supplies and as a base for parties seeking Prudhomme. In the course of their search, the Frenchmen met two Chickasaws. La Salle sent presents and a peace message by them to their villages situated a few days' journey east. The searchers finally found Prudhomme, and La Salle's party proceeded to the Gulf.[5]

La Salle's appearance in the lower Mississippi Valley signaled a determined attempt by France to develop the vast resources of that region and to exploit the water route connecting French settlements in the Northwest with the Gulf. In addition, French officials regarded it as essential to establish French presence and power in that region to thwart the English thrust which had nearly reached the Mississippi. Reports from French traders in the Northwest warned that "the English are coming," confirming the English traders' relentless march from their base at Charleston to the West. French and English traders inevitably were the vanguard of troops, fortifications, and settlements. Their daring and intensively competitive attempts to establish commercial relations with tribes in the lower Mississippi Valley prompted the early incidents in the long and bloody contest for control of this region which lasted from the 1680's to 1763. At times Spain was a reluctant participant in this power struggle which centered on the Chickasaws.[6]

[5] Francis Parkman, *La Salle and the Discovery of the Great West*, II, 41–42.
[6] Clarence W. Alvord, *The Illinois Country*, 120–21.

The Chickasaws noted an increase in European traffic through their domain, both on water and land, following La Salle's visit to Chickasaw Bluffs in 1682. By 1698, Charleston-based English traders, such as Thomas Welch and Anthony Dodsworth, arrived in the tribe's Tombigbee settlements leading horse trains packed with Limburg cloth, guns, powder and shot, beads, knives, hatchets, hoes, scissors, vermillion, axes, brass wire, Bengal silk, brass kettles, and "Dutch pretties." The Chickasaws' fascination with the frontier merchants' wares quickly turned to practical application. The Indian women used the hoes to cultivate their corn patches, the axes to gather firewood, and the textiles to make more comfortable and attractive garments for their families. The warriors prized the merchants' guns, knives, and hatchets to improve their hunts and to make them deadlier on the warpath and used brass wire for arm and ankle bracelets and earrings. In return the English took Chickasaw pelts, especially deerskins (called "leather" and traded by the pound) and Indian captives, to be shackled and marched to Carolina and there sold as plantation slaves.[7]

The French were alarmed by the presence of this English commercial enclave among the Chickasaws and in 1698 began earnest attempts to establish French dominion over the lower Mississippi Valley. The Bishop of Quebec claimed the region as his diocese and sent Francis Jolliet de Montigny and Anthony Davion to establish missions among the tribes. Davion visited the Chickasaw towns but concluded that "no mission could be attempted in a tribe already devoted to the English."[8]

Davion's judgment on Chickasaw commitment was premature, for the English influence, though soon a compelling force among the Chickasaws, was, as yet, slight. At this time the Chickasaws were tied to no nation, but, knowing little about the Europeans, they were naturally curious. During 1699 a party of Chickasaws watched the French establish their first station on the Gulf at Fort Biloxi. Governor Pierre Le Moyne d'Iberville founded additional settlements on the Gulf, including Mobile, which became the ad-

[7] Verner W. Crane, "The Southern Frontier in Queen Anne's War." *American Historical Review*, Vol. XXIV (April, 1919), 379–82.

[8] John G. Shea, *History of the Catholic Missions Among the Indian Tribes of the United States, 1529–1854,* 439–41.

ministrative center for the province of Louisiana in 1702. In an attempt to check the extension of English trade and influence in the lower Mississippi Valley, Iberville invited the leaders of various tribes to meet with him in council. The French invitation found the Chickasaws engaged in one of their regular wars with the Choctaws. They agreed to suspend hostilities and meet with the French and Choctaws at Mobile.[9]

In 1702 seven Chickasaws journeyed down the Tombigbee to Mobile to attend Iberville's council. The governor pointed to French power and generosity as he presented each Indian delegate with beads, a kettle, a knife, a hatchet, powder, ball, and a gun. He urged the Chickasaws to end their war on the Choctaws and warned representatives of both tribes about the evil English design. And he told the Chickasaws that if they did not end relations with the English, he would be forced to arm neighboring tribes against them. If the Chickasaws ended their war on the Choctaws and rejected the English, Iberville promised to protect them, to send French traders to them, and to request that the Bishop of Quebec send them missionaries. The Chickasaw delegates agreed to accept French protection and French traders and promised to eschew the English. However, they wanted no missionaries whose teaching would attempt to overthrow their tribal gods.

Iberville's proposal to supply missionaries to the Chickasaws was an attempt to fulfill his government's policy of integrating the Indians into the colonial format. Missionaries were a part of the French apparatus to control the tribes. Missionaries and traders were to concentrate the Indians in compact villages where instruction could be given, the English influence checked, and a closer surveillance maintained. French officials had found that missionaries were essential for successful management of the tribes, "for in addition to the knowledge of God that they would impart to them . . . nothing is more useful than a missionary to restrain the Indians, to learn all that is happening among them [and] to inform the commandants of the neighboring posts about it." Even in the early years when the Chickasaws had no

---

[9] Dawson A. Phelps, "The Chickasaw, the English, and the French," *Tennessee Historical Quarterly*, Vol. XVI (June, 1957), 120–21.

international commitment and were carefully watching both the English and the French, they refused to accept missionaries. This caused French colonial administrators to lament, "We do not know at all what has happened among the Chickasaws." The Choctaws did accept missionaries, thereby making their villages strategic listening posts for the French. Before he closed the council of 1702, Iberville, anxious to have a representative among the Chickasaws, offered to send them St. Michel, a fourteen-year-old French youth. Ostensibly he was to live among the Chickasaws to learn their language, but actually his mission was to watch this tribe and report to Iberville on their activities. The Chickasaws agreed to accept St. Michel.[10]

Apparently the Chickasaws made a conscientious attempt to abide by the pledges they made to Iberville at the Mobile council. They waited for the French to establish a trading station convenient to their villages. And they waited for the French to protect them from attack by other tribes. All the while the number of English traders in their villages increased. Their presence and their goods galvanized the Chickasaws and revolutionized their economy. To obtain the appealing trinkets, tools, fabrics, weapons, and other wares the tribe so deeply desired, Chickasaw hunters shifted from gatherers of food and skins for their families to commercial hunters, collecting an ever-increasing quantity of marketable pelts. When an occasional French trader turned up in their towns, the Chickasaws noted that his goods were of lower quality than English items and that his prices were higher, sometimes twice that for goods from Carolina. The English were making a serious attempt to win the Chickasaws to something more than a commercial alliance by regularly distributing gifts among them. The French seldom brought gifts and shrugged at reports in 1704 that four Englishmen with eight horses loaded with gifts

10 "Iberville's Journal, December 15, 1701–April 15, 1702," in Pierre Margry (ed.), Decouvertes et Etablissements des Francais (1614–1754), IV, 503–23; Pontchartrain to Bienville, November 4, 1705, in Dunbar Rowland and Albert G. Sanders (eds. and trans.), Mississippi Provincial Archives, 1704–1743, French Dominion, III, 30–31; Extract of Bienville Letter from Louisiana during 1706, July 28, 1706, in Rowland and Sanders, Mississippi Provincial Archives, 1678–1707, French Dominion, Series 4, General Correspondence, I; and Memoir on Louisiana for 1726, in Rowland and Sanders, Mississippi Provincial Archives, French Dominion, III, 495.

had arrived in the Chickasaw towns. The governor stated, "I doubt very much that the Chickasaws will receive them well since they have always seemed to me very zealous for the French." On another occasion, in response to a report of the distribution of gifts to the Chickasaws, he admitted that "the English have spared nothing to attract the nation of the Chickasaws to themselves." And he assured his superiors in the French Colonial Office "but it is in vain. Although, to tell the truth, I do not give them any presents at all they are more attached to us than to them."[11]

Clearly French officials at Mobile miscalculated and underestimated the growing English influence among the Chickasaws. Perhaps this was due to the emergence of a small but determined group of Chickasaws who resented the English intrusion and the favored attention which certain clan chiefs received from the Carolina agents and who expressed their pique by maintaining regular contacts with the French. It is possible that French officials assumed that this minority expressed tribal consensus. This anti-English clique can be called the French party among the Chickasaws. They regularly opposed tribal actions unfavorable to the French. As Chickasaw-French relations deteriorated, they attempted to ameliorate the breach. During the French-Chickasaw wars they interceded for captives, saved the lives of many Europeans, and delivered them to French officials. This cleavage marked the beginning of the decline of the Chickasaws—a tribal schism, at first slight but eventually severe, built up from alignment in either the dominant English party or the French party. Invasion by European things and ways certainly contributed to the ultimate debauchment and displacement of Chickasaw natural ways. But it was the presence of European powers, the pressured necessity of alignment and involvement in their power struggle, and the accompanying recrimination and intertribal conflict, that eventually eroded the age-old resources and traditions of tribal unity and self-reliance. It weakened the Chickasaws, subtly at first, later devastatingly, and by the nineteenth

11 Bienville to Pontchartrain, September 6, 1704, in Rowland and Sanders, *Mississippi Provincial Archives, French Dominion,* III, 18–29; and Bienville to Pontchartrain, February 25, 1708, *ibid.,* 111–24.

century made them easy marks for every form of public and
private exploitation. These schisms engendered by the French-
English power struggle endured long after the European rivalry
ended, were transferred to other causes, and comprised a major
part of the composite of eventual tribal decline.

The genesis of Chickasaw disenchantment with the French
and the alignment of most of that nation with the English began
in 1703 when a Chickasaw party arrived in Mobile to accuse the
Choctaws of breaking Iberville's peace of the year before. The
Choctaw domain was situated between the Chickasaw Nation
and the Gulf. In passing from their settlements on the upper
Tombigbee to Mobile, the Chickasaws customarily took the most
direct route: through the Choctaw towns. The Choctaws had
closed this trail, forcing the Chickasaws to make a long detour.
When the Choctaws claimed that the Chickasaws had burned
young St. Michel, the Chickasaws promptly brought him to
Mobile to prove that he was alive and safe. Two years later, a
Chickasaw delegation visiting Mobile requested and received a
twenty-six-man French escort through the Choctaw Nation. Despite the presence of French soldiers, the Choctaws attacked
from ambush and killed several Chickasaws.[12]

This harassment continued. At first the Chickasaws blamed the
Choctaws, but as French officials continued to pressure them to
drive the English traders from their nation, warning that otherwise they would arm neighboring tribes, the Chickasaws began
to suspect that these incidents were French-inspired. Jean Baptiste Le Moyne d'Bienville, Iberville's successor as governor of
Louisiana, finally gave up in his attempt to win the Chickasaws.
By 1711 he admitted, "The Chickasaws . . . have let themselves be
won over to the English and have excused themselves to me for it
on the ground that not being able to obtain from us the needs
which have become indispensable to them find themselves
obliged to take from the English." The Chickasaws' growing acceptance of the English, due largely to the English attentiveness
to expanding Chickasaw trade needs which the French were
never able or willing to supply, caused Bienville to regard the
Chickasaws as a threat to the achievement of the French design

[12] Penicault's Account, in Margry, *Decouvertes*, V, 433–40.

in the lower Mississippi Valley. Also, with limited European manpower resources, he saw the necessity of utilizing the populous and complaisant Choctaw Nation to insulate French settlements in the lower Mississippi Valley from the threat of Chickasaw-English raids. It followed that the Choctaw Nation had to be strengthened militarily, for, as he advised the French Colonial Office, "if the Choctaws who serve as a rampart for us should once happen to be destroyed, we should be in a very insecure position." As early as 1706 he had begun secretly to distribute arms and ammunition to the Choctaws, and each year he increased the amount of support.[13]

The first Chickasaw war with the French began in 1720. The decade preceding formal hostilities was a time of small but bloody and frequent actions which prepared the Chickasaws for the larger operations that began in 1720. The French kept Choctaw mercenaries in the field watching for isolated Chickasaw parties and lurking along the Carolina trader paths ready to plunder the English caravans. The only effect of these French attempts to intimidate the Chickasaws was to drive that tribe closer to the English.

The decade preceding the outbreak of the first French-Chickasaw war was also a time of sustained change in the Chickasaw Nation. The number of Englishmen in Chickasaw towns increased with a concomitant strengthening of English influence. Several Carolina traders married Chickasaw women and started mixed-blood families. This fusing of Anglo and Indian bloodlines provided an additional and compelling reason for Chickasaw support of the English cause.[14]

Also during the period 1710 to 1720 a commercial surge occurred in the Chickasaw Nation which heightened the effects of the economic revolution set in motion in 1698 by pioneer English traders. Just as European modes were subtly displacing Chickasaw natural ways, European consumer goods were altering the tribe's simplicity of taste and traditional self-sufficiency. The Chickasaws' increasing consumption of European goods and

---

[13] Bienville to Pontchartrain, October 27, 1711, in Rowland and Sanders, *Mississippi Provincial Archives, French Dominion*, III, 158–71.
[14] See Adair, *The History of the American Indians*.

their growing reliance on English tools, weapons, and fabrics transformed the primitive Chickasaw subsistence hunter into a frontier businessman who energetically searched for items to exchange for the esteemed European goods.

Englishmen transported their goods from Charleston warehouses over the trader traces to the Chickasaw towns on pack trains and occasionally on the backs of Negro slaves. The trader compounds in the Chickasaw towns consisted of dwellings, storehouses, and trading rooms for displaying goods and negotiating exchanges. Their business houses became centers for tribal life, gradually displacing the council house and sacred ground. To obtain traders' goods, the Chickasaws collected deerskins and bearskins, wolf, panther, and otter pelts, some buffalo robes and tallow, as well as beeswax, wild honey, salt, and hickory nut oil. For several years Indian captives were important trade items in the English-Chickasaw traffic.[15]

The expansion of European trade in the lower Mississippi Valley and the growing addiction of the tribes to trader goods forced Indian hunters to range more widely in their quest for pelts. This intensified competition "for hunting grounds with an accompanying increase of hostilities." The stronger tribes, ever deadlier with firearms, expanded their hunting preserves by waging war on the smaller tribes. A grim result of these conquests was the substantial increase in the number of captives. The Chickasaws had enslaved captives from other tribes before the Europeans came. But trader presence and encouragement and the trade value of captives committed the Chickasaws to deliberate slave-hunting enterprises, and they became the most notorious of the lower Mississippi Valley tribes in this loathsome traffic.[16]

In early years of the Indian slave traffic, the Chickasaws raided the Choctaws, Acolapissas, Chawashas, Yazoos, and other neighboring tribes for captives. But as the English trader demand increased, they ranged into the Illinois country, falling on the hapless Cahokias and other tribes. West of the Mississippi, the Chickasaws devastated the small tribes residing along the lower

[15] As late as 1768 hunters were reported killing buffalo on both banks of the Mississippi River two leagues below the Chickasaw Bluffs. Samuel C. Williams, *Beginnings of West Tennessee*, 11.
[16] Cotterill, *The Southern Indians*, 17.

Arkansas and Red rivers. The fury of their slave raids in 1717 caused a Caddo chief to mourn to French officials that the Chickasaws had captured so many of his nation that the surviving remnant had taken refuge among other tribes in their area.[17]

English traders delivered the Indian slaves to Charleston markets. Local planters purchased some, but most of them were shipped to the West Indies. The English rationale for abetting the Chickasaws in this human traffic, aside from the economic return, was that these were French Indians, and it reduced the number of warriors the French could arm and turn on the Chickasaws and the English. Also it liberated them from the baneful influence of French Catholic missionaries. As English slaves they were better assured of the proper civilizing influence.[18]

French officials in Louisiana countered by offering their Indian mercenaries bounties for Chickasaw captives. Governor Bienville reported that these slaves were "very good for cultivating the earth but the facility that they have in deserting prevents the colonists from taking charge of them. These colonists ask permission to sell slaves in the . . . islands in order to get negroes in exchange since the English follow the same practice with the Indian allies of the French who are captured, and this commerce is quite necessary." In 1713, officials in Louisiana were authorized to send captured French Indian enemies, especially the Chickasaws, to French West Indian planters for sale as slaves.[19]

Two other noteworthy developments occurred in the Chickasaw Nation during the prelude to their wars with the French. It was in this period that the Chickasaws were introduced to Negro slaves, brought into their nation by English traders as bearers and servants. The number of Negro slaves owned by Indians, especially the mixed bloods, increased appreciably, and by 1861 the

[17] Lauber, *Indian Slavery in Colonial Times*, 30–37; P. F. X. de Charlevoix, *History and General Description of New France* (trans. with notes by John G. Shea), V, 124; and Penicault's Account, in Margry, *Decouvertes*, V, 505–11.

[18] Crane, "Southern Frontier," *American Historical Review*, Vol. XXIV (April, 1919), 381. Also see journal entry for November 29, 1716, and Instructions for Theophilus Hastings, July 19, 1718, in W. L. McDowell (ed.), *Journals of the Commissioners of the Indian Trade*, 134–310.

[19] Bienville to Pontchartrain, July 28, 1706, in Rowland and Sanders, *Mississippi Provincial Archives, French Dominion*, II, 20–29; and Du Clos to Pontchartrain, May 2, 1713, *Mississippi Provincial Archives, 1713–1714, French Dominion*, Series 4, General Correspondence, IV.

Chickasaw Nation was an intensely dedicated slaveholding community.

English traders also introduced horses to the Chickasaw Nation. The De Soto expedition had exposed this tribe to horses in 1540, but the Spanish residence in the Province of Chicaza was brief, and the Chickasaws regarded the invaders' horses as frightening curiosities. Extended exposure to the English mounts and pack animals caused the Chickasaws to appreciate their value and to adopt them. Once mounted, the Chickasaws searched for horses as widely as they did for Indian slaves, stealing or trading for them in their contacts with horse-owning tribes west of the Mississippi River. The Chickasaws became singular horsemen and are credited with developing a special breed—the Chickasaw horse—famous all along the Mississippi Valley for its long stride, endurance, and striking appearance and esteemed by Indians and frontiersmen alike. During their wars with the French, beginning in 1720, they exchanged French captives for horses, the exchange rate being one Frenchman for one horse.[20]

The first Chickasaw-French war began in 1720 when the Chickasaws executed a Frenchman who lived in their nation under the protection of the Chickasaw French party, ostensibly as a trader. The pro-English faction among the Chickasaws put him to death because they claimed he was spying on them and reporting to Governor Bienville. Until this time the Chickasaws had warred only on Indian tribes under French influence. Continuing their raids on the Choctaws and other French tribes, they now struck French settlements as far south as the mouth of the Yazoo, taking European captives, burning farms, and running off livestock. Chickasaw bands hit at the French lifeline connecting Illinois and Louisiana settlements by preying on supply boats on the Mississippi. This tactic closed the river to French shipping for nearly four years. Besides capturing great quantities of food, munitions, and trade goods, these Chickasaw river raids netted numerous French boatmen. Through intercession of the French party, these European prisoners were exchanged for horses and Chickasaw captives held by the French. Leaders of the French party in the nation met with Bienville in 1723 to negotiate the

20 Swanton, *The Indians of the Southeastern United States*, 312–20.

exchange of two French prisoners for a Chickasaw child, held as the slave property of the Company of the Indies, and a Chickasaw woman who had "been sold on credit to a German."[21]

By 1723 commerce in Louisiana was at a standstill. Frenchmen who dared travel by land or on the Mississippi did so at great risk. Governor Bienville noted that peace with the Chickasaws was not too likely for he would have to set as a condition that they renounce the English and trade only with the French. He conceded that "it is impossible for us to do this because, in addition to the fact that we never have enough merchandise, the English . . . trade for their peltries at a rate higher than that at which the French receive them." Except for organizing his few French regular troops and the colonial militia into defensive forces, Bienville fought the Chickasaws only with Choctaw mercenaries. He seemed to take great satisfaction from the fact that he was fighting the war "without shedding one drop of French blood," adding that Chickasaw "destruction is the sole efficacious means of insuring tranquillity to the colony." French officers organized the reluctant Choctaws into companies and occasionally led them against the Chickasaws. To fire his Indian troops to greater campaign efforts, Bienville pledged to pay them a bounty of a gun, one pound of powder, and two pounds of bullets for each Chickasaw scalp delivered to French officials. For each Chickasaw slave he agreed to pay the Choctaws in goods at the rate of eighty livres each.[22]

The French-supported Choctaw offensive had slight effect on the Chickasaws. Their ambushes on the Carolina trader paths did reduce the quantity of goods entering the Chickasaw Nation and the amount of pelts and Indian slaves reaching Charleston. Thus the motion for cessation of Chickasaw-French hostilities came from the English traders. Also, with the Chickasaw Nation tied up as one great market, they longed to capture the Choctaw trade. In 1723, at the prompting of English traders, Chickasaw leaders attempted a diplomatic coup by sending peace calumets and messages to the Choctaws, admonishing them to stop being

[21] Minutes of the Superior Council of Louisiana, July 23, 1723, in Rowland and Sanders, *Mississippi Provincial Archives, French Dominion,* II, 355–57.

[22] Minutes of the Council of Commerce of Louisiana, February 8, 1721, *ibid.,* III, 302–304.

French lackeys, to make peace with the Chickasaws, and to open their towns to English traders. Several Choctaw leaders were receptive and urged the French to end hostilities. The Louisiana Council of War debated the issue of ending the Chickasaw war, and one council member, alarmed at the possible defection of their Choctaw defenders, said he "hoped that it [the war] will continue to the extent of the entire destruction of both [Choctaw and Chickasaw] nations if it were possible because the Choctaws are numerous and may cause us uneasiness on account of the fact that they are near the English, on account of their numbers and because the more of them who are killed on both sides the greater will be our safety." The council voted not to end the war.[23]

By 1724 the Chickasaw diplomatic offensive to separate the Choctaws from the French was close to success. English traders were reported ready to enter the Choctaw Nation when Choctaw chiefs could assure protection to them and their goods. Also, Chickasaw pressure on the French was having telling effects. Illinois settlements dependent on Louisiana for supply were suffering, and French officials admitted that the Chickasaw fury was "obliging our voyageurs to go and do their hunting on the upper part of the Wabash River, whereas in time of peace they would do it beyond the Arkansas." Therefore, during late 1724, the Louisiana Council of War again debated the question of ending hostilities with the Chickasaws. First it was admitted that life in the colony was uncertain, trade and industry were languishing, and the Illinois settlements were perilously isolated. Worse yet, the council members admitted,

> Our enemies the Chickasaws had sent calumets accompanied with presents to our allies the Choctaws in order to make the proposals of peace that the latter seem to accept. . . . The continuation of the war with Chickasaws has appeared indispensable to us until the present, in the first place because it was advisable for the honor of our nation and the maintenance of its authority in this country to punish these mutinous people who had wished to shake off the yoke of French dominion. . . . The Council will first consider whether the honor of our nation is satisfied and whether the Chickasaws have been sufficiently punished for their temerity,

23 Minutes of the Council of War of Louisiana, September, 1723, *ibid.*, 378.

by the losses that they have incurred and by the continual alarms to which they have been exposed for the almost five years that this war has been lasting.

On December 2, 1724, the council decided that the Chickasaws had "been sufficiently punished," that "the honor" of France had been sustained by their brave Choctaw troops in the field, and that it "was to the advantage and welfare of the colony to accept the proposals of peace that these Indians are having made to us and that in order to maintain this peace and prevent this nation from joining that of the Choctaws for the purpose of making an alliance and trading with the English."[24]

The first Chickasaw-French war ended early in 1725 when French officers led their Choctaw companies from ambush positions on the Carolina trader paths back to the Choctaw Nation. Several officers remained in the Choctaw towns to stiffen resistance to Chickasaw-English attempts to detach the Choctaws and open their nation to English trade. A deceptive calm settled over the lower Mississippi Valley. Once again French boatmen navigated the Mississippi, and hunters and traders roamed the prairies and forests unmolested. During 1726, French officials exulted in the pleasant turn of events, but admitted anxiety about Chickasaw intent: "We do not know at all what has happened among the Chickasaws." But they assured the colonial office that they would be vigilant because "these people breathe nothing but war ... are unquestionably the bravest of the continent," and with their British liaison were capable of doing irreparable harm to French interests.[25]

Actually the Chickasaws were busy applying a craft they had learned from the British—intrigue and diplomacy as alternatives to outright warfare—and their successes set the stage for the second Chickasaw-French war. Chickasaw tactics in the recent French war revealed to British colonial officials the strategic potential of the Chickasaw Nation in fulfilling their western design, that is, wresting control of the Ohio and lower Mississippi valleys from the French. A report on British resources in the West confirmed this. The report disclosed that the Chickasaw villages were

[24] Minutes of the Council of War of Louisiana, December, 1724, *ibid.*, 457–59.
[25] Memoir of Louisiana, 1726, *ibid.*, 495.

situated about 780 miles from Charleston and 80 to 90 miles east of the Mississippi River. "In point of Situation without Doubt there is none other in the Western parts of No. America [than the Chickasaw Nation] of so much Importance to the English to be possessed of. For it lies in a central place about the middle of the Mississippi, and commands all the water Passages between New Orleans and Canada, and from that River to the backs of our Colonies." The report rated the Chickasaws as "expert Horsemen (having perhaps the finest breed of Horses in No. America); by much the best Hunters; and without Exception . . . the best Warriors." Chickasaw river raids, launched from the shore of their nation between 1720 and 1725, paralyzed shipping and communication on the Mississippi and demonstrated the value of the Chickasaw Nation as a base for driving a wedge between the French settlements in Louisiana and Illinois and isolating them for easy conquest. Thus plans were made for the Chickasaw Nation to function as a British military enclave and to serve that nation's drive for supremacy in the West.

For over twenty years the Chickasaws had proved their constancy and attachment to the English, and their energy, resourcefulness, and success as hunters had enabled Charleston-based trading enterprises to prosper. It was planned to greatly expand trade in and through the nation. Besides accommodating the thriving local Chickasaw trade, their towns were to become entrepôts for trade goods to be introduced into tribes tributary to the French. The expansion of commerce would bring increased prosperity to the trading companies, the goods would serve as vehicles for insinuating English influence, and the French hold over these tribes would be weakened, thus making easier the ultimate conquest of the region. The Chickasaws were to serve as commercial and paradiplomatic agents in the contact work with other tribes, the British shrewdly managing the scheme on an Indian-to-Indian basis.[26]

The Chickasaws found factions in many of the tribes ready to listen. French dominion over them had never produced economic

[26] Wilbur R. Jacobs (ed.), *Indians of the Southern Colonial Frontier*, 66–68; and John W. Monette, *History of the Discovery and Settlement of the Valley of the Mississippi*, I, 252–62.

satisfaction. French trader goods generally were lower in quality and more expensive than English goods and were always in short supply. Limburg cloth, a popular trade commodity, was exchanged by English traders at the rate of ten skins for one fathom of cloth. French traders charged twenty skins for the same quantity of cloth.[27]

Chickasaw agents surreptitiously worked to detach the French Indians. Their emissaries to the tribes in the Illinois country were rejected, but they found receptive tribes south of their nation. Certain Choctaw bands received them and began to trade for English goods. Chickasaw agents also found the Natchez receptive. The French Company of the Indies had colonized great numbers of settlers in the lower Mississippi Valley. In one year this enterprise imported one thousand Europeans and five hundred Negro slaves. Many settled on rich lands near the Mississippi which were claimed by the Natchez tribe. This intrusion and growing pressure made the Natchez easy marks for Chickasaw blandishments.[28]

The Chickasaw-British intrigue among the Natchez exploded on the French in November, 1729. A French observer provided the setting for the bloody outburst. "The tranquillity enjoyed in Louisiana since peace had been granted to the . . . Chickasaws was but a delusive calm which lulled the inhabitants, while there was gathering around them a storm, whose most disastrous effects were averted only by mere chance, saving the country from becoming in a single day the tomb of all the French."[29]

On the morning of November 28, 1729, Natchez warriors struck the unsuspecting garrisons at Fort Rosalie and Fort St. Peter. First they slaughtered the soldiers defending the French settlements, then they turned their fury on the civilians. The Natchez killed at least 250 Frenchmen and gathered up nearly 300 women and children as hostages. A combined French-Choc-

[27] Perrier to Director, June 22, 1729, in Rowland and Sanders, *Mississippi Provincial Archives, French Dominion*, II, 610–24.

[28] Joseph Wallace, *The History of Illinois and Louisiana Under the French Rule*, 289; and William O. Scroggs, "Early Trade and Travel in the Lower Mississippi Valley," *Proceedings of the Mississippi Valley Historical Association*, II, (1908–1909), 248–49.

[29] Charlevoix, *New France*, VI, 79–80.

taw force marched on the Natchez in February, 1730, avenged the Fort Rosalie massacre several times over, and recovered most of the hostages. The Natchez survivors fled their country. Most of them, perhaps 200, took refuge among their patrons, the Chickasaws.[30]

Governor Perrier, temporarily Bienville's successor as head of the French government in Louisiana, demanded that the Chickasaws surrender the Natchez. The Chickasaws refused. During 1731, the French party among the Choctaws, at Perrier's urging, burned three captured Chickasaw agents at the stake. The Chickasaws and their Natchez allies retaliated by raiding French shipping on the Mississippi. Perrier responded by organizing several Choctaw companies under French officers to harass the Chickasaws by blockading their towns. Forty "faint hearted" Chickasaw families left to settle in the safety of the Carolina settlements, but most of that nation stood firm in its determination to defy the French.[31]

Perrier attempted to intensify French pressure on the Chickasaw Nation by turning the Indian tribes of the Illinois country on them. At Vincennes, French officers supplied arms, munitions, and bounties to raider parties made up of warriors from the Wea, Piankashaw, Potawatomi, Miami, Iroquois, and Illinois tribes. The Iroquois drew most of the bounties. During 1732, they invaded the Chickasaw Nation and returned with a tally of thirty-four Chickasaw men, women, and children killed or captured. The following year, their take in slain and captured Chickasaws was forty-two.[32]

The northern Indian invasions stirred the Chickasaws to counter with retaliatory forays north of the Ohio and along the Wabash and other vital arteries in French Illinois. During the winter of 1732, a Chickasaw party on the Wabash captured a pirogue, its trade goods, and its *voyageur* crew. A French officer on the Wabash reported in 1733 that he was "more embarrassed

[30] Monette, *Valley of the Mississippi*, I, 264–67; and Charlevoix, *New France*, VI, 97–102.
[31] King to Bienville, February 2, 1732, in Rowland and Sanders, *Mississippi Provincial Archives, French Dominion*, III, 540.
[32] Bienville to Maurepas, April 8, 1734, *ibid.*, 656–67; and Alvord, *Illinois Country*, 177.

than ever, at this place, by the war with the Chickasaws who have come twice since spring. Only two days ago the last party took away three people; and since the French took up the tomahawk against them I am obliged every day to put up a defense." And the Chickasaws partially nullified the French-Choctaw blockade of their towns by two tactics: sending out decoy parties followed by furious assaults on invader camps and distributing gifts and peace messages which eroded the Indian mercenaries' morale.[33]

Chickasaw and Natchez raiders also preyed on French shipping on the Mississippi, and Chickasaw agents, well-supplied with British goods, increased their intrigues among the Choctaws to alienate that nation. This campaign never won a majority of the Choctaws, but it did create divisions causing this populous nation to waver. And the appeal of British goods, introduced into the Choctaw Nation by Chickasaw agents, attracted an increasing stream of Choctaw traffic into the Chickasaw Nation to trade at the British stores. Thus there was the paradox of Choctaws coming in peace to trade while French-officered Choctaw mercenaries attempted to maintain the siege on the Chickasaw towns. Governor Perrier's program to destroy Chickasaw power, rather than intimidating this tribe, had provoked the Chickasaws to more intensive and successful efforts to thwart the French purpose. They had extended their range of attack and their intrigues were having a frightening impact. When Bienville returned as governor of Louisiana during the winter of 1732–33, his assessment of the French position was gloomy: "The English have made infinite progress. . . . the Chickasaws entirely belong to them, a part of the Choctaws is wavering." The "Choctaws do not seem so animated [as reported] to make war" on the Chickasaws.[34]

Chickasaw successes, which increased the British threat to the French hold on the lower Mississippi Valley, made Bienville desperate. It appeared that, due to Chickasaw intrigues, the French were losing their principal source of defense, the Choctaws. While a core of French support remained in this tribe, a

[33] Salmon to Maurepas, May 20, 1733, in Rowland and Sanders, *Mississippi Provincial Archives, French Dominion*, I, 205–207; and Williams, *West Tennessee*, 20.

[34] Bienville's Memorandum, August 25, 1733, in Rowland and Sanders, *Mississippi Provincial Archives, French Dominion*, I, 193–204.

disturbing number were wavering. The French commandant at Mobile warned that Choctaws in his area were becoming increasingly "insolent and less tractable." During the summer of 1734, the prominent Choctaw chief Red Shoes went to Carolina to meet with British officials. Chickasaw river raids again threatened to sever connections between Louisiana and Illinois via the Mississippi. And the Chickasaws refused to surrender to the French the Natchez refugees residing in their nation. Bienville revealed his desperation to the French Colonial Office: "As long as the Chickasaws exist we shall always have to fear that they will entice away the others from us in favor of the English. . . . The entire destruction of this hostile nation therefore becomes every day more necessary to our interests and I am going to exert all diligence to accomplish it."[35]

Driven to the ultimate step—mustering all available French military resources and personally leading a campaign of annihilation against the Chickasaw Nation—Bienville collected military stores and provisions and alerted French regulars and militia in Louisiana. He selected a corps of six hundred Choctaws whose loyalty to the French was unquestioned. And he sent spies to the Chickasaw country to study the towns and their defenses and to map his invasion route. Their reports revealed that one large fort, made of tree trunks and with four bastions, protected the enemy towns, while a palisade with loopholes enclosed every ten households. The Chickasaw defenses also included shoulder-deep trenches. Bienville ordered troops and workmen up the Tombigbee to construct a fort on the north edge of the Choctaw Nation, Fort Tombeckbe, as the forward depot for his campaign. And he sent couriers to the Illinois country with dispatches ordering Major Pierre D'Artaguette to assemble local French forces and to rendezvous with his army in the Chickasaw Nation for the campaign which he planned to begin at the end of March, 1736. Waiting for provisions and mortars from France to arrive on storm-slowed ships, delayed Bienville. Finally on April 4, 1736, he collected his army at Mobile—six hundred men in nine companies of French regulars, one Swiss company, two militia companies,

[35] Bienville to Maurepas, April 14, 1735, *ibid.*, 254–60; Bienville to Maurepas, August 26, 1734, *ibid.*, 229–337; and Alvord, *Illinois Country*, 171.

one volunteer company of *voyageurs* and forty-five Negroes, all to be joined later by six hundred Choctaw mercenaries. The army moved up the Mobile River in pirogues and bateaux, arriving at Fort Tombeckbe on April 20. The Choctaw force joined him there.[36]

D'Artaguette's army from the Illinois—thirty French regulars, one hundred French militia, and parties of Miami, Iroquois, and Kaskaskia warriors totaling four hundred—left Fort Chartres and Kaskaskia in late February, 1736. The northern army landed at Chickasaw Bluffs. D'Artaguette had his men construct a small fort and, detaching an officer and twenty-five men as the garrison force, he led his column toward the Chickasaw towns. After nearly three weeks of marching and searching, D'Artaguette could find no trace of Bienville and, the provisions nearly gone, he decided to return to his post on the Chickasaw Bluffs. His scouts, however, had located a Chickasaw town, Chocolissa, and several in his party urged that before departing they capture and plunder it for meat and grain. D'Artaguette placed his baggage and munitions under guard and led the French charge against Chocolissa on the morning of March 25. From loopholes in their palisades, the Chickasaws poured a deadly fire into D'Artaguette's troops, pinning them down while a relief force from a neighboring town flanked the Frenchmen. This threat caused the Miami and Kaskaskia troops to flee. The Chickasaws cut D'Artaguette's army to pieces. Most perished or were captured. Only twenty escaped. Most of the prisoners, including D'Artaguette (who had been wounded three times) and Father Antoine Senat, were burned alive by the incensed Chickasaws. The victors captured D'Artaguette's baggage train which included 450 pounds of powder, 12,000 bullets, and 11 horses.[37]

The Chickasaws, fresh from their victory over the French northern army, strengthened their defenses to receive Bienville's invasion force. Papers taken from D'Artaguette and other captured officers which the Chickasaws delivered to British traders

---

[36] Bienville to Maurepas, September 9, 1735, in Rowland and Sanders, *Mississippi Provincial Archives, French Dominion*, I, 270–74; and Narrative of the War against the Chickasaws, April 1, 1736, *ibid.*, 316–20.

[37] Bienville to Maurepas, June 28, 1736, *ibid.*, 311–14; and Williams, *West Tennessee*, 21–23.

yielded information concerning the French movement from the south. The supreme commander of French forces arrived in the Chickasaw country in late May. On the morning of May 26, his troops could see the Chickasaw villages looming on small rises in the broad prairie just west of the Tombigbee. As Bienville placed his army in battle order, five Chickasaws appeared in his camp, one carrying the peace calumet. These were leaders of the French party. They had met with Bienville the year before and promised to work for peace and to persuade the British party to bow to Bienville's demand that they surrender the Natchez residing in their nation. A squad of Choctaw troops appeared and fired at the emissaries. Three with wounds fled to their town. The Choctaws handed the slain Chickasaws' scalps to the supreme commander.[38]

Bienville's army waited near the Chickasaw town of Akia. He and Chevalier de Noyan studied the town's defenses and chose a triangular extension of stockaded houses near the French camp for the initial assault. De Noyan selected a force of 120 regulars including detachments from the Karmer Grenadier Regiment and the Halwill Regiment, and 60 Swiss. At three o'clock on the afternoon of May 26, the Battle of Akia began as the invaders marched on the Chickasaw defenses with rattling drums and flying flags.[39] De Noyan's troops captured and burned the first three fortified compounds, then carried a forward palisade which they used as a screen to ready themselves for a rush into the town's center. There they were checked. The inner defenses caught the French troops in a deadly crossfire: the "head of the column and the grenadiers were exposed and were badly handled." Charge after charge melted in the withering fire which seriously wounded de Noyan and fifty-two others and killed twenty-four regulars. Bienville rushed reenforcements into the town, but they were driven back with losses. Finally, after three hours of French bloodletting, the supreme commander ordered the drummers to beat retreat, and the French invasion force hurried to safety beyond the Tombigbee. Bienville claimed that dur-

[38] Bienville to Maurepas, February 10, 1736 in Rowland and Sanders, *Mississippi Provincial Archives, French Dominion*, I, 274–94; and Bienville to Maurepas, June 28, 1736, *ibid.*, 297–310.
[39] *Ibid.*

ing the battle his Choctaw troops hid under the cover of a hill "waiting for the outcome, then rose and fired several volleys." They lost twenty-two killed and wounded. In excusing his shameful defeat, Bienville placed much blame on the Choctaws and also pointed to Chickasaw marksmanship. "It is true that the Chickasaws have the advantage of shooting more accurately than perhaps any other nation."[40]

The French disaster at the Battle of Akia only intensified France's determination to destroy the Chickasaw Nation. In the period between 1736 and 1763, French officials maintained sustained pressure on the Chickasaws with their Choctaw and northern Indian mercenaries. Their raids caused some migration from the Chickasaw Nation to safety near the English settlements in South Carolina and Georgia. But by Bienville's calculation there remained a deadly core of at least 450 Chickasaw and perhaps 150 Natchez warriors. Besides extended raids by French Indians, the Chickasaw Nation also bore the brunt of two additional invasions by sizable French armies before 1763. Soon after his defeat at Akia in 1736, Bienville began planning the second invasion of the Chickasaw Nation. He ventured to officials in France that "an honest war would be better than a bad peace." And he added that because of "the love they [the Chickasaws] have for their country, their recent successes and the great number of hostile nations with which they are surrounded will make them remain in their country until the last and it is on that we must depend in order to strike them a blow from which they will never recover." For this decisive blow Bienville asked the French Colonial Office to send him sufficient reenforcements, about five hundred troops, to enable him to muster an army of twelve hundred regular and militia forces to which he planned to add fifteen hundred northern and southern Indian mercenaries.[41]

The French minister of colonies informed Bienville that the King was so anxious to restore the "honor of France" in the lower Mississippi Valley that he authorized seven hundred regular reenforcements to insure success "in accomplishing the destruction of the Chickasaw Indians." Bienville's attention was directed to

40 *Ibid.*; and Bienville to Maurepas, September 1, 1736, *ibid.*, 314–16.
41 Bienville to Maurepas, September 1, 1736, *ibid.*, 320–26.

the "great expenditures that he [the King] is willing to make on this occasion" which indicated "how much he has at heart the success of this undertaking. It is so much the more necessary that, in addition to the new expense which doubtful success might cause, that will assure the tranquillity of the colony and reestablish in this country the glory of his arms. His Majesty recommends to him to give it all his attention to take the most proper measures for success."[42]

Pressure from the crown for success drove Bienville to make elaborate preparations for the second Chickasaw Nation invasion. He decided to strike at the Chickasaws from a landing at the Chickasaw Bluffs, and sent a party of 150 soldiers and workmen up the river to the site of old Fort Prudhomme, La Salle's former base on the Chickasaw Bluffs, to construct a fort and depot to receive military stores. The new post was named Fort Assumption. Quapaw scouts led French engineers inland near the Chickasaw towns to map the country and mark the routes for the invasion army. Bienville sent detailed instructions to French officers on the Arkansas, in the Illinois country and Canada, directing them to collect regular, militia, and Indian troops and to be ready to rendezvous at the Chickasaw Bluffs on the appointed day. Ordnance officers collected vast stores of munitions and weapons. Bienville's artillery included four eight-pounder cannon, eight four-pounders, and large and small mortars, the former capable of firing twenty-pound demolition bombs. A large supply of mines arrived from France with a detachment of six demolition experts from the Turmel Company. Bienville believed that the mines and twenty-pound bombs could be used with good effect on the strong Chickasaw defenses. Ordnance stores for the Chickasaw campaign included two thousand grenades, fifty thousand pounds of powder, sixty thousand pounds of bullets, and bombs. Workmen constructed fifty river boats, each forty feet long, to transport troops and stores. Officers collected eighty yoke of oxen to pull subsistence and ordnance wagons and two hundred horses to draw artillery and to "relieve the officers who will be inconveni-

[42] Memorandum from King to Bienville about Preparations for the Chickasaw Expedition, 1739, *ibid.*, 376–79.

enced by the march." Bienville also ordered fifty light wagons to be drawn by Negro slaves. Finally, after three years of preparation, Bienville was ready to redeem "the honor of France." He ordered his troops to rendezvous at the Chickasaw Bluffs during September, 1739.[43]

During the early autumn of 1739, Chickasaw spies watched an armada of river boats, arriving from both the north and south, land Bienville's thirty-six-hundred-man army at the bluffs. Heavy and sustained rains set in. French officers, faced with a march of about one hundred miles to the Chickasaw towns with a huge baggage and artillery train, found the planned invasion routes impassable and bivouacked their troops near Fort Assumption. The only action for three months was an occasional brush between French patrols and Chickasaw spy parties, resulting in a few casualties and the capture of several prisoners by both sides. Bienville, waiting for optimum operational conditions was finally pressured by his officers into sending Captain Pierre Celeron with six hundred Canadian troops and Iroquois and Choctaw mercenaries toward the Chickasaw settlements. Celeron's mission was to capture a Chickasaw town, arrange for an exchange of prisoners, and urge the Chickasaws to send a delegation to Bienville to negotiate a peace. Celeron's column held a Chickasaw town under a two-day siege but was forced to retreat with losses. He did succeed in delivering Bienville's invitation for a council. During February, 1740, a Chickasaw delegation arrived at Fort Assumption and negotiated a peace with the French. Both sides agreed to end hostilities and exchange prisoners. The Chickasaws informed Bienville that the Natchez living among them had fled during the French landings. Bienville did not press this point. Meanwhile, the French commander convened his officers in a council of war at Fort Assumption for advice and opinions on the policy "advisable to adopt in a situation as thorny as this one in which we find ourselves." The consensus was that, in view of the condition of the roads and continuing rains, "we cannot without exposing the honor of the King's arms to receive a defeat, march

[43] Bienville to Maurepas, February 16, 1737, *ibid.*, 332–34; and Bienville to Maurepas, May 12, 1739, *ibid.*, 389–95.

against the enemy, since we are not able to carry the artillery and the provisions necessary for their [Chickasaw] subjugation."[44]

After his council with the Chickasaws, Bienville ordered a general withdrawal. Thus, the French had failed a second time to conquer the Chickasaw Nation. One officer reflected the contempt and scorn which coursed through the Louisiana settlements following Bienville's evacuation of Fort Assumption: "What a triumph for these barbarians when they see such a large force abandon the expedition when it has gone almost to their forts! What an opinion the other Indians especially the Choctaws will have of the valor of the French. . . . Now they will treat us as women, and in a way they will be right."[45]

Bienville's second failure to conquer the Chickasaws caused his removal as governor of Louisiana. During 1743, when his successor, the Marquis de Vaudreuil, arrived at New Orleans, he found the Chickasaws to be his most serious problem. Their vicious forays against French settlements, their retaliatory attacks on French Indian villages, their sustained intrigues among Choctaws and other French tribes, and their destructive river raids drove the French in 1752 to again attempt the annihilation of the Chickasaw Nation. Vaudreuil mustered an army of seven hundred regulars and a large number of Indian mercenaries and marched on the enemy nation by way of the Tombigbee, Bienville's invasion route of 1736. The Chickasaws wisely remained in their fortified towns. The French could not dislodge them and withdrew with some losses after setting fire to the deserted villages, destroying crops, and running off livestock.[46]

The long struggle between France and Great Britain for colonial supremacy, climaxed by the Seven Years' War, ended with the Peace of Paris on January 1, 1763. The triumph of British arms in

[44] Deliberations of the Council of War held by Bienville at Fort Assumption, February 9, 1740, *ibid.*, 428–31; and Beauchamp to Maurepas, March 19, 1740, *ibid.*, 438–41.

[45] Beauchamp to Maurepas, March 12, 1740, *ibid.*, 433–38.

[46] Vaudreuil to Rouille, September 22, 1749, in Theodore C. Pease (ed.), *Illinois on the Eve of the Seven Years' War, 1747–1755*, 111–18; Bienville to Maurepas, August 5, 1742, in Rowland and Sanders, *Mississippi Provincial Archives, French Dominion*, III, 771–73; Raymond to Jonquiere, January 5, 1750, in Pease, *Illinois on the Eve of the Seven Years' War*, 149–56; Charles Gayarre, *History of Louisiana*, II, 64–65; and Journal of John Buckles, in W. L. McDowell (ed.) *Documents Relating to Indian Affairs*, 382–85.

that war marked the fulfillment of the Anglo design in the West. By the terms of the peace treaty the British received Canada, the Illinois country, and the rich prize of the eastern half of the Mississippi Valley. The Chickasaw Nation had been an enduring enclave of emerging British power in the West, and Chickasaw warriors, by serving their nation's purpose in thwarting the French drive to link the Illinois and Louisiana settlements and thus to build a position of strength in the West, also served the British. A preliminary agreement, signed on November 3, 1762, by French and Spanish representatives at Fountainbleau, provided for the cession of Louisiana from France to Spain and injected into Mississippi Valley affairs a new force which affected the stream of Chickasaw history until the turn of the century. Soon after the signing of the Peace of Paris, French-allied tribes in the lower Mississippi Valley transferred their fealty to representatives of Great Britain. For the Chickasaw Nation this ceremony was unnecessary.

CHAPTER THREE

SERVING THREE MASTERS

THE period 1763 to 1786 was a confusing and divisive time for the Chickasaws. The insinuation of European ways and things into Chickasaw life, begun as a determined commercial thrust in 1698, became a deadly international contest between France and Great Britain for control of the Chickasaws and other tribes of the lower Mississippi Valley. By 1763, through conquest, diplomacy, and aid from the Chickasaws, the British had won Florida from Spain, and Canada, the Illinois country, and the trans-montane territory east of the Mississippi between the Ohio River and Florida, from France. Despite the fact that a single power claimed dominion over this region, there was continued controversy over the question of control of the land, its resources, and its peoples. The transfer of Louisiana by France to Spain in 1762 introduced a new and disturbing force. Confusion as to control and allegiance was compounded in the mid-1770's when the American independence movement added another force to the struggle for the support of the tribes of the lower Mississippi Valley. Thus in less than twenty-five years, the Chickasaws and their neighbors found themselves in the midst of a great international rivalry. Each nation especially exerted itself to win over the Chickasaws. In the process, each country, by seeking out tribal partisans and creating loyal factions, contributed to the subtle conquest of personal and public Chickasaw honor and independence.

The Chickasaws and neighboring tribes were subjected to a noticeable administrative tightening at the close of the Seven Years' War. This was accomplished in two ways. British officials held a series of councils with Indian leaders to incorporate the new lands and peoples into the British imperial system and to inform the tribes of their place in the new order. Also, the British government formulated a policy to govern the lands and the tribes. This was a new thing for the Chickasaws. Until 1763, France had claimed suzerainty over all lands and peoples of the lower Mississippi Valley. The Choctaws and most other tribes nominally accepted French dominion. Except for the small French party in the tribe, the Chickasaws regarded themselves as free and independent of all foreign nations and therefore refused to acknowledge fealty to France or any other power. The Chickasaws received British traders and served the British purpose in the Mississippi Valley. They did so not because they considered themselves British mercenaries, but rather because the British furnished them with the technical assistance and arms and ammunition necessary to thwart France's sustained drive to destroy their independence and to force them to accept vassal status in the French colonial system. Thus the new British mode for governing the tribes had the effect of creating a second level of government for the Chickasaws. The first level, their tribal government, was becoming increasingly turbulent and disorganized by factionalism created by the intrusion of alien forces. If the rank and file Chickasaws found it increasingly confusing and difficult to understand their own government, in their unsophisticated state they could hardly be expected to comprehend this new level of government.

British councils with the lower Mississippi Valley tribes, designed to receive the tribes into the new order and to inform their leaders of the new system for administering trade and land and for regulating tribal affairs, began with the Augusta council in 1763 and closed with the Mobile council in 1765. Chickasaw delegations attended several of these councils. Officials pointed to their unwavering loyalty to the British king and admonished the Choctaws and other tribes to emulate them. This exploitation of Chickasaw constancy to British purpose became a common device in the conduct of councils: "As the Chickasaws have ever been faithful to us they shou'd be distinguished by our favours to them before any other Nation & Showing a partiality for them before other Indians might inspire others with a resolution of imitating their fidelity." At the 1765 Mobile council, Governor George Johnstone, addressing Chickasaw and Choctaw delegations, prefaced his denunciation of Choctaw duplicity with recognition of Chickasaw dedication:

> You generous friends of the Chickasaw nation, who have so long adhered to the interests of the English, whom neither dangers could startle nor promises seduce from our interest. I hope there is little more necessary with you than to renew our ancient alliance, which as it has continued for many ages to the mutual advantage of both nations, so I hope it will continue until this earth is dissolved.[1]

The second level of government over the Chickasaws was established by the British in 1764 by dividing Florida at the Chattahoochee River into East and West Florida. West Florida, bounded on the north by the thirty-first parallel and extending to the Mississippi River, had jurisdiction over the territory south of the Ohio River. Its governmental apparatus had to accommodate both European settlers and Indian tribes. Governor Johnstone reached Pensacola, capital of West Florida, in February, 1764, with a regiment which he dispersed at Fort Charlotte (Mobile), Fort Bute (Manchac), and Fort Panmure (Natchez). Johnstone and John Stuart, superintendent of Indian affairs for the tribes south of the Ohio River, drew on established British policy, law, and experience to fashion the governmental structure for administering the Chickasaws and other tribes in their jurisdiction.

Besides trade, Indian leaders were most concerned about settlers invading tribal lands. Johnstone and Stuart attempted to assuage these fears by pointing to the Royal Proclamation of October 7, 1763, which they were bound to enforce. It declared the region between the Appalachian Mountains and Mississippi River and the Ohio River and thirty-first parallel reserved for the exclusive benefit of resident tribes. Private land purchases and settlement were prohibited. The domain of each Indian nation was to be surveyed, the boundaries marked, and each tribe pro-

---

[1] Fraser to Haldimand, May 4, 1776, in Clarence W. Alvord and Clarence E. Carter (eds.), *The New Regime, 1765–1767*, II, 266; and Mobile Council Proceedings, March, 1765, in Dunbar Rowland (ed.), *Mississippi Provincial Archives, English Dominion*, I, 188–225.

tected in the tenure, occupancy, and exploitation of that domain. The supervision and administration of this royal province, a huge Indian reserve, was placed with the superintendent of Indian affairs and ranking military officials where appropriate.[2]

Another source for this second level of government was a royal document, titled "Plan for the Future Management of Indian Affairs," devised "to place commercial and political relations with all of the Indians under a general system, administered by Crown officials, independent of provincial interference." It provided for the organization of two huge Indian reservations, one north of the Ohio River, the other south of the Ohio River. Each was governed by a superintendent who·had exclusive authority to regulate trade. The plan provided for a close supervision and licensing of traders who were under substantial bond. Traders were forbidden to traffic in rum or other spirits, "swan shott," or rifle-barreled guns. Credit to Indians was limited to fifty shillings per person. The superintendent was authorized to appoint a deputy to each tribe (called a commissary), an interpreter, and a gunsmith. The superintendent and his deputies were delegated judicial powers and commissioned as justices of the peace with the power to commit offenders in capital cases. Indians were brought under British law in that the superintendent and his deputies presided in actions involving Indians and traders. To integrate the Chickasaws and other tribes into the governmental apparatus, each Indian town was to select a "Beloved Man" approved by the superintendent. In a very real sense he was to be the local royal representative. The approved "Beloved Men" elected a chief who served as the supreme royal representative for the tribe. He was "to live in the same town as the commissary, to sit at all trials and to express the opinion of the Indians upon all important affairs." This plan was never submitted for parliamentary approval, but Stuart and Johnstone applied it to their Indian province to provide a structure for governing the many tribes of their jurisdiction and to defeat the seaboard colonies in their attempt to control Indian lands and trade.[3]

[2] Helen L. Shaw, *British Administration of the Southern Indians, 1756–1783*, 26–32.
[3] *Ibid.*

Stuart appointed John McIntosh as his deputy or commissary for the Chickasaws. They accepted him and looked to him for direction in their time of mounting confusion. One of McIntosh's first public acts as Chickasaw commissary was to muster a force of warriors to assist in taking over the Illinois country. A conspiracy in the Northwest—the British claimed it was French inspired—threatened to incite the entire Indian community of that region to thwart the British takeover. One British officer reported that a French agent who "has taken considerable presents for Pontiac from New Orleans" had arrived in the Illinois country, and "Indians have also left our side [of the river] and gone to the Spanish side." One "great chief of the Illinois," on his way to New Orleans "with no good intentions I believe," was intercepted by a Chickasaw party guarding the river. The British official reported that "the threats of the Chickasaws brought him back. . . . That Nation can be very Usefull in case of Disturbances amongst the Northern Indians, as would not only cut off all Supplies, but would also Strike upon them with as many Men as we would Choose."[4]

During December, 1765, the Thirty-fourth British Regiment moved up the Mississippi from the Gulf to occupy the Illinois country. McIntosh and a party of 125 Chickasaws met the regiment at the Chickasaw Bluffs. Major Robert Farmar, in charge of the operation, met in council with the Chickasaws. When the British army moved upstream, 14 Chickasaws joined the British for the movement to the Illinois country. Farmar had high praise for their service as flankers and hunters: "Had it not been for the buffalo meat they supplied us, the expedition must have failed, being about five weeks short of provisions. . . . They were of great Service here likewise; both French & Indians stand in great Awe of them. I have made them join hands with the Illinois Indians; but only in consequence of their good behavior to the English."[5]

With the British in control of the country between the Atlantic and the Mississippi and with no hostile foreign power then present to wage war or to stir neighboring tribes against them, the Chickasaws enjoyed a brief time of relative peace. The northern

[4] Fraser to Gage, December 16, 1765, in Alvord and Carter, *New Regime*, 130.
[5] Farmer to Stuart, December 16, 1765, *ibid.*, 79.

tribes which had made the Chickasaw Nation a bounty-hunting ground through French encouragement temporarily halted their raids due to Major Farmar's intercession. And the Chickasaws made a permanent peace with the Choctaws.

The Chickasaws did wage and win at least one war, which had no direct European connection, with another tribe before the outbreak of the American War of Independence. For several years the Chickasaws had been in league with the Cherokees to check Shawnee attempts to occupy territory they claimed along the Cumberland and Tennessee rivers. In 1715 and again in 1745 the Chickasaws and Cherokees joined to expel the Shawnees. Around 1765 the British peace encouraged some Chickasaws to leave their compact, fortified towns on the Tombigbee and to scatter along the Tennessee River near the original Chickasaw Old Fields. During 1769 a Cherokee force challenged this eastward extension of Chickasaw settlement and was soundly defeated.[6]

This dispersal of Chickasaw settlements toward the Tennessee River was but one manifestation of a number of significant demographic alterations occurring in the tribe. There had been a sustained scattering of Chickasaws before 1763, and it continued, but for different reasons, after that date. The Chickasaws had extended their hunting and depredation range before 1763 in part through retaliatory wars on French Indians and in part because economic pressures forced an ever-widening search for Indian slaves and pelts to meet the English trader demands. Chickasaws had roamed north of the Ohio into the Illinois country and west of the Mississippi along the Arkansas and Red and their lower tributaries. Bernard de la Harpe met a Chickasaw trader in the Wichita villages on the Canadian in 1719. But in this broadened range the Chickasaws hunted and traded from temporary bases, returning to the Tombigbee settlements for the exchange of pelts and slaves. In the period of the British peace Chickasaws continued to hunt and trade on the Arkansas and Red and their lower tributaries.

Just as there was a scattering of Chickasaw settlements and a widening of their economic range during the period of the British

---

[6] Nina Leftwich, *Two Hundred Years at Muscle Shoals*, 12; and Swanton, *The Indians of the Southeastern United States*, 117.

peace, there was also a return of dispersed bands. The French wars had caused some Chickasaw families to move to the safety of the English settlements. About 1723 a band under the Squirrel King settled on the South Carolina side of the Savannah River, and through the years of bloody strife in the lower Mississippi Valley other Chickasaw bands joined this group. Some *émigrés* settled across the river in Georgia. Another Chickasaw band, containing about eighty warriors, was colonized in the Creek Nation near the head of the Coosa River, probably to guard British packtrains bound for the western trade. With the British peace in 1763 most dispersed bands returned to the Chickasaw Nation, although some were returning as late as 1786, and a few Chickasaw stragglers were reported in South Carolina and Georgia in 1795.[7]

Another important demographic alteration occurring in the Chickasaw Nation was a mixing of Indian bloodlines, produced by absorbing neighboring tribes to maintain tribal population and to offset losses caused by the extended wars with the French and their Indian mercenaries. The Chickasaws had absorbed a large number of Natchez following the French attempt to exterminate that tribe in 1730. Several small tribes, the Quinipissa (Napissa), the Taposa, and the Ibitoupa, situated just south of the Chickasaw Nation, united with the Chickasaws. The Chakchiumas on the upper Yazoo River, once friendly to the French, had suffered heavy losses at the hands of the Chickasaws in the 1740's. After 1763 the Chickasaws blended peacefully with the surviving Chakchiumas.[8]

Just as the mixing of Indian bloodlines continued during the period of British peace, there was also an acceleration of the blending of Indian and white. The growing mixed-blood community in the Chickasaw Nation had far-reaching effects on the tribe's economic, social, and political life. The mixed bloods, more like their Anglo fathers than their Indian mothers, better understood the ways of the British, Spanish, and later the Americans. They were more assertive than their full-blood counterparts and

[7] Swanton, *The Indian Tribes of North America*, 93; and Jacobs, *Indians of the Southern Colonial Frontier*, 45, 64.

[8] John R. Swanton, *Indian Tribes of the Lower Mississippi Valley and Adjacent Coast of the Gulf of Mexico*, B.A.E. *Bulletin 43*, 279–97.

came to comprise a sort of aristocracy in the tribe. More and more the avenues to tribal leadership shifted from clan association based on wisdom and bravery to mixed-blood parentage based on accommodation with the emerging order. As the times became more confused, the innocent full bloods increasingly withdrew or transported themselves out of their confusion with rum and brandy supplied by the traders. Thus by default as well as by deliberate action, the mixed bloods moved in and gradually took over management of tribal affairs. One of the leading mixed-blood families was established by James Logan Colbert, a Scotsman who in 1729 began a forty-year residence in the Chickasaw Nation. Colbert married three Chickasaw women who bore him many children. His sons, William, George, Levi, Samuel, Joseph, and Pittman (James), were the principal Chickasaw spokesmen for well over a century. The elder Colbert, with his "rich lodging" and one hundred and fifty Negro slaves, set the economic and social tone for Chickasaw mixed blood emulation. The growing Chickasaw mixed-blood community also changed settlement patterns. John McIntosh, the British commissary appointed by Superintendent Stuart, established his headquarters at Tokshish, a Chickasaw town on the Indian trail which became the Natchez Trace. The town's name was changed to McIntoshville. Mixed-blood families gathered there, and McIntoshville became a model for other mixed-blood settlements as this growing community separated itself more and more from the primitive full bloods.[9]

By 1800 the mixed bloods had completely taken over the management of Chickasaw tribal affairs. But in the period 1763 to 1786 some full-blood leaders, notably Payamataha and Piomingo, attempted to turn back the tide of change and to preserve the power of their group as the directing force in Chickasaw government and society. To accomplish this, they regarded it as essential to restore and preserve the old ways. Distressed and alarmed at the growing corruption of their young warriors and at the mounting tribal confusion and deterioration, they blamed the trader abuses and the exposure of their people to the encircling Anglo

[9] John W. Caughey, *Bernardo de Galvez in Louisiana, 1776–1783*, 228; and Harry Warren, "Missions, Missionaries, Frontier Characters and Schools," *Publications of the Mississippi Historical Society*, Vol. VIII (1904), 585.

settlements. Payamataha, Piomingo, and other full-blood leaders regularly voiced their concerns to Superintendent Stuart, Commissary McIntosh, and Governor Johnstone and his successors. They pointed to their tribal government, beset with pressures from ambitious mixed bloods and powerful trader cliques and faltering in its attempt to govern the nation. And they pointed to the second level of government imposed upon them by the British, ostensibly to better protect and preserve their local determination, but seemingly abetting those who turned it to their selfish purposes.

Chickasaw leaders were very sensitive to the threat of envelopment by Anglo settlements. They insisted that British officials survey their domain, mark it, and assist them in excluding intruders. Payamataha and Piomingo had the sad example of Squirrel King's band in South Carolina to warn them of the contaminating influence of settlements. A British report issued in the 1750's admitted the corrosive impact of too close contact. It read: "These Indians are not less brave, or less good Hunters than the Nation they come from . . . altho from the great Ease wherewith they acquire all necessaries, and too much Liquor ever at Hand, they have been much debauched. The constant and too great Familiarity added thereto, which they have been used to among the Settlers, and the many Indian Traders daily in that Neighborhood, hath made them somewhat insolent and mischievous."[10]

Because of its remoteness the Chickasaw Nation had escaped the Anglo settler invasion which had occurred before 1763 in portions of the Cherokee, Creek, and Choctaw nations. The British action in 1763 of reserving the land west of the mountains and north of Florida as off limits to settlers exercised only a nominal check on the extension of this menace. Following the British takeover of West Florida there occurred a rush of immigrants from the British Isles, the West Indies, and the American seaboard colonies to the lower Mississippi Valley and Gulf. A favorite route to the West Florida settlements was by way of the Ohio or Tennessee rivers, then across Chickasaw territory to the Mississippi. Many immigrants squatted on Chickasaw lands. Another

[10] Jacobs, *Indians of the Southern Colonial Frontier*, 45.

settlement type, more subtle, also developed in the Chickasaw Nation after the British takeover. The resident European community, ostensibly traders, greatly increased. But many were settlers in a real sense in that they brought their families or formed mixed-blood families and opened plantations with slave labor. The traffic across their territory, the squatters, and the growing trader-settler community disturbed and alarmed the full-blood Chickasaw leaders. Conscientiously and persistently they appealed to British officials for the protection their nation had been promised. The government at Pensacola had to accommodate both European settlers and adjacent Indian tribes. With limited resources, providing just administration for these two disparate communities was nearly impossible. But officials made the attempt. As late as 1778, Governor Peter Chester urged the West Florida Provincial Assembly to inflict the severest legal penalties on persons settling in the Chickasaw Nation and other Indian lands reserved by the 1763 proclamation. He also pressed for a completion of the survey and marking of the Chickasaw Nation.[11]

Another serious problem facing the Chickasaws in the post-1763 period was the mounting abuse by traders. Soon after 1763 the number of traders in the Chickasaw Nation increased in less than a year from under thirty to over one hundred, and there occurred a concomitant increase in their influence. This generated widespread resentment, and the tribal council threatened to expel them. To avoid this the trader clique tampered with Chickasaw politics and installed a complaisant clan chief, Mingo Houma, in the position of principal chief.[12]

Superintendent Stuart intervened through his Chickasaw deputy John McIntosh and reduced Mingo Houma to his lesser clan position, but the baneful influence of the traders in tribal politics continued. Stuart attempted to reduce the number of traders in the nation by exercising his authority under the "Plan for the

11 Wilbur H. Siebert, "The Loyalists in West Florida and the Natchez District," *Proceedings of the Mississippi Valley Historical Association*, Vol. VIII (1914–15), 103; and George C. Osborn, "Relations with the Indians in West Florida During the Administration of Governor Peter Chester, 1770–1781," *Florida Historical Quarterly*, Vol. XXXI (April, 1953), 265.
12 John R. Alden, *John Stuart and the Southern Colonial Frontier*, 323.

Future Management of Indian Affairs" and by licensing a single trader for each town. But they nullified its effect and maintained their numbers by hiring the horde of non-licensed traders as assistants. The trader population increased even more in 1768 when Stuart was required to share his licensing power with the colonial governments.[13]

At every council held with the Chickasaws by Stuart and the West Florida governors between the Augusta Congress of 1763 and the Mobile Congress of 1777, the full-blood leadership complained of the growing trader presence and their corrupting influence and appealed for aid in ridding their nation of this scourge. Stuart attempted unsuccessfully to reduce their numbers by a strict licensing system and to control their transactions with Indians by setting a price list for peltries and merchandise. At the Mobile Congress of 1772, Payamataha said his nation was "once great but now much diminished" largely because traders corrupted his people and cheated them with "short weights and measures." The fabric pieces used by the warriors for breech-cloths were reportedly so flimsy and narrow that "they don't cover our secret parts, and we are in danger of being deprived of our manhood by every hungry dog that approaches." He charged that the traders made his people disrespect old ways, corrupted their "manners," and "rendered them ungovernable." Sharp trader practices often took advantage of the growing Chickasaw addiction to rum and brandy. For example traders exchanged generously, as ten skins for a fathom of cloth, and "when they have gathered in all the skins they bring out their brandy and get back their . . . cloth with this beverage, which they sell dearly."[14]

Once British traders had flooded the Chickasaw towns with goods, they became hard pressed to find new and appealing things to keep hunters in the field after pelts. Thus, more and more traders turned to brandy and rum as their principal trade items. As early as 1750 the colonial governments had allowed rum

[13] Shaw, *British Administration*, 23.
[14] Mobile Council Proceedings, March 26, 1765, in Rowland, *Mississippi Provincial Archives, English Dominion*, I, 215; Osborn, "Relations with the Indians in West Florida," *Florida Historical Quarterly*, Vol. XXXI (April, 1953), 247–51; and Perrier to Director, June 22, 1729, in Rowland and Sanders, *Mississippi Provincial Archives, French Dominion*, II, 610–24.

in the Indian traffic in "such moderate Quantities as they [the traders] shall think convenient." West Florida governors and Superintendent Stuart had made serious attempts to ban intoxicants in the Indian trade. In 1765, Governor Johnstone called on Chickasaw leaders to assist him in checking the rum traffic:

> Bringing that Poisonous Liquor called Rum into your Country . . . has distracted your Wise Nation to such a Degree that I never expected to have heard Concerning the Chickasaws . . . [and] they are our People who carry the Liquor which is the Cause of the Mischief. I consider them as the real Agressors. Those men who are Guilty of carrying that Liquor amongst you ought to be Considered as your real Enemies much more than if they lifted the Hatchet against you. . . . It is therefore my Request . . . that you will Seize . . . every drop of Spirituous Liquors which may be introduced amongst you.[15]

Working with Commissary McIntosh, the Chickasaw full-blood elders banished all traders trafficking in rum. But rum traders lurked in the woods, tempting Chickasaw hunters with their strong drink and cheating them out of their pelts. One renegade trader was reported to have returned surreptitiously with twenty-six kegs of rum which "inebriated" a large portion of one of the nation's principal towns "for a long Time to the damage of the . . . Quiet & security of the Nation."[16]

A British official who had just completed an inspection of the Indian country observed that all the tribes seemed addicted to rum and brandy. He reported, "They are in general great Drunkards." The Chickasaws used rum and brandy but were not "so passionately fond of drink as other Nations are. . . . Drink is the Occasion of all our troubles amongst them, and it were much to be wish'd that the Assemblies or Councils of the neighboring Provinces would restrict the Vending of it, as has been done to the Northward."[17]

Banishing the rum vendors from the Chickasaw Nation, rather than inducing a more temperate state among the warriors, seemed

---

[15] Mobile Council Proceedings, March, 1765, in Rowland, *Mississippi Provincial Archives, English Dominion*, I, 215.

[16] McIntosh to Richardson, April 15, 1766, in Alvord and Carter, *New Regime*, 214.

[17] Fraser to Haldimand, May 4, 1766, *ibid.*, 266.

to make them more determined to pursue this folly. In 1770 an official estimated that four-fifths of the skins brought in by traders were obtained with rum. And when renegade traders were unable to fill their intoxicant needs, Chickasaw drinkers journeyed to the settlements to trade for rum. In 1772 a Chickasaw band carried a load of pelts to Kaskaskia in the Illinois country which they exchanged with local tavern keepers for rum. Soon wild drunk, they turned on the town, plundered stores, killed one citizen, and wounded another. Only the timely arrival of a company of soldiers stopped them from putting the torch to the town.[18]

Superintendent Stuart and the West Florida governors persisted in their efforts to protect the Chickasaws from rum traffic, exploitation by traders, and invasion by settlers. But, the enormity of their problems compounded by the power of callous business interests which profited from the contraband trade and by the general lack of co-ordination in regulating trade and settlement with other colonial governments, doomed their efforts to failure. The enforcement and protection problem, especially as related to the rum traffic, was made worse by the innocent and unwitting co-operation of the average Chickasaw warrior who, confused by the rapid changes occurring in his nation, took refuge in strong drink. Also, increasingly the energy and attention of West Florida officials had to be addressed to the broader problem of securing their portion of the lower Mississippi Valley from the threat posed by Spain and the emerging United States.

Slowly, almost reluctantly, Spanish officials took over French Louisiana, completing the formal process in 1769. Spain followed a cautious policy of exploiting the power resources of the region and by 1770 was mildly intriguing with the Choctaws. About this time representatives of the old French party in the Chickasaw Nation made occasional trips to New Orleans and St. Louis soliciting Spanish officials to serve as their protectors, much as the French had in earlier times. Increasingly after 1770 the British-Indian congresses with Chickasaw and Choctaw leaders at Mobile and Pensacola served as forums to counter Spanish intrigue.

[18] Magistrates to Todd, May 21, 1779, in Clarence W. Alvord (ed.), *Kaskaskia Records, 1778–1790*, II, 88–132; and Alden, *John Stuart*, 315.

Superintendent Stuart and the governors regularly warned these Indian leaders of the evil Spanish design, reminded them of their treaty obligations to Great Britain, and assured them of continued protection by the British king.[19]

Spanish meddling with the tribes on the east side of the lower Mississippi Valley increased each year. British officials worked to counter this, but by the mid-1770's they had to give greater attention to the war generated by the seaboard colonies. During 1774, crown officials directed Governor Chester to muster the resources of his region and prepare to defend it. Chester replied that of all the tribes under his jurisdiction the Chickasaws could be expected to provide major support. They "have always been very good friends to the English and . . . we may rely (in case the War becomes general) that they will join us."[20]

In the early stage of the American Revolution, British strategy was to concentrate operations on the Atlantic seaboard and to establish a defensive system in the West to guard against an American thrust to the Mississippi. For the western defense the British planned to rely largely on warriors drawn from the tribes of the lower Mississippi Valley. This was confirmed in an order issued from Boston in October, 1775, by General Thomas Gage to Stuart which directed him to rally the Chickasaws and other tribes in his area and "when opportunity offers . . . to make them take arms against his Majesty's enemies." Thereupon Indian Superintendent Stuart became a military co-ordinator. He collected arms and ammunition at St. Augustine, Pensacola, and Mobile and dispatched them to his commissaries in the Indian nations for distribution to the warriors. During December, 1775, a packtrain containing three thousand pounds of powder and a large supply of lead arrived at the Chickasaw towns. Stuart expected that to reach British positions on the Gulf any American invasion force would cross the Chickasaw Nation via the well-blazed immigrant traces. Thus he concentrated his Chickasaw troops on the trails funneling into the upper Tombigbee Valley.[21]

19 Chester to Hillsborough, December 28, 1771, in Rowland, *Mississippi Provincial Archives, English Dominion*, V. 1771–73.

20 Chester to Dartmouth, June 4, 1774, in Rowland, *Mississippi Provincial Archives, English Dominion*, VI, 1774–76.

21 Shaw, *British Administration*, 111–21; and Philip M. Hamer, "The Watau-

During February, 1778, an American force did invade the lower Mississippi Valley, but it came by way of the Ohio and Mississippi. Captain James Willing and a force of about one hundred men packed in two boats slipped past the Chickasaw Bluffs, raided British plantations and settlements between Natchez and Walnut Hills, then proceeded to the sanctuary of Spanish New Orleans. The Willing raid caused Stuart to shift his defenses. He positioned Chickasaw squads along the Mississippi from the mouth of the Ohio to below the bluffs. Chickasaw bands also marched with British regulars and West Florida militia guarding the land routes into the region.[22]

The Chickasaws' bloodiest action against the Americans occurred in 1780. It grew out of George Rogers Clark's conquest of the British Northwest. To provide the Americans with a base to launch a similar campaign into the British Southwest, Clark was ordered by Governor Thomas Jefferson of Virginia to build a fort below the mouth of the Ohio in Chickasaw territory. Jefferson also intended for the post to serve as a depot for arming northern Indians. His plan was to send them into the Chickasaw Nation to harass the towns and soften the Chickasaws for conquest. He regarded them as the stalwarts of the British defenses south of the Ohio River and thus the key to destroying British power there. The post, completed in April, 1780, and garrisoned with one hundred men, was named Fort Jefferson. Settlers collected around the post and opened farms. Chickasaw squads on the upper ring of Stuart's defenses discovered the American invasion, notified Stuart's deputy in their nation, and urged reenforcements. James Colbert led a Chickasaw army to Fort Jefferson, ran the settlers inside the post, burned their houses, and set up a siege. For nearly a year Chickasaws "swarmed around the fort, cut off its supplies, killed and captured stragglers from the garrison and at one time subjected the fort to such a close and protracted siege that only the timely arrival of reenforcements saved it from destruction." Clark's American army retreated from Fort Jefferson in June, 1781.[23]

---

gans and the Cherokee Indians in 1776," *East Tennessee Historical Society Publications* (January, 1931), 108–109.
22 Shaw, *British Administration*, 118–19.

The stiff Chickasaw action at Fort Jefferson checked American plans to invade the British Southwest, and the Chickasaw presence stabilized the American conquest line on the Ohio River for the remainder of the war. But a new threat to the British Southwest developed on the Gulf. In 1779, following a declaration of war on Great Britain by Spain, Louisiana Governor Bernardo de Galvez led a Spanish army into West Florida, captured British settlements at Baton Rouge and Natchez, and, in March, 1780, conquered Fort Charlotte at Mobile. Pensacola, the last British stronghold in West Florida, fell to Spanish arms on May 9, 1781.[24]

Thereafter, the Chickasaw Nation, as the only unconquered tribe in the Southwest, served as the last British stronghold. Many Britishers from the West Florida settlements took refuge in the Chickasaw Nation thus further increasing the size of the Anglo community there. These refugees teamed with Chickasaws to raid American positions north of the Ohio River, Spanish positions in West Florida, and Spanish settlements along the Red and Arkansas rivers in Louisiana. They did their deadliest work, however, on the Mississippi, virtually closing that river to Spanish shipping between New Orleans and St. Louis. Of the resistance forces based in the Chickasaw Nation, James Colbert's Chickasaw company continued to be the most active and devastating. Their most famous raid occurred on May 2, 1782, when they captured a Spanish river convoy bound for St. Louis. This strike netted great quantities of shot, powder, provisions, and Doña Anicanora Ramos and her four children—the wife and family of Francisco Cruzat, lieutenant governor of Spanish Illinois. Colbert held Doña Anicanora and the children in the Chickasaw towns, treated them with proper courtesy, and later voluntarily released them.[25]

For the remainder of the war the Americans took no military

[23] Jefferson to Clark, January 29, 1780, in Alvord, *Kaskaskia Records*, II, 144–49; Guy B. Braden, "The Colberts and the Chickasaw Nation," *Tennessee Historical Quarterly*, Vol. XVII (September, 1958), 222–49, and (December, 1958), 318–35; and Robert S. Cotterill, "The Virginia-Chickasaw Treaty of 1783," *Journal of Southern History*, Vol. VIII (November, 1942), 483–84.

[24] Shaw, *British Administration*, 149.

[25] Labbadie to Miro, May 1782, in Lawrence Kinnaird (ed.), *Spain in the Mississippi Valley, 1765–1794*, in *Annual Report for the American Historical Association for 1945*, II, 15–16; and Declaration of Labbadie, July 5, 1782, *ibid.*, 21.

initiative against the Chickasaws. But the Spaniards persisted in attempting to throttle the Chickasaws even after the close of hostilities with Great Britain. This determined, if futile, effort included use of Spanish troops, northern Indian mercenaries, and diplomacy. In the summer of 1782 a Spanish force landed at Chickasaw Bluffs and located the base used by Colbert's Chickasaw company. It was unoccupied at the time. The Spaniards burned the camp and returned to St. Louis. Also, Spanish officials at St. Louis organized northern Indians, notably the fierce Kickapoos, into attack forces and turned them loose on the Chickasaw towns.[26]

At no time were the Spaniards able to invade the Chickasaw Nation with sufficient strength to accomplish any substantive military objective. The Spanish-inspired Kickapoo raids, although destructive, simply stirred the Chickasaws to more vicious retaliatory strikes against Spanish settlements and shipping on the Mississippi. By 1783 the Chickasaw towns held over fifty Spanish captives. Only through intrigue and diplomacy did the Spaniards make even mild headway with the Chickasaws. Spanish agents courted the old French party which had survived as the anti-British faction through the American War of Independence. The British community in the nation, swelled by émigrés from West Florida, was a source of growing resentment among certain leaders and their partisans. Even Principal Chief Payamataha, who equated Chickasaw corruption with the British presence, joined the old French party leaders on several trips to St. Louis for councils with Spanish officials. In 1782, Payamataha assured Lieutenant Governor Cruzat that he sought peace with Spain and that he would work for the expulsion of the British from his nation. Cruzat assured Payamataha that if he succeeded, the Chickasaws "would find that our friendship would be reciprocal and generous."[27]

As the American War of Independence drew to a close, the Chickasaws found themselves in an increasingly confused and divided state. The British, who had claimed dominion over their

[26] Grand Pre to Miro, May 6, 1782, *ibid.*, 13.
[27] Cruzat to Miro, August 8, 1782, *ibid.*, 49–54; and Du Breuil to Miro, November 8, 1783, *ibid.*, 89–91.

nation since 1763, had suffered defeat by Spain and the United States. And both Spanish and American agents were urging the Chickasaws to sign treaties of alliance. These pressures crystallized the factions in the nation. One, led by Piomingo, was favorably disposed toward the Americans, perhaps because they were so much like the English whom he and his following revered. Also, they hated the Spanish for stirring up the Kickapoos and other northern Indians against them. The old French party consorted with the Spaniards. Principal Chief Payamataha was ambivalent, attentive to the Americans and the Spaniards. Thus after 1782 one stream of Chickasaw diplomacy was east with the United States, the other west with the Spaniards in Louisiana.

The first postwar treaty of alliance signed by the Chickasaws was made by the emerging American faction led by Piomingo in response to invitations from representatives of Virginia. They announced their intentions in a letter drafted by Simon Burney, an Englishman residing in the nation:

> We mean to conclude a peace with you. . . . Thereafter, you'l observe at the same time our making a Peace with you doth Not Intitle Us to Fall out With Our Fathers the Inglish for we Love them as They were the First People that Ever Supported Us to Defend Our Selves Against Our former Enimys the French & Spaniards & All their Indians. & We are a People that Never Forgets Any Kindness done Us by Any Nation. . . . We are Not Like White people for when they fight they Sends A flagg to Each Other & then Renews the Fight But I this day Send you a Flagg for a Peace not to Renew Any more Battles As there never was much fight Between you & us, As to Our parts We Never Have done you much Harm its True Some of Our young fellows has Stole Some of your Horses. . . . what damage Was done by Reason you Settled A Fort in Our Hunting ground without Our Leave And at that place you Suffered Most from Us. . . . I hope youl Send An Agreable Ansr To this that you & us may Set down in Safety & plant.[28]

Virginia officials responded to the Chickasaw letter by appointing Joseph Martin and John Donelson commissioners to meet at

[28] Piomingo to U.S. Commanders, July 9, 1782, in James A. James (ed.), *George Rogers Clark Papers, 1781–1784*, IV, 73–75.

French Lick with Chickasaw delegates headed by Piomingo. The council opened on November 5, 1783, and lasted for two days. The resultant treaty provided for peace between Virginia and the Chickasaw Nation and obligated the Chickasaws to expel Europeans hostile to the United States and to free American captives held in their towns. The Virginia commissioners acceded to Piomingo's demand that Virginia assist in ejecting intruders and in checking the stream of immigrants crossing his nation. The Chickasaw-Virginia treaty also defined the eastern boundary of the Chickasaw Nation as a line running along the Cumberland-Tennessee divide from the Ohio River to Duck River and up that stream to its source.[29]

Spanish officials, fearful that the Chickasaw-Virginia treaty was but a preliminary for comprehensive negotiations with the new United States government, moved to integrate the Chickasaws into their emerging scheme for constructing a position of strength in the lower Mississippi Valley. This included erecting a buffer zone, consisting of lower Mississippi Valley tribes in commercial and political alliance with Spain, to check American expansion in the Southwest and to insulate the L-shaped line of Spanish settlements extending from Natchez to New Orleans and east along the Gulf through Mobile and Pensacola. Spain worked first on the Creeks to initiate this buffer. It was expected that the Creeks would be receptive because of the pressure of American settlements on their eastern flank. Also the Creek Nation was strategically situated to serve the Spanish purpose in that it thrust northward between the southern American settlements and the Chickasaw and Choctaw nations.[30]

To accomplish the commercial phase of their defensive plan, Spanish officials granted trade monopolies to the British firms of Panton, Leslie and Company at St. Marks and Mather and Strother at New Orleans. Thus Spain exploited Anglo commercial experience and the acknowledged quality of trade goods produced in Great Britain. Panton and Leslie succeeded to the Mather and Strother franchise and dominated all Indian trade in

[29] Bowman to Harrison, August 30, 1782, *ibid.*, 99–101; and Cotterill, "Virginia-Chickasaw Treaty," *Journal of Southern History*, Vol. VIII (November, 1942), 494.

[30] Arthur P. Whitaker, *The Spanish-American Frontier, 1783–1795*, 42–43.

the Southwest. Spain obtained the Creek alliance in 1784 by a treaty negotiated with that nation's leaders at Pensacola. The key figure in the Creek Nation for winning the other tribes of the region to a Spanish alliance was Alexander McGillivray, a shrewd mixed blood who was a Panton-Leslie partner and intensely anti-American. Through McGillivray's influence and the activity of Spanish agents a Chickasaw delegation was persuaded to attend a council at Mobile in June, 1784.[31]

The Chickasaw-Spanish treaty negotiated during the Mobile council provided for the prompt release of Spanish captives, acknowledged the Chickasaw Nation to be under the protection of Spain, and pledged Chickasaw fidelity to the king of Spain. By this treaty the Chickasaws obligated themselves to keep peace with neighboring tribes and to accept no traders except those sent by Spain. For its part Spain extended protection over the Chickasaws, promised to assist the Chickasaws in expelling intruders, and pledged to supply all goods required by the tribe at moderate prices. Spain promptly fulfilled the commercial clause of the treaty. By late summer, 1784, Panton-Leslie agents were importing trade goods from Pensacola and Mobile into the Chickasaw Nation.[32]

By the Treaty of Paris, 1783, Great Britain ceded to the United States the territory west to the Mississippi and north of thirty-one degrees. Completing the organization of the new national government and administering the new nation so absorbed the attention of American officials that not until word arrived that the Chickasaws and other southern tribes had signed comprehensive treaties with Spain did they initiate steps to establish relations with these tribes. The Confederation Congress on March 15, 1785, passed a resolution providing for appointment of a commission to negotiate treaties. American agents went to the Chickasaw, Cherokee, Choctaw, and Creek nations to invite tribal

---

[31] See John W. Caughey, *McGillivray of the Creeks.*

[32] Miro to Grimarest, February 10, 1784, in D. C. and Roberta Corbitt (eds.), "Papers from the Spanish Archives Relating to Tennessee and the Old Southwest, 1783–1800," *East Tennessee Historical Society Publications* (1937), 115; Manuel Serrano y Sanz, *España y Los Indios Cherokis y Choctas en las Segunda Mitad del Siglo XVIII*, 82–85; and McGillivray to Panton, August 10, 1784, in Caughey, *McGillivray*, 79.

leaders to attend a council to be held at Hopewell on the Keowee River in South Carolina.[33]

When McGillivray learned of American plans to open negotiations with the southern tribes, he set to work to hold them fast to the Spanish alliance. His approach was to play upon their deep fear that the United States government intended to appropriate their lands for settlers. He recalled·for the benefit of Chickasaw and other Indian leaders "past Injurys & the Strong Jealousy which Subsists among them lest they Should be deprived of their hunting Grounds (the greatest Injury an Indian can form an Idea of) affords a favorable opportunity of effecting a total Separation of those Nations from the Americans & establishing an Interest Among them for the Spanish Nation which will not be easily dissolved, and which it is my most ardent wishes to accomplish."[34]

At McGillivray's invitation, Chickasaw, Creek, and Cherokee leaders met at Little Tallassie in the Creek Nation during July, 1785. The delegates signed a statement, probably drafted by McGillivray, denouncing any claims to Indian lands which the United States government might presume to derive from its recent treaty with Great Britain. The chiefs objected that the transmontane cession defined in the treaty

> includes the whole of our hunting Grounds to our Great injury and ruin—It behoves us therefore to object to, and We Chiefs and Warriors ... do hereby in the most solemn manner protest against any title claim or demand the American Congress may set up for or against our lands, Settlements, and hunting Grounds in Consequence of the Said treaty of peace between the King of Great Britain and the States of America declaring that we were not partys, so we are determined to pay no attention to the Manner in which the British Negotiators has drawn out the Lines of the Lands in question ceded to the U.S. his Brittanick Majesty was never possessed by session or purchase or by right of Conquest of our Territorys and which the Said treaty gives away.[35]

[33] Hawkins to Lee, December 2, 1785, *American State Papers, Indian Affairs,* I, 38–39; and Walter H. Mohr, *Federal Indian Relations, 1774–1778,* 140.
[34] McGillivray to O'Neil, July 24, 1785, in Caughey, *McGillivray,* 93–94.
[35] Statement of Chickasaw, Creek, and Cherokee Nations at Little Tallassie Council, July 10, 1785, *ibid.,* 90–93.

Despite McGillivray's machinations, a Chickasaw faction led by Piomingo responded to the American invitation and journeyed to Hopewell. The council, conducted by Commissioners Benjamin Hawkins, Andrew Pickens, Joseph Martin, and Lauchlin McIntosh (and William Blount as North Carolina commissioner) got underway in October, 1785. The commissioners negotiated with the Cherokees, Choctaws, and on January 10, 1786, they completed the Chickasaw agreement. Piomingo, Mingatushka, and Latopoia signed for the Chickasaws. By the Treaty of Hopewell, which marked the beginning of official relations between the Chickasaw Nation and the United States, the Chickasaws declared themselves at peace with that government and "under the protection of the United States of America, and of no other sovereign whosoever." The Chickasaw national boundaries were defined as beginning on the Cumberland-Tennessee divide in a northeast line striking the Tennessee at the mouth of Duck River, thence westerly along the divide to the Ohio River, down that stream to the Mississippi, and along the Mississippi to the Choctaw line or Natchez District, thence east "as far as the Chickasaws claimed and lived and hunted" on November 29, 1782. The United States reserved a circular tract, five miles in diameter, on the lower Muscle Shoals for a trading post site. And the United States also reserved the "exclusive right of regulating trade" in the Chickasaw Nation.[36]

An ominous clause in the Treaty of Hopewell—its awesome possibilities probably little understood or appreciated at the time by either the national government or the Chickasaw Nation—stated that "for the benefit and comfort of the Indians" the United States government was authorized to manage all their affairs in such manner as it might "think proper."

[36] Treaty with the Chickasaw, 1786, in Charles J. Kappler (comp. and ed.), *Indian Affairs: Laws and Treaties*, II, 14-16.

CHAPTER FOUR

TWILIGHT OF THE FULL BLOODS

THE years 1786 to 1818 probably were the most crucial in the history of the Chickasaw Nation. It was in this period that the erosion of Chickasaw independence and the corruption of their old ways, subtly begun by the Spanish, French, and British, were completed by the Americans. By 1818 tribal independence was a fiction, and the people of this proud nation had been reduced to the status of government wards. Thereafter Chickasaw history is, for the most part, a chronicle of confused existence in a world which few of the Indians understood.

Tribal factionalism, present since French times, had intensified during the American War of Independence. The old French party had accepted Spain as its patron. It was led by Ugulaycabe (Wolf's Friend) who was flamboyant, assertive, and shrewd. A large man of "dignified appearance," Wolf's Friend attended councils and other state functions in garments of "scarlet and silver lace, and in the heat of day with a large crimson umbrella over him." Piomingo (Mountain Leader), described as tall, quick of movement, forceful in personality, intense in oratory, and fierce as a warrior, headed the old British party, now the American party. Mingatuska (Hair Lip King), the high minko or principal chief, vacillated—embarrassingly eager to serve both Spain and the United States. A third faction in the nation consisted of the mixed bloods. Most of them were preoccupied with the business of developing farms and plantations, increasing livestock herds, and dominating the commercial life of the nation. One mixed-blood family, the Colberts, did dabble a bit in Chickasaw politics, generally lining up with the American party. But for the most part this was a time of full-blood leadership. It was their twilight, however, for the mixed bloods were on the threshold, ready to move in and take over management of tribal affairs.[1]

This schismatic condition placed the Chickasaws in a precarious position. Wolf's Friend had signed a treaty at Mobile in 1784, assigning the Chickasaw Nation to the protection of Spain. Less than two years later, at Hopewell, Piomingo had signed a treaty placing the Chickasaw Nation under the protection of the United States. Also by the Hopewell Treaty the Chickasaws began formal diplomatic relations with the new American nation. Because of these commitments the Chickasaws from 1786 to 1797 were caught up in a competitive struggle between the United States and Spain for control of the lower Mississippi Valley. This contest intensified the Chickasaw dichotomy and on several occasions nearly precipitated civil war. But it had some passing benefits for the Chickasaws. Courted by the United States and Spain, they received special attention, treatment, and favors from both. Thus Spain for a time served as a sort of counterpoise. Spanish presence in the lower Mississippi Valley forced a cautious posture on the United States, causing this new government to defer its ambitions in the Southwest and to accord better treatment to the Chickasaws and other tribes than otherwise would have been the case. After the United States bested Spain for control of the region, after it no longer needed the southern tribes to defend and further its interests, American callousness surfaced. Controls over the Chickasaws and other tribes noticeably tightened and demands and exactions increased.

Chickasaw citizens must have been perplexed and confused by the comings and goings in their nation during the late 1780's and early 1790's. Spanish and American agents regularly visited their towns. They received annual gifts of tobacco, blankets, rum and whisky, knives and hatchets, and sometimes guns and powder from both Spanish and American emissaries. Spain was closer geographically to the Chickasaws, Choctaws, and other southern tribes, and for a time seemed certain to win the contest for control of the region.

[1] Chickasaw Council Proceedings, August 7, 1792, *American State Papers, Indian Affairs*, I, 284–88; and Malcolm McGee report on Piomingo, Draper Collection, Frontier Wars Manuscripts, Southern Tribes, Typescripts, X, 25–28.

First of all Spain had a precise plan for accomplishing its goal of winning permanent control of the lower Mississippi Valley. The United States had no particular plan for wresting the region from Spain. And the new nation was beset with serious competition from certain of its component states which were determined to exercise assumed or real prerogatives in handling Indian affairs and lands in the Southwest. This internecine conflict dissipated the strength of the young nation. Also the stated intentions and actual attempts by North Carolina and Georgia officials to open the southwestern lands to settlement gave the Spanish persuasive evidence to woo the Chickasaws and their neighbors.[2]

Basic to the Spanish plan was the erection of a barrier or buffer, composed of the Chickasaws and other southern tribes, between the American settlements and Spanish Louisiana. Great Britain had ceded to the United States the land to the Mississippi River and north of Florida. But Spain claimed that the lands of the Chickasaws, Choctaws, Cherokees, and Creeks could not be trafficked by international agreements and posed as the protector of the southern tribes in keeping their lands free of American settlements. Spain's plan called for trade, the cement to hold the tribes fast to the Spanish alliance, and diplomacy. Spanish officials regularly held councils at Mobile, Nogales, and Natchez to remind Chickasaw, Choctaw, Creek, and Cherokee leaders of their obligation and commitment to Spain and to negotiate new and increasingly binding treaties of alliance. Also, as very special favors and at appointed times, Wolf's Friend and other high chiefs received invitations to journey to New Orleans for an awesome audience with the Spanish governor, in the course of which they received their annual pensions. Wolf's Friend reportedly was paid $500 each year for promoting the Spanish interest in the Chickasaw Nation.[3]

Those most active in promulgating the Spanish plan were Francisco Luis Héctor, Baron de Carondelet, who became governor of Spanish Louisiana and West Florida in 1791, and Manuel

[2] Williams, *Beginnings of West Tennessee*, 42.
[3] Manuel Serrano y Sanz, *España y Los Indios Cherokis y Choctas, en las Segunda Mitad del Siglo XVIII*, 43–62; Gayoso to Carondelet, July 25, 1793, Draper Collection, Clark Manuscripts, 42 A (Microcopy); Abraham P. Nasatir, *Spanish War Vessels on the Mississippi, 1792–1796*, 12, 253.

Gayoso de Lemos, governor of the Natchez District. Their deputies living among the Indian tribes included Captain Juan de la Villebeuvre, Spanish agent to the Chickasaw Nation. Without question the most devoted and successful Spanish agent was Alexander McGillivray, a Creek mixed blood. From his Creek Nation headquarters at Little Tallassie he directed a surprisingly extensive apparatus of intrigue and military power to bolster the Spanish-Indian buffer and to check the westward thrust of American settlements.[4]

McGillivray's immediate concern was the invasion of eastern Creek territory by American settlers. He appealed to Spanish officials and received regular shipments of arms and powder from the Pensacola and Mobile arsenals. For several years McGillivray kept Creek raider bands in the field attacking Americans, burning their settlements, and temporarily checking their advance.[5]

It was apparent to McGillivray that the weakest link in the Spanish-Indian buffer was the Chickasaw Nation and, next to the threat of invasion of the Creek Nation by American settlements, he gave his greatest attention to forcing this tribe into its full and proper role in the Spanish-Indian alliance. Its strategic exposure along the Ohio River to the north and along the Mississippi River to the west invited the Americans to view the Chickasaw country as a base for entrenching themselves in the lower Mississippi Valley. Also Piomingo's American party, though numbering only two hundred fighting men out of a warrior community estimated at seven hundred, contained the Chickasaw elite and comprised a hard core of resistance, unremitting in its hostility to Spain and thwarting fulfillment of Spanish designs in the Southwest. Therefore McGillivray closely watched the Chickasaw Nation.[6]

Spies from the Wolf's Friend faction kept McGillivray informed of Piomingo's activities and of the presence and movement of American agents and traders residing in the nation under Piomingo's patronage and protection. Thus in 1786, McGillivray

---

[4] See Jack D. L. Holmes, *Gayoso: The Life of a Spanish Governor in the Mississippi Valley, 1789–1799*; and Caughey, *McGillivray*.

[5] Whitaker, *The Spanish-American Frontier*, 58.

[6] Wellbank to McKee, April 12, 1794, in Philip M. Hamer, "The British in Canada and the Southern Indians, 1790–1794," *East Tennessee Historical Society's Publications* (1930), 129–32.

learned that a group of Americans headed by William Davenport, a Georgia commissioner and trader, had arrived in the nation. Davenport distributed gifts and medals to Chickasaw leaders. McGillivray's instructions from Spanish officials were to pressure the Chickasaw chiefs to expel Davenport and his party, turn in their American medals, and promise that they would "admit no other Americans."[7]

McGillivray found the Chickasaws dilatory in carrying out the Spanish order to expel Davenport and complained to the Spanish governor that "the Chickasaws have behaved in a most ungrateful manner . . . 'tis my opinion that if ammunition & other necessarys be stopt or prohibited to them for a season it will effectually open their eyes & understandings to behave as they in duty bound ought to do, for the great favors that have been extended to them from your Excellency's good will."[8]

Impatient at the Chickasaw slowness in meeting his demands, McGillivray sent a squad of Creeks into the Chickasaw Nation. The intruders watched until they found the Georgians separated from Piomingo's protection, then ambushed them and slipped away undetected. Creek war parties, also watching the trails connecting the Chickasaw Nation with American settlements on the Cumberland, tormented Indian travelers, often robbing them and occasionally killing one if he could not prove that he belonged to the Spanish party. During 1789, McGillivray's Creeks ambushed two Chickasaw messengers carrying letters written for Piomingo to the national government. One of the slain Chickasaws was Piomingo's nephew. The letters were taken to McGillivray who reported their contents to the Spanish governor. He said they contained

> the Strongest professions of friendship to the Americans requesting a trade of Goods, offering to admit them to Settle & build a fort at Chicasaw Bluffs on Wolf River. . . . The Chicasaws can have little to say for the fall of their Countrymen as tis a maxim with all Indians to have no regard to any found in an enemys Camp, & if they resent it, they will be Soon destroyed between this nation

[7] Miro to McGillivray, April 26, 1786, in D. C. and Roberta Corbitt, "Papers from the Spanish Archives," *East Tennessee Historical Society Publications* (1938), 310.

[8] McGillivray to Miro, June 20, 1787, *ibid.*, 83–84.

& its Indian allies, who are all eager to chastize the Chickasaws for their defection from the general league.[9]

McGillivray also used intrigue in his attempt to weaken the American party, reduce Piomingo's power and influence, and completely integrate the Chickasaw Nation into the Spanish alliance. He advised Governor Carondelet that he had sent Creek agents into the Chickasaw country to "endeavor to set up an opposition by Stirring up Colberts party of which the Mingo [Mingatuska] is principal against the american party, as dividing them would have its good effects." His plan, he believed, stood "a good chance to succeed at this time as I find the Mingo is much affronted at the americans because they do not take any notice of him, & pay all their attention poy Mingo [Piomingo]; & a little Courtship now to the old Mingo from our Side will I trust its good effects, & an attempt will be made to get him & his friends to pay Your Excellency a Visit."[10]

McGillivray's pressure on the American party and his intrigues and growing influence with the Wolf's Friend faction caused Piomingo to appeal to the United States for aid. He warned that Creek harassment and Spanish pressure would either drive his group to war on both or to a capitulation and acceptance of the Spanish alliance. He made regular visits to New York, Philadelphia, and the Cumberland settlements urging that the Americans assist him in his determination to crush the Creeks, thwart the Spanish design, and bring his nation totally into the American orbit. At Philadelphia in 1787, Piomingo told United States officials that his greatest need, besides military assistance, was trade, and that McGillivray's surveillance of American traders in his nation made it impossible for the Chickasaws to receive much needed items from United States sources. Thus the only goods his people could receive came "by way of the Spaniards. This makes us very uneasy. . . . The Spaniards are often sending talks to us,

[9] McGillivray to O'Neil, June 25, 1787, in Caughey, *McGillivray*, 158–59; O'Neil to Miro, September 8, 1787, in D. C. and Roberta Corbitt, "Papers from the Spanish Archives," *East Tennessee Historical Society Publications* (1938), 100–101; and McGillivray to Miro, June 24, 1789, in Caughey, *McGillivray*, 238–40.
[10] McGillivray to Carondelet, November 15, 1792, in Caughey, *McGillivray*, 344–46.

but we want to have nothing to say to them if we can help it, but we must have trade from some place. . . . Necessity will oblige us to look to new friends if we cannot get friends otherwise."[11]

Piomingo found American officials not particularly receptive to his appeals. They put him off with various excuses, including their preoccupation with a serious Indian uprising in the Northwest. Piomingo, perhaps reasoning that once this threat was removed the Americans would have little excuse for not helping him, offered his services against the insurgent Northwest tribes. Piomingo and a party of fifty Chickasaws joined St. Clair's army for the 1791 campaign.[12]

Piomingo finally got the attention of American officials who possibly saw how they could use his faction to serve the United States purpose in the Southwest against Spain and McGillivray's insurgent Creeks. The president and secretary of war lavished praise on Piomingo. President Washington thanked him and the Chickasaws for service against American enemies and sent as gifts great silver medals and "rich uniform clothes." The secretary of war wrote Piomingo that "General Washington invites Piomingo and three other great chiefs to repair to Philadelphia. He wishes to convince them, by a personal interview, how desirous he is of promoting the happiness of the Chickasaws."[13]

By 1792, American goods flowed to the Chickasaw Nation via the Ohio and Mississippi for distribution at Chickasaw Bluffs. And at Piomingo's urging, United States officials moved to detach the southern tribes from the Spanish alliance. On August 7, 1792, William Blount, governor of the territory south of the Ohio and superintendent of Indian affairs for the region, convened a council near Nashville. Delegations of Chickasaws, Choctaws, Cherokees, and Creeks attended. Blount assured the leaders of the southern tribes that the "purpose of the meeting is not to alter the Hopewell Treaty but to strengthen and keep alive that friendship of which the treaty is the basis of and to beg your acceptance

[11] Samuel Cole Williams, *History of the Lost State of Franklin,* 141–42.
[12] Secretary of War to Blount, February 16, 1792, *American State Papers, Indian Affairs,* I, 246; and Malcolm McGee report on Piomingo, Draper Collection, Frontier Wars Manuscripts, Southern Tribes, Typescripts, X, 25–28.
[13] Message of the Secretary of War to the Chickasaw Nation, February 17, 1792, *American State Papers, Indian Affairs,* I, 249.

of a quantity of valuable goods as proof of the sincere friendship of the United States." He added that another purpose of the council was "to present Piamingo, the Colberts, and their followers, who joined the arms of the United States last year, and fought against their enemies, hearty and sincere thanks for their services, and to present them each with a rifle." Blount's staff drafted a treaty committing tribal leaders to peace and amity with the United States. As the chiefs assented to the treaty, Blount said that he was aware that the Spaniards had told them that "we want, and will ask you for land; we shall not; we wish you to enjoy your lands and be as happy as we ourselves are; nor do we want the land of any red people; the United States have land enough."[14]

Blount's treaty brought quick action from McGillivray. His Creek raiders depredated along the Cumberland settlement line to isolate the Chickasaws and to check assistance from that direction. And they stepped up their raids on the Chickasaws, hitting the eastern edge of their towns and lurking along the trails leading to the Tennessee and Cumberland. In February, 1793, four Chickasaw hunters were ambushed fifteen miles from their towns. The Creek party killed one, scalped him, "hacked and mangled his body, and threw it into a pond." This incident provoked Piomingo to convene his council. The American party unanimously decided to wage a war of retaliation on the Creeks and readied their towns for defense.[15]

American party leaders informed officials in the Cumberland settlements of their action and appealed for aid: "When you get this talk, speak strong to your young warriors, and let us join, to let the Creeks know *what war is*. You made whiskey; If war, it is good to take a little at war talks; please send me some." In addition, they asked for guns and ammunition—"Many of our young men have none; such as muskets, rifles, and smooth-bores will do; and flints we want, six swivels, ten blunderbusses." And "as it is now a war, I desire you will send a blacksmith and tools, to keep our guns in order, likewise a bombardier to work our swivels."

---

[14] Council Proceedings with Southern Tribes, August 7, 1792, *ibid.*, 284–87.
[15] Blount to Robertson, March 28, 1793, *ibid.*, 452; and Blount to Knox, March 23, 1793, *ibid.*, 441.

Because hostile Creeks controlled the trails into the Chickasaw country, the Americans were advised to send the supplies by "guarded boats to the bluffs."[16]

The Chickasaws received a response to their appeal. During the spring of 1793, American boats delivered to Piomingo at Chickasaw Bluffs five hundred stands of arms, two thousand pounds of powder, four thousand flints, four thousand pounds of lead, one hundred gallons of whisky, and an armorer and tools. Freshly armed Chickasaw warriors drove intruding Creek bands from their country and searched for the enemy along the eastern trails, on their hunting grounds east of the Tombigbee, and near the Cumberland settlements.[17]

Alexander McGillivray died in February, 1793, and the Spanish-Creek leadership faltered. Spanish officials interceded to stop the Chickasaw war on the Creeks, but Piomingo was adamant. They showered him with a commission and gifts, including a horse and saddle, and invited him to visit Nogales and New Orleans, "but he, at all times . . . refused to any connexion with them."[18]

The growing power of Piomingo's faction, the increase of American goods and influence in the Chickasaw Nation, and the damage the American party warriors were inflicting on the Spanish-supported Creeks caused Spain to take corrective steps. From the Wolf's Friend faction Spanish officials obtained authority to establish a military post in Chickasaw territory. In the spring of 1795, Wolf's Friend received his patrons at the Chickasaw Bluffs. Spanish troops felled trees and erected the post, named San Fernando de las Barrancas, on the fourth Chickasaw Bluff. When completed, its palisade walls formed a square with a bastion in each corner. The inner structure contained a barracks, a "handsome house for the commander," and a powder magazine. Each bastion at Fort San Fernando was fitted with two eight-pound cannon. The garrison consisted of 150 men. The firm of Panton and Leslie opened a store in the fort, managed by John

[16] Chickasaw Chiefs to Robertson, February 13, 1793, *ibid.*, 442–43.
[17] Secretary of War to Blount, May 14, 1793, *ibid.*, 429–30; Robertson to Blount, January 13, 1795, *ibid.*, 556; and Blount to Robertson, January 20, 1795, *ibid.*, 557.
[18] Robertson to Blount, March 12, 1793, *ibid.*, 441–42.

Forbes, and stocked it with a boatload of goods from Pensacola. Many of the Chickasaws allied with Wolf's Friend established a settlement near Fort San Fernando to escape recrimination from Piomingo's faction for granting the Spanish a foothold in their nation.[19]

Three things nullified the effect of Spain's initiative in establishing this military base in the Chickasaw Nation. First, there was the general inertia of the Wolf's Friend faction. Rather than taking advantage of the close Spanish presence to counter the rising power of Piomingo's American party, the Spanish party Chickasaws seemed content to reside in their new settlement near Fort San Fernando, basking in the beneficence of their Spanish protector, consuming rations issued from the post commissary stores, and generally remaining inactive.

Second, Piomingo's American party kept up its vicious war on the Spanish-supported Creeks (the old McGillivray faction) and carried the conflict into the enemy's settlements. A massive Creek force, estimated at over one thousand warriors, retaliated in 1795 by invading the Chickasaw settlements. Their objective was Long Town, Piomingo's headquarters. Piomingo had expected an invasion for some time, and in correspondence with American officials pointed to his alertness and preparations—"I have not received any damage lately but expect it." He had hoarded the powder and lead supplied by the United States, contending that it was public property. According to one observer, "This very ammunition saved the nation." Piomingo's scouts had detected the Creek army crossing the Tombigbee. In a drizzling rain the invading host invested the Long Town stockade. The main Chickasaw force was secreted outside the town defenses in the timber. At a signal they "dashed into the action with great spirit." Taken completely by surprise the Creeks fled in disorder, losing forty dead and over one hundred wounded. Five Chickasaws were slain in the defense of their town. By December, 1795, the Spanish-supported Creeks were suing for peace with the Chickasaws. Soon leaders from the warring factions of the two tribes be-

[19] Nasatir, *Spanish War Vessels*, 105–18, 253; Whitaker, *Spanish-American Frontier*, 59–60; Gayoso to Carondelet, July 25, 1793, Draper Collection, Clark Manuscripts, 42 A (Microcopy); and Victor A. Collot, *Journey in North America*, II, 22.

gan meeting in peace councils. Sporadic sorties by both Creeks and Chickasaws, generally ending in stealing horses, continued for three years. Finally in July, 1798, a lasting peace was established between the Creeks and Chickasaws.[20]

The third factor which blunted the Spanish initiative to integrate the Chickasaw Nation into their Indian buffer was an international agreement—the Treaty of San Lorenzo—negotiated between the United States and Spain in 1795. Its provisions included an acknowledgement by Spain of United States title to all southwestern territory north of thirty-one degrees and west to the Mississippi River, the region which Spain had attempted to occupy and use as a part of its Indian confederation and buffer scheme. Spain was obligated to evacuate military posts in the area including Fort San Fernando de las Barrancas on the Chickasaw Bluffs. However, local Spanish officials were dilatory in carrying out this provision of the San Lorenzo Treaty. Not until the spring of 1797, when they learned that Captain Isaac Guion and an American force was en route to take possession of the military stations on the Mississippi River's east bank, did they order their troops to evacuate. Guion arrived at the Chickasaw Bluffs in July, 1797, and established an American military station which he named Fort Adams. From this base his troops marched to Walnut Hills and Natchez. Governor Carondelet refused to completely abandon the Chickasaws. He ordered the construction of a new Spanish post just across the river from the Chickasaw Bluffs, Fort Esperanza, so "that the Chickasaws might look across the river and see the flag of their Spanish father and know that he had not deserted them."[21]

---

[20] Piomingo to Robertson, September 1, 1795, Robertson Papers, Tennessee State Archives; Malcolm McGee report on Piomingo, Draper Collection, Frontier Wars Manuscripts, Southern Tribes, Typescripts, X, 25–28; Haywood to Overton, May 8, 1821, Claybrooke Collection, Overton Papers, Tennessee State Archives; Hawkins to Chickasaw Chiefs, May 21, 1797, in Benjamin Hawkins, *Letters of Benjamin Hawkins, 1796–1806*, IX, 176–77; Cotterill, *The Southern Indians*, 123; and Pickering to Blount, March 23, 1795, in Clarence E. Carter (comp. and ed.), *The Territory South of the Ohio River, 1790–1796, The Territorial Papers of the United States*, IV, 386–93.

[21] Treaty between the United States and Spain, 1795, *American State Papers, Foreign Relations*, I, 546–49; Whitaker, *Spanish-American Frontier*, 215; and Mary A. M. O'Callaghan, "The Indian Policy of Carondelet in Spanish Louisiana, 1792–1797" (Ph.D. dissertation, University of California, 1941), 72.

After besting Spain in the contest for control of the Southwest, the United States created a system for administering the peoples and lands of that region. To more effectively integrate the Chickasaws and other southern tribes into American dominion, the federal government developed three broad policies, each backed by law and administrative fiat. One policy had as its purpose the assertion of federal supremacy in the conduct of Indian relations. The states, earlier as colonies and more recently as powerful components of the Confederation, were "accustomed to handling" their "own Indian affairs."[22]

Chickasaw leaders had been confused by the presence and activity of agents from both state and national governments. States with colonial charters or grants for western lands, notably North Carolina and Georgia, occasionally had presumed to dispose of lands within the defined bounds of the Chickasaw Nation by sale to speculators or by grants as settlement for War of Independence claims. Before 1797, Spain had used this presumptive appropriation of tribal lands by the states as a threat to bring many Indians into the Spanish camp.

In 1791 Secretary of War Henry Knox issued a memorandum to quiet the fears of the southern tribes and to assert the federal government's constitutional supremacy in the management of Indian affairs and tribal lands. First he pointed out that the Hopewell treaties defined the boundaries of the southern tribes. Knox also observed that Georgia claimed the right of pre-emption to nearly all the lands belonging to the Chickasaws, Cherokees, and Choctaws and that the Georgia legislature had passed a law which granted to three companies that state's presumed right of pre-emption to these tribal lands, amounting to 15,500,000 acres. He warned that any attempt by a state or company to extinguish Indian claims to land, unless authorized by the United States, would be repugnant to treaties, the United States Constitution, and federal laws regulating trade and intercourse with the Indian tribes.[23]

Federal supremacy in dealing with the Chickasaws and other

[22] Merritt B. Pound, *Benjamin Hawkins—Indian Agent*, 44.
[23] Secretary of War Memorandum, January 22, 1791, *American State Papers, Indian Affairs*, I, 112–13.

tribes triumphed, but territorial and state interference in tribal affairs remained a problem. Soon after Spain's expulsion from the Southwest, the federal government erected new territories and states astride the Indian domains, and inevitably legislatures extended local laws to certain aspects of Indian relations. Another problem grew out of the fact that in the organization set up by the federal government for managing Indian affairs, the governor also served as the superintendent of Indian affairs for the tribes in his territory.

A second policy developed by the federal government to guide the management of Indian affairs was concerned with the creation of an administrative apparatus to deal directly with the tribes. Responsibility for Indian affairs in these times resided with the War Department. Each tribe was administered by two federal appointees—the territorial governor, who also served as the superintendent of Indian affairs, and the agent. The first, and probably the most successful, United States agent assigned to the Chickasaws was General James Robertson who resided in the Cumberland settlements. Robertson was one of the few white men Piomingo trusted. He recognized and esteemed Piomingo's value to the American purpose while Spain was all-powerful in the Southwest and was attentive to Piomingo and his demands for munitions and other aid. One very important favor he granted Piomingo and other full-blood Chickasaw leaders was assigning them clerks and interpreters. Thus they could communicate with Robertson and other American officials and could partially understand what to expect and what was expected of them. Having their personal staff of clerks and interpreters made them independent of the assertive and ambitious mixed bloods in the nation, many of whom were literate. The domination of tribal affairs by the full bloods was therefore extended longer than otherwise would have been the case.[24]

In 1797, Samuel Mitchell was appointed United States agent for the Chickasaws and Choctaws. He administered both tribes from headquarters in the Choctaw Nation. Four years later he was appointed Chickasaw agent and became the first agent to

[24] Piomingo to Robertson, September, 1795, Robertson Collection, Tennessee State Archives.

reside among the Chickasaws. Robertson had remained in the Cumberland settlements and only occasionally visited the Chickasaw Nation. Mitchell erected the first Chickasaw agency buildings in 1801, situated nine miles south of Tokshish on the Natchez Trace. The agency compound included the agent's office and quarters, a blacksmith shop, and store houses. Other Chickasaw agents to 1818 included William Hill (1806–1808), Thomas Wright (1808–10), James Neeley (1810–14), and William Cocke (1814–18). James Robertson served briefly as Chickasaw agent during 1812.[25]

The agent had many duties. He represented the United States in the Indian nation and in the early years was expected to watch for tribal defection from the United States. As the federal government's representative, he had the duty of enforcing federal laws in the Indian country with regard to intruders, traders, contraband traffic, and Indian treaty provisions. It was the intent of the federal government to "civilize" the Indians, and the agent was expected to instruct them in those arts which would accomplish this goal. In President Thomas Jefferson's view the Indian agent's function was to promote peace and acquire more land for the settlers by leading the Indians to agriculture as the tribe's primary industry. "When they shall cultivate small spots of earth, and see how useless their extensive forests are, they will sell from time to time, and help out their personal labor in stocking their farms, and procuring clothes and comforts from our trading houses."[26]

The Chickasaws looked forward to annuity distribution. Their first annuity, $3000 paid in goods, was distributed in 1795. This increased to $3100 for the period 1806 to 1816. Then in 1817 and 1818 it ran $15,100 for each year and increased in 1819 to $35,100.[27]

The Chickasaws found the agent's handling of their relations with the United States generally unsatisfactory. The tribal council frequently sent delegations to the national capital where it was

[25] Dawson A. Phelps, "The Chickasaw Agency," *Journal of Mississippi History*, Vol. XIV (April, 1952), 119–37.

[26] *The Writings of Thomas Jefferson* (ed. by H. A. Washington), IV, 464.

[27] Statement of annuities ... payable in each year under Indian Treaties to the year 1819, *American State Papers, Indian Affairs*, II, 215–16.

expected that more direct and satisfactory solutions would be achieved. Piomingo also was a frequent visitor to the capital. In 1802, Captain Rabbit, a clan chief, led ten Chickasaws to Washington. Along the way they lost their interpreter and credentials, so federal officials could not learn the object of their mission. However, President Jefferson was reported to have received Captain Rabbit and his warriors with great "cordiality" and because of the tribe's "friendly disposition" to the United States he "desired to give them particular attention." After entertaining Captain Rabbit's party, he had them supplied with new clothes and trinkets and sent them back to the Chickasaw Nation in a wagon drawn by four horses.[28]

A third policy developed by the federal government to guide the management of Indian affairs was concerned with trade. It was derived from the maxim that "trade with the Indians is the principal means of their political management." After the Panton-Leslie store at Chickasaw Bluffs closed with the evacuation of Fort San Fernando de las Barrancas in 1797, the Chickasaws obtained their goods from itinerant American traders and at the Panton-Leslie establishment at Spanish Mobile. Also some Chickasaws traded in the Spanish towns on the west bank of the Mississippi River. In an attempt to completely detach the Chickasaws from Spanish contact, the federal government laid plans to establish a trading station for them. In 1796 Congress passed an act providing for the construction of public supported and operated trading houses. The law permitted licensing of private traders and forbade traffic in ardent spirits. In 1797 federal trading houses were established at Coleraine in Georgia and at Tellico Blockhouse at Hiwasse, Tennessee. It was hoped that the Chickasaws would trade at Tellico in the Cherokee country, but several officials, including the secretary of war, doubted that the Chickasaws would patronize this station because of its distance from their towns. This was the case, for the Chickasaws continued their traffic with local unlicensed traders and in the Spanish towns.[29]

[28] Dearborn to Mitchell, November 27, 1802, Governors' Records, Series A, III, Mississippi State Archives.

[29] Mohr, *Federal Indian Relations*, 164; An Act for Establishing Trading Houses with the Indian Tribes, 1796, *United States Statutes at Large*, I, 452–53;

Finally in 1802 the federal government established a trading house at Chickasaw Bluffs. The site selected for its construction was near the United States military station on the bluffs, first called Fort Adams, then Fort Pike, and in 1802 designated Fort Pickering. Thomas Peterkin was the first factor or manager of the Chickasaw Bluffs Trading House.[30]

The Chickasaw agent reported that warriors increasingly were turning to agriculture, but the record of exchanges at the Chickasaw Bluffs Trading House indicates that by no means had they abandoned the chase. In 1809, when fourteen federal trading houses were in operation, the Chickasaw Bluffs Trading House exceeded all others with a business of $12,070 worth of pelts. And in 1815, at a time when government officials were urging them to surrender their hunting grounds because the game had been destroyed, Chickasaw hunters brought in $23,812 worth of skins compared to $6,486 worth of pelts traded at the Choctaw Trading House and $19,301 at the Natchitoches House which was situated west of the Mississippi River and closer to fresh hunting grounds. The Chickasaw take in 1815 included 36,000 gray deerskins, as well as wolf, elk, panther, beaver, otter, raccoon, fox, and bear and cub skins, 1,223 pounds of tallow and 330 pounds of beeswax. The Chickasaw Bluffs Trading House records show only a portion of the Chickasaw pelt traffic inasmuch as private traders in the nation also carried on exchanges with the hunters.[31]

In the years between 1800 and 1818, the most conspicuous development in the expanding relationship between the Chickasaw Nation and the United States was the negotiation of four treaties for the sale of tribal lands. But before considering these treaties and their impact on the Chickasaw Nation, it might be well to survey the Chickasaw role in the War of 1812.

As disturbing for the United States as the British threat from

and Pickering Report on Indian Trade, 1795, *American State Papers, Indian Affairs*, I, 583–84.

[30] Claiborne to Mitchell, August 15, 1802, Dunbar Rowland (ed.), *Official Letterbook of W. C. C. Claiborne, 1801–1816*, I ,155–56; and Secretary of War to Peterkin, July 28, 1802, Letters Sent, Secretary of War relating to Indian Affairs, National Archives, Microcopy 15, Roll 1.

[31] Abstract of peltries . . . forwarded . . . to . . . New Orleans, 1809, *American State Papers, Indian Affairs*, I, 772; and Abstract of furs . . . forwarded to New Orleans, March 31, 1815, *American State Papers, Indian Affairs*, II, 56.

Canada and the Atlantic was the intensely anti-American Indian confederation forged by the brilliant and articulate Shawnee Tecumseh among the tribes of the Northwest. During 1811 he evangelized the tribes south of the Ohio River with his doctrine of resisting the advance of American settlements to the death. Indian councils from the Wabash to the Chattahoochee had been galvanized by his oration:

> The white race is a wicked race. Since the day when the white race had first come in contact with the red men, there had been a continual series of aggressions. Their hunting grounds were fast disappearing, and they were driving the red men farther and farther to the west. Such had been the fate of the Shawnees, and surely would be the fate of . . . [all tribes] if the power of the whites was not forever crushed. The mere presence of the white man was a source of evil to the red man. His whiskey was destroying the bravery of their warriors, and his lust corrupting the virtue of their women. The only hope for the red men was a war of extermination against the paleface. Would not the . . . [warriors of] the . . . southern tribes unite with the warriors of the Lakes.

With a Kickapoo escort, Tecumseh crossed into the Chickasaw Nation and stopped at Chokkillissar. He visited with George Colbert and other prominent Chickasaws, delivered his oration, and urged them to lead their nation in joining his Indian confederacy and making war on the whites. The Chickasaw headmen, though impressed with his oratory, firmly declared that their nation was at peace with the Americans. They did supply him a mounted Chickasaw escort to guide his party to the Choctaw Nation.[32]

Tecumseh's doctrine appealed to a Creek faction, the Red Sticks, causing federal officials concern that the entire southern Indian community might defect from the United States. To reassure themselves that the defection was isolated and not widespread, officials held councils with the Chickasaws and their neighbors during 1812. James Robertson conducted the Chickasaw council on August 15, 1812. He reported that he had just

---

[32] Tecumseh Oration, Draper Collection, Tecumseh Manuscripts, Typescripts, IV, 59; Coleman Cole to Draper, June 18, 1884, *ibid.*, 74–75, 82; and Coleman Cole to Draper, December 1, 1884, *ibid.*, 15–16.

completed "the greatest council ever held in this nation. The Chickasaws profess to be devoted to me as I am to them. There cannot be a people more determined to observe peace with the United States than the Chickasaws, and if the professions of the Creeks are real there will be no danger with the southern Indians. This nation is determined to put their warrior force in the strictest manner should an enemy pass through their country."[33]

In the early stages of military operations in the Southwest, the Chickasaws played only a secondary role. Their nation served as a strategic land bridge connecting Cumberland and Ohio River settlements with the lower Mississippi Valley and Gulf. On several occasions during late 1812 and early 1813, American army units passed over the Chickasaw country's well-marked traces. One officer commented on the treatment he and his men received from the Chickasaws during their march to Natchez in February, 1813: "We are now one hundred miles south of Colbert's Ferry in the heart of the Indian country. The Indians are remarkably kind, and furnish us with everything they have. We do very well, get plenty of corn and fodder, meat, etc."[34]

As the Red Stick Creeks became more daring and devastating in their raids on American settlements, the federal government called on the southern tribes to furnish warriors to help General Andrew Jackson's Army of the Southwest crush the renegades. On March 9, 1813, Agent Robertson announced that the Chickasaws had met in council to consider the request: "The Chickasaws are in a high state for war. They have declared war against the Creeks . . . and declared that if the United States will take a campaign against the Creeks they are ready to give their aid."[35]

From 1813 to 1814 a reported 350 Chickasaw warriors were attached to various companies of Jackson's army. Many served as scouts and messengers. Some Chickasaws served with Cherokee, Choctaw, and loyal Creek companies at the Battle of Horseshoe

[33] Robertson to Davis, August 15, 1812, Miscellaneous Collections, Tennessee State Archives.

[34] Coffee to Mary Coffee, February 4, 1813, Coffee Papers, Tennessee State Archives.

[35] Robertson to Davis, March 9, 1813, Miscellaneous Collections, Tennessee State Archives.

Bend where the Red Stick Creeks were nearly annihilated. An American officer's account depicts the role played by the Indian troops in this battle. According to him, the

> victory obtained over our enemy, at the . . . bend of the Tallipossey . . . we attacked the enemy, on the 27th of last month, the enemy were about one thousand in number, enforted in a bend of the river, with very strong works. I crossed the river with 700 mounted men and 600 Indians and took possession of the other bank to prevent them swimming over the river and escaping—all was executed well, the enemy fought with their usual desperation, but we overpowered them, and after cannonading them about two hours, we charged their works by storm, and put the whole to death but a few that hid under the banks of the river, the slaughter was great we counted 557 dead bodies on the ground besides about 300 was shot and sunk in the river; . . . took about 500 prisoners, Squaws and children.[36]

During late 1814 a Chickasaw force attached to the Thirty-ninth Infantry was ordered to "march and scour the Escambia for hostile Creek Indians." The Chickasaws, commanded by William Colbert, marched to Fort Montgomery on the Alabama toward Pensacola, then across the Escambia where they found hostile signs. On contact Colbert's Chickasaws destroyed a Creek fortification, slew several defenders, and returned to Fort Montgomery with eighty-five prisoners.[37]

General Jackson's negotiations with Creek Nation leaders which ended the Red Stick War should have been instructive for southern Indian leaders. Jackson used Indian troops, including loyal Creeks, to crush the hostiles. Then he callously exploited the victories to punish all Creeks for a minority defection by exacting from them as a sort of reparations a vast cession of Creek land. Jackson exulted to a friend: "I finished the convention with the Creeks . . . it was fully executed, and cedes to US 20 million of

---

[36] Malcolm McGee report on the Colberts, Draper Collection, Frontier Wars Manuscripts, Southern Tribes, Typescripts, X, 7–11; and Coffee to Mary Coffee, April 1, 1814, Coffee Papers, Tennessee State Archives.

[37] General Orders for November 16, 1814, in John S. Bassett (ed.), *Correspondence of Andrew Jackson*, II, 100; Malcolm McGee report on the Colberts, Draper Collection, Frontier Wars Manuscripts, Southern Tribes, Typescripts, X, 7–11; and *Niles Register*, June 15, 1816.

acres of the cream of the Creek Country, opening a communication from Georgia to Mobile."[38]

The 1814 Creek cession was but one instance of an extended series of actions by the federal government to reduce the estates of the southern tribes for the purpose of opening their lands to settlers. The Creek rebellion during the War of 1812 simply provided the United States with a convenient and persuasive excuse to appropriate what its citizens so ardently desired. In this period the Chickasaw estate also was drastically reduced by federal action. But because of the loyalty of this tribe to the United States, federal commissioners had no cause to use coercion as they had with the Creek Nation. In their negotiations with the Chickasaws, however, American officials gained valuable experience, finding vulnerable points to exploit and techniques to use time and again.

Jackson and other federal commissioners who dealt with the Chickasaws noted that by 1800 the mixed bloods had pretty well taken over the management of tribal affairs. And the Colberts, as the leaders of this group, dominated the nation. Officials first noted this development during the 1801 negotiations. The Chickasaw council received the requests of the American commissioners and then went into session. When the Indians returned to respond to the commissioners, Chinubbee Minko, the principal chief, pointed to George Colbert and announced that Colbert had been "fully empowered by the council" to negotiate and to give "its deliberations."[39]

When meeting with the Chickasaws to discuss their rather regular requests for land cessions and other favors, the American commissioners found it necessary to negotiate first with the Colberts. A charade, repeated again and again, was for the Colberts to insist that the Chickasaws had no land to sell and that any negotiation on this subject would be very difficult. By interposing themselves as an obstacle, but a negotiable obstacle, this Chickasaw mixed-blood family was assured special treatment and consideration by the commissioners. Colbert shrewdness was illustrated during the essential preliminary negotiations held with

[38] Jackson to Overton, August 20, 1814, Claybrooke Collection, Overton Papers, Tennessee State Archives.

[39] Wilkinson to Dearborn, October 25, 1801, *American State Papers, Indian Affairs*, I, 651–52.

his family to accomplish full-scale negotiations in 1805 with the Chickasaw Nation. One of the commissioners appointed for this negotiation passed on the secretary of war's comment that "the average price paid for Indian lands . . . does not amount to one cent an acre." George Colbert answered, "My friend you know very well that land is very expensive."[40]

General Jackson accepted Colbert family power as the most strategic element in Chickasaw negotiations and bragged that he knew how to manage them. His formula was "touching their interest, and feeding their avarice." In the prelude to the 1818 Chickasaw treaty, George Colbert advised the American commissioners that the Chickasaws would "part with their lands for the price the U. States gets for theirs." Jackson exploded. "These are high toned sentiments for an Indian and they must be taught to know they do not possess sovereignty with the right of domain." Negotiations went slowly in completing the 1818 treaty, and Jackson admitted, "We soon found (to be successful) we must address ourselves to their fears and indulge their avarice. . . . The Colberts wielded the nation and of course laid several hundred per cent on their own influence."[41]

Just as government commissioners had to negotiate with the Colberts before they could expect to negotiate with the Chickasaws, once a treaty council got underway the commissioners found it necessary to make gifts and payments as a part of the official proceedings. These consisted of awards published in the treaties and secret payments and gifts. The official records for the 1801 treaty show $700 worth of goods dispensed. But a commissioner's private report indicates that certain Chickasaws had received $2,696 worth of gifts and goods, including 200 gallons of whisky and 1,000 pounds of tobacco. Selected references from treaties, journals of councils, and commissioners' reports show that in the 1805 negotiations, George Colbert and Tishumastub-

---

[40] Colbert to Jackson, July 17, 1816, *ibid.*, II, 102–103; Hawkins to Colbert, September 26, 1801, in Hawkins, *Letters of Benjamin Hawkins*, 387; Dearborn to Robertson, March 20, 1805, *American State Papers, Indian Affairs*, I, 700; and Colbert to Robertson, January 25, 1805, Robertson Collection, Tennessee State Archives.

[41] Shelby and Jackson to Calhoun, October 30, 1818, Coffee Papers, Tennessee State Archives; Jackson to Shelby, August 11, 1818, in Bassett, *Jackson Correspondence*, II, 387.

bee each received $1,000 for "services rendered their nation," and Chinubbee Minko, the "King of the Nation," was awarded an annuity of $100 for life "as a testimonial of his personal worth and friendly disposition." By the 1816 treaty, George Colbert was granted a tract of land north of the Tennessee River in the ceded area opposite the Colbert Ferry which he reportedly sold for $40,000. Jackson claimed that the 1816 treaty was nearly lost because of Chickasaw reluctance, so "we were therefore compelled . . . to apply the sole remedy in our power. It was applied and presents offered to the influential chiefs, amounting to $4,500 to be paid on the success of the negotiation. . . . We have drawn upon the Department of War for the amount of those presents distributed to the principal chiefs, and which could not appear on the treaty." To assure the 1818 treaty, American commissioners made gifts to signatory chiefs of from $100 to $150 each, and paid $1,089 to James Colbert, "the amount of a sum of money taken from his pocket, in the month of June, 1816, at the theatre in Baltimore."[42]

Occasional collusion between certain Chickasaw leaders and American commissioners was evident from the care officials used in guarding the identity of recipients of special gifts and payments. Commenting on the 1816 treaty negotiations, Jackson said, "Secrecy was enjoined as to the names" of persons receiving special gifts because "Secrecy is necessary, or the influence of the chiefs would be destroyed, which has been, and may be useful on a future occasion."[43]

Other devices used by American commissioners to gain Chickasaw cession treaties included feting the Indians. Weeks before a council convened at Long Town, government contractors began stockpiling beef, whisky, and flour. The commissioners used food and drink to grease the negotiation machinery and to dull the

[42] Treaty . . . between the United States . . . and the Chickasaws, October 24, 1801, *American State Papers, Indian Affairs*, I, 648–49; Hawkins to Dearborn, October 28, 1801, in Hawkins *Letters of Benjamin Hawkins*, 390–92; Malcolm McGee report on the Colberts, Draper Collection, Frontier Wars Manuscripts, Southern Tribes, Typescripts, X, 17–19; Manuscript Treaty with the Chickasaws, 1805, Robertson Collection, Tennessee State Archives; and Treaty with the Chickasaw, 1818, Kappler, *Indian Affairs: Laws and Treaties*, II, 174–77.

[43] Jackson to Crawford, September 20, 1816, *American State Papers, Indian Affairs*, II, 104–105.

growing suspicion of the rank and file Chickasaws that mysterious things transpired each time their leaders met with Jackson, John Coffee, and Isaac Shelby. There is evidence that commissioners used threats to exploit Indian ignorance and fear if tribal negotiators proved especially resistive. During the 1818 council Jackson instructed one commissioner to tell the Chickasaws that "Congress will pass a law, authorizing them to take possession" of the land in question if they refused to meet American demands. Also, commissioners attempted to accomplish a quick settlement, hoping to obtain assent to a treaty before the tribesmen could understand what was happening. By 1818 even the rank and file Chickasaws were becoming wary of the repeated American demands for land and other concessions. Thus the council of that year took much money, gifts, and time, and still negotiations lagged. Commissioner Shelby complained that, "the Indians have been very litigous and slow in the decisions; the business which might have been done in two or three days, it has taken twenty days to effect."[44]

Perhaps the most callous practice used on the Chickasaws, a practice approved at the highest level of government, was the deliberate withholding of annuity payments for the purpose of forcing the Indians to negotiate. It was expected that the 1818 negotiations would be difficult, so officials began two years early to soften tribal resistance. They used various empty excuses for not paying the 1816 and 1817 annuities. The correspondence between officials in Washington and the commissioners reveals the devious intent of the government. Secretary of War John C. Calhoun wrote General Jackson during the summer of 1818 that "it is possible that the payment of so large an amount at the time of negotiating the treaty might be turned to some account." And Jackson, advising the commissioners assigned to the difficult 1818 negotiations with the Chickasaws, stated, "Believing that great advantage might result from so large a sum being distributed, at the time of the treaty, as well as a great saving of expense to the government, I have wrote the agent to postpone the payment of the annuity to the first of October next. This will ensure us a full

[44] Jackson to Shelby, August 11, 1818, Bassett, *Jackson Correspondence*, II, 387; and *Niles Register*, December 12, 1818.

delegation from the Nation." When all was ready to apply this tactic, Jackson advised Calhoun that the Chickasaw agent had been instructed "to withhold the payment of the sums which may be due the Indians until that time, as the payment of so large an amount at the time of negotiation, will, no doubt, have considerable effect in forwarding the objects of the treaty, and will also be a saving of considerable expense."[45]

Between 1801 and 1818, General Jackson and his fellow commissioners accomplished American goals in the Chickasaw lands of the Southwest. Their treaties opened vital lines of communication in the Chickasaw Nation and extinguished Chickasaw title to nearly twenty million acres. If in the process they added substantially to Chickasaw corruption and prostituted American honor, perhaps their defense is found in the maxim "nothing succeeds like success."

Chickasaw land cessions to the United States began in 1786 by the Treaty of Hopewell—a tract on the Tennessee River at Muscle Shoals, five miles in diameter for a trading post site. Next Chickasaw chiefs met commissioners James Wilkinson, Benjamin Hawkins, and Andrew Pickens at Chickasaw Bluffs during October, 1801. Wilkinson told the Indians,

> On the part of your white brethren, we have to represent to you that the path from the settlements of Natches (thro' your nation) to those of the Cumberland is an uncomfortable one and very inconvenient to them in its present unimproved condition, and we are directed to stipulate with you to make it suitable to the accommodation of those who may use it, and at the same time beneficial to yourselves.

Principal Chief Chinubbee Minko, after conferring with the council, said, "I am very glad that does not require the cession of land or any thing of that kind: I consider the propositions to be made for the benefit of our women and children." The Chickasaw council added,

[45] Calhoun to Jackson, July 30, 1818, *American State Papers, Indian Affairs,* II, 178; Jackson to Shelby, August 25, 1818, in Bassett, *Jackson Correspondence,* II, 391; and Jackson to Calhoun, August 18, 1818, *American State Papers, Indian Affairs,* II, 179.

The nation agrees that a waggon road may be cut thro' this land, but does not consent to the erection of houses for the accommodation of travelers. We leave that subject to future consideration, in order that time may enable our people to ascertain the advantages to be derived from it. In the meantime travelers will always find provisions in the nation sufficient to carry them through.

For this concession the Chickasaws received, as stated by the treaty, goods valued at $700.[46]

Federal commissioners returned to the Chickasaws in 1805 to obtain title to Chickasaw lands north of the Tennessee River. Interestingly, these negotiations represented fulfillment of the announced intent of President Thomas Jefferson: "Establish among the Chickasaws a factory for furnishing them all the necessaries and comforts they may wish (spirituous liquors excepted), encouraging them and especially their leading men, to run in debt for these beyond their individual means of paying; and whenever in that situation, they will always cede lands to rid themselves of debt." The Chickasaw Bluffs factory was established in 1802. At the time of the 1805 negotiations the Chickasaws were in debt to the amount of $12,000. By the 1805 treaty, the Chickasaw Nation ceded to the United States all claim to lands north of the Tennessee River. In return, the federal government allowed the Chickasaws $20,000, much of which was required to pay their trade debts. This agreement was negotiated by James Robertson and Silas Dinsmoor.[47]

General Jackson, David Meriwether, and Jesse Franklin negotiated a treaty with the Chickasaws in September, 1816, which extinguished tribal title to all land from the south side of the Tennessee River to the west bank of the Tombigbee River. This gave the United States "undisputed navigation of the Tombigbee River to Cotton Gin Port, which is the highest point of unob-

---

[46] Treaty with the Chickasaw, 1786, in Kappler, *Laws and Treaties*, II, 14–15; Minutes of a Conference held at Chickasaw Bluffs, October 21, 1801, in Hawkins *Letters of Benjamin Hawkins*, 387; Treaty between the United States and the Chickasaws, 1801, *American State Papers, Indian Affairs*, I, 648–49; and Treaty with the Chickasaws, 1801, in Kappler, *Laws and Treaties*, II, 55–56.

[47] *The Writings of Thomas Jefferson* (ed. by Andrew A. Lipscomb), XVII, 374; Manuscript Treaty with the Chickasaws, 1805, Robertson Collection, Tennessee State Archives; and Treaty with the Chickasaw, 1805, in Kappler, *Laws and Treaties*, II, 79–80.

structed navigation upon that river," and connected "the settlements of Tennessee with those upon the Gulf of Mexico." For this cession the Chickasaws were to receive $12,000 per year for ten years.[48]

Two years later Jackson and Isaac Shelby extracted a treaty from the Chickasaws, completed October 19, 1818, which extinguished their claim to all land north of the southern boundary of Tennessee. The United States committed itself to pay the Chickasaws $20,000 per year for fifteeen years for this cession. All that remained of the once vast Chickasaw Nation was their territory in northeastern Mississippi and a small tract—495,936 acres—in northwestern Alabama. Concentrated on a drastically reduced domain, the Chickasaws were easy marks for the final pressure which would appropriate all that remained of their eastern homeland and would cast the nation into the trans-Mississippi wilderness.[49]

[48] Crawford to Commissioners, July 5, 1816, *American State Papers, Indian Affairs*, II, 100–102; William Cocke Memorandum relating to Chickasaw Treaty of 1816, Documents Relating to the Negotiation of Ratified and Unratified Treaties with Various Tribes of Indians, 1801–69 (hereafter cited as Ratified and Unratified Treaties with Indians), National Archives, Microcopy T-494, Record Group 75, Roll 1; and Treaty with the Chickasaw, 1816, in Kappler, *Laws and Treaties*, II, 135–37.

[49] Estimate of land ceded, *American State Papers, Indian Affairs*, II, 499; Treaty with the Chickasaw, 1818, in Kappler, *Laws and Treaties*, II, 174–77; United States Commissioners' Journal of Proceedings re Negotiation of Chickasaw Treaty, September, 1818, Ratified and Unratified Treaties with Indians, National Archives, Microcopy T-494, Record Group 75, Roll 1.

CHAPTER FIVE

CONQUEST OF CHICKASAW GODS

C ORROSIVE forces subtly insinuated into Chickasaw culture by the Europeans had done their deadly work by
1800. Decay in Chickasaw natural ways and law, corruption of
personal and tribal honor, and disintegration of institutions and
society were conspicuously evident. It seemed that these degenerative processes were about to destroy the Chickasaw Nation.
Several groups—traders and frontier merchants, state officials
from Mississippi and Alabama, and federal officials—were determined to precipitate the process. Within the Chickasaw Nation
certain ambitious mixed bloods, deceitfully turning tribal interests to personal purpose, contributed to the destructive process.
Around 1800, missionaries entered the Chickasaw Nation. By the
very nature of their program for the Chickasaws they too were
destroyers, for they sought to overthrow tribal deities and replace
myths and folkways—superstitions and heathenism—with Bible
teachings and church doctrine. The one saving grace of the missionaries was intent. While other groups were hypocritical, men-
dacious, and at times disgustingly callous in their schemes to
destroy the Chickasaw Nation, take Chickasaw lands, and elimi-
nate the tribe as a barrier to local and national purpose, the
missionaries, even though benighted, were of good intent.

From the Christian missionary viewpoint the Chickasaws were
heathens, and the missionaries' heavenly ordained charge was to
overthrow the tribal gods and convert the pagans to Christianity.
The Chickasaws in their natural state had a system of religion
adequate for their needs. It permeated their personal and group
life. Through their religion the Chickasaws found satisfying explanations for natural phenomena and answers to the vexing

questions of life origin, purpose, and the nature of existence after death. So attached were they to their natural religion that they adamantly refused to permit French officials to locate Christian missionaries in their towns. The Chickasaws had occasional contact with English divines. In 1737 a Chickasaw delegation met with John Wesley in Savannah and shared concepts of religion.[1]

After the British takeover of French territory south of the Ohio River in 1763, no attempt was made to provide English missionaries for the Chickasaws. In 1769 trader James Adair wrote to British officials objecting to this neglect of a people he esteemed and urging (unsuccessfully) that they receive the benefits of Christian instruction. The Chickasaws were frequently exposed to Christian ritual and practice during their regular councils with George Johnstone, British governor of West Florida, a deeply religious man who spiced his talks to the Chickasaws with Christian admonitions and prayers. They were reported to have listened attentively and to have called these ecclesiastical utterances "The Beloved Speech."[2]

In the late eighteenth century the missionary society of the New York Presbyterian churches decided to send a missionary to the Chickasaw Nation. Their choice was Rev. Joseph Bullen, a Yale graduate from Vermont. Bullen arrived in the Chickasaw towns in June, 1799, with his young son. He visited with Chickasaw leaders, surveyed what he regarded as their needs, preached several sermons to an attentive but uncomprehending audience, and departed for the East. Soon he returned to the Chickasaw Nation with his family and another missionary, Ebenezer Rice.[3]

Bullen made no attempt to establish a school or church among the Chickasaws. He relied chiefly on personal visitation and won many Chickasaws as listeners to religious instruction by first teaching them to write their names. His son taught reading and writing to Chickasaw children in their homes. The Chickasaws were hospitable to Bullen, treated him with kindness throughout his sojourn in their nation, and were attentive when he preached. He conveyed the doctrines of his faith through an interpreter and

[1] Charles C. Jones, *The History of Georgia*, I, 283.
[2] Adair, *History of the American Indians*, 24.
[3] William L. Hiemstra, "Early Presbyterian Missions Among the Choctaw and Chickasaw," *Journal of Mississippi History*, Vol. X (January, 1948), 11.

reported that the favorite subjects of Chickasaw listeners were "history of creation, Noah's flood, and the confounding of the languages." The women appeared more interested in his work than the men. Christian baptism was too esoteric for the Chickasaws, but Bullen did report on one occasion that he baptized five Negro slaves, the property of James Gunn, an old Loyalist still residing in the nation.[4]

Bullen concluded his work with the Chickasaws in 1803. Nearly twenty years passed before Christian missionaries returned to do battle with tribal gods. Presbyterian, Methodist, and Baptist representatives were active in the Chickasaw Nation from 1819 until the tribe was relocated in the trans-Mississippi wilderness during the late 1830's. In the early days of missionary contact, the Methodists were intensely evangelical and stressed preaching and conversion rather than education and the construction of permanent mission stations. In 1821 the Chickasaws were introduced to Methodist doctrine by Rev. Alexander Deavers who preached through an interpreter. Deavers' ministry was of an itinerant camp meeting type which the Chickasaws found entertaining if not particularly edifying. For several years Deavers made preaching stops in the Chickasaw Nation as he moved through his frontier circuit. In 1827 the Mississippi Conference of the Methodist Church authorized establishment of a mission for the Choctaws and the Chickasaws. Rev. Alexander Talley, the best-known missionary supported by this group, reportedly began his mission with a tent and an interpreter. Most of the Methodist work supported by this conference was concentrated among the Choctaws although the Chickasaws occasionally received attention.[5]

In the period before removal the Baptists also exercised only a light contact with the Chickasaws, but at least the tribe was exposed to the men and teachings of this denomination. In 1819 the Baptist Board of Foreign Missions contemplated a missionary establishment for the Chickasaws and Choctaws. Rev. John A. Ficklin and Rev. Stark Dupuy worked for a time among both

[4] Dawson A. Phelps (ed.), "Excerpts from the Journal of the Reverend Joseph Bullen, 1799 and 1800," *Journal of Mississippi History*, Vol. XVII (October, 1955), 263–76.
[5] Horace Jewell, *History of Methodism in Arkansas*, 391; and S. H. Babcock and J. Y. Bryce, *History of Methodism*, 13.

tribes. The Choctaws were more receptive than their northern neighbors, and in 1825 the Baptists consolidated their activities by establishing the Choctaw Academy and Mission. Several Chickasaw youths studied at this school. The Baptists persevered against the general Chickasaw disinterest and in 1828 sponsored Rev. J. A. Ware as a resident missionary. He located a Baptist mission two miles east of Tokshish.[6]

The Presbyterians accomplished the most enduring and important missionary work among the Chickasaws before removal. During 1819 the South Carolina–Georgia Synod and the Cumberland Presbyterian Association made plans to establish missions for the Chickasaws. In the same year Congress had passed the Indian Civilization Law. Its purpose was to implement a plan to transmit the arts of civilization to the Indian tribes. Missionary societies were invited to participate. The federal government would tolerate religious instruction if an adequate amount of mission attention was given to instructing Indian youth in secular subjects, agriculture, and domestic and mechanic arts. For their work among the Indians, the missionary societies received an annual federal grant as reimbursement for Indian tuition costs. Congress appropriated $10,000 for this purpose.[7]

The educational program of both the South Carolina–Georgia Synod and the Cumberland Presbyterian Association was adapted to the government prescription. The commissions for their missionaries were to "preach the gospel and establish schools for educating . . . [Chickasaw] children both in literate and agricultural and domestic arts." Cumberland Presbyterian Association representatives founded Charity Hall in 1820 near Cotton Gin Port on the Tombigbee River. Two years later, school officials certified to the federal government that it was in operation with twenty-eight pupils and was entitled to a federal tuition grant of $500. Superintendent Robert Bell supervised the erection of log buildings for classrooms, shelter for students, mechanic shops, and barns. The school farmer opened fields and instructed Indian

[6] *Latter Day Luminary*, I, 1818, 42; *Baptist Missionary Magazine*, XXVI, 1846, 240; and E. T. Winston, *Father Stuart and the Monroe Mission*, 60.

[7] An Act Making Provision for the Civilization of the Indian Tribes, March 31, 1819, *United States Statutes at Large*, III, 516; and Rainwater, "Indian Missions," *Journal of Mississippi History*, Vol. XXVIII (February, 1966), 15–39.

boys in agricultural and animal husbandry. Matrons taught Chickasaw girls weaving, spinning, and household operation. Charity Hall was submerged by the national attention received by the Chickasaw schools sponsored by the South Carolina–Georgia Synod and its successor the American Board. But Charity Hall supporters and staff persevered in their attempt to advance the cause of civilization and the gospel. The Cumberland Presbyterian Association closed its school in 1834 in the face of general Chickasaw disenchantment with education and most other things, caused by the devastating removal pressure.[8]

The origins of the extensive educational system provided the Chickasaws by the South Carolina–Georgia Synod go back to June, 1820, when its representatives, Rev. Thomas C. Stuart and Rev. David Humphries, arrived in the Chickasaw Nation. They first called on Levi Colbert. Through his influence the council authorized Stuart to establish a mission. Stuart chose a location near McIntoshville, the Chickasaw Agency, and the Natchez Trace as the site for the mission station. The South Carolina–Georgia Synod advanced $5,000 for construction of buildings. Workmen cleared timber, hewed logs, and constructed the six buildings comprising the missionary compound. The school was named Monroe for President James Monroe. By 1822, workmen had progressed sufficiently to permit the missionaries to open a day school which served children in the immediate neighborhood, and within a year facilities were completed for the boarding school which made it possible for the mission to accommodate students throughout the Chickasaw Nation. These included a demonstration farm of one hundred acres where the boys were instructed in agriculture and where much of the food required to sustain the student body and staff was produced. Enrollment varied from fifty to eighty students. They ranged in age from six to sixteen, and most of them were mixed bloods although the full-blood student population increased in later years. Federal aid to Monroe school for Indian student tuition varied from $500 to $800 annually.[9]

[8] Rainwater, "Indian Missions," *Journal of Mississippi History*, Vol. XXVIII (February, 1966), 39; *Missionary Herald*, XXIV, 1828; Bell to Calhoun, April 9, 1822, Letters Received by the Office of the Secretary of War relating to Indian Affairs, 1800–24, National Archives, Microcopy 271, Roll 4; and Nicholas to Calhoun, April 20, 1822, *ibid*.

Chickasaw leaders apparently were favorably impressed by the results produced at Monroe school for in 1824 the council appropriated $5,000 from tribal funds to finance the construction of buildings for additional schools and $2,500 per year for operating expenses. The direction of these new schools was placed in the hands of the South Carolina–Georgia Synod missionaries. This Chickasaw subsidy made possible the founding of three additional schools. One was located at Tokshish, and called Tokshish school, two miles north of Monroe. Another school, named Martyn, was established at Pigeon Roost. The third new school, Caney Creek, was erected on the western Alabama lands of the Chickasaws.[10]

Tokshish school, constructed in 1824, functioned as a day school and served somewhat over twenty pupils. Rev. James Holland and his wife, both from Pennsylvania, were in charge. Its facilities included a thirty-acre farm. Church officials closed Monroe school in 1830 and its student body, equipment, and livestock were transferred to Tokshish. Removal pressures forced its closing in 1834.[11]

Martyn school at Pigeon Roost was directed by Rev. W. C. Wilson. Construction began in 1825 and it opened the following year with a student body of about thirty. Martyn was a boarding school and, like the other stations, had a demonstration farm and shops for instructing Chickasaw youths in the mechanical arts and agriculture. It operated until 1832, another casualty of tribal disinterest produced by removal pressures.[12]

Caney Creek school in western Alabama opened in 1826 as a boarding institution with a student body of thirty-five. Rev. Hugh Wilson was in charge of the Caney Creek school. His wife and daughter served as teachers. Its location, forty miles from any

[9] Statement in Relation . . . to Civilizing the Indians, 1824, *American State Papers, Indian Affairs*, II, 459.

[10] McKenney to Barbour, December 13, 1825, *ibid.*, 650–52; Smith to Coffee, April 12, 1823, Coffee Papers, Tennessee State Archives; *Missionary Herald*, XXVI, 1830, 284; and Dawson A. Phelps, "The Chickasaw Mission," *Journal of Mississippi History*, Vol. XIII (October, 1951), 230–31.

[11] *Missionary Herald*, XXVI, 1830, 11; Rainwater, "Indian Missions," *Journal of Mississippi History*, Vol. XXVIII (February, 1966), 34–35; and Phelps, "Chickasaw Mission," *Journal of Mississippi History*, Vol. XIII (October, 1951), 230.

[12] Phelps, "Chickasaw Mission," *Journal of Mississippi History*, Vol. XIII (October, 1951), 231.

Chickasaw town, was deliberate in that the missionaries believed that their impact was greater on the students if far enough removed "from the influence of their heathen relatives."[13]

The Chickasaw school curriculum had a three-fold objective: to train the head, heart, and hand of Chickasaw children to accomplish "temporal as well as eternal felicity." For the head or intellect, Indian youth were taught reading, writing, spelling, geography, arithmetic, English grammar, and written composition. The hand or vocational aspect of the curriculum included for the boys instruction in mechanical arts like carpentry and blacksmithing and agriculture and animal husbandry on the school farm. Missionary matrons taught the girls sewing, spinning, weaving, knitting, and household management. The heart or spiritual training included daily prayers, evening devotions, Bible study, and instruction in temperance and church doctrine.[14]

The missionaries' instructional methods included some lectures and much recitation. To offset the general paucity of teaching staff, they also used the Lancastrian plan by which certain older students instructed younger students. Although many mixed bloods understood English, missionary teachers found the language barrier one of the major obstacles to accomplishing learning goals. Chickasaw children were for the most part instructed in English. Thus all students had to develop a working use of this language before they could understand instruction in geography, arithmetic, and other subjects. Choctaw missionaries Cyrus Byington and Cyrus Kingsbury had adapted the Choctaw spoken language to written form by using the English alphabet to capture Choctaw sounds. They produced textbooks in Choctaw for spelling, arithmetic, and reading as well as hymnals and a catechism. These books were printed in Boston.[15]

Since the Chickasaw spoken language was virtually the same as Choctaw, their missionaries made some limited use of these

[13] *Missionary Herald*, XXV, 1828, 151; and Phelps, "Chickasaw Mission," *Journal of Mississippi History*, Vol. XIII (October, 1951), 231.

[14] Stuart to Calhoun, March 28, 1821, Letters Received by the Office of Secretary of War relating to Indian Affairs, 1800–24, National Archives, Microcopy 271, Roll 3; *Missionary Herald*, XXVI, 285; and Sarah Tuttle, *Letters on the Chickasaw and Osage Missions*.

[15] *Missionary Herald*, XXV, 1829, 364.

instructional materials printed in Choctaw. But most of their instruction was in English, and Chickasaw children were expected to learn English. One method used by Chickasaw missionaries to accomplish this was to place Indian children for extended periods in settler homes close to the nation. An 1830 report on the progress of Caney Creek pupils who spent most of the year in settler homes in Tennessee and Alabama revealed that "the object is to give them acquaintance with the English language and the habits of civilized life. All of them can speak English fluently and with a good degree of propriety, and seem thoroughly domesticated. All can read, and most of them write."[16]

The administration of Chickasaw schools was spread among the missionaries, the tribal council, and the Chickasaw agent. Primary field responsibility was placed directly with the missionaries of the Cumberland Presbyterian Association and the South Carolina–Georgia Synod. Most of the school support, staff additions, and general oversight and direction came from these two agencies. During 1827 the South Carolina–Georgia Synod missionaries and their Chickasaw schools and educational programs generally were placed under the control of the American Board of Commissioners for Foreign Missions, a co-operative missionary venture supported by Presbyterian, Associate Reformed, Dutch Reformed, and Congregational Churches of New England, and commonly called the American Board. Charity Hall continued as a mission of the Cumberland Presbyterian Association. Stuart served as superintendent for the American Board operation, co-ordinating work at the four schools—Monroe, Martyn, Tokshish, and Caney Creek—and supervising teachers and curriculum.[17]

The tribal council exercised some supervision over the missionary education program by its members, and sometimes even the principal chief visited the schools. Their appropriations from tribal funds provided an important subsidy for support of education. The Chickasaw agent's role in the administration of Chickasaw schools included regular visits and inspections to determine if the federal government's prescription concerning

[16] *Ibid.*, XXXII, 1836, 110; and *Ibid.*, XXVII, 1831, 352.
[17] *Ibid.*, XXIV, 1828, 56.

academic and vocational training was complied with. Certification to the secretary of war that these requirements had been met was necessary before the missionary society could receive its annual share of federal aid as tuition for Indian students. Just as the missionaries had to face occasional criticism from the tribal council concerning the treatment and training of Chickasaw children, they sometimes encountered difficulties with the Chickasaw agent. Their contest with agent Benjamin F. Smith over curriculum in the Chickasaw schools in 1824 caused South Carolina–Georgia Synod missionaries to appeal through synodal officials to the secretary of war. Their protest charged Smith with opposing the use of tribal funds by the "Benevolent Societies." They claimed that he sought to use the public funds spent on education to establish a thoroughly secular school program which would "exclude the Bible from the schools and introduce Paine's *Age of Reason*, Voltaire, Hume, Gibbon, and other infidel writers. And instead of fatiguing and harassing the children by labour, they are to be pleased and amused by balls, dancing, etc."[18]

A frequent criticism by the tribal council of the missionaries was that they gave too much of their attention to preaching, conversion, and building churches in the Chickasaw Nation and not enough attention to educating Chickasaw children. In 1830, Anson Gleason, a missionary teacher at Tokshish admitted: "The great outcry against the missionaries has been, that they were not teaching school, which, it was said, was their appropriate work, and that, if we kept on this way, we should get the people all crazy and spoiled, like the Choctaws." This criticism was justified in that the missionaries clearly were more interested in evangelism than in education, but this could be expected since they were trained as preachers and not as educators. The promise to provide an educational program for Chickasaw youth had given the missionaries an official presence in the nation. Each year after their entry they devoted an increasing amount of time and effort to preaching and church building.[19]

The Methodists and Baptists maintained an evangelical contact

[18] Barr to Calhoun, June, 1824, Letters Received, Office of Indian Affairs, National Archives, 1824–81, Chickasaw Agency, Microcopy 234, Roll 135.
[19] *Missionary Herald*, XXVI, 1830, 383.

with the Chickasaws in the period before removal. Their representatives preached before the tribal council each year, and they held lively arbor meetings and revivals. But the only enduring resident churches among the Chickasaws before 1837 were established by Presbyterian missionaries. In 1823 the first Presbyterian church was organized in the Chickasaw Nation at Monroe with seven members. Presbyterian missionaries in the Chickasaw Nation and converts, wherever their residence, were carried on the rolls at Monroe for several years. By 1830, Presbyterian churches were in operation at Tokshish and Martyn.[20]

From 1823 to 1829 the Chickasaw Nation churches were a part of the North Alabama Presbytery. The beginnings of a new presbytery, which for a time served the Chickasaws and after their removal to Indian Territory served the frontier settlements which developed in north Mississippi, emerged in 1826 when Presbyterian missionaries met at Monroe to form the Association of Missionaries in the Choctaw and Chickasaw Nations. This association's work led to the formation of the Tombigbee Presbytery in 1829.[21]

The evangelistic phase of Presbyterian work among the Chickasaws focused on the mother church at Monroe. However, regular religious services were held at all Presbyterian schools. Commonly the pattern at the educational stations and churches called for divine services on Sunday and prayer meetings twice each week and on the first Monday of each month.[22]

An important exercise each Sunday afternoon at all churches and educational stations in the Chickasaw Nation, in some respects partaking of adult education, was the Bible study session. Persons of all ages, but chiefly adults, attended. Missionaries presented Bible stories and related them to daily life. They also instructed the Chickasaws in reading so that they could study their Bibles, presented to the Indians by missionary societies, in

---

[20] *Ibid.*, XXV, 1929, 11.

[21] See J. W. Moseley (ed.), *A Record of Missionary Meetings Held in the Chahta and Chikesha Nations and the Records of Tombigbee Presbytery from 1825 to 1838* (n.p., n.d.); and Hiemstra, "Early Missions," *Journal of Mississippi History*, Vol. X (January, 1948), 15.

[22] *Missionary Herald*, XXVII, 1831, 351.

their homes. Many Chickasaw adults became somewhat literate through the Sabbath school study.[23]

At each school and church, missionaries organized a Bible society and a temperance society. Heavy consumption of alcoholic beverages continued to be a problem in the Chickasaw Nation. In some years the missionaries spent about as much time instructing in the evils of intemperance as they did in preaching the gospel. A missionary at Martyn church admitted that while "a respectably large Bible class recites every Sabbath afternoon, his temperance society works drags somewhat heavily; it is uphill work" among the Chickasaws. Another missionary said that despite all his efforts, the "whiskey merchants were more popular and successful than myself." He added, "Strong drink has long been the destroyer of this people. Whiskey, that devouring foe, is the god they adore, and after it they heedless go."[24]

Missionaries preached in English without an interpreter at the Martyn church, which had seventy-five members at its peak, because this was predominantly a mixed-blood settlement and most of the congregation was at least semi-literate. But in most preaching situations the missionaries had to use interpreters. The most successful technique was for the clergyman to read an English sermon, then with an interpreter explain the way of "free salvation through the gospel." There followed the singing of hymns in Chickasaw and the service ended with a prayer and exhortation.[25]

Missionaries found Chickasaw slaves the most useful interpreters for bridging the language barrier. The slaves, purchased from white traders and planters, could speak English. From their Indian owners they learned Chickasaw. Rev. Stuart used Chickasaw slaves as interpreters altogether. His first language aide was "a black woman, the first fruits of the Chickasaw mission, was received on a profession of faith. Being a native of the country, she spoke the Chickasaw language fluently; and having the confidence of the Indians, I employed her as my interpreter, for several years, in preaching the gospel to them."[26]

23 *Ibid.*   24 *Ibid.*, XXVI, 1830, 383.
25 *Ibid.*, XXVII, 1831, 351.
26 Rainwater, "Indian Missions," *Journal of Mississippi History*, Vol. XXVIII (February, 1966), 36.

Woodcut bust of a Chickasaw warrior, from Bernard Romans, *A Concise Natural History of East and West Florida.*

Tishomingo, the last war chief of the Chickasaw Nation.

General John Coffee, a close friend of Andrew Jackson, negotiated an allotment treaty with the Chickasaws in 1832, from Marie M. Owen, *Our State: Alabama.*

Fort Washita (above), erected in 1842, and Fort Arbuckle (below), erected in 1851, were established to protect the relocated Chickasaws from marauding Texans and hostile Plains Indians, from *Harper's Weekly* (March 16, 1861).

Cyrus Harris, first governor of the Chickasaw Nation, 1856–58, 1860–62, 1866–70, and 1872–74.

First Chickasaw council house, Tishomingo.

Ben Colbert

Ben Colbert's ferry, across the Red River from Denison, Texas.

Winchester Colbert, governor of the Chickasaw Nation,
1858–60 and 1862–66.

Louis Johnson, Chickasaw leader, ca. September, 1865.

A young Chickasaw brave, prior to 1868.

Chickasaw freedmen filing on allotments.

James D. James, a mixed blood, 1869.

W. P. Brown, governor of the Chickasaw Nation, 1870–71.

B. F. Overton, governor of the Chickasaw Nation, 1874–78 and 1880–84.

D. O. Fisher, Chickasaw Indian counselor, ca. 1875.

Ah-it-to-tubby, ca. 1875.

Annie Guy, mixed blood, prior to 1877.

Sho-ni-on, mixed blood, prior to 1877.

Ash-ke-he-na-niew, prior to 1877.

For church membership, the missionaries found the Chickasaw slaves much more receptive to evangelizing than the Indians. About two-thirds of those admitted to membership in the Monroe Church were persons of African descent. It was found that "they generally understand the English language and are more constantly accessible than the full Indians; and are of course are more within the reach of religious instruction." Besides serving as interpreters, converted slaves also assisted the missionaries as lay readers in the remote settlements. A Chickasaw slave who lived ten miles from Monroe Church was reported to be conducting prayer meetings in his hut every Wednesday evening. While initially only about six Negroes attended, the missionaries were pleased when the number soon increased to fifty-five, including twenty-three Indians. "The exercises are conducted by Christian slaves, using the Chickasaw language. One of them can read some." They worshiped, read scripture, sang hymns, and offered prayers, but there was no preaching. One mission official said, "I have thought it expedient to discourage lay preaching among the slaves, on account of their ignorance, and for other reasons."[27]

An extension of the missionaries' program for the Chickasaws was the revival meeting. At least once every three months, Presbyterian clergy visited remote Indian towns and conducted extended preaching services. Often they were joined by missionaries from the Choctaw Nation. Also, for many years missionaries attended Chickasaw council meetings and were permitted to preach to tribal leaders.[28]

The missionaries used various ecclesiastical devices in their attempt to hold the Indian and Negro communicants firm in the faith. The "anxious seat" held the faltering subject on the threshold of total acceptance into the faith. And their stern and prying examination of members' personal lives sometimes stirred them to improve. After an extended member examination ordeal, one missionary said, "The members of the church . . . are a little waked up. . . . At the late meeting we excommunicated one, suspended three, and restored two. We have a temperance society, which numbers between 80 and 90 members."[29]

[27] *Missionary Herald*, XXVI, 1830, 115.
[28] *Ibid.*, XXV, 1829, 301.　　　　　[29] *Ibid.*, XXVIII, 1832, 260.

The missionaries faced almost impossible obstacles in attempting to accomplish their goals for the Chickasaws. Probably the one most difficult to deal with came from within the tribe. The Chickasaw natural religious system had declined as a constructive force in tribal life, and in these confused and troubled times it is likely that most tribesmen had only moderate religious sensitivity, if at all. But there was an enduring hard core of conservatives, largely among the full bloods, who were determined to preserve and continue the old tribal ways. They sincerely resented the Christian missionaries' attempt to overthrow their old tribal gods. And they sought ways, sometimes subtly, sometimes overtly, to discredit the missionaries and weaken their churches and schools. They blamed most tribal disasters on the missionaries' presence, claiming their work displeased Chickasaw deities. One missionary said his group had "been standing here a long time between two hot fires. Those Indians who hate missionaries, or the praying people, charge us with the villainy of selling their country." They occasionally harassed and even did violence to the "praying Indians." According to one report, two women who had joined the Tokshish church were "abused by their own unmerciful relatives." One was driven from her house, her persecutors "spoiled all her furniture, beat her off into the woods, and vowed her death."[30]

Another obstacle to missionary success among the Chickasaws, according to the mission teachers and preachers, was action by the state of Mississippi in extending its laws over the Chickasaw Nation between 1828 and 1830. These laws nullified tribal law, forbade tribal officers to exercise the functions and duties of their offices, and made the Chickasaws subject to Mississippi law. Thus tribal laws which forbade traffic in and consumption of whisky in the Chickasaw Nation were abrogated. There followed an orgy of intemperance among the Indians which distracted interest in things religious, desolated congregations, and made the missionaries intense in their denunciation of the state of Mississippi.[31]

The third obstacle to missionary success was tribal reaction to

30 *Ibid.*, XXVI, 1830, 383.
31 *Laws of the State of Mississippi Passed at the Thirteenth Session of the General Assembly*; and *Missionary Herald*, XXXIII, 1832, 260.

the extended pressure applied to the Chickasaws by the federal government to cede their lands in Mississippi and Alabama and relocate in Indian Territory. The Chickasaws finally submitted through a series of treaty negotiations between 1830 and 1837. But the anxiety, tension, and general demoralization generated by the long period of uncertainty, and the bitter intertribal dispute over the question of removal distracted the rank and file Chickasaw. In this dark, troubled period of tribal history Chickasaws turned for solace not to the certitude of their tribal gods or Gilead's balm offered by the Christian missionaries, but to "Whiskey, that devouring foe . . . the god they adore, and after it they heedless go."[32]

The missionary reports covering the period of intense removal pressure reflect despondency even among the divines. One wrote,

This poor people are now expecting to cross the great river, and find a home farther west. . . . They know not where their home is to be, only it is told them that it is to be across the great river. . . . It is now an anxious time with the missionaries here, who have just begun to reap the precious harvest which has cost so many painful years of hard labor, and the loss of many beloved fellow-laborers. Oh that we could have been left unmolested in our delightful work till these tribes should have become the happy people of the Lord. Missionaries may follow them; but who would presumptuously take on himself the responsibility of sowing a field of grain to be reaped and gathered in some far distant clime. If these natives are shoved off, what will be done with us?[33]

Another report reflected the impact of the removal question on church activities by the Chickasaws.

This mission has suffered greatly during the year, from the agitation in which the Chickasaws have been thrown by the apprehension of being removed west of the Mississippi, and the perplexity occasioned by the extension of the laws of Mississippi over them. In the early part of the year the church was in a very cold and backsliden state. Several instances of painful defection among its members occurred. . . . During the spring and summer the state of things has somewhat improved. The church members have manifested an increase of religious feeling. A number who

[32] *Missionary Herald*, XXVI, 1830, 383.
[33] *Ibid.*

were excommunicated or suspended have given very satisfactory evidence of exercising godly sorrow for their past delinquency, and have been restored to church fellowship.[34]

The missionaries were benighted in their approach and intolerant of tribal religion. They denounced esteemed Chickasaw natural ways as heathenish. But this was an age of intolerance, of absolute ideas and attitudes. And in some respects they must be regarded as a force for good among the Chickasaws. The missionaries protected the Chickasaws from exploitation by sharp traders. They interceded many times for Indians afoul of the law in the settlements ringing the Chickasaw Nation. Missionaries pressured the tribal council to adopt laws to ban intoxicants from the nation.[35]

Missionary schools extended literacy in the nation. The shops and farms trained Chickasaw youth in carpentry, blacksmithing, farming, and stock raising. Chickasaw girls learned clothmaking, sewing, and household skills. Mission school graduates became business and political leaders for the nation after removal. Cyrus Harris, the first elected governor of the Chickasaw Nation was a student at Monroe, as were six members of the Chickasaw Senate. The Speaker of the house was a student at Martyn. Training at Monroe, Tokshish, Martyn, and Caney Creek quickened an interest in some Chickasaw youths for additional education with the result that several continued their studies in schools bordering the nation and in the East.[36]

Rev. Stuart who founded the first schools in the Chickasaw Nation and labored for seventeen years "to light the lamp of learning" for this tribe candidly summed up the results of his ministry:

The number who obtained anything like a good English education was comparatively small. Having learned to read and write, many of them left school, supposing they had finished their education. Moreover, the regulations of the school and the requirements of the station imposed such a restraint on their former roving

[34] *Ibid.*, XXIX, 1833, 23.
[35] *Ibid.*, XXV, 1829, 11.
[36] (Vandalia) *Illinois Intelligencer*, January 14, 1825; and Phelps, "Chickasaw Mission," *Journal of Mississippi History*, Vol. XIII (October, 1951), 234.

habits that many of them ran off and never returned. . . . A large number of youths of both sexes were educated; much useful instruction was communicated, and a foundation was laid for a degree of civilization and refinement which never could have been attained without it.[37]

In another connection Stuart recalled, "Comparatively few of our Chickasaw scholars embraced religion and united with our church." He said that at first adult Chickasaws were suspicious of him. He claimed that in a few years he had gained their confidence and removed some of their suspicions, although he said "with few exceptions," the Chickasaws "universally are ungrateful people."[38]

On the eve of the Chickasaw migration to Indian Territory in 1836, the missionaries closed the schools and churches, disposed of all ecclesiastical property in the Chickasaw Nation, and awaited new assignments by their missionary boards. The last missionary report on the spiritual state of the Chickasaws was melancholy: "This mission has been discontinued. . . . The state of the Chickasaws seemed to require this step. Under the influence of strong temptation they give themselves up to idleness, gambling, and intoxication; and are, of course, disinclined and unfit to listen to instruction. . . . The members of the church amounting, a year ago, to nearly one hundred, have been subjected to a fiery trial. Many give fearful evidence of fatal apostasy."[39]

[37] Phelps, "Chickasaw Mission," *Journal of Mississippi History,* Vol. XIII (October, 1951), 234.

[38] Rainwater, "Indian Missions," *Journal of Mississippi History,* Vol. XXVIII (February, 1966), 37.

[39] *Missionary Herald,* XXXII, 1836.

CHAPTER SIX

PRELUDE TO REMOVAL

IN 1830 a federal agent analyzed Chickasaw society for the secretary of war. He observed that "The buffalow, and Bare are gone, and there are but few Deer, not sufficient to justify an Indian to depend upon for support. . . . Consequently the Chickasaws are compelled to subsist by a different means than that of the chase. They have a plenty of Horses of superior quality. . . . They have large herds of cattle, swine, sheep and goats, and poultry of every description. . . . Cotton, beef and pork are the principal articles for exportation." He estimated that Chickasaw planters would export one thousand bales of cotton during the year. From the proceeds of farm produce and livestock sales the Indians purchased "necessaries and luxuries of life" as well as slaves, sugar, coffee, and

> dry goods to render them comfortable and ornament their persons. The time has come when they no longer depend upon the rifle for support, but it is used more for their recreation and amusement than for the means of sustenance. Every family cultivates the earth more or less as his thirst for gain, or his imaginary or real wants increases. Much to the honor of the Chickasaws, for the last eight years, the practice of the men requiring the women to perform all the labour in the field is much changed—the men now (with few exceptions) cultivate the earth themselves, while the female part of the family is engaged in their household affairs. They spin, weave and make their own clothing.

The women made butter and cheese and kept themselves "decent and clean and in many instances particular attention is paid to fashions that are in use by the whites. It is their constant practice to appear in their best apparel at their public meetings, also when they visit the country villages in the white settlements."[1]

This picture of Chickasaw society on the eve of removal made it appear that a thirty-year effort by the federal government to eradicate tribal ways, especially hunting as the principal means of subsistence, and to recast each Chickasaw family in the image of the self-sufficient frontier farm family had at last succeeded. The primary mission of federal agents assigned to the Chickasaws had been to accomplish this metamorphosis. The Chickasaws' first agent, Samuel Mitchell, had been directed to so influence these people that "habits of Industry and of Civil life will soon acquire such an ascendancy in the nation, as to banish from the land, that attachment to Idleness, which has hitherto, so much impeded the progress of Civilization . . . exercise all the Means in your power, to excite the Chickasaw Men to agricultural pursuits, you will be equally Zealous in encouraging a spirit of Domestic Economy among the women."[2]

It is possible that federal officials had a jot of good intent in their determined campaign to reconstruct Chickasaw society. But any trace of humanitarianism was submerged by the callous thrust to appropriate the vast Chickasaw estate. As agriculturalists the Chickasaws would require much less land than as hunters. Typical rhetoric was expressed in a directive from the secretary of war to federal commissioners assigned to negotiate the 1816 treaty with the Chickasaws: "A cession of a considerable portion of their . . . land . . . will diminish the temptation to waste in the chase the time which could be more profitably employed in husbandry. . . . Until the propensity for the chase be checked, until the enterprise of the nation receive a different direction, great and beneficial changes in the situation cannot be expected."[3]

The picture depicting Chickasaw society on the eve of removal perhaps evoked a sense of accomplishment among federal officials. But the agent saw only what pleased him. The things which

[1] Allen to Eaton, February 7, 1830, Letters Received, Office of Indian Affairs, 1824–81, Chickasaw Agency, National Archives, Microcopy 234, Roll 136.

[2] Claiborne to Mitchell, October 4, 1802, in Rowland, *Letterbooks of W. C. C. Claiborne*, I, 194–96.

[3] Crawford to Commissioners, July 5, 1816, *American State Papers, Indian Affairs*, II, 100–102.

he failed to detect and thus left unreported were of great moment for the Chickasaws. Had the agent penetrated beneath the surface of bucolic calm, he would have exposed seething forces and pervasive changes—some constructive, much degenerative. He failed to identify the heterogeneous elements comprising the Chickasaw community and left unnoticed the demise of the tribe's homogeneous society of old. And he conspicuously ignored the different responses by the various elements of Chickasaw society to the new economic order. Likewise he made no mention of the sordid influences at work on the rank and file Chickasaw, saying nothing about the vicious exploitation by government officials and citizens or the devastating pressure applied to the Chickasaws by white intruders and the state governments of Mississippi and Alabama.

The new Chickasaw society consisted of Indians, whites, and Negroes. There survived a small group of British Loyalists who had taken refuge in the Chickasaw Nation after the Spanish conquest of West Florida during the American War of Independence. They included John McIntosh, son of the British agent, James Gunn, Thomas Love, and Christopher Oxbury. One of the most colorful in this group was Gunn. He had married a Chickasaw girl which gave him access to free use of the vast Chickasaw domain. Gunn developed an extensive plantation and became a wealthy slaveowner. Reportedly he allowed no idleness or celebration on his premises on the Fourth of July, and to his dying day he celebrated the birthday of George III. Through the years, the number of white men with a legal right to residence in the nation increased. They could obtain this status under tribal law by adoption into the tribe and by marriage to a Chickasaw.[4]

A component of the new Chickasaw society which played a substantive role in tribal improvement was the Negro. African slaves were introduced among the Chickasaws during the 1750's by British traders. By the time of removal the tribe's Negro population numbered perhaps one thousand. Most of the slaves were owned by the mixed bloods and whites. The presence of slaves

[4] Harry Warren, "Missions, Missionaries, Frontier Characters and Schools," *Publications of the Mississippi Historical Society*, Vol. VIII (1904), 587; and Allen to Eaton, February 7, 1830, Letters Received, Office of Indian Affairs, 1824–81, Chickasaw Agency, National Archives, Microcopy 234, Roll 136.

and the practice of slavery by the Chickasaws had a number of important influences on the tribe. First, slavery fed the aristocratic pretensions of the owners in their drive to emulate white planter neighbors. These attitudes spread into Chickasaw society, which, as a microcosm of the larger American society, generated notions of superiority and a presumed social stratification. Second, the slave performed labor generally scorned by Indians, such as clearing the wilderness, opening fields for agriculture, building roads and bridges, and performing other useful labor which enhanced the value of Chickasaw properties and improvements. This enabled the tribe to obtain a removal settlement from the federal government generally better than that received by other tribes. Third, slaves purchased from English-speaking planters learned the Chickasaw language, served as an important communication bridge, and played an important if unrecognized role in Chickasaw acculturation. When Rev. Joseph Bullen visited the Chickasaw Nation in 1799, he was advised by Malcolm McGee, the tribal interpreter, that the African slaves as well as the resident white men and mixed bloods spoke English and had a great influence with the full bloods. Thus, for Bullen to accomplish his purpose he had best "begin with these, who, he says, as they learn, will have good talks with the Indians, and so the knowledge and practice of these things will soon become national." And fourth, the Negro presence in the Chickasaw Nation and the well established institution of slavery committed that Indian community during the Civil War to an inevitable alliance with the Confederate States of America. Chickasaw armies fought Union troops in Indian Territory to defend that institution. And that part of the reconstruction formula concerning the Negro as a freedman, imposed by the victorious Union government, remained a perplexing problem for the Chickasaw Nation into the twentieth century.[5]

The Indian component of the new Chickasaw society, according to a census taken in 1827, numbered about four thousand. A conspicuous dichotomy existed in the Indian portion of Chicka-

---

[5] Adair, *History of the American Indians*, 410–11; also see Phelps, "Bullen Journal," *Journal of Mississippi History*, Vol. XVII (October, 1955), 254–81; and Annie H. Abel, *The American Indian as Slaveholder and Secessionist.*

saw society. It was derived less from an emotional force like allegiance, which had been the basis of the old French party and British party or the more recent American party and Spanish party. The new alignment was based on degree of Indian blood and divided the Indian community into mixed bloods and full bloods. The mixed bloods by this time dominated the political life of the nation. The full bloods, comprising about three-fourths of the tribal population, had withdrawn. Piomingo, the Mountain Leader, who died in 1795, was the last of the assertive full-blood leaders. Tishomingo attempted to be a latter day Mountain Leader but in most respects was the unwitting tool of the mixed-blood clique.[6]

The mixed bloods had learned to control the full bloods and to manage them to their purpose. The Colberts and others of their group were shrewd enough, however, to operate through the mechanism of tribal institutions. They diligently defended and preserved the form if not the substance of old ways, thereby placing themselves in a good light with the full bloods. Also, they exploited ancient tribal customs which fitted their tastes and met their needs. For example, mixed-blood Levi Colbert imitated a native Chickasaw custom by practicing polygamy, a condition in which, said one observer, he "appeared to live comfortably." And the mixed bloods passionately attached themselves to the practice of common ownership of tribal land. The sparse Chickasaw population and the vast tribal estate (over five million acres) created a most favorable man-land ratio. As Chickasaw citizens the mixed bloods had the privilege of using as much land as they desired at no cost and tax-free.[7]

The mixed bloods also dominated the business life of the nation and used their control of the governmental apparatus to legislate special economic privileges for their group. They were the principal slave owners and emulated the planters on the rim of their nation by developing productive farms and plantations. In their dress, furnishings, and general tone of living they sought to live as the whites did. Not all Chickasaw mixed bloods were members of

[6] McKenney to Secretary of War, October 10, 1827, Letters Received, Office of Indian Affairs, 1824–81, Chickasaw Agency, National Archives, Microcopy 234, Roll 135.

[7] Phelps, "Bullen Journal," *Journal of Mississippi History*, Vol. XVII (October, 1955), 263.

the power clique. But the favored few—serious, energetic, and ambitious—imaginatively exploited the benefits of tribal citizenship and institutions.

Most of the full bloods on the eve of removal appeared desolated by the pressures applied to the tribe by federal and state officials, intruders, and missionaries. The devastating changes occurring in their nation's economic, social, and political life confused them. They reacted in various ways. A few remained attached to the old ways and attempted to preserve and transmit them and to defeat the new forces precipitated by the missionaries and others. Most of them, however, withdrew in some form. Nearly two hundred Chickasaws withdrew from the nation to live a wandering life of hunting, trading, and fighting the Osages in the trans-Mississippi West.[8]

Most of the full bloods remained in the nation and withdrew in a social sense. With the restraints and responsibilities of old ways declining, they lived an abandoned life. More and more they seemed satisfied to exist from one day to the next, preoccupied with the frivolous and entertaining. A visitor to the Chickasaw Nation in the 1820's detected this trend: "The Chickasaws generally appeared to us neater in their persons, than our friends the Choctaws. . . . The Chickasaws seem, however, to expend in ornaments, the savings and annuity of which the Choctaws appropriate a large proportion to their farms or cattle." In another connection the visitor recorded: "As we were riding along toward sunset, we saw many parties of Chickasaws repairing to a dance and ballplay. The magnificence of their dresses exceeded any thing that we had yet seen; and the profusion of silver ornaments was far greater than among the Choctaws. Indeed, they cut a splendid figure as they galloped through the woods . . . it was going to be a 'very gay party'. The women were dressing their husbands' hair along the path-side."[9]

In the period before removal, changes in the Chickasaw economy corresponded with the substantial alterations occurring in Chickasaw society generally. Many Chickasaws, especially the full bloods, were determined to sustain themselves by hunting.

[8] Wilkinson to Dearborn, October 5, 1805, in Carter, *The Territory of Louisiana-Missouri, 1803–1806*, XIII, of *Territorial Papers of the United States*, 234–37.

[9] Adam Hodgson, *Letters from North America*, I, 255–56.

But the appropriation of the tribal estate by the federal government through cession treaties had so drastically reduced hunting grounds that this enterprise declined to virtually nothing. By 1819, those Indians determined to follow the chase east of the Mississippi had been reduced to a pitiful state. This was illustrated by Thomas Nuttall's report of a visit to a Chickasaw hunting camp on the Mississippi River. "We found many of them in a state of intoxication. They are generally well dressed, extravagantly ornamented." This band of Chickasaw hunters traded at a store nearby at the Chickasaw Bluffs. Nuttall rated the prices "exorbitant." A "course Indian duffell blanket four dollars, whiskey, well watered, which is sold almost without restraint, in spite of the law, two dollars per gallon, and everything else in the same proportion. Yet the Indians get no more than 25 cents for a ham of venison, a goose, or a large turkey." Only a few years before, Chickasaw hunters, rated as the best in the Mississippi Valley, had scorned small game and had gone after the large fur-bearing creatures. Turkey and other small game had been left for the Indian children to hunt.[10]

The Chickasaw band living more or less permanently in the trans-Mississippi West, found hunting easier because game was still abundant. From French and Spanish times Chickasaws had raided, hunted, and traded in Louisiana. In later times they temporarily resided on the St. Francis River. An 1806 report called the Chickasaws "vagabonds" and stated that they were "troublesome to the boats descending the river and have even plundered some of them and committed a few murders." However, the Western Chickasaws spent most of the time on the lower Red and Arkansas rivers.[11]

Resourceful Chickasaw traders came to dominate the commerce of this region. They hunted and gathered furs and trafficked with the Quapaws and other tribes for their pelts. They also dealt in horses and grain. One federal official accused them of carrying on a lucrative whisky trade with the Caddoes, Quapaws, and other Red River tribes.[12]

[10] Thomas Nuttall, *Journal of Travels into the Arkansas Territory During the Year 1819*, XIII, of *Early Western Travels, 1748–1846*, edited by Reuben Gold Thwaites, 88.
[11] Eron Rowland, *Life, Letters and Papers of William Dunbar*, 210.

Chickasaws from the nation in Mississippi also were attracted to this trans-Mississippi commerce. Some visiting bands were out for as long as six months, mingling with the Western Chickasaws, "leaving their females at home engaged in raising Corn much of which they dispose in this settlement (Arkansas Post) and the raising of Horses which they also dispose of both to Whites and Indians."[13]

The Chickasaw presence in the trans-Mississippi West and their widespread hunting and trading inevitably brought them into conflict with the fierce Osages who claimed the territory south to Red River. The Osages contested the right of Chickasaws to hunt and trade in this domain, and a bloody feud developed between warrior bands of the two tribes which extended from 1802 to 1821. In their campaigns against the Osages the Western Chickasaws generally allied with the Cherokee community residing on the lower Arkansas River. In 1805 a federal official expressed concern that "the Chickasaws and Cherokees meditate a heavy stroke, at our friends the Osages, pending the present Season, & I know not how to ward the blow." A Chickasaw force "ascended the White River . . . three weeks since, all well armed with Rifles . . . vowed revenge for the loss of four Warriors killed in a late attack of the Osages."[14]

In the removal prelude most Chickasaws continued to reside on the tribe's drastically reduced territory in northern Mississippi and northwestern Alabama. They relied increasingly upon agriculture. The full bloods seemed content to subsist from the production of small patches of corn, beans, squash, pumpkins, and melons tended by the women and children. An economic survey

[12] Treat to Secretary of War, December 31, 1806, in Carter, *The Territory of Louisiana-Missouri, 1806–1814,* XIV, of *Territorial Papers of the United States,* 56; and Gray to Secretary of War, April 6, 1828, in Carter, *The Territory of Arkansas, 1825–1829,* XX, of *Territorial Papers of the United States,* 225-27.

[13] Treat to Dearborn, November 15, 1805, in Carter, *The Territory of Louisiana-Missouri, 1803–1806,* XIII, of *Territorial Papers of the United States,* 276-84.

[14] Francisco de Caso y Luengo to the Chickasaws, August 5, 1802, Governors' Records, Series A, III, Mississippi State Archives; Treat to Dearborn, March 27, 1806, Letterbook of the Arkansas Trading House, National Archives, Microcopy 142, Roll 1; Wilkinson to Dearborn, October 8, 1805, in Carter, *The Territory of Louisiana-Missouri, 1803–1806,* XIII, of *Territorial Papers of the United States,* 234-37; and Brearley to Calhoun, April 26, 1821, in Carter, *The Territory of Arkansas, 1819–1825,* XIX, of *Territorial Papers of the United States,* 285.

of the Chickasaw Nation in 1827 revealed that the typical full-blood household contained five members and owned two horses, two cows, five hogs, and a small flock of poultry. The old family compound—a round winter house, a rectangular summer house, and smaller service structures—had been replaced by the familiar frontier log cabin, consisting of walls formed by hewed timbers placed horizontally and sealed against the weather with mud daub, a puncheon floor, and gable roof covered with split shakes. The fireplace, against an end wall, was served by a chimney made of split sticks placed in a square and plastered inside and out with clay.[15]

Increasingly the mixed bloods turned to commercial agriculture, opening farms and plantations on the rich land of the Chickasaw Nation's public domain. They broke with the old tribal pattern of town living to establish residences on separate fenced properties. The improvements constructed by some of the more enterprising mixed bloods caused an official to note that "comfortable houses were owned" by this segment of Chickasaw society. To encourage agriculture among the Chickasaws, federal officials and missionaries subsidized them by providing training, tools, seeds, and livestock. In 1801 the Chickasaw agent opened a twenty-acre demonstration plot to illustrate the best planting and cultivating methods. Also, the federal government provided a farmer, blacksmith, and carpenter as part of the agency staff. They were teachers as well as craftsmen and were expected to impart their skills to the Indians. In the early years of annuity distribution, officials provided the Chickasaws with ploughs, axes, grubbing hoes, spinning wheels, livestock for herd development, and fruit trees for orchards. Much of the mission school program was vocational. Each school had a demonstration farm and livestock herd, and the staff instructed Chickasaw youth in growing crops, animal care, and the mechanical arts useful in erecting houses, farm buildings, and fences, and repairing tools. By taking advantage of these opportunities, certain mixed-blood leaders set an example for others to follow. Thus, "Major Colbert

[15] McKenney to Secretary of War, October 10, 1827, Letters Received, Office of Indian Affairs, 1824–81, Chickasaw Agency, National Archives, Microcopy 234, Roll 135.

who ranks high in the government of his nation . . . has laboured at the plough and hoe during the last season, and his example has stimulated others. Several families have planted cotton, which grows well, and some of the women spin and weave."[16]

Other enterprises which developed prior to removal and which reflected the revolution occurring in the Chickasaw economy included the rise of service industries, diversification of markets, development of communication links across the Chickasaw Nation, and the rise of a local but rich mercantile monopoly. Soon after 1801, gins made their appearance in the Chickasaw Nation in response to the rapid development of cotton production on local farms and plantations. Another service enterprise, one which displaced the age-old home industry of grinding corn with mortar and pestle, was the grain mill. By 1827, ten mills were operating in the nation. Also it was reported that blacksmiths and mechanics worked in fifty shops.[17]

Chickasaw grain, livestock, and cotton generally moved to Gulf markets. Some shipping was done from Chickasaw Bluffs on the Mississippi, but most Chickasaw exports left the nation at Cotton Gin Port on the Tombigbee River on the eastern edge of the nation. Resourceful Indians created local markets serving traveler needs on the highway grid coursing their territory and supplied grain and meat to the Fort Pickering garrison at Chickasaw Bluffs.[18]

In the years before removal one development which had a great economic and social impact on the Chickasaws was the action by the federal government in opening a network of roads in their nation. The Chickasaw Nation's strategic situation, with the Ohio, Tennessee, and Cumberland rivers as feeder arteries, had from earliest times made it an important land bridge linking the Northeast with the lower Mississippi Valley and Gulf. In early historic times three heavily traveled trails crossed the Chickasaw Nation—the Big Trading Path from Mobile along the Tombigee,

[16] Chickasaw Agent to Dearborn, August 26, 1802, Governors' Records, Series A, III, Mississippi State Archives; and Hawkins to Dearborn, October 28, 1801, in Hawkins, *Letters of Benjamin Hawkins*, 392–94.

[17] McKenney to Secretary of War, October 10, 1827, Letters Received, Office of Indian Affairs, 1824–81, Chickasaw Agency, National Archives, Microcopy 234, Roll 135.

[18] Claiborne to Madison, November 24, 1801, in Rowland, *Claiborne Letterbooks*, I, 9–12.

later used as a horse path by traders; the Great Charleston–
Chickasaw Trail which crossed the Savannah River near Augusta
and coursed westward to the Chickasaw Crossing on the Tombigbee; and a diagonal trail connecting the Ohio and Cumberland
with the lower Mississippi near the mouth of the Yazoo River,
which became the Natchez Trace. By the late 1780's, Ohio Valley
settlers transported their furs, grain, and other products by flat-
boat to Natchez and New Orleans. They marketed their commodities, sold the flatboats as salvage lumber, and turned home-
ward either afoot or on horseback to Natchez. From there they
traveled northeasterly on the Natchez Trace to the Cumberland
and on to their homes. After 1797, riders carried government mail
between Nashville and Natchez over this trail.[19]

An 1801 treaty committed the Chickasaw Nation to permit the
federal government to construct a wagon road on the Natchez
Trace. The Chickasaws pledged in this treaty that the road would
be open at all times to the mails and people of the United States.
Soon the Natchez Trace road became the most heavily traveled
highway in the Southwest. As states and territories developed
around the Chickasaw Nation, the Chickasaws were pressured to
permit the construction of additional roads. But the Natchez
Trace remained the basic route, and most of the new roads trun-
cated as laterals from it or crossed it.[20]

In 1807, General Edmund P. Gaines and a party of United
States troops surveyed a route for a road from the head of Muscle
Shoals on the Tennessee River to Cotton Gin Port on the Tombigbee River. The road constructed on this route was called
Gaines' Trace. By connecting Cotton Gin Port, the head of navigation on the Tombigbee, and the Tennessee settlements, citizens
had a connection with Mobile and the Gulf. Goods were floated
on the Tennessee to Muscle Shoals, transported by wagon to the
Tombigbee over Gaines' Trace, and floated to the Gulf.[21]

Other roads lacing Chickasaw territory included one con-

[19] Dawson A. Phelps, "Travel on the Natchez Trace," *Journal of Mississippi History*, Vol. XV (July, 1953), 157–63; Leftwich, *Muscle Shoals*, 22; also see Arminta Scott Spalding, "The Natchez Trace Parkway: A Study of Origins of an Interstate Federal Highway" (M.A. thesis, Stephen F. Austin College, 1965).
[20] Treaty with the Chickasaw, 1801, in Kappler, *Laws and Treaties*, II, 55–56.
[21] Notes of a survey from the head of Muscle Shoals, Tennessee River to the

structed in 1811 connecting the Chickasaw Agency on the Natchez Trace with Runnolds Ferry on the Tennessee River. It was to serve the Kentucky settlements. Four years later the Chickasaws assented to the construction of a road from Reynolds-burg on the Tennessee River through the nation intersecting the Natchez Trace near the south end of Chickasaw Old Town. The promoters of this route declared, "The advantages arising from this road to the citizens of the western part of Tennessee, Kentucky, Ohio and the Territories, are obvious." As late as 1828, citizens at Helena, Arkansas, memorialized Congress to open a road across the river from Helena at Chickasaw Bluffs running east to the Alabama towns and connecting those communities with Helena, Little Rock, and Fort Smith on the Arkansas River.[22]

The impact of traffic on these roads was considerable. Chickasaws and travelers mingled, and even the most isolated tribesmen were exposed to new people, things, and ways. Some had a good influence on the Indians; most had an unfavorable influence. The most obvious effect of this traffic on the Chickasaws was in their economy. In 1815 their agent said that "many thousands trading to and from New Orleans, Mobile, &c." and immigrants bound for new lands in the Southwest crossed the Chickasaw Nation each year. The Indians prospered from this traffic. They operated the ferries on the rivers, and kept the public inns (called stands) which provided lodging, food, refreshment, and entertainment for travelers. Many Chickasaws opened farms along the roads and "raised corn and other necessaries to sell to travelers."[23]

The most intriguing feature of the Chickasaw economy in the

Cotton Gin Port, Tombigbee River by Edmund P. Gaines, 1808, Miscellaneous Collections, Tennessee State Archives; and Leftwich, *Muscle Shoals*, 25.

[22] Hampton to Secretary of War, August 16, 1811, in Carter, *The Territory of Mississippi, 1809–1817*, VI, of *Territorial Papers of the United States*, 218; Mc-Minn to Congress, November 15, 1815, Miscellaneous Collections, Tennessee State Archives; Cocke to Crawford, October 24, 1815, *American State Papers, Indian Affairs*, II, 79–80; Graham to Clay, December 5, 1816, *ibid.*, 401–402; and Memorial to Congress, Inhabitants of Arkansas Territory, February 17, 1829, in Carter, *The Territory of Arkansas, 1825–1829*, XX, of *Territorial Papers of the United States*, 844–45.

[23] Cocke to Crawford, October 24, 1815, *American State Papers, Indian Affairs*, II, 79–80; Notes of a survey from the head of Muscle Shoals, Tennessee River to the Cotton Gin Port, Tombigbee River by Edmund P. Gaines, 1808, Miscellaneous Collections, Tennessee State Archives; and Dawson A. Phelps, "Stands and Travel Accommodations on the Natchez Trace," *Journal of Mississippi History*, Vol. XI (January, 1949), 1–54.

period before removal was its complete domination by a mixed-blood clique headed by the Colbert brothers. It is wondrous to behold the imagination, ingenuity, initiative, and unmitigated brass which this group of Chickasaws brought to the joyous business of integrating the nation's productive enterprises into a combine which they shrewdly managed. The methods used by this board of directors of Chickasaw business life were surprisingly sophisticated and perhaps could have been illuminating and instructive for entrepreneurs of a later age. They wrote treaties which contained special privileges and concessions for their group. And through their control of the Chickasaw government, they drew legislation which protected and preserved their monopoly of tribal economic life. So successful was this Colbert-led clique that by 1830 the Chickasaw Nation was in fact their commercial fief. They operated the best farms and plantations in the nation with slave labor. This alone would have made them wealthy, but they strove to integrate all the nation's productive enterprises under their proprietorship. They prospered from farming, stock raising, and shipping, but their greatest profits came from the mercantile business. Getting what they desired from the Chickasaw government was perfunctory since they ran it. Obtaining special concessions from the federal government conceivably could have been difficult or impossible. But the Colberts knew what the federal government wanted most from the Chickasaws, so in a sense they managed federal officials by making it impossible to obtain a cession treaty until it carried the Colberts' stamp of approval. The crass but piddling personal gratuities found in Chickasaw treaties between 1801 and 1834, such as compensating James Colbert for money lost in a Baltimore theater; granting George Colbert a $1,000 award for "services rendered the nation"; giving special land reservations or pensions for life—not to mention the side arrangements which General Jackson declared were essential to obtain the desired Chickasaw treaties but which could not show in the official proceedings, screened the clique's bolder and more substantive strokes. The 1801 treaty and collateral papers, written by the Colberts, provided that, rather than having white men receive concessions to establish and operate the ferries, inns, and other income-yielding public accommodations on the Natchez Trace, these were reserved for the Chickasaws. The Colberts divided the concessions among relatives and friends.[24]

The Chickasaw treaty of 1805 contained the seemingly innocent proviso requiring that annuity payments to the Chickasaws "be made in specie." The government had the custom of paying its annual obligation to this tribe with goods. The mass distribution by government contractors of blankets, guns, trinkets, knives, axes, ornaments, and provisions materially reduced sales in the local mercantile establishments operated by the mixed bloods. By inserting the clause requiring payment in specie, Chickasaw businessmen were assured of prosperity rather than disaster at annuity time.[25]

The Chickasaw treaty of 1816 contained a proviso which prohibited white men from trading in the Chickasaw Nation. Chickasaw spokesmen at the treaty council complained that their nation was overrun by a "crowd of pedlars." Banishing non-Indian merchants from the nation tightened the Colbert mercantile monopoly. The Chickasaw agent in 1824 announced that in compliance with the 1816 treaty he could report "no white man has an establishment of any kind in this nation."[26]

There remained one last obstacle to this Chickasaw Nation mercantile combine achieving a total monopoly. In 1802, United States officials had established a trading post at Chickasaw Bluffs. This federally operated store competed with local businessmen for the Chickasaw trade. During 1819, federal officials received a remonstrance from the Chickasaw government—"The Chickasaws have petitioned that the United States trading post at Chickasaw Bluffs be closed and that they be permitted to manage their own trade." Federal officials responded by moving the station and goods to Arkansas Territory.[27]

---

[24] Jackson to Crawford, September 20, 1816, *American State Papers, Indian Affairs*, II, 104–105; and Treaty with the Chickasaw, 1801, in Kappler, *Laws and Treaties*, II, 55–56.

[25] Treaty with the Chickasaw, 1805, in Kappler, *Laws and Treaties*, 79–80.

[26] Smith to McKenney, July 14, 1824, Letters Received, Office of Indian Affairs, 1824–81, Chickasaw Agency, National Archives, Microcopy 234, Roll 135; and Treaty with the Chickasaw, 1816, in Kappler, *Laws and Treaties*, II, 135–36.

[27] McKenney to Calhoun, March 17, 1819, in Carter, *Territory of Louisiana-Missouri, 1815–1821*, XV, of *Territorial Papers of the United States*, 360–63.

Through the years critics denounced the Chickasaw combine. Two samples should suffice to illustrate the resentment certain outsiders felt toward the Colbert-led clique. One letter to the secretary of war contained the comment that "through the avarice of a few chiefs . . . they contrive to keep our mails and citizens who travel through their country, exposed to all the dangers and inconveniences of an extensive wilderness, by opposing the erection of stations on the road." By 1808, the year of this complaint, there were adequate accommodations for travelers on the roads crossing the Chickasaw Nation. What the writer resented was that these businesses were operated by Chickasaws rather than his white friends.[28]

Another critic wrote in 1826: "There exists in this nation, a resolution of the Chiefs, that no person except one of their own blood, shall offer for sale any merchandise, within the limits of the nation, which has thrown the whole business of the Nation into a few hands, thereby creating a monopoly to the few, who have means, to draw into their coffers a great portion of the surplus monies that come into this nation. . . . A few half breeds who enjoy this monopoly and who have been educated and are more enlightened, have great influence with these people, and that it has been used to keep the nation together for their own benefit and interest."[29]

This denunciation of Chickasaw business success was in part a reflection of the bigotry of the age towards Indians. Presumptive whites publicly subscribed to the program of civilizing the Chickasaws and other tribes, but they meant by their support of the government and mission civilization programs that tribesmen should advance only to the level of performing the menial tasks of tending crops, herding livestock, and perhaps the less sophisticated mechanical crafts. It was inconceivable for many that an Indian could function successfully in a business situation. Also this denunciation of Chickasaw entrepreneurial success reflected the resentment of white businessmen, traders, and government contractors who profited from the easy entree they enjoyed in

[28] Gaines to Dearborn, January 29, 1808, in Carter, *The Territory of Mississippi, 1798–1817*, V, of *Territorial Papers of the United States*, 598–602.
[29] Hinds to Barbour, November 2, 1826, Letters Received, Office of Indian Affairs, 1824–81, Chickasaw Agency, National Archives, Microcopy 234, Roll 135.

every Indian nation except the Chickasaw Nation. Rather than denunciation, the Colberts should receive praise for their imagination, energy, and initiative. They were part Indian, and it is to their credit that they saw the opportunities and had the intelligence and courage to assert themselves and to appropriate those benefits which in other Indian nations went to enrich contractors and friends of federal officials.

Despite the extension of Mississippi jurisdiction over Chickasaw territory and the attempts of the federal government to integrate the tribe into the national purpose, the Chickasaw Nation continued as a self-governing community in the period before removal. The apparatus for governing the Chickasaw Nation followed the old system of hereditary principal chief and council of clan chiefs only in form, for the real power in Chickasaw politics resided with the mixed bloods. They preserved the old form out of deference to the full bloods who comprised three-fourths of the tribal population. The mixed bloods managed the innocent full-blood leaders as protégés and puppets. An 1829 report on the Chickasaw government confirmed this. Levi Colbert was identified as being "to the Chickasaws, what the Soul is to the body. They move at his bidding. They agree or disagree to any measure that he, and those over whom he knows how to exercise his authority as the Speaker of the Nation may bid. As to their *King*, he is without power. Like all Indian kings, or the most of them, he is but the subject of some more able and intelligent mind—Levi Colbert is that mind."[30]

The Chickasaw council in a simple way performed those customary functions of legislative bodies. It appropriated portions of the annuity for public purposes, including subsidies for the support of mission schools. In 1824 the council divided the nation into four districts—Pontotoc, Chesafaliah, Choquafaliah, and Big Town—to accommodate an emerging public judicial system and to improve administration of the nation. Under mixed-blood tutelage, the council took an important step in 1829 by adopting a code of written laws. These statutes improved law and order enforcement and gave special protection to private property, a concern of the nation's business community. Theft was punished

[30] McKenney to Eaton, June 27, 1829, *ibid.*

with thirty-nine lashes, "without regard to color, age, or sex." The offender was required to restore the stolen property or its equivalent. In the interest of peace and order, the code banned whisky from the nation. Enforcement of the Chickasaw code was performed by a mounted police force of one hundred men, twenty-five from each district. The agent reported in 1830 on the workings of the Chickasaws' new written code. "The Municipal Laws of the Chickasaws consists in written laws or resolutions commanding that which is right; and prohibiting that which they conceive to be wrong. Their laws are few, easily understood; and rigidly inforced, and are highly calculated to promote peace, and good order among themselves."[31]

In the removal prelude several groups brought great pressure on the Chickasaw Nation. These included missionaries, white intruders, and officials from the federal government and the state of Mississippi. The missionaries, though committed to destroying Chickasaw old ways, especially tribal religion, had constructive intentions and did produce some good. The intruders and federal and state officials were committed to the baneful goal of liquidating the Chickasaw estate and forcing the Indians to emigrate to Indian Territory.

The federal government was obligated to keep the Chickasaw Nation clear of intruders. Intruders coveted the rich agricultural lands in Chickasaw territory and were willing to risk expulsion and destruction of improvements for the benefits of an uncertain tenure. Many intruders admitted that they expected the federal government to succeed soon in its negotiations for all Chickasaw territory, and it was their intent to be present and pre-empt the best land. Tribal officials complained to federal officials that "these people are not only suffered to remain undisturbed—but others are coming on daily, and these intruders are even selling land to each other." In 1810 the Chickasaw agent reported that four to five thousand white intruders were scattered in settlements on Chickasaw lands, "determined to remain there in opposition to the laws of the United States until removed by force." As late as 1830, agents revealed that for several years intruders had

31 Long to McKenney, November 5, 1824, ibid.; Allen to Eaton, February 7, 1830, ibid., Roll 136; and Missionary Herald, XXV, 1829, 31–32.

planted corn and cotton on Indian land and that each winter they pastured herds of cattle in Chickasaw territory. Intruders poached prime timber in the eastern portion of the Chickasaw Nation and cut huge logs on their lands below Memphis to make rafts for hauling goods to New Orleans. Intruders also were accused of stealing Indian cattle and horses, slaves, and other property and carrying on a clandestine whisky trade with the Indians. Only occasionally did the federal government act to protect the Chickasaws. In 1810 the intruders were so troublesome that Chickasaw leaders threatened to raise a force, drive them off, and burn their homes. This brought a quick response by the federal government. Troops entered the nation and cleared the territory of intruders. In 1828 a Chickasaw was tied to a tree by several white men who "whipt him most unmercifully" in a dispute over livestock. This incident infuriated the Chickasaws, and to keep them from retaliating the federal government again sent in troops. A detachment of troops patrolling the nation in 1830 arrested several hundred "obstinate intruders" and burned their improvements. But their presence, evil influence, and depredations had a telling effect on Chickasaw morale.[32]

Leaders in Mississippi and Alabama were strongly attached to the cause of driving the Chickasaws and other tribes from their domains and were inventive in their methods to accomplish this. Only the federal government was constitutionally qualified to achieve this, and the local governments regularly reminded the Congress through resolutions and memorials of the unfavorable effect that the presence of Indian nations had upon local progress. Three documents illustrate their sustained appeals to Congress to liquidate the Chickasaw estate and relocate the Indians west of the Mississippi. During 1817, the Mississippi Constitutional Convention prepared the following memorial for Congress: "The quantity of Land to which the Indian title is extinguished is very small, and it is to be feared that many years will elapse before the

---

[32] Freeman to Gallatin, March 4, 1809, in Carter, *The Territory of Mississippi, 1798–1817*, V, of *Territorial Papers of the United States*, 720–22; Holmes to Eustis, February 7, 1810, *ibid.*, VI, 44–45; Smith to Barbour, February 5, 1828, Letters Received, Office of Indian Affairs, 1824–81, Chickasaw Agency, National Archives, Microcopy 234, Roll 135; Allen to Eaton, February 7, 1830, *ibid.*, Roll 136; and Allen to Eaton, October 23, 1830, *ibid.*

Tribes of Choctaws and Chickasaws who now occupy the Country to its Northern extremity, can be induced to dispose of it to the Government. This circumstance alone will confine the growth and population of the State, until it shall be overcome by some exercise of executive authority, which will lead to the extinguishment of Indian title over this tract of Country."[33]

On January 7, 1818, the Mississippi General Assembly resolved that United States senators and representatives from Mississippi "use their best endeavours . . . to procure the extinguishment of Indian title, to as much lands, within the limits of this state, as can be procured from the different nations owning the same."[34]

Ten years later the Mississippi General Assembly memorialized Congress, reminding that body that a large part of the most valuable territory in the chartered limits of the state was occupied by "savage Indian tribes, interspersed with disorderly whites, whose vicious and intemperate habits give the example, and afford the facility of indulging in intoxicating liquor, a practice rapidly extinguishing their numbers and entirely hostile to the progress of civilization." The memorialists urged removal of the whites and negotiation with the Indians to liquidate their title to the land.[35]

Federal officials labored mightily to bring the Chickasaws to the point of surrendering their eastern lands. Tribal leaders were very difficult to deal with. To nudge them, the Mississippi and Alabama legislatures adopted a series of laws between 1819 and 1830 which abolished tribal government and incorporated the Chickasaw Nation into state jurisdiction. That this action had the desired effect was manifested in an agent's report to the War Department on the anxiety and distress of the Chickasaws. He revealed that tribal leaders

> had no belief that they would be placed upon an equal footing with the whites; and if they were made so by Law, all the officers

[33] Memorial to Congress by the Mississippi Constitutional Convention, December 14, 1817, in Carter, *The Territory of Alabama, 1817–1819*, XVIII, of *Territorial Papers of the United States*, 209–13.

[34] *Acts Passed at the First Session of the First General Assembly of the State of Mississippi* (n.p., 1817).

[35] *Laws of the State of Mississippi Passed at the Eleventh Session of the General Assembly.*

of the Law would be composed of white men, and as they were unskilled in Lawsuits; and the whites would be partial to each other, they had no belief that they would be able to withstand the encroachments of the whites upon them, and if they did attempt it, that in a few years they would not have a vestige of property left. Consequently they would exchange their Country for any they could get rather than as they conceived, lose their native freedom.[36]

The final negotiations between the Chickasaw Nation and the federal government which provided for this exchange of "Country" were not completed until 1837. Meanwhile the Chickasaws languished on their Mississippi lands, scorned and imposed upon by their white neighbors. About the only sources which provide a candid look at Chickasaw life for the latter days of the removal prelude were the missionary reports, and these were tinged with lugubrious tones and indicated the futility of resisting the settler juggernaut. "The expectation of a removal beyond the river seems to have concentrated every thought to that one point. . . . Judging from what has passed since the extension of the laws [of Mississippi and Alabama] over the nation, they cannot promise themselves much undisturbed enjoyment." Rev. Stuart, the august divine who served the Chickasaws for seventeen years, lamented: "Let the Chickasaws have daily intercourse" with their white neighbors "for several successive years, purchase as much whiskey as their appetites may crave at the white man's prices, and in my opinion, they will not need a new country beyond the Mississippi river. The church is suffering dreadfully from the intense anxiety which all feel for their temporal concerns. The Spirit of God has been grieved away by the worldliness that generally prevails, and some, we fear, have been permitted to draw back to perdition. We have never felt so entirely discouraged."[37]

[36] *Laws of the State of Mississippi Passed at the Thirteenth Session of the General Assembly*; and Allen to Eaton, February 7, 1830, Letters Received, Office of Indian Affairs, 1824–81, Chickasaw Agency, National Archives, Microcopy 234, Roll 136.

[37] *Missionary Herald*, XXVIII, 1832, 16; and *ibid.*, XXIX, 1833, 133.

CHAPTER SEVEN

LIQUIDATING THE CHICKASAW ESTATE

THE Chickasaws marched west in 1837 on their "Trail of Tears," a melancholy hegira which marked their reluctant capitulation to intense state and federal pressures. Of all the southern tribes the Chickasaws were the most difficult to bring to terms. The Choctaws in 1830, the Creeks and Seminoles in 1832, and the Cherokees in 1835 signed final removal treaties. The Chickasaws were the last tribe of this Indian community to sign a final agreement, the Treaty of Doaksville in 1837, accepting a new home in the West. Since the Chickasaw Nation had bowed to federal government demands in the 1806, 1816, and 1818 cession treaties, apparently officials believed that old and tried methods for obtaining Chickasaw land would work one last time. Besides, the earlier cessions had concentrated the Chickasaws into a much reduced territory in northwestern Alabama and northern Mississippi, presumably setting them up for the final liquidation. But there was an important difference between the lands ceded in these previous treaties and the territory sought after 1826. The remaining territory was the Chickasaw homeland. To certain orthodox full bloods this core area of the once vast Chickasaw Nation was the bounty of the Great Spirit, granted to the Chickasaws by sacred ordinance. To part with it was unthinkable blasphemy. The lands their leaders had ceded were tangential to this homeland, lands held by conquest and strength of arms and used as a hunting range. As game became depleted, the Chickasaws used that territory less and less. Those tribesmen committed to hunting for subsistence roamed the trans-Mississippi West. An increasing number of Chickasaws had turned to agriculture. Many mixed bloods had developed substantial farms

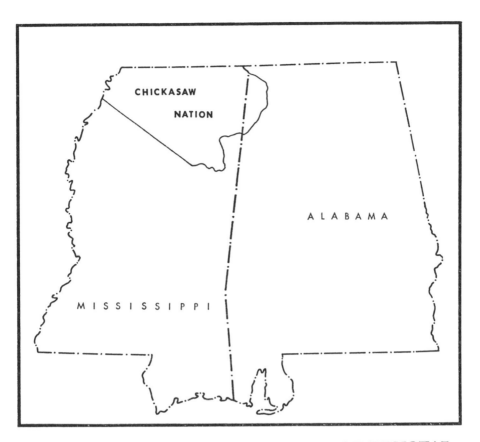

CHICKASAW NATION ON THE EVE OF REMOVAL

and plantations and prospering businesses in the reduced Chickasaw Nation. In the past this group had been consistently amenable to federal government purpose. A cabal of federal commissioners and the Colbert-led mixed-blood clique had time and again produced treaties which surrendered the land coveted by settlers and the states and territories adjacent to the Chickasaw Nation. Thus federal officials were surprised to find this group as determined as the orthodox full bloods not to surrender the Chickasaw homeland.

During the 1820's the press of white settlement onto Indian lands in the frontier region east of the Mississippi River prompted demands that the resident tribes be relocated west of the Arkansas and Missouri. These settler demands were translated into memorials, resolutions, and petitions to state legislatures and transmitted to the national government by United States senators and congressmen from these states. Because of their numbers, strategic territory, and educated leadership, the southern tribes were the most resistive of the tribes faced with the pressures and demands that they surrender their homelands and migrate west of the Mississippi River.

Federal officials responded to these pressures and demands by developing rhetoric to salve the national conscience and policy to effectuate removal. This rhetoric and policy evolved during the mid-1820's. President James Monroe requested counsel from knowledgeable officials on how best to proceed. William Clark, superintendent of Indian affairs at St. Louis, presented the president with a candid statement on resolving the dilemma of providing justice for the Indians and satisfying the settlers.

> The relative condition of the United States on the one side, and the Indian tribes on the other, is, in my opinion, perfectly correct; and the obligation which is imposed upon this government to save them from extinction, is equally the dictate of magnanimity and justice. The events of the last two or three wars, from General Wayne's campaign, in 1794, to the end of the operations against the southern tribes, in 1818, have entirely changed our position with regard to the Indians. Before those events, the tribes nearest our settlements were a formidable and terrible enemy; since then, their power has been broken, their warlike spirit subdued, and themselves sunk into objects of pity and commiseration. While strong and hostile, it has been our obvious policy to weaken them; now that they are weak and harmless, and most of their lands fallen into our hands, justice and humanity require us to cherish and befriend them. To teach them to live in houses, to raise grain and stock, to plant orchards, to set up landmarks, to divide their possessions, to establish laws for their government, to get the rudiments of common learning, such as reading, writing and ciphering, are the first steps towards improving their condition. But, to take these steps with effect, it is necessary that previous measures of great magnitude should be accomplished; that is, that the tribes now within the limits of the States and Territories should be removed to a country beyond those limits,

where they could rest in peace, and enjoy in reality the per-
petuity of the lands on which their buildings and improvements
would be made.[1]

President Monroe uttered the rhetoric and set the policy tone,
revealing federal commitment to settler demands at the sacrifice
of tribal wishes by an address to the Senate early in 1825. "Being
deeply impressed with the opinion that the removal of the Indian
tribes from the lands which they now occupy, within the limits of
the several States and Territories, to the country lying westward
and northward thereof, within our acknowledged boundaries, is
of very high importance to our Union, and may be accomplished
on conditions and in a manner to promote the interest and happiness of these tribes, the attention of the Government has been
long drawn with great solicitude to that object."[2]

Government officials developed an elaborate format in their attempt to break Chickasaw resistance to ceding their homeland
and migrating to the trans-Mississippi West. Chickasaw delegations received regular invitations to visit Washington. Officials,
including the president, feted the Colberts and other tribal leaders and were solicitously attentive to their comfort. During a visit
to the nation's capital in 1824, Secretary of War John C. Calhoun
entertained Levi Colbert and other members of the Chickasaw
delegation. When Calhoun broached the subject of ceding tribal
territory, Colbert informed him that his people were determined
"to sell no more land, despite pressure of the State of Mississippi"
and increasing depredations by intruders. Federal officials had
received this type of response from the Colberts many times and
miscalculated it as the continuing charade, an invitation to provide side inducements to remove their opposition. But this rebuff
was genuine and marked the beginning of a determination not to
negotiate on the subject of the Chickasaw homeland.[3]

Other methods used by federal officials to weaken Chickasaw

---

[1] Clark to Barbour, March 1, 1825, *American State Papers, Indian Affairs*, II,
653–54.

[2] President Monroe's Plan for Removing . . . Tribes West of the Mississippi
River, January 27, 1825, *ibid.*, 541–42.

[3] Colbert to Calhoun, December 7, 1824, Letters Received, Office of Indian
Affairs, 1824–81, Chickasaw Agency, National Archives, Microcopy 234, Roll 135.

resistance to removal included assigning a special agent to the tribe and harassing the Chickasaws with periodic visits by federal commissioners who had full authority to negotiate on the subject of removal if the tribe could be pushed to that point. The special federal agent assigned to the Chickasaws was Colonel John D. Terrell, an Alabama planter. His mission was to agitate removal, watch for breaks in Chickasaw decision not to cede their home-land, and maintain a close and continuing liaison with officials in Washington. One report on his energetic fulfillment of the mission disclosed: "The special agent Colonel John D. Terrell seems to have been active and zealous in communicating with the Chiefs and leading men of the nation, endeavouring to prepare their minds for a cession of their lands."[4]

During May, 1826, Congress appropriated $20,000 to pay the costs for a council with the Chickasaws and Choctaws where it was hoped the two tribes would agree to surrender their eastern lands and migrate to the West. Federal officials issued commissions directing William Clark, Thomas Hinds, and John Coffee to meet with the leaders of the two tribes and to undertake comprehensive negotiations. All through that summer special agents worked on the Chickasaws and Choctaws to create a receptive atmosphere. Agent Terrell was described as "zealously engaged" in the "duties allotted," but leaders of both tribes appeared impervious to the official pressures.[5]

The special agents' reports disclosed that "more time will be required to ascertain the feeling of the tribes in regard to the contemplated purchase of their lands than was expected by the Department [of War]." Special agent George P. Gaines attended a Chickasaw-Choctaw council where the subject of removal was discussed. He reported that "they have in common with all other men a strong regard for the land of their nativity and they cannot very suddenly reconcile to themselves the idea of parting with it."

[4] Hinds to Barbour, November 2, 1826, *ibid.*
[5] An Act to enable the President . . . to hold a treaty with the Choctaw and Chickasaw nations of Indians, *United States Statutes at Large*, IV, 188; Mc-Kenney to Coffee, May 26, 1826, Coffee Papers, Tennessee State Archives; Benton to Clark, Hinds and Coffee, May 24, 1826, *ibid.*; Clark to Coffee, August 14, 1826, *ibid.*; and Coffee to Clark, September 6, 1826, *ibid.*

Levi Colbert and other Chickasaw leaders were described as "silent on the subject of the treaty."[6]

In early September, special agents' reports announced that "prospects with the Chickasaws were most flattering." This caused the commissioners to make definite plans to travel to the Indian country and begin negotiations. Their strategy was first to work on the Chickasaws, then proceed to the Choctaws, "believing the first will influence the other."[7]

The Chickasaw council opened on October 16, 1826. Commissioners Clark, Coffee, and Hinds opened with the statement: "We have met you here in council, by order of our great father the President of the United States. Like a kind and good parent, he is ever mindful of the best interests and true happiness of all his children. . . . You have been apprized of the object of holding this treaty. It is the policy and interest of our Government to extinguish the Indian title to all lands on this side of the Mississippi. We must have a dense and strong population from the mouth to the head of this father of rivers." The commissioners warned that if the Chickasaws opposed this

and prolong the time of its consumation by throwing obstacles in the way, they must be prepared to expect the speedy adoption of the only alternative which is left to the Government to protect its citizens. If the different tribes are permitted to hold their lands on this side of the Mississippi, the laws of the United States must be extended to the Indian country. . . . which of these alternatives will our red brothers, the Chickasaws, choose? . . . Your father the President proposes to give his Chickasaw children a fine tract of country on the other side of the Mississippi river, of *equal extent*, in exchange for their present lands. We know that you are attached to the country of your birth, and the lands in which the bones of your fathers are buried; but if the United States offer you one of equal or greater advantages, and are willing to pay you liberally for your improvements, would not the nation best consult its real interest by making the exchange? By removing to that country, you will be freed from the intrusions and interruptions of

[6] Gaines to Coffee, August 13, 1826, *ibid.*; and Clark to Coffee, August 14, 1826, *ibid.*

[7] Coffee to Clark, September 6, 1826, *ibid.*

your white brethren. You will then be enabled to live in peace and quietness; nor will you be ever asked for any portion of the lands which will be given to you. The Government will guaranty to you and your children forever the possession of your country, and will protect and defend you against all your enemies. Your father the President will also, in addition to what has already been promised, defray all expenses of removing you to the country on the west side of the Mississippi, and furnish you with all things necessary for your comfort and convenience, should you think it your interest to accept his liberal offer.[8]

The Chickasaw response, presented by Levi Colbert, was direct and negative:

We never had a thought of exchanging our land for any other, as we think that we would not find a country that would suit us as well as this we now occupy, it being the land of our forefathers, if we should exchange our lands for any other, fearing the consequences may be similar to transplanting an old tree, which would wither and die away, and we are fearful we would come to the same. . . . We have no lands to exchange for any other. We wish our father to extend his protection to us here, as he proposes to do on the west of the Mississippi, as we apprehend we would, in a few years, experience the same difficulties in any other section of the country that might be suitable to us west of the Mississippi. . . . Our father the President wishes that we should come under the laws of the United States; we are a people that are not enlightened, and we cannot consent to be under your Government. If we should consent, we should be likened unto young corn growing and met with a drought that would kill it.[9]

The commissioners were bitter over their defeat at the Chickasaw council. Coffee chastized the Indians with "a few words expressive of his astonishment at the headstrong obstinacy of his red brothers; he said that he feared that, at some future day, they would bitterly lament the existence of that influence by which he believed them to be at present so much deluded." The commissioners received a similar rejection by the Choctaws, and to justify their failures before officials in Washington they heaped

[8] Journal of Chickasaw Council, October 16, 1826, to November 1, 1826, *American State Papers, Indian Affairs*, II, 718–27.
[9] *Ibid.*

all blame on the mixed bloods. They pointed to the wealth and power of the mixed bloods among the Chickasaws and Choctaws. The mixed bloods, they charged, "have been enlightened by education and otherwise" and use this to dominate the tribes' political and economic life. "It is . . . their interest to continue things as they now are." This was true. The changes produced by the proposed removal would cause their businesses to suffer. They had developed economic patterns, including markets, which they understood and which abetted their prosperity. The remoteness of a new western home would produce serious dislocations. Also, the political power of the mixed bloods in the tribal governments, if not destroyed, at least would be disturbed. The commissioners should have perceived that the education and enlightenment which they ascribed to the mixed bloods made them less susceptible to the domineering, arrogant council proceedings. More sophisticated, the mixed bloods could be expected to be more sensitive, and thus perhaps secretly to resent and take insult at the commissioners' patently crude presentation.[10]

The failure of the 1826 mission to the Chickasaws only intensified the determination of federal officials to win from the tribe an agreement to cede their homeland and remove to the trans-Mississippi West. Every year until 1837, representatives from the government in Washington made some attempt to negotiate. Thomas L. McKenney, commissioner of Indian affairs, journeyed to the Chickasaw Nation in 1827. Unlike most federal officials he apparently was genuinely concerned about tribal welfare. He regarded removal less as a means of obtaining their eastern lands and more as a compassionate solution to the problem of tribal desolation. In his view the Chickasaws relocated in the West could resume their progress in civilization free from the intense and disturbing pressure from federal and state officials and the contaminating influence of settlers. Before McKenney departed Washington he presented a memorandum to the secretary of war containing his views on why the 1826 removal negotiations with the Chickasaws had failed. Coffee, Clark, and Hinds were unsuccessful, he wrote, because they made "the proposition direct

---

[10] *Ibid.*; and Clark, Hinds and Coffee to Barbour, November 19, 1826, *ibid.*, 709.

to the enlightened" Chickasaws who had deep prejudices against surrendering their homeland. "Those prejudices, it must be conceded, are natural. They arise out of a review of the past. Those enlightened half-breeds, from whom the opposition to emigration generally comes, read in the history of the past the effect of this mode of acquiring lands. They see the entire country of the east has been swept of their brethren who once inhabited there; and that, as the chiefs in the middle and northern States have listened to proposals to treat with them, they also have disappeared, until only a remnant of their once mighty race is left." McKenney added, they "enjoy the preciousness of domestic life; and, in the absence of game, have, to a very great extent at least, turned their attention to the soil and to manufacturing. They dread a rupture of those ties; and, from the moment a proposition is made in the Congress to appropriate the means to treat" for their homeland, "those intelligent and lettered Indians exert an influence over the headmen, and over as many of the body of their people as they can reach, which has resulted, as we have seen, in their refusal to acquiesce in the terms proposed to them. 'The obstacles to their removal' are, in my opinion, in great part, those which arise out of the *mode* of approaching them."[11]

McKenney's "mode" or style was to visit the Chickasaw leaders and address them, not with threats and demands, but with friendly, relaxed conversations. He urged Levi Colbert and other Chickasaw leaders at least to consider the proposition to "exchange their lands, east, for lands west of the Mississippi." Such a step, though painful and costly for the Chickasaws, would relieve "them from the . . . increasing causes that had operated to render them miserable where they were." He commiserated with the Chickasaws on their being trapped in a "collision with state sovereignty, and state rights" which he said prevented the federal government from providing them "adequate protection."[12]

McKenney attempted to assuage the very conspicuous tribal anxiety with the soothing comment: "Brothers—Whilst then you cherish a sacred remembrance for the bones of your Fathers, forget not to provide for your children, and never stop a moment, but

11 McKenney to Barbour, December 27, 1826, *ibid.*, 699–702.
12 Thomas L. McKenney, *Memoirs, Official and Personal*, 160.

hasten with all speed to place them in a situation that will secure them against the evils that your Fathers endured. . . . This Brothers, is Wisdom. The past I know has been cloudy and dark enough, but, brothers, be not discouraged. The Great Spirit will yet open your way."[13]

The Indian commissioner succeeded in obtaining one important commitment from the Chickasaw leaders. Levi Colbert, Tishomingo, and William McGillvery drafted a response to McKenney's talk. "Brother you would not wish us to move away and into a Country where we could not live as well as we live here. . . . We agree to go and look at it."[14]

This marked a significant break in Chickasaw determination not to discuss the subject of removal, and McKenney could write the secretary of war as he ended his council with the Chickasaws that he had concluded a "conditional arrangement" with tribal leaders. It was his view that this might lead to ultimate cession of their eastern lands.[15]

Government officials followed up the Chickasaw commitment to McKenney that they would visit the West and examine the country. For several years officials had hoped that they could persuade the Chickasaws to settle in territory assigned the Choctaws. By the Treaty of Doaks Stand, 1820, the Choctaws had received a vast tract west of Arkansas and bounded by the Arkansas and Canadian rivers on the north and the Red River on the south. In 1825, Secretary of War Calhoun had pointed out that the western Choctaw domain was ample for both tribes and recommended that the Chickasaws be assigned a portion of it.[16]

The Chickasaws refused to consider any particular area as a possible future home, insisting that they had agreed only to explore the West generally. Officials pushed them for a time when they would go, but the Chickasaws refused to be hurried. Congress appropriated $15,000 to finance the expedition. The Chick-

[13] McKenney's Talk to the Chickasaw Council, October 9, 1827, Letters Received, Office of Indian Affairs, 1824–81, Chickasaw Agency, National Archives, Microcopy 234, Roll 135.
[14] Chickasaw Council's Response to McKenney's Talk, October 9, 1827, *ibid.*
[15] McKenney to Secretary of War, October 10, 1827, *ibid.*
[16] Calhoun to Monroe, January 24, 1825, *American State Papers, Indian Affairs*, II, 542–44.

asaw agent and several special agents pressured tribal leaders for action, and finally in the early autumn of 1828, twelve Chickasaws journeyed to St. Louis to meet Isaac McCoy, a Baptist missionary hired by the government to conduct the search for a western home for the Chickasaws. The Chickasaw party, headed by Levi Colbert, included mixed-blood and full-blood leaders. Colbert was accompanied by his Negro servant. The Chickasaws reached St. Louis on October 12, and joined a delegation of six Choctaws and four Creeks.[17]

McCoy's column, all mounted, departed St. Louis on October 17. His train included wagons loaded with flour, bacon, tents, and camp equipment. A military detachment commanded by Captain G. H. Kennerly formed an escort. The line of march was southwesterly to the Neosho River, thence south to Cantonment Gibson. Along the route, Chickasaw, Creek, and Choctaw hunters bagged buffalo and deer to enrich the coarse government rations. McCoy's party established a base camp on the Arkansas at the mouth of the Verdigris on November 26. The Creek and Choctaw delegations visited their tribesmen already settled in the area, while Levi Colbert led the Chickasaws on a reconnaissance along the Arkansas and Canadian. On December 7, the Chickasaws returned to the base camp and prepared to depart for their eastern home.[18]

McCoy was disappointed that, although "the principal design of the exploration was to satisfy the Chickasaws," the Indians were noncommittal. Indeed, he advised officials in Washington that "on the whole route . . . the Chickasaws were reserved in conversation of the subject of *country*, their removal, &c." Colbert and others "all plainly enough expressed their dislike of the country we had seen previous to our arrival at Fort Gibson."[19] McCoy also reported that he had encouraged the Chickasaws to consider settling west of Missouri but that they "manifested less

[17] *Arkansas Gazette*, September 9, 1828; "William Clark's Diary" (ed. by Louise Barry), *Kansas Historical Quarterly*, Vol. XVI (May, 1948), 161; Smith to Coffee, September 11, 1828, Coffee Papers, Tennessee State Archives; and Isaac McCoy, *History of Baptist Indian Missions*, 349.

[18] John F. McDermott (ed.), "Isaac McCoy's Second Exploring Trip in 1828," *Kansas Historical Quarterly*, Vol. XIII (February, 1945), 400–62.

[19] *Ibid.*

inclination to settle in the more northern parts of the country under consideration than in the southern. It therefore became the more perplexing on the tour, that almost all the country of Arkansas and its waters had been previously assigned to other tribes so that there remained, in a manner, none vacant for the examination of the Chickasaws. The Choctaws own a great deal of excellent country. . . . They could spare country fully sufficient for the use of the Chickasaws on Arkansas & Canadian rivers."[20]

The Chickasaw explorers reported to the tribal council that the country visited in no wise matched their homeland. The council then presented to federal officials its view concerning the quality of the western country and its refusal to consider removal.

> Our opinion is different to that of a portion of our White Brethren who accompanied us on the expedition, respecting the *vacant country* through which we passed—They have represented it as a Country suited to the convenience of Indians & one in which all the wants and necessaries of life could be secured with facility. But of this, we are disposed to doubt. . . . The country in which we now live, is one that pleases us. . . . We cannot consent to remove to a country destitute of a single corresponding feature of the one in which we at present reside.[21]

This unyielding Chickasaw determination not to sell their homeland and migrate West was broken in 1830 by two things. One was the passage of the Indian Removal Act. It authorized the president to negotiate with tribes for the exchange of their lands in any state or territory for new lands outside of a state or organized territory west of the Mississippi River. The act committed the federal government to compensate Indians for improvements on lands ceded and to bear removal costs and provide emigrating tribesmen subsistence for one year after their arrival in the West. The Indian Removal Act produced nothing new, since the federal government for years had been relocating eastern tribes on western lands. The act did consolidate and solidify an emerging

[20] *Ibid.*

[21] Report of Chickasaw Chiefs on Expedition to West, June 19, 1829, Letters Received, Office of Indian Affairs, 1824–81, Chickasaw Agency, National Archives, Microcopy 234, Roll 135.

policy. And it expressed in dramatic form the federal government's intent and formalized the procedure for removal.[22]

The other development which eroded Chickasaw determination not to remove, its impact far more direct and devastating to Chickasaw recalcitrance than the Indian Removal Act, was the extension of Mississippi and Alabama state laws to the Chickasaw Nation. As early as 1820, Mississippi had begun the process of extending its jurisdiction over the Chickasaw Nation in such areas as fugitive slave recovery. During 1829 and 1830, in the face of continued Chickasaw reluctance to vacate lands in Mississippi and Alabama and migrate West, these states adopted comprehensive statutes which erased tribal government and destroyed the power of the chiefs. Tribal leaders faced a $1,000 fine and imprisonment for exercising the functions and powers of their offices. The statutes abolished tribal law and declared all Indians subject to state law.[23]

Tribal leaders appealed to President Andrew Jackson for succor. They urged him to deliver the Chickasaws from the application of these laws and accord their nation the protection promised them by treaties with the United States. They got little sympathy or support from Jackson. He told them:

> To these laws, where you are, you must submit;—there is no preventive—no other alternative. Your great father cannot, nor can congress, prevent it. The states only can. What then? Do you believe that you can live under these laws? That you can surrender all your ancient habits, and the forms by which you have been so long controlled? If so, your great father has nothing to say or to advise. He has only to express a hope, that you may find happiness in the determination you shall make, whatever it may be. His earnest desire is, that you may be perpetuated and preserved as a nation; and this he believes can only be done and secured in your consent to remove to a country beyond the Mississippi, which for the happiness of our red friends was laid out by the government a long time since, and to which it was expected,

[22] An Act to Provide for an Exchange of Lands with the Indians . . . and for their Removal West of the River Mississippi, *United States Statutes at Large*, IV, 411–12.

[23] *Laws of the State of Mississippi Passed at the Thirteenth Session of the General Assembly*; and *Alabama Acts*.

ere this, they would have gone. Where you are, it is not possible
you can live contented and happy. Besides the laws of Mississippi
which must operate upon you, and which your great father cannot
prevent, white men continually intruding are with difficulty kept
off your lands, and difficulties continue to increase around you.[24]

The moment the president rejected their appeal, Chickasaw
leaders were ready to negotiate. Years of sustained and intensive
pressure by special agents working on the Chickasaws had failed
to produce a willingness to emigrate. Similarly, they had endured
harassment by intruders. The Chickasaws were incensed at the
impunity with which settlers committed depredations on Indian
land and property, noting that only on rare occasions did federal
troops enter the Chickasaw Nation to eject squatters. And it appeared this was more to protect settlers from Indian wrath than to
fulfill treaty assurances of a tribal domain free of squatters. Instead of persuading them to emigrate, this unofficial pressure
applied by the settlers simply pushed them to appeal to the federal government for official remedies. Also the Chickasaws had
suffered through extended councils with federal commissioners,
quietly brushing aside insulting, abusive fulminations at their
unwillingness to co-operate. But these pressures, depredations,
and insults did not weaken their resolve to remain on their homeland. It was the simple but very direct action by Mississippi and
Alabama which succeeded where all other attempts failed. The
federal government was a secret party to this final and successful
coup in that it did not intervene to provide treaty-guaranteed
protection to the Chickasaws. The federal government's position
on the question of state sovereignty and states' rights was shame-
fully ambivalent—energetic, prompt, and active to defend the
principle of federal supremacy in the case of South Carolina nul-
lification but indifferent and deferential in the realm of Indian
relations and state law. Where all other efforts to drive the
Chickasaws to negotiate had completely failed, this succeeded
magnificently.

Federal officials promptly exploited the Chickasaw readiness
to negotiate. During late August, 1830, United States treaty commissioners John A. Eaton and John Coffee summoned tribal

[24] *Niles Register*, September 18, 1830.

leaders to Franklin, Tennessee. President Jackson came down from the nation's capital to lend prestige and force to the proceedings by his presence and his address at the council. Even in defeat Levi Colbert and other Chickasaw leaders did not submit supinely. Throughout the council they presented bold proposals in an attempt to extricate the maximum benefits for their people and themselves. They urged that each Chickasaw man, woman, and child receive a reservation or allotment of one hundred sixty acres in fee simple. Each head of a family not choosing to take a reservation for himself and family was to receive a suitable cash settlement. Emigrants were to be compensated for improvements, livestock, and furniture which could not be removed. When Eaton and Coffee said that reservations for women and children "could not be thought of," the Chickasaws countered with the proposition that each man, woman, and child of the nation be paid twenty dollars annually for ten years in lieu of reservations. The commissioners estimated the tribal population at five thousand and calculated that this plan would cost one million dollars, a "demand which exceeded what they considered liberal and could not be admitted. They could not think of providing them a country equal to that which they should leave, removing them, supporting them for one year, compensating them for their improvements and stock, and then having to pay them, besides, so large an amount by way of annuity . . . they must make their propositions reasonable, but not exorbitant."[25]

As finally signed, the Franklin treaty provided for the cession of the Chickasaw eastern homeland in return for a western home for the tribe. Each warrior, widow with family, and each white man with an Indian family was entitled to a half section of land. Single persons were entitled to a quarter section of land. The reservations or allotments were to be granted in fee simple and sold if the grantee emigrated. If he remained, he would be subject to state laws. The United States agreed to pay the nation an annuity of $15,000 for twenty years. Levi Colbert and four other tribal leaders were to receive reservations of four sections each. Lesser leaders received reservations of from one to two sections

[25] Proceedings of Chickasaw Council, August–September, 1830, *Correspondence on Subject of Indians*, II, 242–43.

each. The United States agreed to pay the cost of removal and to subsist the emigrating Chickasaws for one year after arrival in the new land. The Chickasaws pledged to send promptly a delegation west to find a new home, but "if, after proper examination, a country suitable to their wants and condition can not be found; then, it is stipulated and agreed, that this treaty, and all its provisions, shall be considered null and void."[26]

Announcement of the federal commissioners' success at Franklin brought rejoicing across the Southwest. Mississippi political and business leaders gathered at Parker's Hotel in Natchez "to testify their joy" concerning the Chickasaw treaty. Toasts, speeches, and cheers preceded the sumptuous dinner. Their toast to President Jackson proclaimed: "He found one half of our territory occupied by a few wandering Indians. He will leave it in the cultivation of thousands of grateful freemen." To the "able negotiators" of the treaty: "Their wisdom has combined justice to the Indian, with immense advantage to our country. No room is left . . . for the political fanatic to murmur." Even the Chickasaws received a toast: "Our departing brethren, destined where they are going, to learn the right of individual property, and self government." And they closed with a toast to "The newly acquired Territory—the dawn of civilization now beams on its horizon. The wilderness shall blossom as the rose."[27]

This exultation at being rid of the Chickasaws was premature. The Franklin treaty could not be submitted for ratification until the Chickasaws had examined the western territory and selected "a country suitable to their wants," a clause which gave the Chickasaws a peculiar and unsuspected advantage. Apparently the commissioners had little knowledge of how difficult it could be to satisfy the Chickasaws. As matters worked out, the Chickasaws were able to defer emigration for seven years. But they did promptly organize an exploring party to make a second reconnaissance of the western country.[28]

[26] Treaty with the Chickasaw, 1830, in Kappler, *Laws and Treaties*, II, 1035–40; and Moseley to Coffee, November 15, 1830, Coffee Papers, Tennessee State Archives.

[27] *Public Dinner, given in honor of Chickasaw and Choctaw Treaties at Mr. Parker's Hotel in the city of Natchez, on the 10th Day of October, 1830*, Pamphlet in Pitchlynn Collection, Gilcrease Museum.

[28] Allen to Eaton, October 23, 1830, Letters Received, Office of Indian Affairs,

On October 15, 1830, a Chickasaw delegation headed by Levi Colbert and accompanied by agent Benjamin Reynolds set out to explore the West. Arriving at Fort Gibson, they moved up the Arkansas and Canadian rivers then turned southeast along the Boggy and Blue rivers. Colbert then led his party across Red River and explored Mexican territory in eastern Texas. The Chickasaw explorers were out two months. In May, 1831, Levi Colbert wrote President Jackson that no section of American territory which they had examined was acceptable. He added that they were favorably impressed with the Mexican land along the Sabine River and "if that country can be purchased for us our nation will remove and be satisfied. We see no other country which we think would suit us so well."[29]

This report nullified the Franklin treaty, but the dreadful impact of the extension of state law to their nation created a readiness by the Chickasaws to negotiate again. The Monroe County circuit court which claimed jurisdiction over the Chickasaw Nation declared those laws of Congress regulating trade and intercourse with the Indian tribes "obsolete by the extension of the laws of Mississippi over the Chickasaw tribe." The Chickasaw agent reported that as a consequence "whiskey traders and pedlers—with other intruders upon the Indian land are over running the Country to the manifest injury of the Chickasaw tribe."[30]

Many ugly incidents occurred, but one will suffice to illustrate the precarious legal position of the Chickasaws. Two white men opened a store in the Chickasaw Nation in defiance of treaty proscriptions and federal law. Chief Tishomingo, principal full-blood leader in the tribe next to Ishtehotopa, the Chickasaw king, seized and sold the traders' goods. The traders brought charges under Mississippi law. Chief Tishomingo was thrown in

---

1824–81, Chickasaw Agency, National Archives, Microcopy 234, Roll 136; and *Arkansas Gazette*, November 3, 1830.

[29] Reynolds to Eaton, January 29, 1831, Letters Received, Office of Indian Affairs, 1824–81, Chickasaw Agency, National Archives, Microcopy 234, Roll 136; Chickasaw Chiefs to Jackson, May 28, 1831, *ibid.*; and *Arkansas Gazette*, December 22, 1830, and February 9, 1831.

[30] Reynolds to Cass, December 9, 1832, Foreman Collection, Gilcrease Museum.

jail, and a Mississippi court rendered a judgment against him for nearly $500.[31]

Chickasaw agent Benjamin Reynolds, ostensibly committed to protecting and promoting tribal interests, performed more like a bureaucratic expediter. His true commitment was revealed in his letter to the secretary of war concerning the Chickasaw readiness to negotiate: "I take great pleasure in saying that the leading Chiefs of this nation are becomeing more sencible of there situation and the situation of there people and I have good reason to believe that they will act more efficiently in aiding the Government to procure them a home beyond the Mississippi, and should one be procured I have no hesitation in saying that the People will remove with greate cherfulness."[32]

In response to the Chickasaw readiness to negotiate, the federal government issued commissions to Eaton and Coffee to meet with tribal leaders. Only Coffee was able to fulfill the commission. Singlehandedly he beat back Chickasaw reluctance to accept his terms and drove a treaty down their throats with threats and the old government trick of withholding the Chickasaw annuity until the chiefs had signed the treaty. Thus tribal leaders were pressured from two sides during the negotiations: by Coffee on the one side and by the rank and file Chickasaws eager for the annuity payment on the other. Also, negotiations were made easier for Coffee because the principal Chickasaw spokesman, Levi Colbert, was gravely ill and therefore unable to attend the council.[33]

The treaty, signed October 20, 1832, at the Chickasaw council house on Pontotoc Creek, contained this preamble: "The Chickasaw Nation find themselves oppressed in their present situation; by being made subject to the laws of the States in which they reside. Being ignorant of the language of the laws of the white man, they cannot understand or obey them. Rather than submit to this great evil, they prefer to seek a home in the west, where they may live and be governed by their own laws." The Pontotoc

---

31 *Mingo and Allen* v. *Goodman*, Proceedings, 1832, *ibid.*

32 Reynolds to Cass, February 4, 1832, *ibid.*

33 Eaton and Coffee Commissions, October 19, 1831, Letters Received, Office of Indian Affairs, 1824–81, Chickasaw Agency, National Archives, Microcopy 234, Roll 136; and Colbert to President, November 22, 1832, Foreman Collection, Gilcrease Museum.

treaty was the basic Chickasaw removal document providing for the cession of all tribal land east of the Mississippi River. The tribal domain was to be surveyed at once and placed on the market to be sold as public lands. This was fulfillment of an idea long held by the Colberts. They had told American commissioners in 1805, "You know very well that land is very expensive. If we were disposed to sell that land we would not sell it by wholesale. When we are disposed to sell that land we will have it surveyed and have so much an acre for it, the same as the white people does to one another with these lands."[34]

The Pontotoc treaty provided that the land could be sold both at public auction and private sale. While their leaders searched for a western home, each adult Chickasaw was to be assigned a temporary homestead, on which he was to reside until he emigrated. A single man, twenty-one and over, received a homestead of one section, each family of five persons and under received two sections, and each family of ten persons and over was assigned four sections. Families owning under ten slaves received an additional half section; over ten, one section. Each Chickasaw was to be compensated for improvements on his homestead. Proceeds from the sale of vacated homesteads and surplus lands were to go to the general fund of the Chickasaw Nation, to be held for the tribe by the federal government. From the proceeds the federal government was to deduct the expenses for surveys and land sales. The federal government agreed to advance the Chickasaws the funds required to pay removal expenses and subsistence for one year after emigration. But this expense was to be deducted from the land sales proceeds. Thus the Chickasaws were to pay for their removal.[35]

Between 1833 and 1837, Chickasaw leaders spent much time traveling to Washington and to the trans-Mississippi territory. In 1833 a delegation was in the nation's capital attempting to persuade federal officials to alter the Pontotoc treaty. They de-

[34] Chickasaw Chiefs to Robertson, January 25, 1805, Robertson Collection, Tennessee State Archives.

[35] Treaty with the Chickasaw, 1832, in Kappler, *Laws and Treaties*, II, 356–64; and Chickasaw Treaty of October 20, 1832, Ratified and Unratified Treaties with Indians, 1801–69, National Archives, Microcopy T-494, Record Group 75, Roll 2.

nounced Commissioner Coffee and charged that he ruthlessly exploited them when their principal spokesman, Levi Colbert, was deathly ill and unable to speak for them at the council. The Chickasaw delegation was especially concerned that the treaty contained no provision for orphans, and they urged that the size of temporary homesteads be increased. Federal officials flatly refused to discuss amending the Pontotoc treaty. Also during 1833 a Chickasaw party explored the West for a new tribal home. Choctaws were emigrating at this time and leaders of that tribe invited the Chickasaws to settle in their vast territory south of the Arkansas and Canadian rivers. Choctaw leaders, however, were unwilling to sell any portion of their western domain and the Chickasaws said they would settle only on land which they could purchase and own.[36]

The Chickasaws' difficulty in finding a suitable western home and their continued occupancy of allotments coveted by settlers caused the federal government to be more receptive to Chickasaw demands for changes in the Pontotoc treaty. A delegation met with officials in Washington during May, 1834, and negotiated an agreement which amended the Pontotoc treaty. One clause increased the size of the temporary homesteads. Families of ten or more persons received four sections as provided in the 1832 agreement, but families of at least five members but less than ten were to receive three sections and families containing less than five members, two sections. Persons owning less than ten slaves were to receive an additional half section and owners of ten or more slaves an additional section. Orphans were to receive a half section each. A basic change was that title to the temporary homestead was granted in fee simple. Proceeds from the sale of surplus lands, as provided in the Pontotoc treaty, were to go into a general tribal fund held and invested in income-producing stocks by the United States government. To this fund the federal government was to charge the cost of survey and land sales. Also, the Chickasaws were to pay their emigration expenses from this fund. But proceeds from the sale of temporary homesteads were

---

[36] Reynolds to Herring, October 31, 1833, Foreman Collection, Gilcrease Museum; Reynolds to Herring, November 14, 1833, *ibid.*; and Chickasaw Chiefs to the President, December 27, 1833, *ibid.*

to go to individual allottees. A tribal commission was created to supervise negotiations between purchaser and allottee to assure "that a fair consideration has been paid." Proceeds from temporary homestead sales were to be controlled by the tribal commission which determined the competency of the allottee, thus holding the money in trust or paying it over to the individual.[37]

Levi Colbert died during the summer of 1834. This removed the most formidable opponent to emigration. Unable to prevent the inevitable Chickasaw removal, his shrewd tactics slowed the process, and his judicious management of tribal affairs in this dreadful time brought his people generally the best possible terms.

As the Chickasaw territory underwent the process of survey, assignment of temporary homesteads, and sale of surplus lands, Chickasaw explorers searched the trans-Mississippi West for a home. One party was in the field during much of 1835. Another group was in the West during late 1836. Finally on January 17, 1837, at Doaksville in the Choctaw Nation, Chickasaw leaders concluded an agreement with Choctaw spokesmen. By the Treaty of Doaksville the Chickasaws agreed to pay the Choctaws $530,000 for the central and western portion of that tribe's vast grant. At last the Chickasaws had a western home. They began emigration preparations as soon as notice of the Treaty of Doaksville was received.[38]

[37] Treaty with the Chickasaw, 1834, in Kappler, *Laws and Treaties*, II, 418–25; Chickasaw Treaty of May 24, 1834, Ratified and Unratified Treaties with Indians, 1801–69, National Archives, Microcopy T–494, Record Group 75, Roll 3.

[38] Chickasaw Chiefs to the President, September 26, 1836, Foreman Collection Gilcrease Museum; Treaty with the Choctaw and Chickasaw, 1837, in Kappler, *Laws and Treaties*, II, 486–88; and Choctaw-Chickasaw Treaty of January 17, 1837, Ratified and Unratified Treaties with Indians, 1801–69, National Archives, Microcopy T–494, Record Group 75, Roll 3.

CHAPTER EIGHT

CHICKASAW TRAIL OF TEARS

THE period 1834 to 1837 was a busy time for the Chickasaws. While tribal leaders ranged the trans-Mississippi
West searching for a suitable home, surveyors sectioned the
Chickasaw Nation, and federal officials supervised the assignment of temporary homesteads to Chickasaw allottees. A roll of
the tribe prepared for this purpose disclosed a population of
6,070—4,914 Chickasaws and 1,156 slaves. Homestead sales proceeded swiftly. Speculation companies formed to negotiate for
vast blocks of tribal land made most of the purchases, paying
$1.25 (the required minimum) to $1.60 an acre. Two companies
reportedly obtained title to about one-fourth of all temporary
homesteads. By the Pontotoc treaty the Chickasaws had ceded to
the United States their entire domain of 6,422,400 acres. The
temporary homesteads absorbed about one-third of this. There
remained over 4,000,000 unassigned acres which were disposed
of at public sale, the first held at Pontotoc in January, 1836. The
final block of unallotted Chickasaw land was sold in 1854.[1]

Proceeds from temporary allotment sales went to the Chickasaw allottees. Those Chickasaws classed as competent—that is, as
presumably capable of understanding and managing their affairs
—received their money at the time of the sale. Monies due incom-

---

[1] Mary E. Young, *Redskins, Ruffleshirts, and Rednecks: Indian Allotments in
Alabama and Mississippi, 1830–1860*, 118–20, 162–68; and Statement Showing
the Quantity of Lands Ceded by the Indian Tribes to the United States . . . since
. . . 1829, *Report of the Commissioner of Indian Affairs for 1836*, 424. At the early
sales of unallotted Chickasaw land, buyers paid slightly over two dollars an acre
for choice tracts. Because of the application of the graduation principle, prices for
this class of land declined to about twenty-five cents an acre in 1839, and at the
final sale held in May, 1854, the remaining land sold for what it would bring,
some for as low as two to ten cents an acre.

petent tribesmen were held in trust by the Chickasaw Commission, composed of tribal leaders. The Chickasaw Commission ruled that incompetents would receive no money until the tribe had reached its western home, at which time a token payment to each would be made. The Chickasaw Commission invested most of the incompetent monies in public bonds. Proceeds from the sale of unallotted lands, amounting to about $3,300,000, were assigned to the Chickasaw Nation general fund and held in trust and invested by the federal government.[2]

The land sales brought flush times to the Chickasaw Nation. For nearly three years the Indian country swarmed with surveyors, land locators, speculators, auctioneers, and interpreters—negotiating between tribesmen and buyers. The vast sums of gold and silver necessary to complete the land purchases attracted hordes of traders. One federal official commented that "a very large amount of gold and silver was brought to this place about the first of September—and the amount actually paid for lands already sold is about one million dollars. . . . The Chickasaws are a rich people—Their permanent fund will exceed in amount all calculations which have heretofore been made. It will not be short of three millions of dollars after all expenses are paid." As he contemplated the tent and log stores and the taverns which sprang up in the Chickasaw Nation when the land sales began and the many white men eagerly watching for opportunities to separate the Chickasaws from their new found wealth, he added, "Allow me to say that it is highly important to the future welfare of the Chickasaws that they be removed west of the Mississippi as soon as possible."[3]

The inevitable exploitation and cheating progressed. Tribal leaders accused merchants and tavern keepers of purchasing allotments with cheap goods and whisky instead of money, observing that these commodities "will not benefit our people much." and adding that "a great deal of unfair means are used to defraud

[2] Statement Exhibiting investments for Indian Account in State Stocks, *Report of the Commissioner of Indian Affairs for 1838*, 472. Most of the proceeds from the sale of incompetent allotments, nearly $500,000 aggregate principal, was invested in Indiana, New York, Maryland, Kentucky, and Arkansas state bonds at interest ranging from five to six per cent.

[3] Carroll to Harris, November 11, 1836, Foreman Collection, Gilcrease Museum.

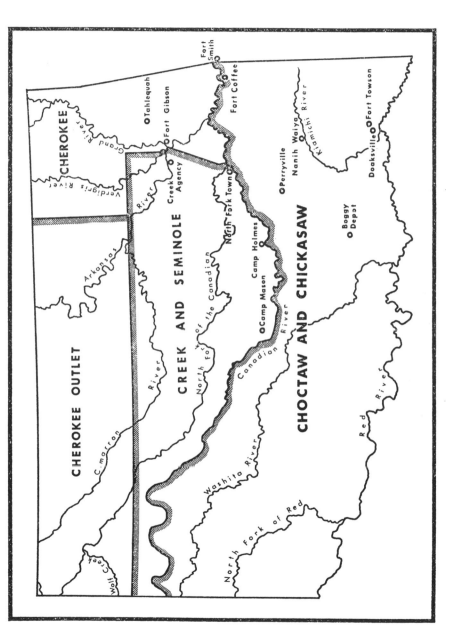

CHOCTAW-CHICKASAW NATION, 1837

the Indians . . . and they carry on with such secrecy it is difficult to detect." Many Chickasaws classed as competent were easy prey for the merchants and tavern men. But a good number sensibly managed their wealth, purchasing teams, wagons, cattle, slaves, tools, plows, and other items useful in opening their wilderness home in the West.[4]

By early 1837, when Chickasaw leaders finally made a decision on their people's western home, much of their nation had been occupied by settlers. State officials from Alabama and Mississippi organized counties in the ceded area, towns grew up, and the erstwhile owners of this territory increasingly became intruders and squatters. The attitude of officials and settlers at the impending evacuation of the old Chickasaw Nation by these tribesmen had been plainly expressed in an earlier statement: "Mississippi will now be freed from the obstruction of Indian claims, in settling their territory, so important to their strength and respectability."[5]

One month after the Chickasaw delegation returned from its negotiations with the Choctaws at Doaksville, tribal leaders informed President Jackson that they were "pleased with the prospect of obtaining, among . . . the Choctaws, a new and, as they hope a permanent home for their people, now almost destitute and houseless." They asked the president to aid them in arranging a "speedy removal to their new home, and thereby prevent the many evils which they now suffer."[6]

Federal officials moved quickly. The secretary of war appointed A. M. M. Upshaw of Pulaski, Tennessee, superintendent of the Chickasaw removal and assigned him a staff to assist him in evacuating the Chickasaws from Mississippi and Alabama. Lieutenant J. D. Seawright traveled to Cincinnati to contract for 1,300,000 rations. Specifications required that each ration—the daily issue to an emigrating Indian—consist of one pound of fresh

[4] Dukes to Folsom, July 8, 1841, Pitchlynn Papers, Gilcrease Museum; and Harris to Butler, December 1, 1836, *Report of the Commissioner of Indian Affairs for 1836*, 380–407.

[5] Overton to Coffee, December 6, 1832, Coffee Papers, Tennessee State Archives; Dunbar Rowland, *History of Mississippi*, II, 678; and *Natchez Courier*, August 9, 1833.

[6] Chickasaw Chiefs to President, February 17, 1837, 27 Cong., 3 sess., *House Report No. 271*, 60–61.

beef or fresh pork, or three-fourths pound of salt pork or bacon, three-fourths quart of corn or corn meal or one pound of wheat flour, and four quarts of salt for every one hundred emigrants. Each ration cost eight and one-half cents. Officials were to place the rations at depots along the Chickasaw emigration trail—200,000 rations were to be delivered to Memphis, the depot near Little Rock was to receive 100,000 rations, and Fort Coffee on the Arkansas River was to receive 1,000,000 rations. War Department officials estimated that this quantity of subsistence would be sufficient to provision the Chickasaws on the trail and for four months after their arrival in the West.[7]

Upshaw met regularly with Chickasaw leaders and developed an emigration plan. His staff enrolled tribesmen in each of the four districts of the old Chickasaw Nation, each district bearing the name of the district chief—Tishomingo, McGilbery, Alberson, and Sealy. Upshaw's plan called for assigning each party of emigrating Chickasaws a conductor, a physician, and a disbursing officer who had charge of the commissary train which transported subsistence stores between depots and supervised the ration issue. Upshaw hoped to have one thousand Chickasaws enrolled and ready to emigrate by June 1, 1837. He commented, "Indians are slow in their movements and will take time." He urged haste for "an average of 50 to 100 are drunk each day" and "as long as they have a cent" the tavern keepers and "petty merchants will use all exertions to keep them here. I think it would have expedited their movement if the competent Indians could not receive their money until their arrival west."[8]

About 450 Chickasaws responded to Upshaw's call for emigrants. Most were recruited from Chief Sealy's district. Upshaw appointed John M. Millard conductor for this first group of Chickasaws to migrate west. The emigrants moved out of their settlements in the old Chickasaw Nation in late June. Their long train of slaves, herds of horses and cattle, and wagons crammed with baggage, household utensils and furnishings, plows, and

[7] Harris to Chickasaw Chiefs, March 30, 1837, *ibid.*, 62; and Harris to Upshaw, April 15, 1837, *ibid.*

[8] Upshaw to Harris, May 15, 1837, Letters Received, Office of Indian Affairs, 1824–81, Chickasaw Agency, National Archives, Microcopy 234, Roll 143; and Upshaw to Harris, April 15, 1837, 27 Cong., 3 sess., *House Report No. 271*, 63.

children, were ferried across the Mississippi River from the Memphis landing on July 4. Heavy rains after July 8, washed out the primitive Arkansas road. Wagons mired and sunk to the axles. Even in their camps on high ground the Chickasaw emigrants were wet and miserable because water-soaked wood made fires for cooking and drying out clothing and bedding impossible. Each day the number stricken with dysentery and fever increased as the column sloshed along the boggy emigration trail. When the road dried out Millard's party was able to average about thirteen miles a day. Near the Little Rock depot several small groups of late starting Chickasaws arrived and increased the size of the first Chickasaw migration to near five hundred. At the Little Rock depot Millard engaged steamers to transport the old people and the sick via the Arkansas River to Fort Coffee.[9]

At the Little Rock depot most of those Chickasaws able to travel decided to depart from the line of march along the Arkansas River valley set by Millard and strike southwesterly for the Choctaw settlements on the Red River near Fort Towson. Millard remonstrated to no avail against this route change, finally ordering his disbursing officer, Lieutenant Gouverneur Morris, to accompany the "recalcitrants." The emigration conductor then boarded a steamer to see his charges, numbering one hundred and seventy, to Fort Coffee. The vanguard reached this depot on August 1, and seven days later the remainder arrived. The entire party drew rations and camped near Fort Coffee.[10]

After seeing this section of the first Chickasaw emigration party to the Fort Coffee depot, Millard rushed off to join the larger group angling toward Fort Towson. He found them straggling, some days progressing only three miles and on others making no advance. He explained that their slowness was due to fatigue which sapped their will to proceed. Each day the number of ill travelers increased. Even on those days when some advance was made, the Chickasaws were slow in starting. The women claimed that they were delayed because the men had to spend much of

[9] John M. Millard's Journal of a Party of Emigrating Chickasaw Indians, 1837, Letters Received, Office of Indian Affairs, 1824–81, Chickasaw Agency, National Archives, Microcopy 234, Roll 143.
[10] *Ibid.*; and Kingsbury to Harris, August 8, 1837, *ibid.*

the morning recovering horses which had broken away during the night. Millard observed that deer were plentiful on the line of march and that searching for horses was a ruse in that the men spent each morning hunting. The most melancholy reason for the slow march was a daily increase in the number of burials. Whereas during the early phases of the migration only an occasional death, burial, and extended family mourning had occurred, by early August the number of daily burials had increased to as many as four or five in a single day.[11]

Millard's compassion was submerged by his determination to achieve an "efficient and orderly movement." Each day he pushed them harder, and the Chickasaws responded by moving even slower. This exhausted Millard's minimal patience. And on August 19, he denounced his charges, accused them of being "refractory and ungovernable" and issued an ultimatum to the tribal leaders in the group. He said the Chickasaws had "their own time and manner to get to their country and seem to take great satisfaction in disregarding all directions and orders they receive from us. . . . They hunt and loiter." Lieutenant Morris drafted a request to the commanding officer at Fort Towson for two companies of infantry. This was read to the Indians, and they were warned that in less than six days the troops would arrive. Then the Chickasaws "would be compelled to march at the point of the bayonet." Emigration officials said they would not make the request for troops if the Indians would follow instructions. Chickasaw spokesmen agreed that the emigrants would comply. On September 5, this group of the first Chickasaw migration arrived in the Choctaw settlements near Fort Towson.[12]

The first Chickasaw removal caused federal officials to take firm steps to assure a more "efficient and orderly movement" of those Indians yet to be removed from Mississippi and Alabama. The commissioner of Indian affairs wrote Upshaw that "before you start another party of Chickasaws to their new country west, you will give them distinctly to understand that they are to pursue the route prescribed for them and will not be permitted to deviate from it. Their course will be direct to Fort Coffee. . . . Should the

[11] *Ibid.*
[12] *Ibid.*

Indians . . . become refractory and refuse to pursue the course indicated," Upshaw was directed to call for troops from local posts to drive the dilatory Chickasaws to Indian Territory. Removal officials also were authorized to withdraw assistance, including rations, if the Chickasaw emigrants refused to cooperate.[13]

During the summer and autumn of 1837, federal officials enrolled four thousand Chickasaws and concentrated them in four emigration camps in northwestern Alabama and northern Mississippi. This progress caused Upshaw to inform officials in Washington, "I speak with confidence when I say I shall be able to get off fifteen-twentieths of the Chickasaws" by early November. He decided to move most of the four thousand Indians by steamer and engaged Simeon Buckner, a Kentucky boatman, to transport the Chickasaws from Memphis to Fort Coffee. Buckner was allowed $14.50 per passenger plus an added charge for baggage. Baggage was to be loaded on flatboats and keelboats and towed by Buckner's six steamers. The horse and cattle herds were to move by land with Indian drovers. The long Chickasaw train, collected from the four emigrant camps, marched toward Memphis in late October, the first group arriving at the landing on November 9. While he awaited Buckner's steamers, Upshaw visited their camps on the river bank and observed that only about five hundred Chickasaws remained in Mississippi, and "they would emigrate in the spring."[14]

Just before Buckner's fleet docked at Memphis landing, a rumor swept the Chickasaw camps telling of a riverboat disaster —a steamer carrying several hundred Creek Indians to their western home had been shattered by a boiler explosion. This caused some one thousand Chickasaws to decide to travel by land. Upshaw remonstrated, raged, and threatened to withhold rations. Konope, spokesman for those choosing to go by land, told the emigration superintendent that he doubted this drastic step was possible because the Chickasaws were paying the emigration expenses. Upshaw capitulated, loaded those Chickasaws willing

13 Harris to Upshaw, September 2, 1837, *ibid.*
14 Upshaw to Harris, September 12, 1837, *ibid.*; and Upshaw to Harris, November 9, 1837, *ibid.*

to go by water aboard Buckner's steamers, then assigned conductors, physicians, and disbursing officers with a commissary train to the land-bound group. His report to the commissioner of Indian affairs on the launching of the second Chickasaw removal stated that four steamboats had left the Memphis landing for Fort Coffee on November 25. "Those going by land have been crossing the river for several days—a great many Chickasaws have fine wagons and teams and 4 or 5,000 horses. I have used all the influence that I had to get them to sell their horses, but they would about as soon part with their lives as to part with a horse."[15]

A traveler stopped at an evening camp of the land-bound party during its march across Arkansas. His description of the spectacle of this vast gathering of Chickasaws resting about their campfires from the tiring day's march is one of the few extant accounts of the second Chickasaw removal. He commented:

> Much money could not compensate for the loss of what I have seen. . . . With all, there was mixed sympathy for the exiles—for they go unwillingly—whether it be for their good or not—moreover the agents & officers all concurred in speaking of the integrity of the men & the good behavior of the women. . . . They said that it rarely happened that any violence was committed by them against the whites, but after receiving the worst & strongest provocation. . . . I do not think that I have ever been a witness of so remarkable a scene as was formed by this immense column of moving Indians . . . with the train of Govt. waggons, the multitude of horses; it is said three to each Indian & besides at least six dogs and cats to an Indian. They were all most comfortably clad—the men in complete Indian dress with showy shawls tied in turban fashion round their heads—dashing about on their horses, like Arabs, many of them presenting the finest countenances & figures that I ever saw. The women also very decently clothed like white women, in calico gowns—but much tidier and better put on than common white-people—and how beautifully they managed their horses, how proud & calm & erect, they sat in full gallop. The young women have remarkably mild & soft countenances & are singularly decorous in their dress & deportment. . . . It was a striking scene at night—when the multitudes of fires kindled, showed to advantage the whole face of the country covered with

[15] Upshaw to Harris, November 25, 1837, *ibid.*

the white tents and white covered waggons, with all the interstices
. . . filled with a dense mass of animal life . . . the picturesque looking Indian negroes, with dresses belonging to no country but
partaking of all, & these changing and mingling with the hundreds
of horses hobbled & turned out to feed & the troops of dogs chas-
ing about in search of food . . . then you would hear the whoops of
Indians calling their family party together to receive their rations,
from another quarter a wild song from the negroes preparing the
corn, with the strange chorus that the rest would join in . . . this
would set a thousand hounds baying & curs yelping—& then the
fires would catch tall dead trees & rushing to the tops throw a
strong glare over all this moving scene, deepening the savage
traits of the men, & softening the features of the women.[16]

Those Indians moving by boat in this second Chickasaw removal reached Fort Coffee in eight to ten days, while the land-
bound party, traveling at a leisurely pace, required a month to
six weeks to reach the Arkansas River depot. By early 1838 most
of the Chickasaws had arrived in the West. However, small bands
emigrated every year for over a decade, and not until 1850 could
it be said that this Indian nation's removal was completed. During June, 1838, King Ishtehopa, the principal chief, and 130
Chickasaws arrived in the West, and early the following year 300
additional Indians emigrated. This led Upshaw to the mistaken
notion that the Chickasaw removal was completed. He discharged his staff of conductors, physicians, and disbursing officers
and reported to the commissioner of Indian affairs that "the
Chickasaws are now all West with the exception of eighteen or
twenty families," owning about three hundred Negroes. In his
judgment these families were "competent to move themselves."[17]

Mississippi and Alabama newspaper editors commented on the
Chickasaw evacuation with tones of exultation and relief. The
Chickasaw Union, published at Pontotoc, praised Upshaw for
making a "clean job of it. The presence of an Indian village, but
recently the great place of rendezvous of the redman, is now al-

[16] John E. Parsons (ed.), "Letters on the Chickasaw Removal of 1837," *New
York Historical Society Quarterly*, Vol. XXXVII (1953), 273–83.
[17] Upshaw to Harris, June 5, 1838, Letters Received, Office of Indian Affairs,
1824–81, Chickasaw Agency, National Archives, Microcopy 234, Roll 143; and
Upshaw to Crawford, February 2, 1839, *ibid.*, Roll 144.

most a curiosity. The demoralizing, brutalizing effects of contact between the white man and the savage, which but a few weeks since were most painfully conspicuous in our streets, are now removed, and our town presents the same quiet orderly appearance which is always to be seen in the inland villages of the Atlantic States." And the *North Alabaman*, published at Tuscumbia, announced that "the whole of this tribe has left that place in the early part of last month under Col. Upshaw. The Chickasaw Indians have ever stood high as a nation. They have ever been found the friend of the white men, and have often poured out their blood in his behalf."[18]

The *Chickasaw Union* editor wrote in late 1837 that those few Chickasaws escaping Upshaw's vast Indian roundup would "in the course of another year . . . be numbered among their Brethren west of the Mississippi." His estimate of the completeness of the Chickasaw evacuation was faulty. Also, Emigration Superintendent Upshaw had revealed his ignorance of Chickasaw population when he announced that the task of relocating the Chickasaws was completed in 1839 because only "eighteen or twenty families" remained. And his action in discharging the removal staff was premature in that the record reveals that Chickasaw emigration continued to 1850. As late as April, 1841, federal officials in Mississippi reported that over 500 Chickasaws remained to be relocated in Indian Territory. During that year 145 Chickasaws emigrated. In late 1842, a party of 188, including 138 slaves, arrived in the west. Ten Chickasaws reached Fort Coffee in January, 1842, 62 the following year, and in January, 1844, 138 Chickasaws with 56 slaves arrived. Thereafter, small parties, sometimes consisting of a single family, continued to straggle into Indian Territory as late as 1850.[19]

After Upshaw discharged his removal staff, the federal government adopted the policy of paying an emigration allowance of

[18] *Chickasaw Union* (Pontotoc), November 23, 1837; and *North Alabaman* (Tuscumbia) as quoted in *Commercial Bulletin* (St. Louis), December 6, 1837.
[19] Armstrong to Crawford, April 24, 1841, Letters Received, Office of Indian Affairs, 1824–81, Chickasaw Agency, National Archives, Microcopy 234, Roll 144; Love to Crawford, September 1, 1841, *ibid.*; James Colbert to Secretary of War, August 1, 1842, *ibid.*; Armstrong to Crawford, April 9, 1843, *ibid.*; and Emigration Rolls, 1838–50, *ibid.*, Rolls 143 and 144.

thirty dollars, from the Chickasaw fund, for each Indian or Chickasaw slave delivered to the Fort Coffee depot. Enterprising Chickasaw mixed bloods exploited this policy in several ways. Some went into the emigration business, collecting scattered Chickasaw families and removing them to Indian Territory. Others drew the emigration allowance to reimburse themselves for expenses connected with overseeing their properties in Mississippi and Alabama. The Colberts, Loves, Overtons, and certain other prominent mixed-blood families held their temporary homesteads for an expected increase in value. They came to Indian Territory early in the removal period, made choice locations on the open tracts along Red River or purchased improvements from Choctaw settlers, and put their slaves to work planting cotton, corn, and other crops. Regularly they returned to Mississippi to look after their gins, mercantile operations, and temporary homesteads. Their names appeared on the emigration rolls several times because their return trips to Indian Territory were financed from the emigration allowance fund. As they liquidated their business interests, they commonly invested the proceeds in slaves and received the customary allowance for transporting each slave to their Indian Territory plantations.[20]

Sadly, there were certain Chickasaws who could not migrate to Indian Territory. A number of widows and orphans, trapped in an exploitive web of Mississippi and Alabama state law, had been assigned guardians by local courts. This came to light during a Chickasaw council at Boiling Springs in Indian Territory. Tribal leaders drafted a petition urging that federal officials intercede and assist in removing "to this country all the Chickasaws, that are now in those states, for there are some of our own people there that cannot get away, several of them are very poor and some of them have property. But their husbands have died and some persons have been appointed to administer their estates, and it appears their object is to keep the Indians there until all of their property is destroyed." Certainly several of the trips to Mississippi made by Chickasaw leaders—for which, on return to Indian Territory, they were reimbursed from the emigration fund—were

20 Colbert to Secretary of War, August 1, 1842, *ibid.*; and Emigration Rolls, 1838–50 found in *ibid.*, Rolls 143 and 144.

errands of mercy to extricate these hapless Indian victims of oppressive state law.[21]

Compared to the Cherokee and Creek "Trail of Tears," the Chickasaw removal to Indian Territory was tranquil and orderly, but grave difficulties developed after they reached their new home. First there was the problem of safety in their district, situated west of the Choctaw settlements. Marauding bands of Kickapoos and Shawnees had established villages in the Washita valley in the heart of the Chickasaw district, and the fierce Kiowas and Comanches roamed its western margins. Thus Chickasaw leaders regarded any attempt to settle in their district perilous, and their people remained in eastern Indian Territory near the Choctaw towns. Except for those enterprising mixed bloods who were developing plantations on the Red River, the Chickasaws lived in emigrant camps, sheltered by tents, until 1842 when the federal government established Fort Washita in the heart of their district to provide protection from the wild tribes. The first emigrant camps were at Eagletown, Doaksville, and Fort Coffee. A later Chickasaw emigrant settlement was situated on the lower Canadian. The fifth and most western camp was on Clear Boggy River near the eastern edge of the Chickasaw District. On December 21, 1837, a party of five Chickasaws accompanied by Captain G. P. Kingsbury set out from Fort Coffee to search for a camp location near their district. One hundred twenty miles south of Fort Coffee on Clear Boggy River they chose a site which became the fifth Chickasaw settlement. Workers cut a road through the wilderness connecting the Boggy River camp with Fort Coffee.[22]

Many Chickasaws suffered in these camps. Fevers and dysentery raged among the emigrants. One of the Chickasaw parties moving by steamer was exposed to smallpox during a stop at one of the river towns on the lower Arkansas. Soon after reaching the emigrant camps they were stricken with the disease. They infected others, and a devastating epidemic swept the portion of

[21] Chickasaw Chiefs to Crawford, July 15, 1843, *ibid.*, Roll 144.

[22] Armstrong to Harris, April 30, 1838, *ibid.*, Roll 143; and Kingsbury to Armstrong, January 11, 1838, *ibid.*

Indian Territory south of the Arkansas and Canadian. Over five hundred Chickasaws and Choctaws died from smallpox.[23]

The most needless suffering inflicted upon the Chickasaws after their arrival in Indian Territory was malnutrition and occasional hunger caused by the poor planning by federal officials and the callousness of contractors. The emigration agreement provided that federal officials would supervise the removal, and the Chickasaws would pay their removal expenses. The Chickasaws were to be subsisted at their own expense until they could produce their first crop. Curiously, federal officials seemed committed to accomplishing an "efficient and orderly movement" to the point of driving the Chickasaws to Indian Territory with bayonets. Also, in view of the fact that the Chickasaws were paying for their removal, it would appear presumptive for federal officials to threaten to withdraw all removal aid, including the drastic step of withholding rations, if the Indians failed to abide by the government's removal formula. In fulfilling the agreement to subsist the Chickasaws (at the tribe's expense) until they produced their first crop, federal officials were shockingly derelict. However, in their administration of the Chickasaw emigration fund government officials were prodigiously generous. Sustained Chickasaw complaints generated by abuses connected with the quality and distribution of rations issued in the post-removal period finally caught the attention of certain compassionate congressmen. Their belated but illuminating investigation revealed not one but two sordid scandals of monstrous proportions, consumated through shameful collusion between government officials and contractors.

Soon after the Chickasaws signed the Treaty of Doaksville whereby they accepted a home in the Choctaw Nation, federal officials began collecting vast stores of salted pork, flour, and corn at Fort Coffee to subsist the Chickasaw emigrants, expected momentarily. There was no co-ordination between the collection of the rations and the arrival of Indian emigrants. Thousands of barrels of flour, salt pork, and corn on the Fort Coffee landing spoiled from the long exposure to hot sun and heavy rains. The cost of these spoiled rations was charged to the Chickasaw ac-

[23] Upshaw to Harris. June 7, 1838, *ibid.*

count. Finding their system for provisioning the Chickasaws faltering, officials entered into contracts with private parties to ration the emigrants. The principal contractor was the firm of Harrison and Glasgow. The contractor, with a staff of fifty workers, established a depot at each of the five Chickasaw emigration camps. Vast wagon trains hauled barrels of salt pork and flour, bushels of corn, slabs of bacon, and tons of salt from Arkansas River ports to the depots. Drovers delivered herds of cattle for slaughter at each ration issue.[24]

One of the earliest complaints by the Chickasaws concerning the contractor's service came in June, 1838, from the Boggy River camp. According to Superintendent of Emigration Upshaw, the Indians were "suffering" from lack of food. Some were "starving" because of "gross mismanagement on the part of the contractors. . . . I begin to think we will have to starve to death, or abandon the country. There has been corn within forty miles of this place for four or five days without moving a peg to relieve the suffering of the people."[25]

Upshaw also charged:

> The rations . . . issued at Fort Coffee consisted of damaged pork, damaged flour, and damaged corn, with salt . . . not regularly issued. The provision was so bad that, on distributing it to the party, many would not receive it. The corn appeared to have been shelled in its green state, and had been mildewed. A part of the corn was weevil-eaten. Some of the corn was so much injured that horses would not eat it. The flour was sour, but occasionally a barrel of it could be used. Those of us who were able were obliged to buy provisions. The pork was so bad that Doctor Walker told me that, if the emigrants continued to use it, it would kill them all off. It gave those who eat it a diarrhoea, and it was always my opinion that many of our poor people died in consequence of it.[26]

Chickasaw leaders charged that short weights in grain, salt, and meat issues were a daily occurrence at the emigrant camps. Cattle

[24] Harrison to Collins, January 5, 1838, 27 Cong., 3 sess., *House Report No. 271*, 158.

[25] Upshaw to Harris, June 7, 1838, Letters Received, Office of Indian Affairs, 1824–81, Chickasaw Agency, National Archives, Microcopy 234, Roll 143.

[26] Love to Hitchcock, February 20, 1842, 27 Cong., 3 sess., *House Report No. 271*, 120–21.

were not slaughtered, weighed, then issued, but "issued on the hoof at an estimate weight." On-the-spot checks showed the contractor estimate of weight one-third above the true weight.[27]

One witness declared that the contractor issues were so irregular and the suffering from want of food so great that "I have known them [the Chickasaws] to pay as high as four dollars a bushel for corn, buying it themselves from the older settlers in the country. . . . On one occasion I was in the country, about fifty miles from Fort Coffee, where an issue of corn from some wagons that were on their way to Boggy. The teams had been fed over night. . . . Indian women came about and picked up the kernels of corn that had been left upon the ground where the horses had been fed."[28]

Angry charges by Chickasaw leaders against their subsistence contractor eventually received official notice. The Chickasaws received assistance, curiously enough, from an element of the mercantile-trader community on the southwestern frontier which had lost the contest for the rich Chickasaw subsistence contract. The Chickasaw subsistence contract was unusual: the federal government assumed the emigration and subsistence expenses for other eastern tribes and paid for them from public funds; the Chickasaws paid their removal and subsistence expenses from tribal funds. Thus it was expected that the federal auditor's surveillance over the Chickasaw contract would be less vigilant than the contracts for the Cherokees, Creeks, and other tribes subsisted at public expense, permitting the contractor greater latitude for exploitation. Later investigations disclosed the procedures followed by contractor companies, generally formed by members of the frontier mercantile-trader community, when a tribe was to be removed from the East to Indian Territory. Federal officials advertised through newspapers inviting sealed proposals for furnishing rations.

If the time is short, there is always danger of a combination among the bidders. A company is usually formed, embracing all those who are disposed to enter into the business; and one or two propose for the contract—sometimes putting in fictitious bids

27 Hume to Hitchcock, February 17, 1842, *ibid.*
28 Crocket to Hitchcock, February 10, 1842, *ibid.*, 116.

above their own to save appearances. . . . If the company finds an individual disposed to bid against them, a proposition is made to him to take an *interest* in the contract, and the proposition is accommodated to his means and situation, and so adjusted as to compensate him for relinquishing his power of interference with the company. The bid of the company is increased to meet all demands of this sort. If the plan succeeds, the company generally realizes a large income, and (subsidizes under the form of an interest in the contract) every one who might have been disposed to bid into their support, or into silence.[29]

The contractors, generally frontier people with little or no capital, negotiated with large eastern banks for loans to finance their operations. The benefits were mutual. The banks benefited from rich interest rates, and contractors, drawing on the power and influence of prominent bankers over politicians, were assured payment by federal officials for services rendered under the contract, regardless of the charges of irregularities. In the case of the Chickasaw ration contract held by Harrison and Glasgow, this company negotiated with Philadelphia banking houses for advances of capital to fulfill their contract.[30]

Despite precautions taken by contractor companies to absorb or silence competition, they often overlooked or miscalculated elements of opposition. This apparently occurred in the case of the Chickasaw contract. Later investigations revealed that A. J. Raines, a frontier merchant trading between the Arkansas River towns and Chihuahua, wrote the commissioner of Indian affairs in early 1840 charging Harrison and Glasgow with "bribery, fraud, and corruption" in subsisting Indians. He claimed that two years earlier he had informed federal officials that this company was committing gross irregularities against the Chickasaws. He said:

> At that time, the evidence against the contractors could have been obtained without much trouble; at present the witnesses are scattered . . . and it would be almost impossible for an individual, unassisted by the Department, to collect the evidence. . . . Consider, too, that these men have wielded a moneyed influence

[29] Hitchcock Statement, 1843, *ibid.*, 32–33.
[30] Armstrong to Hitchcock, March 12, 1842, *ibid.*, 141–45.

amounting to a million and a half dollars, thereby gaining an interest heretofore unknown in this country. I am able to prove the charges I have laid before the Department against these contractors, and will unfold a tissue of fraud and bribery to an alarming and unheard-of extent. But, sir, I want some assistance from the Government to collect the evidence.

Raines threatened to appeal to Congress that the matter be investigated.[31]

Apparently Raines's charges did cause federal officials momentarily to hold up payment to Harrison and Glasgow for services allegedly performed under the Chickasaw subsistence contract. Subsequently it was reported that A. Harris, a sutler at Fort Gibson, was "authorized by Glasgow & Harrison to bring about a compromise between them and Major Raines, by which they might be enabled to receive from the Government the amount of their contract for furnishing the Indians with provisions, and that he [Harris] did so by paying Major Raines thirteen thousand five hundred dollars, though Raines might as well have had twenty thousand, for he was authorized to give that amount." In February, 1840, Raines wrote federal officials that he had withdrawn all charges against Harrison and Glasgow, and that officials had made final payment from the Chickasaw emigration fund to this company.[32]

Recurring charges, largely originating with Chickasaw leaders, that fraud had been committed in connection with their removal finally stirred the War Department to undertake an investigation. Secretary of War J. C. Spencer sent Major Ethan Allen Hitchcock to Indian Territory for this purpose. Later events demonstrated that the War Department really did not wish for an investigation, at least not the penetrating, probing type of inquiry made by Hitchcock, who proved to be a tenacious, indefatigable sleuth. Arriving in Indian Territory in early December, 1841, he spent three months collecting evidence. Hitchcock noted that word had passed of his coming, and prominent persons in the lower Arkansas River towns were "exceedingly anxious to know

31 Raines to Crawford, January 27, 1840, *ibid.*, 124–26.
32 Lear to Hitchcock, March 8, 1842, *ibid.*, 137; and Raines to Armstrong, February 21, 1840, *ibid.*, 135.

B. C. Burney, governor of the Chickasaw Nation, 1878–80.

Jonas Wolf, governor of the Chickasaw
Nation, 1884–86 and 1892–94.

William M. Guy, governor of the Chickasaw Nation, 1886–88.

Chickasaw council, prior to 1890.

Chickasaw House and Senate in 1890, in front of the second Chickasaw council house at Tishomingo, erected 1858.

Palmer S. Mosely, governor of the Chickasaw Nation, 1894–96 and 1902–1904.

William L. Byrd, governor of the Chickasaw Nation, 1888–92.

Jackson Fish, mixed blood, 1896.

Third Chickasaw capitol at Tishomingo, erected 1896.

Ahshawlatabi, sometimes known as C. A. Burris, in 1896. Burris was a
mixed blood who represented the Chickasaws in the 1887 session of
the International Council, a meeting called by the Five Civilized
Tribes to oppose the move of the federal government to organize a
unified government for the Indian Territory.

Robert M. Harris, governor of the Chickasaw Nation, 1896–98.

Douglas H. Johnston, governor of the Chickasaw Nation, 1898–1902 and 1904–1906.

Members of the Chickasaw Senate, 1899.

Bloomfield Academy for girls, opened in 1852.

Bloomfield Academy and pupils, ca. 1900.

Two Chickasaw boarding schools, Sulphur, Indian Territory.

Shunahoyah or Roaming Woman, also called Mrs. Mary High-
tower, 1907.

Last Chickasaw legislature, 1907.

Chickasaw paying party, September, 1908.

my business in this country, suspecting that some of their rascalities may come to light."[33]

Hitchcock found evidence that "worn-out oxen and bulls were forced upon the half-starving people at an exorbitant price. Various white men are pointed out as having made $10,000 to $20,000 each in a year in this plunder of the helpless. Bribery, perjury, and forgery were the chief agents in these infamous transactions." He found that "spoiled rations to the value of $200,000 had been sold to the Chickasaws," and that they were charged for rations valued at over $700,000 which were never delivered. Short weights in grain and beef occurred daily at each of the issue depots. He found that in 1836, contractors were charging six cents per ration to subsist emigrating Indians. The Chickasaw contractor was allowed from fourteen to sixteen cents per ration. He also found reason to look into the "shockingly high" transportation charges made against the Chickasaw emigration fund. Hitchcock declared, "The air is full of scandals." Expressing "astonishment, disgust, and indignation," he promised "that the foul transactions shall be probed to the bottom and the thieves punished." As he prepared his report for the secretary of war he observed, "It will certainly appear very extraordinary that the portion of the Indians over whom the Govt. assumed a guardianship should be precisely those fixed upon for a sacrifice."[34]

Hitchcock was surprised at the reception accorded him and his report when he returned to Washington. Secretary of War Spencer routed it to Solicitor of the Treasury Charles B. Penrose for an opinion. He admonished Penrose that the report's contents were "strictly confidential—not to be exhibited to any one; nor are its contents to be made known without the authority of this Department; and it is to be returned as soon as you have become familiar with it." Penrose returned Hitchcock's report with the comment that the "contract with Harrison & Glasgow was an improvident one. . . . [they] did not faithfully perform their agreement; for I think it may be clearly established that the rations

[33] Ethan A. Hitchcock, *Fifty Years in Camp and Field: A Diary of Major Ethan Allen Hitchcock* (ed. by W. A. Croffut), 137.

[34] *Ibid.*, 142–44; Ethan A. Hitchcock, *A Traveler in Indian Territory: The Journal of Ethan Allen Hitchcock* (ed. by Grant Foreman), 169; and Hitchcock Statement, 1843, 27 Cong., 3 sess., *House Report No. 271*, 34.

delivered to the Indians were first, inferior in quality; second, insufficient in quantity; and, third, irregular and fraudulent in issue."[35]

Several congressmen urged Spencer to make the findings of the Hitchcock report public. The secretary of war refused. Hitchcock suspected collusion, saying that he was "convinced" that high officials were attempting "to screen" important persons "from the effect of my examination in the Southwest." He also detected "a marked change of manner in the Secretary of War, who seems to avoid conversation with me" and reported Indian Commissioner Crawford as remarking that "Indians can be made to say anything, etc." Finally, because his report implicated officials in the government, Hitchcock concluded that "the administration . . . [has] hesitated to charge its own party's officials with felonious acts, and adopted dilatory measures. . . . I am told that the chairman of the Committee on Indian Affairs, H. of R., has called for my report to the Secretary of War. This morning I talked with the Secretary about the matter. He says he will not furnish the report."[36]

Congressmen persisted in their demand that the secretary of war permit them to examine Hitchcock's findings. Spencer was adamant, and before long the report was lost in the War Department files. The House Committee on Indian Affairs and the Committee on Public Expenditures finally proceeded to collect evidence and investigate charges that fraud had been committed in the execution of the Chickasaw subsistence and transportation contracts. Committee findings confirmed the charges made by tribal leaders and revealed that the Chickasaw removal had cost nearly $1,500,000.[37]

The transportation contract also came in for strong criticism. The Committee on Public Expenditures reported "that in this case there has been an unpardonable neglect of all prudence and economy" by officials who deserved "the severest censure." The committee found in its review of the transportation contract that

[35] Spencer to Penrose, June 3, 1842, *ibid.*, 195–96; and Penrose to Spencer, July 20, 1842, *ibid.*, 196–97.
[36] Hitchcock, *Fifty Years in Camp and Field*, 156–58.
[37] 27 Cong., 3 sess., *House Report No. 271*; and 27 Cong., 2 sess., *House Report No. 454.*

the federal officials had signed a contract with Simeon Buckner to transport the Chickasaws and their baggage in steamboats, with keel boats attached, from Memphis to Fort Coffee. The rate from Memphis to Fort Coffee was to be $14 a person. The freight on all Indian baggage was at the rate of $2.50 to Fort Coffee. The contract allowed Buckner a demurrage of $100 a day for each boat while waiting at the Memphis landing for passengers. For this service Buckner was paid $108,544 ($37,652 for transporting Indians, $54,520 for baggage, and $14,370 for demurrage). The committee challenged the payment of $54,520 for 1,064 tons of baggage: "With the knowledge that the stock of the Indians had been driven across by land, we are at loss to conceive what items of Indian property could have constituted this large total of baggage.... The regulations of the Indian department, in other cases, have assumed that 30 pounds per capita was a *fair average* of the baggage of Indians." And the committee was shocked to learn that in addition to the $108,544, "Captain Buckner was allowed by the accounting officers of the Treasury out of Chickasaw funds and ... was paid the further sum of $37,749!" Only 3,001 Chickasaws went by boat. For those who went by land "Captain Buckner charged the same price for transportation as if they had gone in his boats; and for this he was allowed and paid ... the sum of $37,749." The committee observed that the vice president's "almost daily" visits to the accounting office probably "had a more persuasive influence with the accounting officers in passing this claim, than the strength of the testimony by which it was sustained."[38]

Nearly fifty years passed before the Chickasaws received a settlement which in a modest way redressed some of the wrongs inflicted on them during their removal to Indian Territory. Meanwhile they had to overcome the trauma of exile from the land of their ancestors and face up to the problem of building a new life in the southwestern wilderness.

[38] *Ibid.*

CHAPTER NINE

CHICKASAWS IN
THE WESTERN WILDERNESS

THE ancient Chickasaw society—its lifeways and sense of community—had been disintegrating for centuries. The tribe's removal to the Indian Territory wilderness accelerated the fragmentation process. Chickasaw emigration began in 1837 and continued into the 1850's. This extended relocation made it impossible for tribal leaders to accomplish a prompt consolidation of the Chickasaw community.

After removal, disruptive forces continued to buffet the Chickasaw community. One disruptive force was the personal and group trauma produced by the ruthless uprooting of the Chickasaws from the land of their ancestors. Perceptive observers claimed that removal was especially hard on the full bloods who felt a strong spiritual attachment for their homeland, although the practical mixed bloods also felt some trauma at being forced to abandon farms, plantations, businesses—all the familiar things —for that which was new and uncertain.

The Chickasaw settlement pattern in the West also fed the fragmentation process. The emigrants scattered in five relocation camps, some over one hundred miles apart, to escape the threat of smallpox and other diseases which raged in the Arkansas and Canadian river settlements. When subsistence contractors established a supply depot at each of the five emigrant camps, the camps became semi-permanent Chickasaw settlements where many emigrants were content to eke out a miserable existence from their rations.

The fragmentation process was abetted by the state of Chickasaw politics. Concomitant with removal there occurred a general decline in Chickasaw leadership. The creative direction provided by the mixed-blood clique headed by Levi Colbert, ruling through the ancient apparatus of Chickasaw king and council, had faltered at Colbert's death in 1834. No one seemed capable of succeeding Levi Colbert, and the mixed-blood community in the Chickasaw Nation disintegrated into factions, each striving for power. Another development in Chickasaw politics, which at first compounded the tribe's confusion and divisiveness, but by 1855 provided some synthesis and direction, was the passing of the ancient Chickasaw government form—the principal chief or king and his council of clan and town chiefs—and the emergence of new administrative forms. Chickasaw politics also were drastically altered by the promulgation of the Treaty of Doaksville. This compact, signed by Chickasaw and Choctaw leaders in 1837, provided a western home for the Chickasaw Nation. By its terms the Chickasaws received the privilege of forming a constituency in Choctaw territory, to be called the Chickasaw District, roughly comprising the western two-thirds of the Choctaw domain. Choctaws and Chickasaws were permitted to settle anywhere in the Choctaw or Chickasaw districts of the Choctaw Nation. For "these rights and privileges" the Chickasaws were to pay the Choctaws $530,000.[1]

All five Chickasaw emigrant camps were in the Choctaw District. Choctaw leaders had graciously received the Chickasaws and were willing to permit temporary residence in their district, believing that as soon as the shock of removal had passed the new-comers would move to their district. Also, as provided by the Treaty of Doaksville, they were willing to permit some Chickasaws to settle permanently in their district. Certainly they did not contemplate the entire Chickasaw community taking up more or less permanent residence there. The Chickasaws seemed content to remain, and as the months and years passed and they made no move to settle their district, Choctaw leaders became alarmed and repented their 1837 covenant which committed them to receive and provide a home for the Chickasaws.

Chickasaw reluctance to settle and develop their district had

[1] Kappler, *Laws and Treaties*, II, 486–88; and Papers relating to the Convention between the Choctaw and Chickasaw Indians, January 17, 1837, Pitchlynn Papers, Gilcrease Museum.

several causes. The principal one was tribal and personal wealth. Levi Colbert's shrewd negotiations with federal commissioners for the sale of the Chickasaw homeland had yielded rich returns both to individuals and to the tribal fund. This legacy of wealth, rather than a blessing, became a curse. Proceeds from the sale of unallotted portions of the old Chickasaw domain—the surplus lands—were paid into the tribal fund, the principal controlled and invested by federal officials. It was expected that income from surplus land sales would amount to over $3,000,000. As a part of their removal agreement, the Chickasaws were to pay their emigration expenses. Much of the early money in this account was generously, at times frivolously, dispensed by federal officials to pay the exorbitant transportation and subsistence charges connected with removal. This drained the funds accumulating in the Chickasaw account to the extent that it was not until 1844 that the Chickasaws received their first annuity payment. But even the reduced common fund could be expected to yield a handsome per capita return, perhaps the highest ever paid Indians to that time. From an annual interest payment of from $60,000 to $75,000 a year each Chickasaw could expect to receive from $14 to $18, whereas the average Choctaw per capita payment was from $2 to $5 a year. Thus each year a Chickasaw family of five would draw from $75 to $100, "enough to keep its members in easy circumstances for a whole year without further income" or effort. While it was seven years before the Chickasaws began to receive these payments, just the prospect of having the means of existing without labor cast a pall over Chickasaw self-reliance, initiative, and resourcefulness. And until the annuity payments began, they had other resources which sustained them without labor. For a year after removal, most Chickasaws were content to draw expensive rations from contractors acting under federal authority and paid from the Chickasaw tribal fund. Thus the Chickasaws' nonproductive cycle was sustained by their own funds—the income from the sale of their allotments in Mississippi and Alabama. When their allotment proceeds were spent, the Chickasaws received easy credit for food and whisky from traders who took notes for advances of goods.[2]

2 Muriel H. Wright, "Brief Outline of the Choctaw and Chickasaw Nations in

This easy life sapped Chickasaw resolve. They became the butt of scorn and rejection by the more energetic Choctaws who perhaps coveted the newcomers' easy life. Choctaw leaders complained to federal officials that the emigrants were "settling promiscuously" near their towns and showed no inclination to bestir themselves, move to the Chickasaw District, and open farms and plantations. "The question is yet to be settled whether the removal of the Chickasaws to this nation will prove a valuable accession or not, as they have been so long living under no restraint, in possession of large sums of money, subject to all the temptations laid before them by cunning white men among them, that many of them have become addicted to intemperance, and all the accompanying vices, making the worst kind of members of society."[3]

Church and government officials reported on the Chickasaw plight. Isaac McCoy, the Baptist leader, wrote that as late as 1838 "few of the Chickasaws have settled permanently; large companies are yet residing in tents. . . . This unsettled condition is attended with deterioration in every thing that belongs to civilization, comfort, and morals." Their money from land sales and investments "are such as to make the tribe uncommonly rich. It proves a great evil to them that Government is under the necessity, upon their demands, of paying them large sums of money, in their unsettled condition. It tends greatly to intemperance and idleness, and their kindred evils. It is hoped that Government will withhold from these . . . moneys . . . until the recipients are in a condition to apply these considerations to their benefit. Otherwise, while whiskey sellers, and others of vulturine principles will be benefited, the Indians will be injured by such unseasonable payments."[4]

Major Ethan Allen Hitchcock, who visited the Chickasaw settlements during the early 1840's to investigate alleged irregularities in their removal, reported on the Chickasaws at Boggy

Indian Territory, 1820 to 1860," *Chronicles of Oklahoma*, Vol. VII (December, 1929), 401.

[3] Report of the Acting Superintendent of the Western Territory, 1837, *Annual Report of the Commissioner of Indian Affairs for 1837*, 538–44.

[4] Isaac McCoy, *Annual Register of Indian Affairs Within the Indian Territory*, 41.

Depot. "Many merely sat down here at first because the Depot for issues was established here, and they have remained without having the spirit to go out and look up better situations. That very few cultivate corn enough for their own use and, depending upon payments anticipated from the Government, they have lived upon credit until that has gone, and a number have been obliged to sell their horses and cattle and other property." He added, "All accounts seem to agree that the Chickasaws are perhaps in a worse condition than either of the other emigrant tribes in part from their dependence upon what seemed in fact a more favorable treaty than that made by any other tribe." They emigrated "and in their new country under the delusive expectation of wealth from their trust fund have been exposed to a double evil. Their reliance upon their trust fund for money has induced a general neglect of industry and has resulted in a dependence upon external resources. This has thrown the . . . greater portion of the tribe, into the hands of creditors who on their part having looked to the prospective wealth of the tribe, have willingly brought them into debt. No annuities having been paid, the creditors are gradually stripping the thoughtless of everything which constitutes an Indian's wealth; even . . . to their very rifles in some instances. Their cattle and hogs are mostly used up—they have cultivated but little corn and while they are reputed to be the most wealthy of the southwest Indians, they are absolutely in the very worst condition, almost to grovelling in poverty and wretchedness."[5]

Another cause of Chickasaw reluctance to move to their district was fear of attack by frontier tribes. The Chickasaw District comprised the central and western portions of the Choctaw Nation. On its western margins roamed the fierce Kiowas and Comanches. Occasionally raider bands from these tribes swept eastward and threatened even the relatively safe Choctaw settlements. Along the Washita and Blue in the central portion of the Chickasaw District resided renegade tribesmen from the Old Northwest—the deadly Kickapoos, who used the broad Washita valley as a highway to penetrate the western country for trade with the wild tribes and southward to raid the thrusting Anglo settlements in

[5] Hitchcock, *A Traveler in Indian Territory*, 175–76, and 259–60.

Texas. The problem of security in the Chickasaw District was compounded by parties of Texan militia crossing Red River into the Chickasaw District in pursuit of hostiles. More often than not the raiders eluded the invading Texans who vented their fury on innocent Chickasaws, burning their cabins, running off horses, and occasionally killing a Chickasaw.[6]

Chickasaw spokesmen, pressured by Choctaw leaders and federal officials to occupy their district, pointed to the threat to life and property posed by marauding parties of Texans, Kickapoos, Kiowas, and Comanches. And they declared that until the federal government made their district safe, settlement there was unthinkable. In 1839, Chickasaw leaders appealed for federal protection: "We are placed entirely on the frontier and surrounded by various bands of hostile Indians . . . and we wish to know of our Great Father if he will not have some of his men placed at some suitable situation in our District to protect our lives and property, both of which are at the mercy of these roving bands." This dependence on others for protection demonstrated how thoroughly the Chickasaws had become dispirited and pacified, emasculated of their ancient martial tradition. Less than a century before their "beloved warriors" were the terror of the Mississippi Valley. Other tribesmen had trembled in their presence, and they had inflicted a series of humiliating defeats on the best armies which France could muster in North America.[7]

Federal agents on the frontier concluded that the Chickasaws would not move to their district until the government provided adequate protection. In 1838, William Armstrong, Superintendent of Indian Affairs for the Western Territory, urged War Department officials to construct a post near the mouth of the Washita, pointing out that until troops were present, the Chickasaws "will not settle in the District of country assigned them." According to him there was but one company of troops at Fort Towson, and it had the monumental task of guarding the ex-

[6] Upshaw to Armstrong, July 10, 1841, Letters Received, Office of Indian Affairs, 1824–81, Chickasaw Agency, National Archives, Microcopy 234, Roll 138; and Upshaw to Spencer, May 9, 1842, *ibid.*
[7] Ishtehotopa to President, September 4, 1838, Documents relating to the Five Civilized Tribes, Western History Collection, University of Oklahoma Libraries.

tended border between the United States and the Republic of Texas, as well as holding the wild frontier tribes at bay.[8]

During 1839, twelve Chickasaw families ventured into their district, settling the rich bottoms between the Blue and Washita. Kickapoo raiders regularly annoyed them, driving off livestock and capturing several slaves. Troops from Fort Gibson marched through the Chickasaw District and forced the Kickapoos to abandon their villages on Wild Horse Creek and Blue River and relocate in north Texas. As soon as the troops departed for Fort Gibson they returned and resumed their raids on the Chickasaw settlements. Chickasaw agent A. M. Upshaw reported this development to Superintendent Armstrong and declared that "the situation of the Chickasaw country is such, that it will be impossible for them to live in peace and safety without the protection from the United States. The southwestern part of their district is the great outlet and inlet to the mean and disaffected of all tribes north, and Spaniards and wild Indians to the south and west."[9]

Finally in the summer of 1841, the secretary of war directed Colonel Zachary Taylor to construct a post in the Chickasaw District at a location best calculated to check the frontier tribes. Taylor's choice was a headland on the left bank of the Washita River, about fifteen miles above its mouth. Captain T. A. Blake and a company of dragoons from Fort Towson occupied the site during late 1841, and construction on the post, named Fort Washita, began the next year. In 1851, Captain Randolph B. Marcy supervised the construction of a second post in the Chickasaw District, named Fort Arbuckle, situated on Wild Horse Creek northwest of Fort Washita. This military station enhanced security in the Chickasaw District.[10]

While troops from Fort Washita and Fort Arbuckle materially

---

[8] Armstrong to Harris, September 4, 1838, *ibid.*; and Armstrong to Crawford, July 15, 1841, Letters Received, Office of Indian Affairs, 1824–81, Chickasaw Agency, National Archives, Microcopy 234, Roll 138.

[9] Report of William Armstrong, 1839, *Annual Report of the Commissioner of Indian Affairs for 1839*, 466–76; and Upshaw to Armstrong, September 13, 1841, *ibid., 1841*, 399–41.

[10] W. B. Morrison, "Fort Washita," *Chronicles of Oklahoma*, Vol. V (June, 1927), 251–58; also see by the same author *Military Camps and Posts of Oklahoma* for sketches of Fort Washita and Fort Arbuckle.

reduced the threat of raids by the frontier tribes in the Chickasaw District, there was still the Texan menace. This was erased in September, 1843, when a Chickasaw delegation headed by Ishehahtubby joined leaders of the Caddo, Tawakoni, and Keechi tribes and Texan commissioners at Birds Fort on the Trinity River and negotiated a peace treaty. The Texas government pledged to control the Indian trade south of Red River and to protect the signatory tribes from depredations by Texans. In 1844, federal agents reported that no depredations had occurred in the Chickasaw District and that they expected the Chickasaws to make a prompt move to their district.[11]

But the Chickasaws did not move promptly. A tribal census taken in 1844 disclosed a population of 4,111, with over three-fourths still residing in the Choctaw District. The occupation of the Chickasaw District was slow. The first settlers to relocate after the construction and garrisoning of Fort Washita were mixed-blood planters who had been farming huge tracts with slave labor along Red River near Fort Towson. They opened new farms and plantations in the fertile Blue and Washita bottoms. As late as 1851, one-third of the Chickasaws still resided in the Choctaw District. Many Chickasaws had become so inured to living without labor and at public—tribal—expense that they were much more concerned with prompt annuity payments than with moving to their district and performing productive labor which would make them again self-reliant. For several years tribal fund and annuity matters dominated the proceedings of Chickasaw councils. Tribal leaders were pressured by rank and file Chickasaws to make certain that federal agents made prompt annuity payment. A typical entreaty read "We have been in the West now for several years; we came to a country uninhabited; we are compelled to give the highest prices for every thing we wanted which soon exhausted what money we brought with us, our people are now becoming naked. They are in great want of the necessarys of life. They have been looking . . . with great anxiety for an annuity

---

[11] Houston Proclamation, September 29, 1843, *Texas Indian Papers, 1825–1843* (ed. by Dorman H. Winfrey), I, 241–46; and Upshaw to Armstrong, September 3, 1844, *Annual Report of the Commissioner of Indian Affairs for 1844*, 469–71.

untill they have become all but beggars; a number of their women and children are on the point of suffering."[12]

For several years well-meaning agents, anxious to get the Chickasaws settled in their district and engaged in constructive activity, found the annuity a bane and curse. Agent Upshaw wrote in 1845, "The large amount of money that the Chickasaws receive does, and is well calculated to keep them from improving. It is the cause of great jealousy and hard feelings, and they will remain in that situation as long as they draw large annuities; and there are at least one thousand, if not more, of the Chickasaws, that depend nearly entirely upon their annuity for clothing and support; but if they had no annuity they would turn their attention to cultivating the soil." As late as 1851, Chickasaw agent Kenton Harper lamented the deleterious influence of the heavy annuity payments on Chickasaw progress. Also he found their scattered condition—one third of the Chickasaws still resided in the Choctaw District—"makes administration of their affairs, peculiarly difficult, and renders any application of their funds for the general good necessarily partial and unequal in its advantages. The effect of such a state of things upon their progress and improvement must be apparent."[13]

At a time when the Chickasaw community seemed to be at its nadir of degradation, forces were at work which gradually generated a renaissance of personal and group pride and produced a fresh sense of purpose and direction. The impact of these forces assuaged the chilling pangs of the Chickasaw Trail of Tears, provoked those resources essential to adjustment in the new land, and committed the Chickasaws to forge a society and way of life to match the challenge of the new land. These new forces included an emergent leader group more committed to promoting tribal than personal interests. This new group's energy and example galvanized rank and file Chickasaws. Another force of

[12] Upshaw to Crawford, October 2, 1842, Letters Received, Office of Indian Affairs, 1824–81, Chickasaw Agency, National Archives, Microcopy 234, Roll 138; Chickasaw Chiefs to Spencer, October 26, 1842, *ibid.*; and Harper to Drennen, September 1, 1851, *Annual Report of the Commissioner of Indian Affairs for 1851*, 397–400.

[13] Upshaw to Armstrong, August 16, 1845, *Annual Report of the Commissioner of Indian Affairs for 1845*, 524–26; and Harper to Drennen, September 1, 1851, *ibid.*, 1851, 397–400.

substantial consequence was the resurgence of Chickasaw nationalism, caused by their status as a minority group in the populous Choctaw community. Some credit for Chickasaw renascence must go to A. M. Upshaw who, serving as tribal agent for twelve years, constantly urged the Chickasaws to move to their district, to act responsibly, and to improve.

By 1853 it appeared that the Chickasaw decline had been checked. A tribal census taken in that year yielded a count of 4,709, and only about one-tenth of them resided outside their district. During the decade of the 1850's there occurred a noticeable economic thrust as the Chickasaws turned their energies to opening the wilderness, developing farms and plantations, and establishing new towns. The principal settlements in the Chickasaw District, those substantial enough to receive a United States post office, were Pontotoc, Fort Washita (Hatsboro or Rugglesville), Colbert, Fort Arbuckle, Tishomingo City, and Burney. These new Chickasaw settlements were trade and administrative centers, quite unlike the ancient communal towns in the East which had served as the focus for the tribal life—religious, political, social, and economic. For many years Chickasaw mixed bloods had been living on detached individual tracts of the tribal domain, apart from the ancient communal towns. In their western domain the full bloods also adopted this style of living, situating their cabins adjacent to their fields and pastures. The Chickasaws had become, for the most part, rural dwellers.[14]

The Chickasaws sustained themselves in various ways in the new country. Certain of the mixed bloods operated grist and lumber mills, cotton gins, and mercantile establishments. Each year some of the more daring Chickasaw merchants drove pack-trains of goods to the plains and traded with the wild tribes for mules and other plunder which had been taken in raids on the Texan and north Mexican settlements. Occasionally the traders were able to ransom Anglo and Mexican captives which they turned over to federal authorities at Fort Towson.[15]

[14] George Shirk, "First Post Offices Within the Boundaries of Oklahoma," *Chronicles of Oklahoma*, Vol. XXVI (Summer, 1948), 179–244.

[15] Upshaw to Lamar, June 18, 1840, *Texas Indian Papers, 1825–1843*, I, 114–15.

Enterprising Chickasaws opened roads, built bridges, operated ferries, and collected tolls from travelers crossing their domain bound for Texas and California. The most lucrative Chickasaw ferry operation was on Red River. Benjamin Franklin Colbert held the ferry franchise granted to him by the Chickasaw council. By its stipulations he was obliged to keep the roads leading to the ferry crossing in "excellent order." His "large gang of slaves" worked on the banks of the river, cutting away sand "so as to make the ascent easy." Colbert's ferry was "simply a sort of raft, pushed across the shallow stream by the aid of poles in the hands of sturdy slaves." Colbert charged $1.25 to transport a four-horse team and wagon or stage. His net annual income from the ferry reportedly was $1,000.[16]

A growing business in the Chickasaw District during the 1850's was operating spas. Resourceful Chickasaws erected tourist facilities at scattered oil seeps and springs on the south edge of the Arbuckle Mountains near the Washita River. They advertised in Arkansas, Texas, and Louisiana newspapers the health-promoting qualities of oil baths provided at the spas as "a remedy for all chronic diseases. Rheumatism stands no chance at all, and the worst cases of dropsy yield to its effects. The fact is, that it cures anything that has been tried. A great many Texans visit these springs, and some from Arkansas."[17]

Virtually all Chickasaws were engaged in agriculture. Even proprietors of mercantile and trading operations, mills, gins, and spas maintained farms and plantations. Upshaw wrote in 1843 that the Chickasaws had "quit the chase for support." Each year Chickasaw hunters went onto the plains to hunt buffalo, "but their attention has been drawn to farming." Also, it was noted that very few of the men had acquired a talent for the mechanical arts or "follow trades of any kind." Most carpenters, wheelwrights, mechanics, and blacksmiths employed in the Chickasaw District were white men.[18]

[16] Waterman L. Ormsby, *The Butterfield Overland Mail* (ed. by H. Wright and Josephene M. Bynum), 34–35.

[17] Smith to Manypenny, August 29, 1853, *Annual Report of the Commissioner of Indian Affairs for 1853*, 400–403.

[18] Upshaw to Crawford, September 4, 1843, Letters Received, Office of Indian Affairs, 1824–81, Chickasaw Agency, National Archives, Microcopy 234, Roll 138; and Josiah Gregg, *Commerce of the Prairies* (ed. by Max L. Moorhead), 401.

Common tribal ownership of the land and the vastness of the Chickasaw domain permitted selective location of farms and plantations, with abundant river bottom land for all. The full bloods opened small fields of three to ten acres each. Their farming was of a subsistence character, although they traded surplus grain and meat. Also they collected a few pelts each season and gathered beeswax and other natural products for trade in the towns. Women worked in the fields, but increasingly the men assumed the outside labor to permit the women to spend more time spinning, weaving, and sewing. Principal crops grown on the subsistence patches owned by full bloods were corn, peas, potatoes, beans, Irish potatoes and yams, pumpkins, melons, turnips, and squash. Each farm included milk cows, hogs, and chickens, and many had small orchards of peaches, plums, apples, and pears.

Many mixed bloods were commercial farmers, specializing in the production of cotton, corn, wheat, oats, and rye. Their farms and plantations ranged in size from one hundred acres to over one thousand acres. Most of the labor on the commercial farms was performed by slaves. Pittman Colbert's farming enterprise included five hundred acres of cotton plus large fields of corn, cultivated by 150 slaves. He reportedly employed "an overseer (white man) at a salary of $1200 a year and does nothing himself at all." Benjamin Franklin Colbert owned twenty-five slaves who operated his ferry and worked his "fine farm." A visitor wrote, "He considers them about the best stock there is, as his increase is about four per year."[19]

Increasingly the Chickasaws turned to stock raising, a natural economic response because of the singular grazing resources of their domain and because this enterprise solved a problem of market logistics. The Chickasaw District contained "extensive prairies, clothed with luxuriant grass . . . capable of sustaining innumerable flocks and herds throughout the whole year." The Chickasaws brought from the East a long and successful experience as horse breeders. They added to their horse herds cattle, sheep, goats, and hogs. Their successes established the founda-

[19] Hitchcock, *A Traveler in Indian Territory*, 190; and Ormsby, *Butterfield Overland Mail*, 35.

tions for the postwar reputation of the Chickasaw Nation as a stock raiser's paradise.[20]

Commercial farmers in the Chickasaw District shipped cotton and grain to lower Mississippi valley markets. Fluctuating water levels on the Arkansas and Red rivers permitted only seasonal shipping. Principal local markets for Chickasaw grain and meat were the military posts in Indian Territory. In 1842, Chickasaw farmers contracted to supply the Fort Towson garrison twenty thousand bushels of corn as well as its meat and hay requirements. Subsistence farmers traded surplus grain, meat, butter, chickens, eggs, peltries, tallow, and beeswax at village stores for flour, coffee, sugar, and ammunition.[21]

The Chickasaw market at Indian Territory posts was destroyed by competition from Texas farmers. Texas grain and meat passed across the international boundary at Red River duty free, but Chickasaw farmers attempting to sell corn in the north Texas towns had to comply with a Republic of Texas tariff law which imposed a tax of twenty cents per bushel. Upshaw reported that Texas products sold cheaply in Indian Territory because money in Texas was "very scarce, and that all persons there, will sell at any sacrifice, in order to obtain possession of current funds. And by being permitted to sell their products on this side of the river free of duty, it not only drains our country, of a large amount of its circulation, but inflicts manifest injury on our own people it is no doubt the policy of the Government to protect." As late as 1859, Texas farmers monopolized the markets at Fort Washita and other Indian Territory posts.[22]

But resourceful Chickasaws developed other markets. Their domain was a grid of transcontinental trails and roads. A principal artery for north-south traffic between the Missouri settlements and Texas was the Texas Road, a portion of which crossed the Chickasaw District. The California Road and the Doña Ana Road, both goldseeker highways, the Canadian valley route to

[20] Harper to Drennen, September 1, 1851, *Annual Report of the Commissioner of Indian Affairs for 1851*, 397–400.

[21] Upshaw to Armstrong, August 25, 1842, Letters Received, Office of Indian Affairs, 1824–81, Chickasaw Agency, National Archives, Microcopy 234, Roll 138.

[22] Upshaw to Crawford, September 4, 1843, *ibid.*; and Upshaw to Armstrong, August 25, 1842, *ibid.*

Santa Fe, and a road that angled southwesterly from Boggy Depot to the Washita valley and then to the Preston ferry crossing were also popular avenues for western travel. Chickasaws settled near these roads and supplied travelers with corn, meat, hay, and barrels of peach brandy. One report stated that three thousand emigrants bound for Texas moved over the Washita valley route in 1859. Along these routes were early Chickasaw livestock markets. Emigrants paid Indian stock raisers fifty dollars for a yoke of oxen, ten dollars for a cow, and twenty dollars for a horse.[23]

The problem of uncertain local markets caused more and more Chickasaws to turn to stock raising, not only because their domain favored this enterprise, but also because cattle and horses were mobile. Each year before 1861 there was a substantial increase in the number of cattle and horses driven from the Chickasaw Nation to markets in Missouri, Arkansas, and Louisiana.[24]

The movement of the Chickasaws to their district produced several discernible improvements in tribal life. These included a resurgence of economic self-reliance and an arrest of the fragmentation process which had nearly destroyed the Chickasaws as an ethnic community. A new Chickasaw society was emerging. It contained elements of the old and the new. Many full bloods continued to observe some of the old customs and rituals, but practitioners followed the form without understanding the substance. Major Ethan A. Hitchcock wrote that "a number of their old dances have gone out of use and they now dance sometimes after the fiddle." He added that the countenances of "both men and women were rather demure and subdued. The spirit of their ancestors is gone." Of all their ancient practices, that which survived in purest form was the ball game. This and horse racing comprised the principal diversions. Horse racing was a natural development because of the Chickasaws' long experience in breeding fine horses. The "Chickasaw horse" was the most esteemed animal in Indian Territory.[25]

[23] Grant Foreman (ed.), *Marcy and the Gold Seekers: The Journal of Captain R. B. Marcy*, 97; and Louise Barry, ed., "With the First U.S. Cavalry in the Indian Country, 1859–1861," *Kansas Historical Quarterly*, Vol. XXIV (Autumn, 1958), 279.

[24] Harper to Drennen, September 1, 1851, *Annual Report of the Commissioner of Indian Affairs for 1851*, 397–400.

[25] Hitchcock, *A Traveler in Indian Territory*, 198–99.

In earlier times the Chickasaws gathered as a nation each year to celebrate the Busk and other ancient festivals. These no longer were observed, and about the only national coming together occurred at an annuity payment. Each year Chickasaw families gathered at the "Pay Ground"—Post Oak Grove near Fort Washita—camping in the timber around the agency. Visiting, horse races, and ball games preceded the payment, and drinking orgies followed. The Chickasaw agent rated the 1850 payment, when "much confusion, drinking and one killing" took place, as the most turbulent of these gatherings.[26]

Just across Red River in Texas were several distilleries and frontier taverns. Texas bootleggers marketed their product with some success in the Chickasaw settlements throughout the year, but at the time of annuity payments their business boomed. Indian light horse police patrolled the border along Red River in an attempt to intercept whisky caravans bound for the Chickasaw settlements. Also, tribal leaders formed temperance societies to commit the Chickasaws against indulgence. The first Chickasaw temperance society, founded in 1842, claimed one thousand members.[27]

The new Chickasaw society had many of the characteristics of Anglo frontier settlers. Perceptive visitors noted "many of them are indistinguishable, except in color, language, and to some degree in costume, from the poorer classes of their white neighbors. Even in dress and language the more civilized are fast conforming to the latter." Great numbers dressed "according to the American fashions; but the ruder portions of even these, the most enlightened nations . . . wear the hunting shirt, sometimes of buckskin, but now more commonly of calico, cotton plaid or linsey." The fashion among the "Chickasaws of full blood" was "a turban, shirt, frock with a cape either fringed or ruffled, a bead belt, pouch worked with beads . . . leather leggings and either shoes or moccasins . . . a knife in the belt." Their women customarily wore a long frock made from a variety of fabrics includ-

---

[26] Fort Smith *Herald*, January 12, 1851.

[27] Upshaw to Armstrong, August 25, 1842, Letters Received, Office of Indian Affairs, 1824–81, Chickasaw Agency, National Archives, Microcopy 234, Roll 138.

ing bed ticking, fine calico, and "sometimes but rarely glossy silk," as well as a "kerchief for the neck," and shoes.[28]

The common Chickasaw dwelling was a double log house with covered passage or "dog trot." Furnishings included "country chairs," table, beds, and crockeryware. The fare consisted of fried and baked chicken, fresh pork, sliced sweet potatoes, wheat flour biscuits, corn bread, and strong coffee.[29]

Compared to the Choctaws, Cherokees, and Creeks, the Chickasaws were conspicuously derelict in providing educational facilities for their youth. Neighboring tribes did much in this regard with quite limited resources, while the Chickasaws, wealthiest of all the tribes at that time, had no schools in their district until after 1850. About the only informational, and in a sense educational, resource available to resident Chickasaws was the newspaper. Literate Chickasaws read several locally published newspapers. The *Choctaw Telegraph*, printed in English and Choctaw, began publication in 1848 at Doaksville. Two years later it was succeeded by the *Choctaw Intelligencer*, also bilingual and published at Doaksville. In 1854, the *Chickasaw Intelligencer* began publication at Post Oak Grove, Chickasaw District, and beginning in 1857, the *Chickasaw and Choctaw Herald* was issued at Tishomingo City.

For years the Chickasaws were content to educate a limited number of their children in Choctaw District elementary schools and upper-level schools in the East. The Chickasaw agent in 1843 chastized tribal leaders for their lack of interest and initiative in establishing local schools and noted that "I think there is not more than seven or eight" children attending school in the Choctaw District.[30]

By the 1834 removal treaty, the federal government was obliged to appropriate $3,000 annually for fifteen years to finance the education of Chickasaw youths. Tribal leaders used this fund to pay educational expenses of Chickasaw children enrolled at Choctaw Academy in Kentucky. Invariably those receiving the

[28] Gregg, *Commerce of the Prairies*, 401–402; and Hitchcock, *A Traveler in Indian Territory*, 199.
[29] *Ibid.*
[30] Upshaw to Crawford, September 4, 1843, Letters Received, Office of Indian Affairs, 1824–81, Chickasaw Agency, National Archives, Microcopy 234, Roll 138.

benefits of this educational support were the mixed-blood sons of tribal leaders. The number of Chickasaw students attending Choctaw Academy each year varied from twelve to eighteen. When this federal subsidy expired, the Chickasaw council negotiated with Plainfield Academy near Norwich, Connecticut, to educate a limited number of their young men. The council paid the educational costs with appropriations from the tribe's national fund.[31]

It was the missionary presence that finally stirred the Chickasaws to establish local schools. No missionaries followed the Chickasaws to the West as was the case for the Choctaws, Cherokees, and Creeks, but soon after the Chickasaws reached the southwestern wilderness, representatives of several religious bodies arrived and attempted to organize churches and schools for them. These included Baptist, Roman Catholic, Methodist, and Presbyterian missionaries. The first Baptist missionary to contact the Chickasaws was Rev. Sidney Dyer. He preached to them during 1844. The following year the Baptist Board of the American Indian Mission Association sent Rev. Joseph Smedley to Indian Territory, to evangelize among the Chickasaws and Creeks. In 1858, Rev. R. J. Hogue organized the Good Spring Baptist Church near Island Bayou with eleven members, the first church established by this religious body among the Chickasaws. The Good Spring Baptist Church existed until the outbreak of the Civil War when the turmoil of that struggle forced its closing.[32]

Roman Catholic missionaries reached the Chickasaws in 1853. Their primary function was to minister to troops at Fort Washita and Fort Arbuckle, but they also worked in the Chickasaw settlements, attempting to instruct the Indians in this faith. Father John Walsh and Father Patrick O'Reilly were with the Chickasaws until 1859.

Presbyterian missionaries had worked among the Chickasaws

---

[31] Colbert to Medill, June 8, 1848, Documents Relating to the Five Civilized Tribes, Western History Collection, University of Oklahoma Libraries; Colbert to Commissioner of Indian Affairs, May 2, 1851, *ibid.*; and Carolyn T. Foreman, "Education Among the Chickasaw Indians," *Chronicles of Oklahoma*, Vol. XV (June, 1937), 139–65.

[32] James W. Moffit, "A History of Early Baptist Missions Among the Five Civilized Tribes" (Ph.D. dissertation, University of Oklahoma, 1946), 140.

before removal; therefore many Chickasaws were familiar with the creed and practice of this religious body. When the Chickasaws reached Indian Territory they settled near the Choctaw towns. Cyrus Kingsbury, C. C. Copeland, and other Presbyterian missionaries assigned to the Choctaws added the Chickasaws to their ecclesiastical responsibility. Kingsbury worked a two hundred-mile circuit with regular preaching points which included Chickasaw settlements. In 1840, he and Copeland organized the first Presbyterian church for the Chickasaws in the West at Boggy Depot. By 1843 they had established several small Chickasaw congregations, aggregating 125 members. Kingsbury was not optimistic over the spiritual prospects of the Chickasaws. Many of the full bloods, he said, are "strongly attached to their ancient habits, are whiskey-drinkers and ball-players, seldom if ever attend on the preaching of the gospel, and manifest no interest in the cause of education." And he pointed out that while the membership of the Chickasaw churches was increasing, "the larger portion of the members" were Chickasaw slaves. "Some of these give good evidence that they are rich in faith, and heirs of the kingdom." By 1840, Presbyterian leaders had organized the Indian Presbytery as part of the Synod of Memphis. This agency persevered despite the dim prospects for Chickasaw conversion and maintained resident workers to minister to this tribe. During the 1850's, Rev. A. M. Watson was in charge of the Boggy Depot Mission, the base for Presbyterian ministry to the Chickasaws. In 1860, Rev. Allen Wright, later Principal Chief of the Choctaws, was assigned this charge.[33]

The most enduring and productive mission work among the Chickasaws before 1861 was accomplished by the Methodists. The Arkansas Conference sent Rev. J. T. Moreland to the Chickasaws in 1842, and reportedly he was "well received." Two years later, when many of the Chickasaws were moving into their district, Rev. E. B. Duncan arrived to serve the new Indian settle-

---

[33] Upshaw to Armstrong, August 25, 1842, Letters Received, Office of Indian Affairs, 1824–81, Chickasaw Agency, National Archives, Microcopy 234, Roll 138; *Missionary Herald*, XXXVI (October, 1840), 483 and 399; *ibid.*, XXXVII (May, 1841), 211; *ibid.*, XXXVIII (November, 1841), 474; and Kingsbury to Armstrong, October 18, 1843, *Annual Report of the Commissioner of Indian Affairs for 1843*, 337–38.

ments with a circuit rider ministry. Duncan established a mission church at Pleasant Grove near Fort Washita as a base for his Chickasaw ministry. His wife operated a day school for Chickasaw children, the first school in the Chickasaw District. Mrs. Duncan's school, with an enrollment of from thirty to forty pupils, received no financial support from the Chickasaw council.[34]

In 1844 the General Conference of the Methodist Episcopal Church authorized establishment of the Indian Mission Conference, which subsequently was organized at Riley's Chapel near Tahlequah, Cherokee Nation, on October 23, 1844. The Indian Mission Conference had seventeen charges or stations, one of which was in the Chickasaw District. At the 1845 Indian Conference meeting Rev. Duncan was reassigned as Chickasaw missionary, and Rev. Wesley Browning was appointed to work with Chickasaw leaders in establishing schools in their district. Delegates from the Indian Mission Conference attended the 1845 convention of the Methodist Episcopal Church in Louisville. At that convention representatives adopted a resolution providing for separation and formation of the Methodist Episcopal Church South. Delegates from the Indian Mission Conference voted for the resolution, thus providing a subtle though forceful influence for the direction of Indian Territory in 1861.[35]

Missionary pressure finally prompted Chickasaw leaders to support the establishment and operation of local schools. In late 1844 they began negotiations with Methodist officials which ultimately led to the creation of a system of local elementary and upper-level schools in the Chickasaw District. The arrangement included joint financing, one-sixth provided by the Methodist Mission Board, the remainder appropriated from the Chickasaw national fund. Methodist missionaries were to be in charge of administration, curriculum, and teaching. Rev. Browning imported to the Chickasaw District a staff of construction workers

---

[34] Upshaw to Crawford, September 4, 1843, Letters Received, Office of Indian Affairs, 1824–81, Chickasaw Agency, National Archives, Microcopy 234, Roll 138; Upshaw to Armstrong, August 16, 1845, *Annual Report of the Commissioner of Indian Affairs for 1845*, 524–26; and Upshaw to Rutherford, September 21, 1847, *ibid.*, 1847, 883–85.

[35] Johnnie B. Chisholm, "Harley Institute," *Chronicles of Oklahoma*, Vol. IV (June, 1926), 116–128.

and selected for the first school a site ten miles northwest of Fort Washita. Construction began in 1848.[36]

The first school in the Chickasaw District, a two-story stone building named Chickasaw Manual Labor Academy, was completed in 1851. A boarding school, the academy in its early years matriculated both male and female students. Its first student body numbered 60 and by 1857 accommodated 140 students. The academy's first superintendent, Rev. J. C. Robinson, established a course of study which included reading, writing, arithmetic, English, Latin, logic, biology, geometry, music, and sacred studies. Part of each day for Chickasaw boys was devoted to instruction and performance of agricultural and mechanical arts on the academy's two hundred-acre farm and several shops. The girls were taught "house-wifery, needle-work, domestic industry," and child care.[37]

Methodist missionaries supervised construction of two additional boarding schools for the Chickasaws. Bloomfield, a school for Chickasaw girls, situated three miles south of Achilles, was directed by Rev. John C. Carr. After completion of Bloomfield in 1854, the Chickasaw Manual Labor Academy became an all-male school. Rev. Carr's instruction included work in the traditional curriculum plus Sunday study in the Bible, catechism, and Mitchell's *Sacred Geography and Atlas*. The third Methodist-operated school for the Chickasaws opened in 1854. Named Colbert Institute, it was situated at Perryville in the Choctaw District to accommodate those Chickasaws residing there. Both male and female students attended Colbert Institute. In 1856 the school was moved fifty miles west into the Chickasaw District on the headwaters of Clear Boggy River.[38]

Presbyterian missionaries also were active in developing Chick-

[36] Chickasaw Chiefs to Secretary of War, May 6, 1843, Letters Received, Office of Indian Affairs, 1824–81, Chickasaw Agency, National Archives, Microcopy 234, Roll 138; Upshaw to Armstrong, August 18, 1845, *Annual Report of the Commissioner of Indian Affairs for 1845*, 524–26; and Browning to Upshaw, August 23, 1848, *ibid.*, 1848, 532–33.

[37] Harper to Drennen, September 1, 1851, *ibid.*, 1851, 397–400; and Carolyn T. Foreman, "Chickasaw Manual Labor Academy," *Chronicles of Oklahoma*, Vol. XXIII (Winter, 1945–46), 338.

[38] "Bloomfield Academy and Its Founder," *Chronicles of Oklahoma*, Vol. II (December, 1924), 366–79.

asaw educational resources. Through an arrangement worked out between the Board of Foreign Missions of the Presbyterian Church and the Chickasaw council, this religious body established a school for Chickasaw girls situated five miles northwest of Wapanucka. Its official name was Wapanucka Female Manual Labour School. To finance Wapanucka School the Chickasaws agreed to furnish three-fourths of the funds, the Presbyterians one-fourth. Wapanucka opened its doors in 1852 with facilities to accommodate a student body of one hundred. School officials hired seven Negro slaves from Chickasaw owners to maintain the school, work the farm, cook, cut wood, and perform other chores. Rev. James S. Allen supervised construction and Rev. Hamilton Ballentine was Wapanucka's first academic superintendent.[39]

In 1857 the Chickasaw council adopted legislation for the erection of a fifth school, Burney Academy, on a site near Lebanon. Tribal officials carried on extended negotiations with the Presbyterians to operate Burney Academy, but before the school could become fully operative the Civil War had begun, a circumstance which arrested all Chickasaw educational progress. Nevertheless, during that pre–Civil War decade of educational thrust, in addition to the upper-level academies the Chickasaws also established a system of elementary neighborhood schools. By 1851, six were in operation with an enrollment of 180 pupils. These were free public schools financed by appropriations from the Chickasaw national fund.[40]

By 1850 it appeared that tribal leaders had checked those destructive processes which for centuries had been at work eroding ancient Chickasaw values and public and personal will. While the merciless uprooting from the land of their ancestors and relocation in the southwestern wilderness had been traumatic and, at the time appeared to signal the end of the Chickasaws as an ethnic community, their Trail of Tears also had been climactic. Yet, at their nadir of personal and group degradation, the Chick-

39 Harper to Drennen, September 1, 1851, *Annual Report of the Commissioner of Indian Affairs for 1851*, 397–400; and Muriel H. Wright, "Wapanucka Academy, Chickasaw Nation," *Chronicles of Oklahoma*, Vol. XII (December, 1934), 402–31.
40 Harper to Drennen, September 1, 1851, *Annual Report of the Commissioner of Indian Affairs for 1851*, 397–400.

asaws seemed to draw on a reserve of determination which enabled them to overcome their difficulties and to recover. They emerged from their crisis committed to forge a society and way of life to match the challenge of the new land. Landmarks in Chickasaw renascence included adoption of new social forms, a reassumption of personal economic responsibility, creation of a school system to develop intellectual resources of tribal youth, and, after much experimentation, the adoption of a new political form. Because this new political form served as a vehicle to accomplish many of the substantive alterations in Chickasaw ways, it merits special attention.

~~~

CHAPTER TEN

THE NEW CHICKASAW NATION

CHICKASAW government—its form and process—had been in ferment for years. The source of much of this turbulence was the mixed-blood community. In the ancient Chickasaw lifeways, mixed bloods enjoyed the same economic rights as full bloods, but their mixed Anglo-Indian heritage made it impossible for them to find status and role in the social context which centered on the clan—the basis for participation in Chickasaw government from local chiefs and town council to principal chief or king and national council. During the late eighteenth century the growing mixed-blood community began to search for ways to contest the full bloods for control of the tribal government. Soon after 1800 shrewd Levi Colbert provided his group with its *modus operandi*. He exploited the full bloods' commitment to the preservation of ancient forms and set the example for his group by being content to retain the ancient apparatus of Chickasaw king and council and to rule the nation through it. The mixed bloods used the Chickasaw government to obtain franchises for ferries, toll roads, and other income-producing enterprises. Mixed bloods also secured special legislation to promote their interests and protect their private property, thus enabling them to pursue their primary interest of achieving business success. The Colbert-led clique used the ancient political apparatus to create a monopolistic society, to support its private interests, and thereby to gain tight control of the business life of the nation.

With all their callous, self-seeking manipulation of the ancient Chickasaw government apparatus, the mixed bloods occasionally turned their talents to serving the public interest. In a sense even their monopolistic management of business life in the Chickasaw

Nation was salutary: the special legislation drafted by mixed bloods and approved by the full-blood national council excluded white men from the customary business privileges which they so easily appropriated from other Indian nations. Also, as the political relations of the Chickasaw Nation became more complex, in part because of periodic negotiations for the sale of the tribal estate, the innocent full-blood king and council needed the acumen which the better-informed mixed bloods could bring to the negotiations. While every negotiation for tribal land might be regarded as an imposition of the strong on the weak, the Chickasaws fared better than all other tribes in their negotiations largely because the full bloods were willing to give the mixed bloods full power to negotiate with federal officials and to support their negotiations once completed.

Several things in the removal period drastically altered Chickasaw politics and government apparatus. First, the removal disturbed and dislocated the Chickasaw governmental apparatus. The settlement pattern of emigrant parties made impossible the resumption of a system of government based on ancient residence sites. The compelling need for food and shelter drew representatives from several clans into each of the emigrant camps. It was expected that these would be temporary and that quite soon the Chickasaws would move to their district and regroup along old clan and town lines. In practice these temporary emigrant camps became semi-permanent Chickasaw settlements. For several years after arrival in the new country, certain Chickasaw leaders attempted to retain the king and national council and to rule the scattered Chickasaw communities through this vestigial structure. The attempts were futile, and the pitiful workings of this reconstructed apparatus proved it a fiction.

In the early post-removal period Chickasaw government and politics also were altered by a problem in leadership. Levi Colbert had created a behind-the-scenes mechanism to control and direct the ancient tribal government. It consisted largely of his forceful personality and vast native talent. For over forty years he was the "soul" of the nation's government. Colbert died in 1834—a disaster for the full bloods who depended on him and his clique for guidance in operating the government and for his mixed-blood following who drew their power and status from his eminence. No one in the mixed-blood community seemed capable of succeeding him as the power behind the government, and this group disintegrated into factions, each striving for position.

Another development which influenced Chickasaw government and politics in the early post-removal period was the Chickasaw Commission, provided for in the 1834 treaty. Organized by Levi Colbert, the commission was designed to guard and administer the property and income of tribal incompetents—orphans, certain minors, and those adults incapable of looking after their interests. The Chickasaw Commission consisted of seven members and, other than the Chickasaw king, was made up of mixed bloods. Besides its great power derived from control of a vast financial resource, the Chickasaw Commission came to arrogate to itself the management of the annuity distribution, supervision of the unsold portion of the eastern tribal estate, and appropriation of monies from the national fund. Eventually the commission served as spokesman for the Chickasaw Nation in all things as the king and council became weaker and less assertive. During the 1840's the Chickasaw Commission in effect was the government for the Chickasaw Nation.

The political arrangement growing out of the Treaty of Doaksville had an immediate impact on Chickasaw government and politics. The new political system not only served as a stimulus for Chickasaw nationalism but also prompted the Chickasaws to experiment with those political forms which culminated in the new Chickasaw Nation of 1856. Signed by Choctaw and Chickasaw leaders in 1837, the treaty provided the Chickasaws with a western home by allowing them to form a constituency in the Choctaw territory to be called the Chickasaw District, roughly comprising the western two-thirds of the Choctaw domain. It permitted Choctaws and Chickasaws to settle in either the Choctaw or Chickasaw District of the Choctaw Nation. For these rights and privileges the Chickasaws were to pay the Choctaws $530,000. The Treaty of Doaksville in effect committed the Chickasaw Nation to dissolve itself politically and to be absorbed into the Choctaw Nation. The territory and political community were designated "Choctaw Nation." Officially "Chickasaw Nation" was erased as a term. Chickasaws became citizens of the Choctaw Nation, were subject to Choctaw law, were guaranteed the rights of Choctaws, and were represented in the Choctaw government by a chief elected from the Chickasaw District of the Choctaw Nation and by representatives on the Choctaw national council. By the 1837 compact the Chickasaws were blended into the Choctaw Nation in all things except their national fund.

In 1834 the Choctaws had adopted a written constitution. It provided for a unicameral legislative body, a general council of twenty-seven elected representatives, and an executive department consisting of three district chiefs, one elected from each of the three districts of the Choctaw Nation. The Choctaws altered their constitution in 1838 to accommodate the Chickasaws. The changes included increasing governmental units to four—Mosholatubbee District, Pushmataha District, Apuckashunnubbee District, and Chickasaw District—with a district chief from each comprising the executive department. The Choctaw national council membership was increased to forty. Ten seats were apportioned to the Chickasaws. This constitution also provided for a district judicial system. Three judges conducting "inferior and superior" courts were elected in each of the four districts. The Choctaw constitution contained a bill of rights which included trial by jury. Further constitutional changes occurred in 1843 when the national council was made bicameral—a senate of four members from each district elected to two-year terms and a house of representatives elected annually and apportioned according to district population. In 1850 the Choctaw constitution was amended to provide for a division of the four districts into nineteen counties. Chickasaw District counties were Panola (southeast), Wichita (southwest), Caddo (northwest), and Perry (northeast). Also at this time the judicial structure was expanded to include a system of county and circuit courts and a national supreme court, made up of four judges who sat annually at the national capital at Tuskahoma as an appellate tribunal.[1]

[1] Angie Debo, *The Rise and Fall of the Choctaw Republic*, 74; Muriel H. Wright, "Organization of Counties in the Choctaw and Chickasaw Nations," *Chronicles of Oklahoma*, Vol. VIII (September, 1930), 314–34; Report of William Armstrong, 1838, *Annual Report of the Commissioner of Indian Affairs for 1838*, 507–16.

Slowly and begrudgingly the Chickasaws came to participate in the government of the Choctaw Nation, but at no time did they accept their defined status as citizens of this constitutional community. It was not until 1841 that they elected a Chickasaw District chief and their quota of representatives to the Choctaw council as provided by the Choctaw constitution.[2]

In 1842, Superintendent of Indian Affairs for the Western Territory William Armstrong announced that "the Choctaws and Chickasaws . . . may be regarded as one people; they speak the same language—have intermarried with each other," and have a common government. What Armstrong failed to detect was an undercurrent of resentment and a growing determination by the Chickasaws to escape the 1837 unification agreement. As the Chickasaws moved into their district, they found Choctaw Nation laws directing their affairs and dividing their district into counties and Choctaw Nation courts settling local disputes. This aroused the Chickasaws, unified them, and generated an intense nationalism.[3]

Chickasaw leaders began to complain that they "[did] not like the idea of losing their name and becoming merged into the Choctaw Nation." They admitted that the Treaty of Doaksville was a mistake, for they "thought they were procuring a country for themselves." They deeply resented the submergence of their nation and were determined "not to part with their name." Chickasaw leaders commented to Major Ethan A. Hitchcock that they "[did not] like the Choctaw laws and [were] overruled in Council." His assessment was, "They have become subordinate to the Choctaw government, a government utterly foreign to their habits and offensive to their national pride. They feel as if they had purchased themselves into degradation . . . they feel humiliated and broken-spirited under the operations of a government which they are told they *share* with the Choctaws." Rank and file Chickasaws also objected to Choctaw pre-eminence and distrusted Choctaw men because of their interest in Chickasaw women. Hitchcock observed that Chickasaw wealth "exposes

---

[2] Armstrong to Crawford, September 30, 1841, *Annual Report of the Commissioner of Indian Affairs for 1841*, 333–39.
[3] Armstrong to Crawford, September 10, 1842, *ibid.*, 1842, 446.

their women to marriage with the Choctaws and this the Chicka-saw men don't like."[4]

By the time the Chickasaws moved to their district several layers of government were in operation, each seeking to direct and manage Chickasaw affairs. As provided for in the Choctaw constitution, one layer of government existed at the district level as a local government. There the elected Chickasaw District chief was the top administrative official. The elected representatives were his captains who served as the legislative and advisory council for the district. The highest level was the national gov-ernment for the Choctaw Nation. The Chickasaw tie to the Choctaw system was through the district chief who worked with the three chiefs from the Choctaw districts to form the executive branch of the Choctaw Nation and through the Chickasaw Dis-trict representatives or captains who served on the Choctaw council and shared in the law-making process for the four districts.

A third level of government, becoming weaker with time but occasionally attempting to assert itself, was the ancient apparatus of Chickasaw king and clan-derived council. Agent Upshaw thought this was the administrative mode most preferred by rank and file Chickasaws. The Chickasaws, said Upshaw, favored "the same kind of government, that they had when they lived East of the Mississippi." He believed they were determined to retain this form because from their viewpoint it was the only means by which they could preserve and protect those "ancient rules and customs" which they so esteemed.[5]

A fourth layer of government striving to control an increasing range of tribal matters was the Chickasaw Commission. Created to oversee and protect the property interests of orphans and in-competents, this group for a time managed all aspects of tribal business life and was in fact the Chickasaw government.

An additional level of government over the Chickasaws was the United States government administered through the Bureau of Indian Affairs. The principal local official was the superintendent

[4] Hitchcock, *A Traveler in Indian Territory*, 172–73, 183, 259–60.
[5] Upshaw to Crawford, September 4, 1843, Letters Received, Office of Indian Affairs, 1824–81, Chickasaw Agency, National Archives, Microcopy 234, Roll 138.

for Indian affairs for the Western Territory. In the early years William Armstrong held this position and served as Choctaw agent. During the emigration the federal government assigned A. M. Upshaw to the Chickasaws as removal agent, responsible for supervising the Chickasaw relocation from Mississippi and Alabama to Indian Territory. As soon as they arrived in the West, the Chickasaws came under the jurisdiction of G. P. Kingsbury, their resident agent. Near Fort Towson during the summer of 1839, Kingsbury died and Upshaw was appointed to replace him. Upshaw served the Chickasaws until 1851. Gabriel Long and Kenton Harper successively were appointed to the position of Chickasaw agent for brief terms. Beginning in 1852, Andrew J. Smith became Chickasaw agent. Douglas H. Cooper, appointed Choctaw-Chickasaw agent in 1856, continued in this assignment until the Chickasaws joined the Confederacy in 1861. The first Chickasaw agency was situated at Fort Towson. In 1842, Upshaw followed the Chickasaws to their district and established a new Chickasaw agency near Fort Washita in Post Oak Grove. Cooper divided his time between the Chickasaws and Choctaws until 1859 when he consolidated the work of both agencies and established his headquarters at Fort Washita.[6]

From an administrative viewpoint the impact of these levels of government on the Chickasaws was nominal. Each Chickasaw lived as he chose, deliberately ignoring those national Choctaw laws which attempted to tamper with polygamy and other esteemed ancient customs. Direction of Chickasaw affairs from the federal government level was thin and permissive. Tribal leaders came to challenge this level, especially its role as trustee for the rich proceeds accumulating in the Chickasaw national fund from eastern land sales by demanding regular accounting for disbursements. Eventually their efforts revealed derelict management and collusive, prodigious expenditures by federal officials in paying contractors for removal expenses from the Chickasaw national fund. In their early post-removal period those layers of govern-

---

6 Upshaw to Crawford, March 23, 1839, *ibid.*, Roll 137; Upshaw to Spencer, May 9, 1842, *ibid.*, Roll 138; Report of William Armstrong, 1839, *Annual Report of the Commissioner of Indian Affairs for 1839*, 446–76; and Fort Smith *Herald*, January 12, 1851.

ment of greatest interest to the Chickasaws were the king and clan council and the Chickasaw Commission.

These two levels of government were erased in 1845. The circumstances which produced their demise demonstrated that the mixed blood's penchant for political inventiveness had survived removal. The circumstances were derived from the rule followed by federal officials in paying the annuity to individuals in the Chickasaw District. The Chickasaw Commission devised this plan and supported it. This method of annuity payment was an inconvenience for those Chickasaws who resided in the Choctaw districts, but the intent of the rule was to encourage non-resident Chickasaws to move to their district. The Chickasaw Commission supervised the per capita payment. Before the 1845 payment was made, a general meeting of the Chickasaws took place at Boiling Springs near Fort Washita. Present were agents of three of the Chickasaw government levels—aged King Ishtehotopa and his council, Chickasaw Commission members, and Chickasaw District Chief Isaac Alberson and his council. Also present were prominent mixed bloods, including Pittman Colbert. During the general meeting Colbert denounced the Chickasaw Commission members, accusing them of mismanagement of incompetents' funds. Colbert added that since the principal assignment of the commission had been fulfilled it should be abolished and that another of the Chickasaw government levels should assume any continuing functions of the commission. Commission members denied Colbert's charges but agreed to resign. The general meeting closed with no decision made on the assignment of the Chickasaw Commission functions. After most Chickasaws had departed the council ground, Colbert convened those few remaining (it was charged later that they were his supporters) and proposed that the Chickasaw Commission functions, including the power to determine the mode of making the annuity payment, be assigned to Chickasaw King Ishtehotopa and his council. Colbert's plan was approved. Thereupon Ishtehotopa announced that the annuity funds would be delivered to him and that he would determine the method of distribution. When informed of Colbert's coup, Chickasaw District Chief Alberson protested and urged Armstrong and Upshaw to assist him in exposing what he charged was Colbert's secret intent. Their investigation revealed that the Chickasaw king and Colbert resided near Fort Towson eighty miles from the Chickasaw District. Armstrong and Upshaw claimed that the king and his council were innocent "dupes," that Colbert in effect would control the annuity and divert substantial portions of the money to satisfy debts allegedly due him from Chickasaws trading at his mercantile establishments. These officials also charged that Colbert was in league with white traders at Fort Towson and Boggy Depot. By controlling the annuity distribution through his management of the Chickasaw king, the officials believed that Colbert could also provide funds to pay Chickasaw debts allegedly due traders and that for this service Colbert was to receive a share. Armstrong and Upshaw also accused Colbert of callousness, charging that Colbert wished to keep as many Chickasaws as possible near him at Fort Towson for selfish business reasons. Alberson on the other hand, according to these officials, urged all Chickasaws to settle in their district, become gainfully employed, participate in their district government, and support the development of schools and other pressing needs. Thus Armstrong and Upshaw refused to deliver the $70,000 annuity to the Chickasaw king. Alberson and his council received the money in the Chickasaw District, and they supervised its payment to individuals.[7]

Although Colbert's coup failed, it had the constructive effect of erasing one level of government—the Chickasaw Commission—thereby assuring the early demise of the anachronistic king and clan-based council. Thereafter, until the rise of the new Chickasaw Nation in 1856, most Chickasaws looked to their elective district chief and council for leadership and direction.

With the elimination of two competing levels of government, the Chickasaw District government could and did proceed to provide the leadership and direction essential to promoting tribal unity, education, law and order, and general advancement. One of the most important steps taken by the district council was to

[7] Armstrong to Crawford, June 10, 1845, Letters Received, Office of Indian Affairs, 1824–81, Chickasaw Agency, National Archives, Microcopy 234, Roll 139; Upshaw to Armstrong, August 16, 1845, Annual Report of the Commissioner of Indian Affairs for 1845, 524–26; Wright, "Choctaw and Chickasaw Nations in Indian Territory," Chronicles of Oklahoma, Vol. VII (December, 1929), 402.

enact legislation providing for a system of schools for Chickasaw youth. Other significant attainments included creation of a mounted law and order corps, the light horse, which improved protection of life and property and enforced district laws regulating the whisky traffic.

In 1849 the Chickasaw District council passed an act creating a Chickasaw Committee of Vigilance. The purpose of the statute was to provide the means to "better watch the interest of our nation and the more securely to protect the rights of our people." By its terms the council elected three "discreet persons who shall constitute a Committee of Vigilance," each to hold office for a two-year term at a salary of eight hundred dollars a year and an expense account of two hundred dollars. The committee's duties included visiting Washington each year to study legislation pending before Congress and rulings coming from the Bureau of Indian Affairs which might affect the Chickasaws, to maintain surveillance over the federal government's trusteeship of the Chickasaw national fund, and to urge the speedy marketing of the tribe's unsold lands in Mississippi.[8]

In its supervision of federal management of the sale of these lands, the Committee of Vigilance found that for some time the expense of maintaining the special land office in Mississippi had exceeded receipts from land sales. The annual cost of maintaining this office including salaries of employees was deducted from the Chickasaw national fund. The Committee of Vigilance charged that federal officials were reluctant to close this office because of the opportunity for patronage it provided at no cost to taxpayers. Vigilance Committee members demanded that the land be sold at once at whatever price it would bring and that the land office be closed. Their demands led to the negotiation of a treaty in 1852. By its terms the federal government was obliged to dispose of the Chickasaws' eastern lands "as soon as practicable" and to submit a regular accounting of the management and disbursement of Chickasaw funds. The Chickasaws were granted the right to file "exceptions thereto," and the secretary of the in-

[8] Act creating Committee of Vigilance, 1849 council session, Letters Received, Office of Indian Affairs, 1824–81, Chickasaw Agency, National Archives, Microcopy 234, Roll 139.

terior was directed to adjudicate all differences. This treaty also formally abolished the Chickasaw Commission which had been inactive since 1845.[9]

Besides meeting immediate leadership and legislative needs, Chickasaw District officials also experimented with constitutional government. By this very act they indicated an intent ultimately to secede from the Choctaw Nation and establish an independent Chickasaw government. And by developing a vigorous Chickasaw District government they were creating a vehicle to accomplish this. The Chickasaws' first effort at constitution making occured in October, 1846, at a general council at Boiling Springs, twelve miles south of Fort Washita. The document drafted by the Chickasaw District council and ratified by the assembled Chickasaws was a simple statement of intent to guard their liberties and protect their property through the guidance of this simple organic law. At the general council of 1848 a second and more elaborate constitution was adopted. Its preamble read:

> We, the Chickasaw people of the Choctaw Nation, having the sole right and privilege to establish our own form of Laws governing the residue of our funds in contracting and managing the same as far as consistant with the late Treaty between . . . the United States and the Chickasaw Tribe . . . 1834 . . . and . . . 1837 between the Chickasaw and Choctaw Tribes of Indians do by our Representatives assembled in convention at Boiling Springs near Fort Washita in the Chickasaw District this the 13th day of October, 1848, in order to secure to ourselves and our posterity justice, insure tranquility, promote the general welfare of the Chickasaw people, we do mutually agree with each other to make ordain and adopt for ourselves the following.

The structure created by this constitution included "a Council established in the Chickasaw District whose power it shall be to reform or abolish these regulations in such manner as they determine as proper and necessary for the Chickasaw people." The council was divided into two "distinct departments—Executive and Legislative." Executive duties and power were vested in the Chickasaw District chief who "shall be styled Chief of the Chickasaw people." His approval was required on all measures passed

[9] Treaty with the Chickasaw, 1852, in Kappler, *Laws and Treaties*, II, 596–98.

by the council, and he was granted the veto power. Legislative power was vested in a council of thirty members elected to two-year terms. The council powers, besides enacting legislation and overriding vetoes with a two-thirds vote, included electing the district chief. Suffrage was granted to all Chickasaw males sixteen and over. That this was potentially a separatist instrument was indicated by the latitude of action given both chief and council. Chickasaw leaders also betrayed their intent by designating their executive leader—"Chief of the Chickasaw people."[10]

The Chickasaws amended their constitution in 1849 to provide for popular election of the Chickasaw District chief at the general election. Constitutional changes adopted in 1851 excluded "white men from holding any office whatever." And as a sop to the full bloods and their preference for the defunct clan-derived council, it was provided that "Thussaway and Elassambe" were to be life members of the council, not subject to election. Also, the term of the district chief was reduced from four to two years, and his election was returned to the council. An indication that the Chickasaw District government was becoming more firmly established and its functions increasingly specialized, was the provision for national treasurer, auditor, and other public officials.[11]

The Chickasaws' success in constitutional government and their new unity produced a resurgence of personal and group pride. This in turn made them sensitive to their status as constitutionally-defined citizens of the Choctaw Nation, which generated nationalism and a determination to rehabilitate the Chickasaw Nation. To accomplish this the Chickasaws had to find justification for dissolving their relationship with the Choctaws established by the treaty of 1837. District Chief Alberson, Winchester Colbert, and other Chickasaw leaders developed a strategy for accomplishing this. They stressed the Chickasaws' "insufferable" status as "intruders" in the Choctaw Nation and concentrated on three sources of friction in their campaign to achieve separation. First was the question of ownership of the

---

[10] Chickasaw Constitutions of 1846 and 1848, Documents of the Five Civilized Tribes, Western History Collections, University of Oklahoma Library; and Chickasaw Constitution of 1848, Letters Received, Office of Indian Affairs, 1824–81, Chickasaw Agency, National Archives, Microcopy 234, Roll 140.

[11] Chickasaw Constitutions of 1849 and 1851, *ibid.*

land in the Chickasaw District. The Choctaw position was that no land had been sold by the 1837 treaty. Rather, by committing themselves to pay $530,000 to the Choctaws, the Chickasaws had merely purchased the right to share in the benefits of Choctaw Nation citizenship. They had obtained an interest in but not absolute title to the district they occupied. The Chickasaw position was that they had in fact purchased the land comprising their district.[12]

Another source of friction was the eastern boundary of Chickasaw District. Chickasaw leaders complained that the line "had never been designated." In question was a twenty-mile-wide strip extending from the Canadian River on the north to Red River on the south. Choctaw and Chickasaw district and county government officials attempted to assert jurisdiction in the disputed zone which created tension, confusion, and controversy.[13]

A third source of friction and the major Chickasaw complaint was their status as a minority community in the Choctaw Nation. Chickasaw leaders acknowledged that they were "entitled to representation in the Choctaw council which makes all the laws; but being in a very small minority their voice is neither felt or heard in that body, practically they have no participation in making the laws to which the whole tribe they are subjected; and often laws are forced upon them to which the whole tribe is unanimously opposed—They are completely at the mercy of the Choctaws, and every Chickasaw feels that he is oppressed by them." Alberson, Colbert, and others accused the Choctaws of treating the latecomers as "intruders, and it is frequently thrown up to them as a reproach that they have no right in the Country— this is the source of many private difficulties, frequently ending in the death of one or the other of the parties, and the number of these is Constantly increasing."[14]

Choctaw tyranny was more imagined than real. The Choctaws

[12] Correspondence on the question of Chickasaw District ownership and Chickasaw separatism from the Choctaw Nation are found in *Ibid.*, Roll 141.
[13] Colbert to Commissioner of Indian Affairs, April 26, 1851, Documents of the Five Civilized Tribes, Western History Collections, University of Oklahoma Library.
[14] Colbert to Commissioner of Indian Affairs, April 24, 1851, Letters Received, Office of Indian Affairs, 1824–81, Chickasaw Agency, National Archives, Microcopy 234, Roll 140.

had received the Chickasaws and provided them a domicile when they were homeless. They had patiently indulged the rich newcomers in their wastrel-style living and fed them when the wealth was dissipated. They could not understand the Chickasaws' restiveness because they enjoyed the same rights as Choctaws. Ironically the Choctaws' magnanimous reception of the Chickasaws into their constitutional society was the very thing which provoked Chickasaw unity, nationalism, and demand for separation. The new breed of Chickasaw leaders were consummate propagandists. They inflated the slightest travesty into an incident of major proportion, and alarmed federal officials with the warning that "we do not believe the Chickasaws will submit to this [tyranny] much longer." And Choctaw aggressions "have estranged the two people very much. The breach is widening every year. . . . Relations between the two people cannot submit much longer in peace. The Chickasaws are dissatisfied with their present political condition; nothing but a separation from the Choctaws will ever satisfy them." This tactic won federal officials to support their drive for independence.[15]

By 1853 the Chickasaws had won official support for separation from the Choctaws at every level of the federal hierarchy. Their agent, A. J. Smith, charged that the Choctaws were "very obstinate in their position, underrating the pretensions of the Chickasaws altogether. . . . The Choctaws have treated the Chickasaws with contempt; they have refused to go even into a correspondence on the subject." Thomas Drew, head of the Southern Superintendency, commented, "The difficulties existing between the Chickasaws and Choctaws are not of recent origin, and are of that character which inevitably result from a forced connection of the weaker with the stronger party upon an attempted principle of equality; and I deem it important to the future peace and harmony of these two tribes that a distinct and separate organization be afforded to the Chickasaws, and that their country be defined with precision, separate from the Choc-

[15] Colbert to Commissioner of Indian Affairs, April 26, 1851, Documents of the Five Civilized Tribes, Western History Collections, University of Oklahoma Library; Harper to Commissioner of Indian Affairs, June 23, 1852, Ratified and Unratified Treaties with Indians, National Archives, Microcopy T–494, Record Group 75, Roll 4.

taws. This I perceive the only sure basis of action on the part of the government to insure future harmony and satisfaction to both parties." And Commissioner of Indian Affairs George W. Manypenny supported separation because in his view "consummation of this reasonable desire would, without doubt, have a decided tendency to promote their advancement and permanent prosperity. It is much to be regretted, however, that the Choctaws, to whom the union is of no advantage whatever, still continue indisposed to yield to the natural and reasonable wishes of their brethren, and those of the government, on this subject."[16]

The Chickasaws had marshaled impressive support for separation, but the Choctaws seemed unimpressed. This caused the Chickasaws to draw on another powerful and potentially persuasive resource—money. The annual income from their national fund ran between $75,000 and $100,000. During the 1850's the Chickasaw District council appropriated substantial portions of this sum in an attempt to expedite separation. An appropriation made in 1851 for $15,000 was designated to pay the cost of what the Chickasaws hoped would be prompt separation negotiations with the Choctaws. The act stated that the $15,000 was to be used to defray negotiation expenses and "for other purposes." Since the negotiations, which did not materialize, were to be held at nearby Doaksville, the maximum commissioners' expenses would not have exceeded $500. This suggests that the Chickasaws expected to purchase Choctaw support. Throughout the early 1850's, Chickasaw money continued to figure in the separation campaign. One report told of an attempt by the Chickasaw Committee of Vigilance to persuade Congress to adopt legislation providing for the dissolution of the Choctaw-Chickasaw community. An observer commented that the Chickasaws "expect to accomplish their object by the influence of money" in that "a large sum of money has been offered to some members of Congress to effect the separation of the Choctaws and Chickasaws."[17]

[16] Smith to Manypenny, August 29, 1853, *Annual Report of the Commissioner of Indian Affairs for 1853*, 400–403; Drew to Manypenny, August 29, 1853, *ibid.*, 371–77; and Manypenny to McClelland, November 26, 1853, *ibid.*, 243–64.

[17] Law of Chickasaw Council, October 16, 1851, Letters Received, Office of Indian Affairs, 1824–81, Chickasaw Agency, National Archives, Microcopy 234, Roll 140; and McKinney to Pitchlynn, April 21, 1853, Peter P. Pitchlynn Collection, Gilcrease Museum.

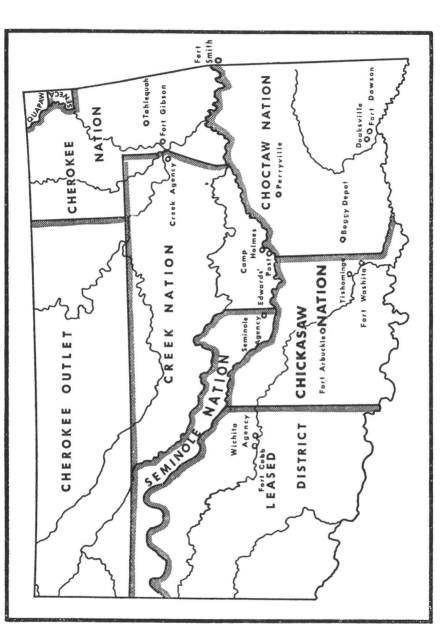

CHICKASAW NATION, 1855

During 1854, Chickasaw and Choctaw commissioners met at Doaksville and nearly reached an agreement on separation. Before the council closed, the commissioners negotiated a treaty which provided the means for removing a principal Chickasaw complaint in that the document precisely described the eastern boundary of the Chickasaw District. By its terms the Chickasaws were to hire a surveyor to run and mark the boundary per the treaty specifications.[18]

Finally in June, 1855, at Washington, Chickasaw and Choctaw commissioners met and negotiated an agreement dissolving their 1837 compact. Its preamble read: "The political connection heretofore existing between the Choctaw and the Chickasaw tribes ... has given rise to unhappy and injurious dissensions and controversies among them, which render necessary a readjustment of their relations to each other and to the United States." The treaty defined the territory of the independent Chickasaw Nation as bounded on the north by the Canadian River, on the south by the Red River, on the east by the boundary defined by the 1854 treaty, and on the west by the ninety-eighth meridian. For a clear title to their territory the Chickasaws were to pay the Choctaws $150,000. That territory formerly a part of the Chickasaw District of the Choctaw Nation between the ninety-eighth and one hundredth meridians was to be held in common by the Choctaws and Chickasaws. The federal government was to lease this area for the purpose of establishing a reserve for the wild tribes. The lease payment of $800,000 was to be divided, the Choctaws receiving $600,000, the Chickasaws $200,000. The 1855 treaty permitted Choctaw and Chickasaw citizens to settle in the territory of either nation. The treaty recognized Chickasaw sovereignty by guaranteeing them "unrestricted right of self government, and full jurisdiction over persons and property within their respective limits" except trade and intercourse which were to be regulated by the United States government.[19]

The ratification process for the treaty by the Chickasaw council, Choctaw council, and United States Senate extended into

---

[18] Treaty with the Choctaw and Chickasaw, 1854, in Kappler, *Laws and Treaties*, II, 652–53.
[19] Treaty with the Choctaw and Chickasaw, 1855, *ibid.*, 706–14.

1856. Anticipating approval of the agreement by all parties, Chickasaw leaders had made preparations for phasing out the Choctaw constitutional government in the Chickasaw District and creating an independent government for the new Chickasaw Nation. On August 1, 1856, the Chickasaws met in a mass convention at Good Spring, the emergent Tishomingo City, on Pennington Creek. Leaders had collected a huge commissary, including five thousand pounds of fresh beef, to subsist the people. Under a large brush arbor the Chickasaws rested on log seats while their leaders conducted business on a crude platform. First the Chickasaw District council met and closed out all old business. The principal item was to determine the manner of receiving and managing the $200,000 due the nation by the 1855 treaty. The council voted to receive the money and turn it over to Agent Cooper for safekeeping until the Chickasaws were ready to expend it for "national purposes." The intent was to use it to pay for the construction of public buildings at Tishomingo City to house the operations of their new national government, and for additional schools.[20]

Then the assembled Chickasaws resolved into a constitutional convention. Jackson Kemp was elected convention chairman. After an extended discussion of constitutional form and substance, Kemp recessed the convention and a drafting committee went to work. The convention reassembled at Tishomingo City on August 30 and ratified the constitution for the Chickasaw Nation. The Chickasaws' organic law defined the geographic extent of the nation and stated the constitution's purpose: to recognize and establish the "general great and essential principles of Liberty and Free Government. . . . All power is inherent in the people and all free governments are founded on their authority and instituted for their benefit." Defined popular rights included freedom of worship; jury trial; protection against unreasonable search and seizure, self-incrimination, and double jeopardy; and prohibition of excessive fine or bail, imprisonment for debt, and cruel or unusual punishment. Each citizen was assured his right

[20] Dean to Manypenny, August 25, 1856, Letters Received, Office of Indian Affairs, 1824–81, Chickasaw Agency, National Archives, Microcopy 234, Roll 142.

to freely speak, write, or publish his opinions on any subject. The document stated that "no religious test shall be required as a qualification to any office of public trust" and that "polygamy shall not be tolerated in this nation." Suffrage was granted to free male persons nineteen years of age and over. The Chickasaw constitution observed separation of powers by providing for a division of government function and power into three branches. It vested the "Supreme Executive power of this nation . . . in a chief magistrate who shall be styled 'the Governor of the Chickasaw Nation'." He was the official spokesman for the Chickasaw Nation and shared in the law-making process through recommendations he might make to the council as to the legislative needs of the nation and the power of veto. The governor was selected by popular election and served for a term of two years. Other officers of the executive branch included an elective national treasurer, auditor, and attorney general and a national secretary appointed by the governor and confirmed by the senate. The constitution also provided for a superintendent of public instruction, selected by a joint vote of the council for a four-year term.

The constitution provided for an elective bicameral legislative body, the council, to consist of a house of representatives and a senate. House members, apportioned by population, served one-year terms; senate members, apportioned by area, served two-year terms. In addition to the customary legislative powers, including impeachment and override of executive vetoes by a two-thirds vote in each house, the council by joint vote elected justices for the supreme court and circuit courts. The president of the senate succeeded to the office of governor on the death, resignation, or removal of the incumbent.

The Chickasaw Nation judiciary, as defined by the 1856 constitution, consisted of a supreme court made up of a chief justice and two associate justices, circuit courts, and county courts. Voters in each county elected the judge at that level of the judicial hierarchy. His term was for two years. County court jurisdiction extended to matters in controversy not exceeding fifty dollars.

This constitution defined the counties of the Chickasaw Nation

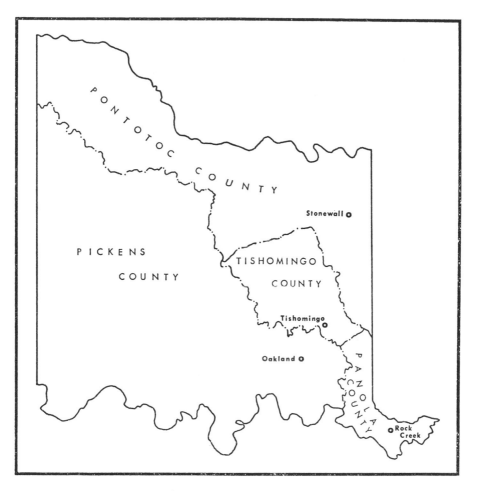

CHICKASAW NATION COUNTIES

—Panola (southeast), Pickens (southwest), Tishomingo (east central), and Pontotoc (north)—and provided a structure of local government. Officials, all elective, included a sheriff and constables.

A constitutional provision forbade the council to adopt legislation emancipating slaves without the consent of owners and compensation at appraised value of each slave. Owners were required to use humane treatment in the management of their slaves. The process for amending the constitution of 1856 consisted of the council by a two-thirds vote proposing a constitutional change and the succeeding council ratifying the proposed change by a two-thirds vote.[21]

The government for the new Chickasaw Nation was organized in the autumn of 1856. The first election saw Cyrus Harris elevated to the position of governor of the Chickasaw Nation. The election method was for Harris and other candidates to take positions in a field near the council house. Voters lined up behind their choice, election judges counted the voters behind each candidate, certified the tally, and declared the victor. During the early years of the new Chickasaw Nation, there were no political parties and candidates campaigned on a personal basis. In the general election of 1858, Winchester Colbert defeated Harris for the office of governor. The Chickasaws' experience in constitutional government as part of the Choctaw Nation and the large measure of independent action allowed them by the Choctaws, augured success for their new venture in self-government. Sadly, the promise of their splendid beginning was dimmed by the Chickasaw Nation's involvement in a brutal and destructive war.

[21] Constitution of the Chickasaw Nation, 1856, *ibid.*

CHAPTER ELEVEN

THE CHICKASAW NATION
IN REBELLION AND RECONSTRUCTION

IN the spring of 1861 the southwestern frontier was in turmoil. Eleven Southern states had seceded from the American Union to form a new political community, the Confederate States of America. The Indian Territory—domain of the Cherokees, Creeks, Seminoles, Choctaws, and Chickasaws—was tangential to the secessionist states of Arkansas and Texas. It was an area coveted by Confederate military planners, for Indian Territory farms and ranches could supply grain, beef, hides, horses, oxen, salt, and lead to the Confederacy. And its strategic location could provide a land bridge connecting east and west to enable the Confederacy to carry out its design for a thrust to the Pacific. Also, as a Confederate province, Indian Territory could serve as a base for launching offensives into Union Kansas and as a buffer to defend and insulate Texas and Arkansas.

In its attempt to win the Cherokees, Creeks, Seminoles, Choctaws, and Chickasaws to the Southern cause, the Confederacy used diplomacy and exploited the federal government's ambivalence and dereliction in fulfilling treaty obligations to these tribes. Except for the Cherokees the tribes of Indian Territory were willing signatories to the proffered Confederate alliance. The anomaly of the so-called Southern tribes signing treaties of alliance with a new government composed of states which less than thirty years before had been instrumental in driving them from their homelands to the remote Indian Territory has been the subject of much speculation. Some writers account for the Southern tribes' alliance with the Confederacy by pointing to blood ties. For example, in the case of the Chickasaws, most mixed bloods were related to Southern white families. Other writers stress the point that the federal Indian agents among the tribes on the eve of the Civil War had strong Southern sympathies. This presupposes that the agents exercised a strong influence over tribal decisions. The Choctaw-Chickasaw agent in 1861 was Mississippian Douglas H. Cooper. The Chickasaws esteemed Cooper, but they regularly followed a line of action quite different from that proposed by him. Economic factors are another explanation given for why tribal leaders committed their nations to the Confederate cause. Much has been made of the fact that the national funds of the Chickasaws and other tribes, held in trust by the federal government, had been invested in securities of Southern states. Confederate agents warned Indian leaders that only a Southern alliance would protect their investments. Other economic factors pointed to in explaining the Southern tribes' commitment to the Confederacy include the stream of Indian Territory trade which generally moved south to the lower Gulf markets. Also in the economic vein is slavery. Triumph of the Southern cause would assure a continuance of the institution of slavery and provide a safeguard for slaveowner investments.

To some degree all these factors influenced the Chickasaw decision for the Confederate cause. Certainly the slavery issue was not an overpowering force among rank and file Chickasaws for in 1861, when the tribal population was less than five thousand, approximately two hundred slaveholders owned about one thousand slaves. It was significant, however, that this small group of slaveowners, largely the mixed-blood elite, dominated tribal politics by their control of the constitutional government. Nonetheless, rank and file Chickasaws were voters, and to obtain their support for a change in allegiance, the mixed-blood leaders had to generate popular issues. These were readily available. The Chickasaws resented the inhumane preremoval actions of Alabama and Mississippi. But perhaps their strong feelings toward these states were exceeded by their resentment toward the federal government for its failure, especially under President Andrew Jackson, to provide treaty-guaranteed protection from state and citizen depredations. And they blamed the federal government for pushing them to remove and then permitting contractors to enrich themselves from the Chickasaw national fund. Also, the

Chickasaws had evidence that federal officials had been derelict in the management of their national fund. Chickasaw leaders accused the federal government of being deliberately slow in fulfilling treaty obligations after removal. They felt insecure in the tenure of their land. The northern half of Indian Territory had been organized as Kansas Territory and opened to settlement. During the 1850's several bills had been introduced in Congress to organize the remainder of the Indian country into a territory, open it to settlement, and prepare it for statehood. Chickasaw leaders became increasingly wary. During the 1860 presidential campaign, when Republican William H. Seward stated, "The Indian Territory . . . south of Kansas, must be vacated by the Indians" to make room for the settlers, Chickasaw leaders transmitted their concern to the rank and file Chickasaws.[1]

The genesis of the Chickasaw alliance with the Confederacy began in early 1861. On January 5, the tribal legislature adopted a resolution calling on the Southern tribes to form a union "not inconsistent with the Laws and Treaties of the United States for the future security and protection of the rights of the Citizens" of the Cherokee, Creek, Seminole, Choctaw, and Chickasaw nations. Governor Cyrus Harris wrote each of the leaders of the five tribes urging that they act with the Chickasaws. Jacob Derrysaw, a Creek leader, responded to the Chickasaw appeal by inviting tribal representatives to meet on February 17 at North Fork Town in the Creek Nation. Creek and Seminole delegations were present, and Cherokee Chief John Ross reluctantly permitted a delegation from his nation to attend. In his response to Harris' letter Ross counseled caution and chided the Chickasaw governor for his nation's impetuous action: "the excitement which has arisen among our White brethren . . . can only be regarded as a family misunderstanding. And it behooves us to be very careful . . . to refrain from adopting any measures liable to be misconstrued . . . and in which . . . we have no direct and proper concern." Ross was respected by the leaders of the other tribes, and perhaps his strong letter to Harris discouraged the Chickasaws. In any event no Chickasaw representative appeared at the North

---

[1] Abel, *The American Indian as Slaveholder and Secessionist,* 58.

Fork Town council. Likewise the Choctaws did not send a delegate.[2]

The next step toward the Chickasaw-Confederate alliance was taken at Boggy Depot in the Choctaw Nation on March 11, 1861. Choctaw and Chickasaw delegates met there "to consult for the common safety of these two tribes, in event of the dissolution of the American Union." A Texas delegation visited the Boggy Depot council and reported that the Chickasaws and Choctaws were "determined to adhere to the fortunes of the South." The Indian delegates planned to raise a "minute company in each county of the two nations, to be drilled for actual service when necessary."[3]

During late April, 1861, a Texas Confederate column crossed Red River into the Chickasaw Nation while Arkansas troops moved up the Arkansas toward Fort Smith. Federal army units were stationed at Fort Smith on the Indian Territory border, at Fort Washita and Fort Arbuckle in the Chickasaw Nation, and at Fort Cobb in the Leased District. Threat of capture by Confederate invaders caused Colonel William H. Emory, regional federal commander, to order his troops to evacuate these posts and rendezvous on the Canadian River. Emory's column fled toward Fort Leavenworth, barely escaping capture by the advancing Arkansas and Texas columns. Arkansas troops occupied Fort Smith while Texas troops occupied Fort Washita, Fort Arbuckle, and Fort Cobb.[4]

Confederate Secretary of War Leroy P. Walker followed up the Union retreat from the Southwest by directing General Ben McCulloch of Texas to establish headquarters at Fort Smith and to recruit a frontier army to guard the Confederate rear. McCulloch's force was to consist of one infantry and two cavalry regiments drawn from Texas, Louisiana, and Arkansas and two or more cavalry regiments recruited from the Chickasaws, Choctaws, and other tribes of Indian Territory. In addition Con-

---

[2] Ross to Harris, February 9, 1861, Documents of the Five Civilized Tribes, Western History Collections, University of Oklahoma Library.

[3] Report of the Texas Commissioners, April 23, 1861, *War of Rebellion: A Compilation of the Official Records of the Union and Confederate Armies* (hereafter cited as *War of Rebellion Records*), Series IV, Vol. I, 322–23.

[4] Ed Bearss and Arrell M. Gibson, *Fort Smith: Little Gibraltar on the Arkansas*, 242–44.

federate officials appointed Albert Pike of Arkansas special commissioner to negotiate treaties of alliance with the Southern tribes.[5]

Before Commissioner Pike began his councils with the tribes of Indian Territory, the Chickasaw legislature took steps which amounted to an act of secession. It declared the Chickasaw Nation independent of the United States. Adopted on May 25, 1861, the Chickasaw declaration of independence read:

> Whereas the Government of the United States has been broken up by the secession of a large number of States composing the Federal Union—that the dissolution has been followed by war between the parties; and whereas the destruction of the Union as it existed by the Federal Constitution is irreparable, and consequently the Government of the United States as it was when the Chickasaws . . . formed alliances and treaties with it no longer exists; and whereas the Lincoln Government, pretending to represent said Union, has shown by its course towards us, in withdrawing from our country the protection of the Federal troops, and withholding, unjustly and unlawfully, our money placed in the hands of the Government of the United States as trustee, to be applied for our benefit, a total disregard of treaty obligations toward us; and whereas our geographical position, our social and domestic institutions, our feelings and sympathies, all attach us to our Southern friends, against whom is about to be waged a war of subjugation or extermination, of conquest and confiscation . . . and whereas we have an abiding confidence that all our rights— tribal and individual . . . will be fully recognized, guaranteed, and protected by our friends of the Confederate States; and whereas as a Southern people we consider their cause our own: Therefore, *Be it resolved by the Chickasaw Legislature assembled* . . . That the dissolution of the Federal Union . . . has absolved the Chickasaws from allegiance to any foreign government whatever; that the current of the events of the last few months has left the Chickasaw Nation *independent*, the people thereof free to form such alliances, and take such steps to secure their own safety, happiness, and future welfare as may to them seem best. . . . Resolved, That the governor of the Chickasaw Nation be, and he is hereby, instructed to issue his proclamation to the Chickasaw Nation, declaring their *independence*, and calling upon the

[5] Arrell M. Gibson, *Oklahoma: A History of Five Centuries*, 196–98.

Chickasaw warriors to form themselves into volunteer companies
. . . and to hold themselves, with the best arms and ammunition,
together with a reasonable supply of provisions, in readiness at
a minute's warning to turn out . . . for the defense of their
country.[6]

Soon after the Chickasaws took this action, Commissioner Pike
reached Indian Territory to negotiate treaties of alliance with the
Southern tribes. At North Fork Town in the Creek Nation the
Confederate commissioner found Creek, Choctaw, and Chickasaw delegates waiting to meet him. On July 10, 1861, Pike concluded an agreement with Creek leaders. Two days later Choctaw
and Chickasaw delegates signed with Pike a joint treaty committing their nations to the Confederate cause. From North Fork
Town Pike traveled to the Seminole Nation and negotiated a
treaty with the Seminoles on August 1. The five Southern tribes
were in the Confederate fold on October 7, 1861, when Pike
completed a treaty with the Cherokee Nation at Tahlequah. The
text of the Confederate treaties with the Southern tribes was
similar. The Chickasaw signatories of the Confederate-Choctaw-
Chickasaw treaty, men elected by the Chickasaw legislature, included Edmund Pickens, Holmes Colbert, James Gamble, Joel
Kemp, William Kemp, Winchester Colbert, James McLish, and
Christopher Columbus. The treaty provided for an offensive-
defensive alliance between the Confederate States of America
and the Choctaw and Chickasaw nations. The Choctaws and
Chickasaws acknowledged themselves to be under the protection
of the Confederate States of America and "of no other power or
sovereign whatever." The Confederate government recognized
Choctaw and Chickasaw title in fee to their lands. The Choctaws
and Chickasaws were committed to raise a regiment of ten companies of mounted men to serve in the Confederate Army. These
troops were to be armed, trained, provisioned, and paid by the
Confederate government and were not to campaign outside of
their respective nations without Confederate consent. The Confederate government agreed to serve as trustee for the national

[6] Resolutions of the Chickasaw Legislature, May 25, 1861, *War of Rebellion
Records*, Series I, Vol. III, 585–87.

funds of both nations and to assume and continue the fiscal obligations of the United States including payment of annuities.[7]

Initially the Confederate fighting force in Indian Territory was to consist of three regiments of Indian troops, one regiment recruited from the Choctaws and Chickasaws, a second from the Creeks and Seminoles, and a third from the Cherokees. The Confederate War Department assigned a white regiment drawn from Louisiana, Arkansas, and Texas troops to operate with the Indian regiments. In the Confederate military command system, troops in the District of Indian Territory were attached to General McCulloch's Army of the Frontier. Former agent Douglas H. Cooper was appointed commanding officer and colonel of the First Regiment of Choctaw and Chickasaw Mounted Rifles. Cooper completed the regimental organization on July 31, 1861. He selected Tandy Walker, a prominent Choctaw, as his second in command with the rank of lieutenant colonel and established regimental headquarters at Buck Creek, about ten miles west of Skullyville in the Choctaw Nation. At Cooper's call for recruits, Choctaws and Chickasaws rushed to fill the ranks of the First Regiment. Chickasaw recruits also were accommodated by additional units authorized for the Indian Territory. These included the First Chickasaw Infantry Regiment, commanded by Colonel William Hunter; Shecoe's Chickasaw Battalion of Mounted Volunteers, sometimes called the "Chickasaw Battalion," commanded by Colonel Martin Shecoe; and the First Battalion of Chickasaw Cavalry, commanded by Lieutenant Colonel Lemuel Reynolds.[8]

Uniforms, weapons, and subsistence stores consigned to regiments in the District of Indian Territory were intercepted at Fort Smith and distributed among the Confederate troops massed about Belle Point. Thus Chickasaw fighting men as well as Choctaws, Creeks, Seminoles, and Cherokees had to equip themselves as best they could. Chickasaw and Choctaw infantry and cavalry were armed with shotguns, "old pattern rifles," and "Colt's six

---

[7] Confederate Treaty with the Choctaws and Chickasaws, July 12, 1861, *ibid.*, Series IV, Volume I, 445–65.

[8] Walker to Davis, August 1, 1861, *ibid.*, Series I, Volume III, 625–26; George Shirk, "The Place of Indian Territory in the Command Structure of the Civil War," *Chronicles of Oklahoma*, Vol. XLV (Winter, 1967–68), 468–69; and Muriel H. Wright, "General Douglas H. Cooper, C.S.A.," *Chronicles of Oklahoma*, Vol. XXXII (Summer, 1954), 163.

shooters." Chickasaw military units subsisted by foraging the countryside and by using beef and flour stores from Texas. Soldiers were permitted to winter at their homes and often were furloughed for brief periods each spring to plow and plant their fields.[9]

The Chickasaw military mission was largely defensive. Through most of the war Chickasaw troops patrolled the Arkansas-Canadian River defense line, garrisoned Fort Washita and Fort Arbuckle in their nation, guarded the huge military camp and depot which Confederate quartermaster officers had established at Boggy Depot, and joined Choctaws to garrison old Fort Towson.[10]

On rare occasions Chickasaw troops operated north of the Arkansas-Canadian defense line. At no time when they met the enemy were Chickasaw fighting men able to accomplish that dashing, daring sortie action which distinguished the Cherokee Mounted Rifles commanded by General Stand Watie. Chickasaw troops saw their first action in November, 1861. McCulloch ordered Colonel Cooper to march the First Choctaw-Chickasaw Mounted Rifle Regiment and a squad of Texas cavalry to the Deep Fork River in the Creek Nation. Their job was to disperse a band of neutral Creeks and Seminoles led by Opothleyaholo. The neutral Indians, however, evacuated their Deep Fork settlement before Cooper arrived, taking refuge at Round Mountain on the lower Cimarron River. On November 19, Cooper's scouts found Opothleyaholo's camp. The Confederate Indians made repeated charges, but a fierce defense caused Cooper to pull back. This allowed Opothleyaholo time to relocate at Chusto Talasah on Bird Creek. On December 9, Cooper again sent his regiment against the neutral Indians. A second time they found the defense unassailable. The Confederate ammunition stores were nearly exhausted, and Cooper moved back toward Fort Gibson, appealing to the Fort Smith headquarters for reinforcements and supplies. In response to Cooper's call, Colonel James McIntosh led a

9 Walker to Davis, August 1, 1861, *War of Rebellion Records*, Series I, Vol. III, 625–26; and Allan C. Ashcraft, "Confederate Indian Territory Conditions in 1865," *Chronicles of Oklahoma*, Vol. XLII (Winter, 1964–65), 421–28.

10 Muriel H. Wright, "Old Boggy Depot," *Chronicles of Oklahoma*, Vol. V (March, 1927), 8.

force of two thousand Confederates against Opothleyaholo. On December 26, McIntosh found the neutral Indians entrenched at Chustenalah. Before Cooper's Choctaw-Chickasaw regiment could move up, the fresh Confederate force smashed Opothleyaholo's defenses, overwhelmed his warriors, and scattered them throughout the rough country along the Verdigris.[11]

Other Chickasaw operations north of the Arkansas-Canadian defense line included peripheral action in connection with the Battle of Pea Ridge (Elkhorn Tavern), March 6–8, 1862, near the northwestern Arkansas border. Chickasaw troops did not participate in the actual battle, which resulted in a smashing Confederate defeat, but, as components of Cooper's regiment, they covered the retreat of the Confederate survivors fleeing west into Indian Territory. Later in 1862, Chickasaw troops were part of a limited Confederate thrust into southwestern Missouri. On September 30, they engaged a Union force at Newtonia and were credited with winning the battle. A Union drive into the Cherokee Nation during October, 1862, brought Cooper's regiment across the Arkansas to bolster local Confederate defenses. At the Battle of Fort Wayne, October 22, Cooper's regiment was soundly thrashed by the Union invaders. For the remainder of 1862 and into the following year, Union pressure increased on Confederate positions in Indian Territory. During the spring of 1863 a Union column drove south along Grand River and captured Fort Gibson. With this post as a base, federal commanders prepared for an assault on Fort Smith. To thwart this, a large Confederate force, which included Cooper's Choctaw-Chickasaw regiment, marched on Fort Gibson. The Union Army moved out to intercept the Confederates, and on July 17 the armies met on Elk Creek. The contest, called the Battle of Honey Springs, ended in Confederate defeat. Union forces followed up this victory by crossing the Arkansas into the Choctaw Nation. On August 22 they struck the Confederate depot at Perryville, drove off the Choctaw and Chickasaw defenders, then rushed east to capture Fort Smith on September 1, 1863.[12]

[11] Cooper's Report of Operations, November 19, 1861 to January 4, 1862, *War of Rebellion Records*, Series I, Vol. VIII, 5–14.

[12] Bearss and Gibson, *Fort Smith*, 268–69.

From the Union conquest of Fort Smith to the close of the war, Chickasaw troops for the most part were used by Confederate commanders to guard the Arkansas-Canadian defense line. After September 1, 1863, this assignment had special significance because Union armies occupied Indian Territory north of the Arkansas and Canadian. During 1864 the Confederate War Department reorganized the command and components of the District of Indian Territory. All Indian units were consolidated with a battery of artillery to make up the Indian Division commanded by Douglas H. Cooper, who was advanced in rank to brigadier general. The Indian Division consisted of the First Indian Cavalry Brigade commanded by Brigadier General Stand Watie; the Second Indian Cavalry Brigade commanded by Colonel Tandy Walker; the Creek and Seminole Cavalry Brigade led by Colonel David McIntosh; a "reserve squadron" of Caddoes commanded by Captain George Washington; and Howell's Texas Battery. The Indian Territory was designated a separate district of the Trans-Mississippi Department.[13]

After 1863, Chickasaw fighting men participated in two engagements before the war ended. The first occurred in early 1864 and consisted of a series of brushes with an invading Union column, the principal encounter occurring on February 13. On February 1, Colonel William A. Phillips had led a Union force of 450 cavalry, a company of infantry, and one howitzer out of Fort Gibson. He slipped by Chickasaw patrols on the river defense line and thrust at Indian settlements on the Middle Boggy. The Chickasaws, scattered in patrols throughout the northern half of their country and as garrison forces at Fort Arbuckle and Fort Washita, were unable to gather in sufficient force to check the lightning-fast Union drive. The daring Phillips ventured as far southwest as the approaches to Fort Arbuckle before returning to his base at Fort Gibson. Along the invasion route he distributed copies of President Lincoln's amnesty proclamation and sent letters to Confederate Indian leaders promising "pardon and peace" if they abandoned the war. His letter to Governor Win-

---

[13] This battery had seventy-five men, eighty-two horses, and six guns of the six-pounder class. Shirk, "Place of the Indian Territory in the Command Structure of the Civil War," *Chronicles of Oklahoma*, Vol. XXXII (Summer, 1954), 471.

chester Colbert of the Chickasaws warned that "their day of grace would soon be over." Phillips' march covered four hundred miles, and he claimed that his men killed 250 of the enemy.[14]

The second Chickasaw engagement in the latter period of the Civil War occurred outside their country. In the spring of 1864 a Union army was driving south across Arkansas towards Texas. Confederate units from Missouri, Arkansas, and Indian Territory were rushed to check this thrust. These included Colonel Tandy Walker's Choctaw-Chickasaw troops. On April 18, 1864, near Camden, Arkansas, at a place called Poison Spring, the armies clashed. Walker's troops turned the enemy's flank, captured an artillery battery and a huge supply train, and were credited with substantially contributing to the Confederate victory. One of the Confederate generals reported that the Southern line "moved forward like a sheet of living fire, carrying death and destruction before it." He praised Walker's Choctaws and Chickasaws who "nobly, gallantly, gloriously . . . did their duty."[15]

A grim and pathetic feature of the Civil War in the Indian Territory was the refugee. The refugee story among the Chickasaws had two aspects. One concerned the Chickasaw exile. Most Chickasaws favored the Southern cause. A few, largely full bloods, did not. When the Chickasaw Nation joined the Confederacy, neutrals found it necessary to flee their homeland. The Chickasaw exiles, numbering 225 men, women, and children, settled near refugee Creeks, Seminoles, and Cherokees on the Neosho River at Le Roy, Kansas. As Union armies drove Confederates south of the Arkansas and Canadian rivers, the Chickasaw refugees returned to Indian Territory. During May, 1864, they resided near Fort Gibson. Shortly thereafter federal agents relocated them near Fort Smith where they remained until the close of the war.[16]

A second aspect of the Indian Territory refugee story con-

[14] Phillips to Curtis, February 24, 1864, *War of Rebellion Records*, Series I, Vol. XXXIV, Pt. I, 108–109; and Phillips to Colbert, February 15, 1864, *ibid.*, 109–110.

[15] General Samuel B. Maxey's Report of Engagement at Poison Spring, April 13, 1864, *ibid.*, 841–44.

[16] Coleman to Coffin, September 30, 1862, *Annual Report of the Commissioner of Indian Affairs for 1862*, 140–41; Coleman to Coffin, September 2, 1863, *ibid.*, *1863*, 181–82; and Coleman to Coffin, September 1, 1864, *ibid.*, *1864*, 313–15.

cerned the Chickasaw Nation as a haven for Confederate exiles. By mid-1863, Union armies had conquered the northern half of Indian Territory. Confederate Cherokee, Creek, and Seminole families fled to the Chickasaw and Choctaw nations and north Texas. A Cherokee exile related that the Union invaders had "burned out" his family and that they had escaped to the Chickasaw Nation in a "hack and carried with us our belongings that had not been burned up." When the state of Texas imposed a head tax on each Indian exile seeking refuge south of the Red River, the result was a concentration of the unfortunates in the Choctaw and Chickasaw nations. The refugees were sustained in various ways. Confederate agents, despite limited means, attempted to subsist them from the army commissary. Most of the subsistence supplies came from Texas, although Choctaws and Chickasaws also generously provided food. Confederate refugee depots in the Chickasaw Nation issued beef, flour, and soap rations to 4,823 Creeks on the Washita, 2,906 Cherokees near Tishomingo, and 574 Seminoles at Oil Springs, situated fifty miles west of Fort Washita. Also, 241 Osages near Fort Arbuckle were furnished rations. During 1864, 4,480 needy Choctaws drew rations from Confederate stores. The Chickasaws were reported to be "faring better," and "many have failed to ask for aid" although 785 qualified "as needy for their men were away fighting." Confederate agents found it impossible to obtain clothing and blankets, either in Indian Territory or Texas, for the destitute Indians. During 1864 they gathered 1,500 bales of cotton raised by Chickasaw, Choctaw, and Cherokee farmers and sent it across Texas to Mexico to exchange for textiles. Confederate agents also established shops to construct looms and spinning wheels for the refugee women to make cloth. One Chickasaw citizen's comment showed resentment towards the exiles:

> During the war here business in the way of improvement or farming was mostly suspended. We raised but little or nothing to sell, but that did not matter much, there was nothing to buy. Our legislature gave the adjoining friendly tribes, Cherokees, Creeks and Seminoles, permission to come into our territory for safety during the War. They came and showed their gratitude by killing

and eating our cattle and hogs at will, stealing our horses . . . .
So at the close of the war we were badly used up.[17]

The war disturbed most aspects of Chickasaw national life, forced the closing of neighborhood schools and academies, and permitted only a shadowy sort of government to function. School buildings were used by the troops for hospitals and barracks. Chickasaw courts ceased to function, and the tribal legislature convened only on an irregular basis from 1862 until October, 1865. One of the legislature's most important enactments was the Conscription Act of October 11, 1864. It directed the governor to call upon "all able-bodied free male citizens of this nation to volunteer in the service of the Confederate States." Those persons between the ages of eighteen and forty-five who failed to volunteer were to be conscripted according to the conscript act of the Confederate States. Most of the nation's manpower was absorbed in the war, either as fighting men or as farmers and stockmen striving to produce food for the troops, the noncombatant population, and the thousands of Cherokee, Creek, and Seminole refugees in the Chickasaw Nation. Thus during the Civil War the government of the Chickasaw Nation focused on the governor. Cyrus Harris had won this office in the 1860 election, and under his leadership the Confederate alliance was consummated. Winchester Colbert was elected governor in 1862 and won reelection two years later. During the Union invasion of the Chickasaw Nation in February, 1864, Colbert fled to Texas where he remained for several months. Horace Pratt, president of the inactive Chickasaw Senate, served as governor during Colbert's absence.[18]

As Confederate fortunes ebbed, leaders of the Southern tribes contemplated the uncertain future of their nations. Their concern and viewpoint were shared and expressed in a series of councils

[17] "Reminiscences of Mr. R. P. Vann, East of Webbers Falls, Oklahoma" (ed. by Grant Foreman) *Chronicles of Oklahoma*, Vol. XI (June, 1933), 837–44; Allan C. Ashcraft, "Confederate Indian Department Conditions in August, 1864," *Chronicles of Oklahoma*, Vol. XLI (Autumn, 1963), 270–85; and Worthington to Worthington, January 31, 1875, Chickasaw Nation Files, Oklahoma Historical Society.
[18] Chickasaw Act of Conscription, October 11, 1864, *War of Rebellion Records*, Series I, Vol. LIII, 1024–25; and John Meserve, "Governor Daugherty (Winchester) Colbert," *Chronicles of Oklahoma*, Vol. XVIII (December, 1940), 348–56.

held between November, 1863, and June, 1865. At the first council convened at Armstrong Academy in the Choctaw Nation in November, 1863, Chickasaw, Choctaw, Creek, Seminole, and Cherokee delegates reaffirmed their commitment to the Confederacy. The Union thrust into the Choctaw and Chickasaw nations in February, 1864, during which Colonel Phillips scattered copies of the amnesty proclamation and warnings to tribal leaders, led to a convening of the Confederate inter-tribal council at Tishomingo on March 16. Cherokee, Creek, Seminole, Caddo, and Osage delegates wavered in their support of the Confederacy and favored submitting to Phillips' invitation to return to the Union. Chickasaw and Choctaw delegates were unmoved. They braced the faltering tribal leaders, and the council reaffirmed the Confederate alliance. The prospect of the collapse of the Confederacy became very real in early 1865. In April, General E. Kirby Smith, Confederate commander of the Trans-Mississippi Department, directed Israel G. Vore to convene the Chickasaws, Choctaws, Creeks, Seminoles, Cherokees, and other tribes of Indian Territory to meet with Confederate officials at Council Grove on the North Canadian River. Threat of interference by a Union force in the area caused Vore to move the council southwest to the Washita River to a place called Camp Napoleon. Chickasaw, Cherokee, Choctaw, Creek, Seminole, Caddo, Osage, Kiowa, Cheyenne, Arapaho, and Comanche delegates met on May 24. Two days later they formed an Indian league and adopted a compact committing them to united action against the expected Union demands which were known to include a plan to take land from the Confederate tribes as a reparation of war. The Camp Napoleon compact included the statement that "peace and friendship shall forever exist between the tribes and bands parties to this compact. . . . The tomahawk shall forever be buried. The scalping knife shall forever be broken. . . . The parties to this compact shall compose . . . an Indian Confederacy." The final inter-tribal council of the Confederate tribes met at Armstrong Academy on June 15, 1865, where delegates adopted resolutions to renew relations with the United States and to present a united front to thwart threatened territorial appropriation by the Union government.[19]

Union General F. J. Herron, commander of the Northern District of Louisiana, formed a surrender commission for the Southern tribes headed by Lieutenant Colonel Asa C. Matthews and directed that it proceed to Indian Territory. Choctaw Chief Peter P. Pitchlynn met with Matthews on June 19, 1865, and surrendered the Choctaw Nation. On June 23, General Stand Watie tendered his sword to Matthews, the last Confederate general to surrender, and signed a truce for the Southern Cherokees. Governor Winchester Colbert did not formally capitulate until July 14. Thus the Chickasaw Nation was the last Confederate community to surrender.[20]

A month after the Chickasaw capitulation, Union officials summoned the leaders of the Confederate tribes of Indian Territory to meet with federal commissioners at Fort Smith to negotiate peace treaties. The Fort Smith council got under way on September 8. Dennis W. Cooley, Charles Mix, Elijah Sells, Thomas Wistar, General William S. Harney, and Colonel Ely S. Parker comprised the United States commission. Indian delegates representing the Creeks, Seminoles, Cherokees, Choctaws, Chickasaws, Osages, Senecas, Shawnees, Wyandots, and Quapaws were present. The Chickasaw and Choctaw delegations were from the small Union factions in the two tribes. The Confederate Chickasaw and Choctaw representatives did not reach Fort Smith until September 15. Commissioner Cooley opened the Fort Smith peace council on September 8 with the statement that the tribes of Indian Territory had been summoned to "renew their allegiance to the United States . . . and make a treaty of peace and amity. . . . Portions of several tribes and nations have attempted to throw off their allegiance to the United States, and have made treaty stipulations with the enemies of the government, and have been in open war with the United States. All such have rightfully forfeited all annuities and interests in the lands in the Indian

[19] Cox to Coffin, March 16, 1864, *Annual Report of the Commissioner of Indian Affairs for 1864*, 331–32; Compact between the Confederate Indian Tribes and the Prairie tribes, made at Camp Napoleon, May 26, 1865, *War of Rebellion Records*, Series I, Vol. XLVIII, Pt. II, 1102–1103; and Resolutions of the Grand Council, Armstrong Academy, June 15, 1865, *ibid.*, 1103–1104.

[20] Treaty Stipulations between Lt. Colonel Asa C. Matthews and Winchester Colbert, July 14, 1865, *ibid.*, 1097.

Territory. But with the return of peace . . . the President is willing to hear his erring children in extenuation of their great crime." Cooley noted that by law of Congress, July 5, 1862, all nations signing treaties with the Confederacy "forfeited and lost all their rights to annuities and lands. The President, however, does not desire to take advantage of or enforce the penalties for the unwise actions of these nations." To return to their former relation with the United States the Indian nations had to negotiate new treaties which provided for "permanent peace and amity with themselves . . . and with the United States." Each Indian nation had to abolish slavery and accept the freedmen "into the tribes on an equal footing with the original members, or suitably provided for." Another condition of peace was that each Indian nation had to surrender a portion of its territory for "friendly tribes now in Kansas and elsewhere." Also the nations and tribes of Indian Territory were expected to eventually accept the consolidation of their governments into a single government for the territory.[21]

The council proceedings were dominated by the Confederate Cherokee delegates. Their articulate objections to the United States' demands made it clear to the federal commissioners that it was hopeless to attempt to conclude a definitive treaty at Fort Smith. Cooley decided to recess the negotiations and handle the representatives of each tribe separately in Washington, far from the local pressures which had stiffened the Indian delegates' resolve. Cooley did salvage from the Fort Smith council a simple treaty of peace and amity. The Union Chickasaw delegates signed this agreement on September 14. On the following day the Confederate Chickasaw and Choctaw delegations arrived at Fort Smith. On September 18, as they prepared to sign the perfunctory treaty of peace, David Burney for the Chickasaws and Robert M. Jones for the Choctaws made the following statement to the United States commissioners:

> [When by the treaty] we admit that we recognize the government of the United States as exercising exclusive jurisdiction over us, we do not consent to, nor do we understand the United States as meaning to assume, the control or jurisdiction over our local

21 Fort Smith Council Proceedings, September, 1865, *Annual Report of the Commissioner of Indian Affairs for 1865*, 312–53.

affairs or national organizations, except as to the question of slavery, which is open to further negotiation; but that we regard the jurisdiction of the United States government as paramount as against all foreign governments. We would further state, that we were not induced by the machinations of the emissaries of the Confederate States to sever our treaty stipulations with the government of the United States, but that we made treaties with the Confederate States, from what appeared to us as our interest seemed to dictate, and as the means of preserving our independence and national identity.[22]

On April 28, 1866, a Chickasaw delegation consisting of Winchester Colbert, Edmund Pickens, Holmes Colbert, Colbert Carter, and Robert Love, and a Choctaw delegation containing Allen Wright, Alfred Wade, James Riley, and John Page met in Washington with United States commissioners and, "because of their common interests," signed a common treaty providing for a definitive peace settlement. The treaty text provided that the Chickasaws and Choctaws "hereby convenant and agree that henceforth neither slavery nor involuntary servitude, otherwise than in punishment of crime whereof the parties shall have been duly convicted . . . shall ever exist in said nations." For payment of $300,000 the Choctaws and Chickasaws ceded to the United States the Leased District. That sum the United States was to hold in trust until the legislatures of the Chickasaw and Choctaw nations had adopted laws "to give all persons of African descent," resident in these nations "at the date of the Treaty of Fort Smith, and their descendants, heretofore held in slavery among said nations, all the rights, privileges, and immunities, including the right of suffrage, of citizens of said nations, except in the annuities, moneys, and public domain" of the Choctaw and Chickasaw nations. Also the Chickasaws and Choctaws were to grant each freedman and descendant a tract of forty acres of land from their national domains. When the Chickasaws and Choctaws had made these provisions for their former slaves and descendants of slaves, the United States would pay over to the two tribes the $300,000, giving three-fourths to the Choctaws and one-fourth to

22 *Ibid.*; and Agreement with the Cherokees and other Tribes of the Indian Territory, 1865, in Kappler, *Laws and Treaties,* II, 1050–52.

the Chickasaws. The United States would deduct from this, at the rate of $100 per capita, and pay same to any freedman who elected to remove from the Chickasaw or Choctaw nations. If, within two years after the ratification of the treaty, the Chickasaw and Choctaw legislatures failed to adopt the laws making provision for the freedmen, the $300,000 held in trust for them would be used by the United States to remove the freedmen from the Chickasaw and Choctaw nations: "the United States agreeing, within ninety days from the expiration of the said two years, to remove from said nations all such persons of African descent as may be willing to remove; those remaining or returning after having been removed from said nations to have no benefit of said sum of three hundred thousand dollars, or any part thereof, but shall be upon the same footing as other citizens of the United States in the said nations."

In the treaty the Choctaws and Chickasaws granted a railroad right-of-way to an east-west line and a north-south line through their nations. For this concession the two Indian nations were allowed to "subscribe to the stock of the particular company or companies such amount or amounts as they may be able to pay for in alternate sections of unoccupied lands for a space of six miles on each side of said road or roads, at a price per acre to be agreed upon between said Choctaw and Chickasaw Nations and the said company or companies . . . Provided, however, That said land, thus subscribed, shall not be sold, or demised, or occupied by any one not a citizen of the Choctaw or Chickasaw Nations, according to their laws and recognized usages." The Chickasaw-Choctaw treaty included a clause providing for the beginning of a consolidated government for the Indian Territory in that these nations agreed to participate in a council "consisting of delegates elected by each nation or tribe." The United States agreed to renew treaty obligations concerning national funds and other Chickasaw and Choctaw fiscal resources and to resume payment of annuities.[23]

Like other Confederate communities, the Chickasaw Nation had to undergo a Reconstruction program, although their period of penance for rebellion against the United States was much

23 Treaty with the Choctaw and Chickasaw, 1866, *ibid.*, 918–31.

milder than that imposed on the eleven Southern states comprising the late Confederacy. For a brief period federal troops occupied military camps and posts in the nation, the army of occupation concentrated at Fort Arbuckle. Reconstruction agencies were active in the Chickasaw Nation. The principal one was the Freedman's Bureau. Major John B. Sanborn was in charge of "Headquarters Regulating Relations Between Freedmen in the Indian Territory and Their Former Masters" with headquarters at Fort Smith. Sanborn dispensed aid to the former Chickasaw slaves and reported to federal authorities in Washington on their treatment by the Chickasaws in the new order. He charged that the former masters still held "most of their negroes in slavery, and entertain a bitter prejudice against them all. They have provided by law for the gradual emancipation of their slaves, and exclude all from the nation who left it during the war. In other words, all negroes who left the country and joined the federal army are prohibited from returning. . . . It is reported to me . . . that Governor Colbert stated to many people, and publicly, before leaving for Washington, that they should hold the slaves until they could determine at Washington whether or not they could get pay for them, and if they could not then they would strip them naked and drive them either south to Texas, or north to Fort Gibson." Later Sanborn modified this report with the statement, "The prejudice on the part of the people of these nations against the freedmen is rapidly passing away, and their treatment of them has not been so bad and cruel as might be inferred from my former report and letters, although there is still much that is wrong and cruel. This wrong and cruelty on the part of these people towards the freedmen is the result of bad and improper laws of these nations—a slave code, which is considered by them as still in force, and executed upon all blacks accordingly."[24]

Governor Colbert in late 1865 reported to federal officers the progress his nation was making toward meeting the freedman problem. The Chickasaw legislature had amended the constitution to abolish slavery and had adopted a resolution authorizing

[24] Sanborn to Harlan, January 5, 1866, *Annual Report of the Commissioner of Indian Affairs for 1866*, 283–85; and Sanborn to Harlan, January 27, 1866, *ibid.*, 285–86.

Colbert to issue a proclamation advising all slaveowners to apprentice all free Negroes under twenty-one to former owners, to "provide for the aged over fifty, infirm, and employ the middle-aged at fair wages." Colbert claimed that this was "the self-same [system] under which Pennsylvania and other northern states got rid of slavery, and it is hoped will meet the approval of the President and people of the non-slaveholding States. . . . Many of our slaveowners have already voluntarily offered to their slaves choice either to go free or remain with them and work as heretofore for their food, clothing, doctor's bill, and the support of the old and the young who cannot work."[25]

One bit of penance which the Chickasaws and Choctaws had to endure was seeing the federal government pay the Union Chickasaws and Choctaws $260,000 as restitution for losses they claimed they had suffered at the hands of their Confederate tribesmen. This payment was derived from the Chickasaw and Choctaw national funds. Federal officials disbursed the money to Union Chickasaws and Choctaws at Fort Gibson in 1868.[26]

The legacy of the Chickasaws' alliance with the Confederacy and of the punishing Reconstruction treaty of 1866 was the recurring threat to national existence. The Chickasaw Nation made a determined but brief recovery from the ruin of war. But their energy and resourcefulness and their tenacious commitment to continue as a quasi-independent community were mocked by the powerful economic and political forces which the federal government abetted in the name of consummating the national purpose. In less than forty years the Chickasaw Nation would be annihilated.

[25] Colbert to Hunt, October 11, 1865, *ibid.*, *1865*, 357–58.
[26] Mix to Smoot, August 25, 1868, Miscellaneous Chickasaw Letters, Gilcrease Museum.

CHAPTER TWELVE

THE LAST DAYS
OF THE CHICKASAW NATION

MUCH of the Indian Territory in 1866 was a wasteland. The Cherokee, Creek, and Seminole nations had been a campaign zone for contesting Union and Confederate armies. Their operations depopulated towns, erased established communication lines and facilities, made impossible the pursuit of any sort of agricultural or commercial activity, and forced governments into exile. Foraging parties from both armies had gathered up most of the cattle, hogs, poultry, grain, and other foodstuffs. Plundering guerrilla bands added to the toll of death, destruction, and desolation. At times the northern perimeter of the Choctaw Nation had been the scene of lively military activity. The Chickasaw Nation, except for Colonel William A. Phillips' swift raid in February, 1864, alone escaped the overt desolation of war.

But the war had absorbed the Chickasaws and had marked them. In 1866 their population was forty-five hundred, about five hundred less than that shown by the 1860 census. Some of this decline was explained by those Union Chickasaws who had not returned to the nation. But it also included men who had died from battle wounds, disease, and exposure while serving in the Confederate Army. And the noncombatant population had suffered loss, largely due to smallpox, measles, and other diseases which the Confederate Cherokees and other refugees brought into the Chickasaw Nation. For five years there had been virtually no business or commercial activity. Farms and plantations had been reclaimed by nature, the once cleared and productive fields choked with underbrush and weeds. Over a million dollars in slaveowner investments had been erased by President Lincoln's

Emancipation Proclamation and the triumph of Union arms. The Chickasaw government, with no funds, barely functioned. Some of its branches, including the courts, had not been in operation since 1861. The nation's schools had closed at the war's outbreak, and a generation of uneducated Chickasaw youth was growing up. The spawn of war included over one hundred orphans, many of whom eventually had to be cared for by the government.

The Chickasaw government served as the principal agency for accomplishing postwar rehabilitation. In the election of 1866, Cyrus Harris defeated Winchester Colbert for the governorship. Harris won re-election in 1868 and thus was the chief executive who guided the Chickasaws through the turmoil of Reconstruction. In 1867 the Chickasaws met in general session at Camp Harris near Tishomingo to adopt a new constitution. This organic law, which consisted of a refinement of the 1856 constitution, served as a guide for Chickasaw government until 1907 when the Chickasaw Nation was absorbed by the state of Oklahoma. The 1867 constitution was silent on the subject of freedmen, and the reason was revealed by subsequent developments associated with this issue.[1]

One of the first recovery steps taken by the Chickasaw government was to reopen the nation's schools. The United States government resumed annuity disbursements in 1867 by paying the Chickasaws $65,735, which enabled Chickasaw officials to open eleven neighborhood schools during that year. The Chickasaw legislature in 1876 adopted a law increasing the number of schools of this class offering elementary-level work to twenty-three—eight schools in Pontotoc County and five each in Panola, Pickens, and Tishomingo counties. Also in 1876 the legislature made provision for reopening four seminaries and academies where Chickasaw students pursued secondary-level studies. When operational, these institutions—Chickasaw Male Academy, Bloomfield Female Seminary, Wapanucka Institute (co-educational), and the Lebanon Orphan School—caused federal officials to comment that "in proportion to their numbers, the Chickasaws have more seminaries and more students in attendance than any of the five

[1] Constitution of the Chickasaw Nation, 1867, *Constitution and Laws of the Chickasaw Nation*, 3–21.

civilized tribes." For several years after the war the nation's schools were totally secularized and supported by public funds. The Chickasaw superintendent of public instruction operated the schools on a contract basis. The neighborhood school contractors furnished the teachers, books, and other supplies and were paid three dollars a student each month. Academy and seminary contractors furnished teachers, supplies, board, room, and clothing for students at an annual rate of $200 a pupil. The contractors were Chickasaw citizens, and most of the teachers were Chickasaws. The superintendent of public instruction conducted normal institutes for training and improving native teachers. In addition, the Chickasaw government provided scholarships at the rate of $350 a year for worthy students to study at colleges and universities in the States. The number of students in this category varied from sixty to one hundred. An indication of the impact of the steady extension of educational benefits to an increasing number of Chickasaws was revealed in an 1880 report—in an estimated 6,000 tribal population, 3,600 could read and write.[2]

Before the war, several religious bodies had established churches for the Chickasaws and assisted in operating the nation's schools. In 1866, missionaries resumed their labors, but the secularization of tribal schools forced them to confine their work to preaching and church building. The Methodist Episcopal Church South, most active of all religious bodies among the Chickasaws from removal to 1861, dominated the Chickasaw religious scene during the early postwar years. The Indian Territory Methodist Conference officially launched its program of rehabilitating the Chickasaw churches through a meeting at Bloomfield Academy on September 1, 1866. John H. Carr, builder of Chickasaw schools and esteemed missionary teacher, was elected presiding elder of the Chickasaw District, and J. T. Talbott was appointed head of the Chickasaw Circuit. Baptist missionaries had maintained a continuing contact with the Chickasaws dating back to

---

[2] James to Olmstead, August 8, 1870, *Report of the Commissioner of Indian Affairs for 1870*, 295–96; Marston to Commissioner of Indian Affairs, September 11, 1877, *ibid.*, *1877*, 107–11; Tufts to Commissioner of Indian Affairs, October 10, 1880, *ibid.*, *1880*, 94–96; and An Act Establishing Chickasaw Schools, October 9, 1876, *Constitution and Laws of the Chickasaw Nation*, 98–102.

preremoval times. In July, 1872, Joseph S. Murrow, who had converted many Creeks and Seminoles in the antebellum period, issued a call which led to the formation of the Choctaw-Chickasaw Baptist Association. Within three years Murrow's labors had produced twenty Baptist churches in the Chickasaw Nation. Nearly all Methodist and Baptist churches, claiming a combined following of five hundred Chickasaw converts, were of log construction, the seats "hewed logs without backs and . . . not well adapted for sleepy Christians." Best attended were the summer revivals, held under brush arbors near the humble log churches. The pulse of religious interest slowed during the mid-1870's, due, according to some observers, to diminishing support of missionaries working among the Chickasaws by state-side churches. For a time religious instruction was provided by Indian preachers directed by the few missionaries residing in the Chickasaw Nation. Then during the 1880's the religious tempo accelerated. Methodist and Baptist support for Chickasaw missions increased, and representatives of other religious bodies appeared. Missionaries were permitted a full mission program of evangelizing and teaching as the Chickasaw government gradually modified its stand on secularization of education. In 1882 the Cumberland Presbyterian Church resumed its work among the Chickasaws by maintaining resident missionaries, and in 1888, Roman Catholic representatives began an earnest effort to serve Chickasaw religious and educational needs. Father Switbert Breeken established a Roman Catholic mission and school at Tishomingo in 1888. Poor attendance forced the closing of this school, but other Roman Catholic schools proved more successful. One of these was St. Elizabeth's School at Purcell on the northern Chickasaw Nation border. In 1884 the Chickasaw government permitted the Methodists to open Pierce Institute at White Bead Hill in Pickens County and Hargrove College at Ardmore in 1895.[3]

It appeared that the Chickasaw Nation would be permitted to resume some measure of the bucolic life of the antebellum years.

[3] Carl C. Rister, *Baptist Missions Among the American Indians*, 93–96; Report to the Secretary of the Interior for 1876, *Annual Report of the Commissioner of Indian Affairs for 1876*, 64, 212; and Sister Mary Ursula, "The Catholic Church on the Oklahoma Frontier, 1824–1907" (Ph.D. dissertation, St. Louis University, 1938), 214, 218.

Its people were making satisfying if not particularly spectacular progress in the arts of civilization. Life was easy for those Chickasaws with simple tastes. Their fertile fields and rich grasslands yielded crops and livestock increases which more than sufficed their needs. Their former slaves, now freedmen, performed the rigorous toil as day laborers and sharecroppers. Most Chickasaws were content and secure in treaty agreements with the United States government which pledged to preserve Chickasaw tenure in their land forever and to insulate their nation from invasion by those disturbing, disruptive forces set loose across the United States in the years following the Civil War. But the Chickasaw sense of security was a mirage. These forces would not be deterred. They at first filtered through, then rushed across the land of the Chickasaws like a mighty flood, producing cataclysmic changes in tribal life and finally destroying the Chickasaw Nation as an ethnic community.

Of these forces the one most responsible for administering the *coup de grâce* to the Chickasaw Nation was a galvanizing, pervasive, economic thrust. As a rich segment of Indian Territory, the Chickasaw Nation, as well as the domains of the Cherokees, Choctaws, Creeks, and Seminoles, comprised one of America's last frontiers and could not escape the invasion and impact of this force. Protective treaty guarantees were twisted or ignored. The federal government, responsible for protecting these tribes and preserving their way of life, must bear much blame for consorting with those business barons who coveted the Chickasaw domain and ached to exploit its riches. But certain ambitious mixed-blood Chickasaws, eager to share in the promise of wealth, and perhaps because they understood the futility of resistance and the inevitability of the Chickasaw demise, were receptive to the overtures of big business. These mixed bloods converted their government into an agency of connivance to aid, legalize, and abet the invasion of the economic thrust.

The railroad was a vital part of this economic thrust. A federal official in 1895 observed that the expanding grid of railways lacing the Chickasaw Nation and connecting it with the outside world "has been fatal to the old order of things, and has forced upon these people much that is found new among them." The first railway to enter the Chickasaw Nation was the M. K. and T. (Katy) line. It received a right-of-way grant from the Chickasaw legislature one hundred feet wide with additional allowances of land for siding and switches within townsites. Completed in 1872, the M. K. and T. crossed the southeastern corner of the Chickasaw Nation. In the early years, Colbert was the only Chickasaw town on this line. Next came the Santa Fe Railway which cut the center of the Chickasaw Nation north to south. Completed in 1887, the Santa Fe ran from Purcell on the Canadian River southward via Ardmore into Texas. A portion of the Chicago, Rock Island and Pacific Railway was constructed across the western Chickasaw Nation in 1892, extending from Minco to Terral. Other lines constructed in the Chickasaw Nation included a branch of the Frisco Railroad, running from Sapulpa in the Creek Nation to Denison, Texas; the Arkansas and Choctaw Railway, crossing the lower Chickasaw Nation east to west; the Oklahoma City, Ada and Atoka Railway; and the Oklahoma Central Railway constructed from Lehigh via Stonewall to Chickasha.[4]

The expanding railroad grid stimulated the urbanization of the Chickasaw Nation. Bustling commercial towns built adjacent to the railroads eclipsed the tranquil Chickasaw settlements. By 1890, eight of these new towns each had a population in excess of 1,000, and four had more than 2,000 each. Chickasha had 3,200. Ardmore with 5,700 was the most populous town in the Chickasaw Nation and ranked as one of the largest inland cotton markets in the South, annually receiving more than sixty thousand bales. To these new towns came business and professional men, craftsmen and laborers, railroad workers, and shopkeepers. A federal report on the urbanization surge in the Chickasaw Nation which began in the 1880's disclosed that the new "towns have all been built and peopled by white residents, whose capital has been invested in large amounts in structures necessary for the great and increasing trade which is being carried on at these centers. Costly and attractive residences have been erected in many of them, and in character they compare favorably with like towns in any of the new States." The report added that the newcomers "with few exceptions are doing a surprisingly large and prosperous business.

[4] *Report of the Commission to the Five Civilized Tribes for 1895,* 56.

And yet those who have built these towns, invested their capital in these expensive structures and have made these beautiful homes, have no title to the land on which they rest. This remains in the nation." Since the Chickasaws held their lands in common, a town could develop only by the patronage of a Chickasaw citizen. First he received authority from tribal government officials "to inclose for his exclusive use any unoccupied territory. He, having first inclosed a prospective townsite, leases town lots at a ground rental, or quitclaims his title for a gross sum to the incoming builder." It was claimed that millions of dollars had been spent on streets and buildings with "no other title than . . . a tenantry of suffrance."[5]   ·

Newcomers settled the Chickasaw rural areas too, and developed vast agricultural and stock-raising enterprises. The United States government was obligated by treaties to preserve the territorial integrity of the Chickasaw, Choctaw, Seminole, Creek, and Cherokee nations. In most respects their tribal domains were legally off-limits to non-Indians, and the United States government was committed to expel intruders. Yet, a 1900 census report disclosed that 300,000 whites resided in the Indian Territory. The greatest concentration of non-Indians was in the Chickasaw Nation where the whites numbered 150,000. Although the Chickasaws never owned more than 1,000 slaves, there were over 5,000 resident Negroes claiming to be Chickasaw freedmen. The number of Chickasaws had remained about constant at slightly less than 6,000.[6]

The Chickasaw government accommodated the invading horde by requiring each male adult noncitizen to purchase a permit "for the privilege of residing and doing business" or laboring in the Chickasaw Nation. The noncitizen permit was obtained from the county clerk, and the proceeds from permit sales went into the Chickasaw Nation treasury. The permit charge, payable each year, varied from twenty-five cents in the early 1870's to one dollar, five dollars, and in 1876 the Chickasaw legislature increased the permit charge to twenty-five dollars a year. Four years later the legislature reduced the annual noncitizen levy to

[5] *Ibid.*, 54, 56–57.
[6] *Twelfth United States Census*, I, Part I, CXII.

five dollars where it remained. Permit holders included physicians, teachers, and other professional persons, farmers, mechanics, and laborers. Merchants and traders purchased the permits and also submitted to an annual tax on all goods offered for sale in the nation. Noncitizens without permits were classed as intruders and were subject to expulsion from the nation by the Chickasaw light horse police.[7]

The permit simply legalized the presence of the noncitizen in the Chickasaw Nation. He also had to observe those Chickasaw laws concerning land use through which he might obtain the privilege of using the land. The permit system was a public relationship between the noncitizen and a government official. The privilege of using land, though covered by law, was a private relationship. As indicated, the Chickasaw citizen had the right to select and use any unoccupied portion of the tribal domain. Chickasaw law permitted him to designate an area for a townsite, and the new commercial towns evolving on the Chickasaw Nation's expanding railway grid were developed on this basis. The same rule applied to agricultural land. The Chickasaw citizen paid no tax on the land he selected for a townsite, ranch, or farm. Chickasaw citizens, most of them mixed bloods, went into the fertile bottoms of the Red, Washita, and Blue and established their claims to huge tracts. As landlords they received permit-holding tenants. In many cases the Indian landlord purchased permits for his tenants. Customarily the Chickasaw proprietors leased or rented their tracts in plots of from 10 to 160 acres. Annual land rent went as high as two dollars an acre for black bottom land. Most land was let to tenants on a share basis— one-third of the "oats in shock," one-third of the "corn piled in field" and one-fourth of the "cotton at gin."[8]

The phenomenal expansion of agriculture in the Chickasaw Nation caught the attention of the superintendent of the Five Civilized Tribes, Robert L. Owen, who reported in 1886 that the

[7] Chickasaw Permit Law, October 17, 1876, *Constitution and Laws of the Chickasaw Nation*, 229–31; Marston to Commissioner of Indian Affairs, September 11, 1877, *Report of the Commissioner of Indian Affairs for 1877*, and Chickasaw Permit Law, 45 Cong., 3 sess., *Senate Report No. 698*.

[8] Agricultural Lease File, Chickasaw Nation Records, Oklahoma Historical Society.

area of farming lands has probably doubled in five years, and is increasing in geometric ratio. The Washita Valley, in the Chickasaw Nation, is almost a solid farm for 50 miles. It is cultivated by white labor largely, with Chickasaw landlords. (I saw one farm there said to contain 8,000 acres, another 4,000 acres, and many other very large and handsome places.) The prairie is being turned to use, and even some of the full-bloods are beginning to take advantage of its opportunities.[9]

Even in the late 1870's substantial changes were occurring in Chickasaw society. Certain inventive and energetic mixed bloods drew great wealth and power from their vast agricultural and ranching estates. Like feudal barons, they exacted annual tribute from their serfs, the tenants who toiled in the Washita bottoms. Federal officials detected the rise of this Indian aristocracy and commented:

> No greater change in any of the conditions existing in these nations is more manifest than in the life of the citizen Indian himself. He no longer depends upon his own labor for his livelihood. The white man, invited to the Territory under laws enacted for that purpose, or the negro, once the slave of the Indian and his children, now labor for him, and he has become a landlord, a trader, or an owner of herds kept for him by others.[10]

Other flourishing enterprises included quarrying for building stone and railroad ballast and lumbering which yielded railroad ties and materials for local building needs. From the Chickasaw Nation's hardwood forests came a type of walnut wood esteemed by furniture makers and gunsmiths (for stocks) in the eastern United States and Europe. A prime market for Chickasaw Nation walnut logs was Hamburg, Germany. The Chickasaw government collected a royalty of five dollars on each one thousand board feet of lumber exported from the nation.[11]

Oil production, a leading twentieth-century industry in that portion of Oklahoma comprising the old Chickasaw Nation—the world-famous Fitts Field and other bonanza zones—was only

[9] Owen to Commissioner of Indian Affairs, September 20, 1886, *Report of the Commissioner of Indian Affairs for 1886*, 146–61.
[10] *Report of the Commission to the Five Civilized Tribes for 1895*, 56.
[11] Fort Smith *Elevator*, December 21, 1894.

limitedly exploited in the antebellum period. Surface petroleum signs and oil springs at many points in the nation aroused interest. In 1872, Chickasaw and Choctaw citizens and a Missouri company formed the Chickasaw Oil Company to drill on leases encompassing what fifty years later became the fabulous Fitts Field. Simultaneous discovery and development of rich coal veins near McAlester in the Choctaw Nation deflected interest in development of Chickasaw petroleum resources. Thus for the time being the bubbling oil springs of the Chickasaw Nation were used only as health spas.[12]

During this period of Chickasaw Nation economic expansion, stock raising ranked with agriculture as the leading enterprise. The Chickasaws had been pre-eminent as breeders of fine horses before removal. In the antebellum years they began the exploitation of the rich grazing resources of their Indian Territory domain, developing substantial herds of horses, cattle, and sheep. After the Civil War the Chickasaw Nation was involved in the flourishing and profitable trans-Mississippi range cattle industry. The Chickasaw Nation served as a great cattle highway for Texas cattlemen driving their herds to market in the Kansas cow towns. Several cattle trails crossed the Chickasaw Nation. Best known of these was the Chisholm Trail. Many Chickasaws resumed stock raising after the war, built substantial herds, and shared in the profitable markets created by an expanding eastern demand for beef. Also, certain Chickasaws appropriated stock ranges on the tribal domain, much as they staked out townsites and valley farms, and leased these to Texas cattlemen. Besides making annual lease payment in cash or animals to their Chickasaw landlord, the noncitizen cattlemen were required by Chickasaw law to purchase the permits which legalized their presence in the Chickasaw Nation and, in addition, to pay to the Chickasaw government an annual tax of twenty-five cents a head for each animal grazing on Chickasaw grasslands. The importance of ranching in Chickasaw Nation economic life was demonstrated by the elaborate stock-raising code adopted by the tribal legislature. In each county of the nation there was a stock superin-

[12] Muriel H. Wright, "First Oklahoma Oil was Produced in 1859," *Chronicles of Oklahoma*, Vol. IV (December, 1926), 322–28.

tendent who rode the ranges in his jurisdiction and collected the tax on noncitizens' stock, examined brands, and enforced the quarantine law which forbade the introduction of steer cattle into the nation except during November and December. The purpose of the quarantine law was to protect local livestock from infection by deadly Texas fever. With assistance from the county sheriff and light horse police, the stock superintendent also enforced the trail-driving law which required trail herds to move across the nation at no less than eight miles a day. Drovers were allowed to graze the herd only over an area one mile wide on each side of the trail upon payment of fifteen cents an animal.[13]

The Chickasaw government struggled through its final years beset with pressures both from within and without. A major source of concern for tribal leaders was the threat that they would have to grant vast tracts of the national domain to railroad companies as subsidies for constructing lines across Indian Territory. In 1870 the Choctaw Council passed an act granting alternate sections of land for six miles on either side of a railroad line to be constructed along the thirty-fifth parallel. Because of the joint Chickasaw-Choctaw interest in tribal lands established by the treaty of 1866, Chickasaw assent was required. The Chickasaw legislature refused to approve the Choctaw action which voided the grant. The Chickasaws and Choctaws granted to the M. K. and T., the first line to cross Indian Territory, a right-of-way only one hundred feet in width. The railroad companies despaired of obtaining tribal assent to land grants for Indian Territory railroad construction and turned to Congress and lobbied intensively for many years to achieve passage of legislation which would require the Chickasaws and other tribes to submit and surrender the desired tracts of land. Through the years the Chickasaw delegation worked with Creek, Seminole, Choctaw, and Cherokee representatives in Washington, countering the railroad lobbyist pressure on Congress. Ultimately the Five Civilized Tribes triumphed on this issue.[14]

[13] An Act in Relation to Stock Being Driven Through the Chickasaw Nation, October 9, 1886, *Constitution and Laws of the Chickasaw Nation*, 180–81; also see Neil R. Johnson, *The Chickasaw Rancher* (edited with an introduction by Arrell M. Gibson).

[14] Grant Foreman, *A History of Oklahoma*, 205–208.

A continuing source of concern for Chickasaw government officials was the sustained mass invasion of the nation by whites and Negroes. Many submitted to the Chickasaw permit system and thereby obtained legal status. Thousands refused. An 1890 report on Pickens County showed 4,934 permit holders and 2,887 white and 152 Negro intruders. Robert L. Owen, superintendent of the Five Civilized Tribes, declared, "The intruders are numerous and a class most difficult to manage. These are the intruding cowmen, farmers . . . vagrants, refugees from justice, professional thieves, and whiskey-peddlers." During 1886, cattle-men from Texas moved 150,000 head of stock onto the Chickasaw ranges and refused to purchase permits or pay the stock tax. Chickasaw officials appealed to Owen who came from his Mus-kogee office to the nation and with a squad of Chickasaw light horse police confronted the intruders. The Texans removed 40,000 head at once and received an abatement of thirty days to remove the remainder. At the appointed time, Owen gave orders to eject the intruders but was informed that they had appealed to the secretary of the interior who granted them an additional forty-day delay. Owen complained that this extension "broke up all that I had done." It gave the cowmen "time to adjust their affairs," which meant that they remained on the Chickasaw ranges by making "bogus sales" to Indian citizens. Some 25,000 head were "manipulated in this way" to evade Owen's removal order.[15]

Aside from the issue of allotment in severalty, the most com-pelling problem facing tribal leaders was the Chickasaw freed-men. By their 1866 Reconstruction treaties the Cherokees, Creeks, and Seminoles agreed to adopt their former slaves as tribal citizens. Federal negotiators attempted to persuade the Chickasaws and Choctaws to include this provision in their Re-construction treaty, but they refused. The Chickasaw-Choctaw treaty permitted these tribes the option of adopting their former slaves within two years following ratification of the treaty or of allowing the United States government to remove their freedmen

---

[15] Chickasaw Nation Census File, Chickasaw Nation Records, Oklahoma His-torical Society; and Owen to Commissioner of Indian Affairs, September 20, 1886, *Report of the Commissioner of Indian Affairs for 1886,* 146–61.

and settle them elsewhere. Also by the 1866 treaty, the United States government appropriated the Leased District, owned jointly by the Choctaws and Chickasaws. The government agreed to pay the tribes $300,000 for this territory, but held the sum in trust until the Chickasaws and Choctaws made provision for their freedmen. If they failed to do this, the federal government was to relocate the freedmen and pay each $100 from this fund. In 1866 the Chickasaw legislature passed a resolution declaring that the Chickasaw Nation had no intention of adopting the former slaves, had no interest in the money, and urged the government to remove the freedmen. In that same year certain Chickasaw freedmen, because of the Chickasaw feeling toward them, petitioned the federal government to relocate them. Two years later the Chickasaw and Choctaw governments repeated to federal officials their determination not to adopt the freedmen and urged removal. The freedmen again asked that they be relocated. Federal officials and the Congress took no action.[16]

The freedmen problem in the Chickasaw Nation was complicated by an invasion of hundreds of newly freed Negroes from Texas. They formed settlements near the Red River and, destitute with no means of support, roamed the countryside stealing cattle, chickens, hogs, and grain from Chickasaw and freedmen farmers. The Chickasaws formed "vigilance committees" which patrolled the troubled zone. Intruder freedmen apprehended any distance from their home settlements were whipped by the vigilance patrols which provoked charges of inhumane treatment. For several years the Chickasaws were regularly investigated and chastened by federal officials for their local handling of the problem of intruding freedmen.[17]

Valentine Dell, an ardent reconstructionist and editor of the Fort Smith *New Era*, and Major S. N. Clark, special agent for the Freedmen's Bureau, were reported to be encouraging freedmen to organize and pressure the Chickasaw and Choctaw governments to grant them citizenship and rights to tribal lands and

---

[16] Chickasaw Freedmen, 55 Cong., 1 sess., *Sen. Doc. No. 157*, 2.

[17] Joseph B. Thoburn and Muriel H. Wright, *Oklahoma: A History of the State and Its People*, I, 375–76; and Olmsted to Parker, September 15, 1870, *Report of the Commissioner of Indian Affairs for 1870*, 291–93.

annuities. And freedmen attitude toward removal changed. In 1869 federal agent George Olmsted attended a convention of three hundred Chickasaw and Choctaw freedmen. He reported that the Negroes no longer desired removal, but considered themselves "full citizens of these nations, entitled to all the rights, privileges and benefits as such, the same as any citizen of Indian extraction."[18]

Chickasaw leaders faced a dilemma. The federal government had not fulfilled its pledge to remove their former slaves, which at the outbreak of the Civil War numbered slightly less than 1,000. Refugee freedmen from Texas and Louisiana were immigrating to the Chickasaw Nation in increasing numbers. The federal government, obligated by treaty to expel intruders, ignored Chickasaw appeals to check this Negro invasion. Attempts by Chickasaw light horse police to turn back the intruders brought charges of inhumane treatment and investigation by federal officials. By the mid-1870's the freedmen population in the Chickasaw Nation had increased to over 2,600. The intruding freedmen were joining former Chickasaw slaves to form a threatening phalanx of pressure and power. In an attempt to separate their former slaves from the growing freedmen community, the Chickasaw legislature passed an act in 1873 which provided for the specific identification of each Chickasaw freedman. After this was established, procedures were set for adoption. This measure was submitted to the federal government for approval to meet a postwar requirement that acts of the tribal legislatures had to be approved by the secretary of the interior and other federal officials and agencies. No action was taken by federal authorities on this law, thus voiding it. In 1877 the Chickasaw legislature repudiated the freedman citizenship act.[19]

Freedmen in the Chickasaw Nation suffered a continuing suppression and rejection similar to that inflicted on former slaves throughout the United States. Freedmen leaders desired, among

18 Debo, *The Rise and Fall of the Choctaw Republic*, 103; and Parthena L. James, "Reconstruction in the Chickasaw Nation: The Freedman Problem," *Chronicles of Oklahoma*, Vol. XLV (Spring, 1967), 48.
19 Chickasaw Legislature's Proceedings File, Chickasaw Nation Records, Oklahoma Historical Society; and Chickasaw Freedmen. 45 Cong., 3 sess., *Sen. Report No. 744*, 3-4.

other things, that Negro children receive some education. The Chickasaw Nation school system was restricted exclusively to Indian children. Baptist missionaries were sensitive to this need and in 1877 organized a freedmen's school at Fort Arbuckle. Congress appropriated $3,500 for Chickasaw and Choctaw freedman schools in 1880. The secretary of the interior signed a contract with Baptist Home Mission Board officials, and missionaries from this religious body opened seven schools during 1880 and 1881. Freedmen furnished the buildings and the mission board provided the teachers and operated the schools. Pressured by missionaries and freedmen leaders for increased educational support, Congress in 1882 appropriated $10,000 from the $300,000 Choctaw-Chickasaw Leased District trust fund for Negro schools. The measure encouraged these tribes to adopt their freedmen by providing that if either took this step, the $10,000 would go to the tribal governments. The treaty of 1866 required joint action by the Chickasaws and Choctaws on matters relating to freedmen and tribal lands, but the measure suspended that requirement in this instance, permitting independent action by either tribe. The Choctaws submitted by adopting their freedmen, and thus the $10,000 was paid over to the Choctaw government. The Chickasaws refused to adopt their freedmen and again urged the federal government to remove those Negroes residing in their nation. The Chickasaw Nation's freedmen problem continued, reaching a climax and finally a solution in the early twentieth century.[20]

All the while that the Chickasaws were struggling with the problems produced by the rapid economic development of their nation, the intruder influx, and freedmen pressure, they were linked in a bitter contest with the federal government which threatened to end their tribal autonomy and to extinguish their identity as an ethnic community. In the postwar years the federal government clearly was committed to a policy of integrating the Indian tribes into the national community. To accomplish this, it first had to erase the Indian governments and liquidate the com-

[20] Smith to Marston, September 3, 1877, Chickasaw Nation Records, Oklahoma Historical Society; Tufts to Commissioner of Indian Affairs, September 30, 1881, *Report of the Commissioner of Indian Affairs for 1881*, 103–105; and Chickasaw Freedmen, 55 Cong., 1 sess., *Sen. Doc. No. 157*, 2.

mon tribal estates. A first step in the annihilation process was taken in 1871 when Congress ended the time-honored practice of conducting relations with the tribes through treaties by adopting an act which stated, "Hereafter no Indian or tribe within the territory of the United States shall be acknowledged or recognized as an independent nation, tribe or power with whom the United States may contract by treaty."[21]

Another step in the annihilation process was accomplished by the extension of federal judicial power over the nations in Indian Territory. The federal district court at Van Buren, Arkansas, and later at Fort Smith had jurisdiction over cases involving offenses committed by non-Indians in the domains of the Five Civilized Tribes and over all cases involving violations of federal laws. The erosion of tribal court jurisdiction, producing a concomitant reduction in tribal autonomy, was continued by an 1889 statute which annexed the Chickasaw Nation to the federal district court at Paris, Texas. The next year Congress adopted an act providing for three Indian Territory courts—one at Muskogee, a second at South McAlester, and a third court, for the Chickasaw Nation, at Ardmore—each with a jurisdiction which encompassed most cases formerly the province of tribal courts. After 1866 most laws adopted by the Chickasaw legislature and other law-making bodies of the tribes of Indian Territory had to be submitted to federal officials for approval. Other instances of the erosion of tribal autonomy included a take-over of tribal schools and the collection of tribal revenues by federal officials. The federal government tightened its administrative noose over the Chickasaws, Cherokees, Choctaws, Seminoles, and Creeks in 1874 by consolidating its relations with these tribes through the creation of Union Agency at Muskogee headed by the superintendent of the Five Civilized Tribes.[22]

In the early postwar years the Chickasaws vigorously resisted the federal government's attempts to annihilate their tribal way of life. It was an unequal contest, but for a time tribal leaders

21 "An Act Making Appropriations for . . . the Indian Department . . . and for other Purposes," *United States Statutes at Large*, Vol. XVI. 544–71.

22 "An Act for the Protection of the People of the Indian Territory and for other Purposes, June 28, 1898," *ibid.*, XXX, 495–519.

showed great initiative and ingenuity in their attempts to thwart federal design. An early indication of their resolve to resist was demonstrated by their railroad policy. The federal government, as the willing agent of the great and powerful railway companies, pushed the Chickasaws and other Indian Territory tribes to surrender substantial blocks of land to the railroads building across the tribal domains. The Chickasaws led the resistance to making land grants, adamantly refusing to negotiate the question. When forced to make some concession, they reluctantly allowed each railway only a ribbon of land one hundred feet wide for construction of a right-of-way through their territory rather than grants six to ten sections wide in alternate strips adjacent to the line as expected by the railroads.[23]

The Chickasaws also were adamant on the freedmen question and evaded great federal pressure to adopt them. By the standards of mid-twentieth-century race relations the Chickasaw Nation would be condemned for its treatment of the Negro, but in the context of the times it certainly was no more derelict in this regard than other former slaveholding communities in the United States. The Cherokees, Creeks, Seminoles, and even the Choctaws succumbed to United States demands and incorporated their freedmen into tribal society. The Chickasaws alone resisted and ultimately won this contest.

The Chickasaws valiantly resisted federal attempts to organize a unified government for the Indian Territory. The reconstruction settlement for Indian Territory committed the tribes to work toward this end. Pushed by United States officials to organize a territorial government, and induced by federal payments of four dollars a day while in session plus mileage, representatives of the Five Civilized Tribes met annually for several years at Okmulgee in the Creek Nation. Representation in the Okmulgee Council was based on the formula of one delegate from each tribe plus one additional delegate for each one thousand population. The Chickasaws were allocated six seats on the council. In 1871 the Okmulgee Council members produced a constitution providing the guide for a unified government for Indian Territory. Chicka-

[23] Olmstead to Parker, September 15, 1870, *Report of the Commissioner of Indian Affairs for 1870*, 291–93.

saw objections nullified the work of the council. A disappointed federal official wrote that

> a prejudice has been created among the Chickasaws against it, on the assumed ground that, as the constitution does not provide for an equal representation of small nations with large in either house, the interests of the smaller nations will be imperiled. At a called session of the [Chickasaw] legislature, convened immediately after the adjournment of the general council, the question of adoption or rejection of the Ocmulgee constitution was submitted to the people, and rejected almost unanimously.[24]

Federal officials continued to pressure the Five Civilized Tribes to organize a unified government for Indian Territory, but tribal leaders, braced by the Chickasaws' rejection of the Okmulgee constitution, refused to accede. The tribes continued to meet regularly in what they called the International Council to develop strategy and oppose federal aggressions on tribal autonomy. They publicized their plight in the eastern press and memorialized Congress and the president to respect treaty promises. At the 1887 session of the International Council, where the Chickasaws were represented by C. A. Burris, the delegates drafted a memorial to the president which stated their alarm at the pressure applied to grant lands to railroads and the attempts to open Indian Territory to settlement, adding that they had "undergone an experience in transactions with the United States of an identical nature in 1830 and 1832." Through their delegations in Washington the Chickasaws and the other tribes of Indian Territory also watched over the increasing flow of bills introduced by congressmen at the behest of railroad lobbyists and other interested groups to open Indian Territory to settlement.[25]

During the 1870's the Chickasaws, in their studied campaign to thwart federal purpose, even toyed with the acceptance of allotments. Common ownership was deeply entrenched in tribal values, but apparently they were willing to sacrifice this ancient

---

[24] Griffith to Clum, August, 1871, *ibid.*, 1871, 569–71.

[25] Owen to Commissioner of Indian Affairs, September 1, 1887, *Report of the Commissioner of Indian Affairs for 1887*, 98–120. The vast body of legislative literature on the subject of opening Indian Territory to settlement includes 46 Cong., 2 sess., *House Report No. 755*; 46 Cong., 1 sess., *House Misc. Doc. No. 13*; and 45 Cong., 2 sess., *Sen. Misc. Doc. No. 82*.

and esteemed practice to escape having to share their land with freedmen and railroads. It was reasoned that by moving swiftly all the tribal land would go to Chickasaws. By the treaty of 1866 they could, with Choctaw co-operation, have their lands surveyed and allotted. In 1871 and 1872 the federal government, at the request of the Chickasaws, surveyed their nation and tribal leaders asked federal officials to proceed with allotment. The Choctaws refused to submit to survey and allotment, causing the Chickasaw scheme to fail.[26]

In their postwar contest with the federal government the Chickasaws won some victories. One victory grew out of the continuing charge by tribal leaders that federal officials had mismanaged Chickasaw trust funds and had shown dereliction and perhaps collusion with contractors during removal, thereby causing expenditures from the Chickasaw national fund far in excess of fair or real removal costs. Federal reluctance to face the matter led to more intense Chickasaw pressure, and finally the secretary of the interior referred it to the United States Court of Claims. In 1877 this tribunal sustained the Chickasaws and directed the federal government to pay them $240,164 for overcharges on removal and mismanagement of their trust fund. The Chickasaws worked with the Choctaws to recover a fair value of the Leased District lands taken from them by the Reconstruction settlement. For that portion of the Leased District assigned to the Cheyennes and Arapahoes, the federal government finally in 1891 agreed to pay the Choctaws and Chickasaws $2,999,450. Their litigation for fair payment for most of the Leased District area, assigned to the Kiowas, Comanches, and other tribes, was not settled so readily and was a source of contention between the United States government and the Choctaws and Chickasaws well into the twentieth century.[27]

Chickasaw political leadership in the period 1866 to 1900 was for the most part competent, bold on occasion, and generally committed to serving the nation's best interests. Governor Cyrus

[26] Commissioner of Indian Affairs to Secretary of the Interior, November 1, 1875, *Report of the Commissioner of Indian Affairs for 1875*, 55–56.

[27] *Chickasaw Nation* v. *United States*, United States *Court of Claims*, XXII, 222–65; Chickasaw Claims, 50 Cong., 1 sess., *House Exec. Doc. No. 42*, 2–4; and the Leased District, 59 Cong., 1 sess., *Sen. Report No. 2516*, 31–32.

Harris (1866–70), the Chickasaws' Reconstruction governor, was succeeded by W. P. Brown (1870–71). There followed Thomas J. Parker (1871–72); Cyrus Harris (1872–74); B. F. Overton (1874–78); B. C. Burney (1878–80); B. F. Overton (1880–84); Hickeyubbee, acting governor (1881); Jonas Wolf (1884–86); William M. Guy (1886–88); William L. Byrd (1888–92); Jonas Wolf (1892–94); T. A. McClure, acting governor (1894); Palmer S. Mosley (1894–96); Robert M. Harris (1896–98); and Douglas H. Johnston (1898–1902).[28]

The Chickasaws grouped into political parties soon after Reconstruction. The two principal partisan associations were the National and Progressive parties. In the early postwar years the National party affiliation generally was based on degree of Indian blood, the full bloods supporting the National party, the mixed bloods the Progressive party. Until the 1880's both parties were committed to preserving the Chickasaw way of life and protecting tribal property, each party candidate campaigning on a pledge to surpass his opponent in accomplishing these goals. By the mid-1880's external political and economic pressures had shattered the Chickasaw Nation's internal unity. The full bloods became aroused at the pervasive changes occurring in their nation—rapid economic development dominated by outsiders, growth of the non-Indian community, and appropriation of vast tracts of the tribal domain by mixed bloods and non-citizens to form towns, farms, and ranches. The full bloods reacted by committing their National party to a program of checking railroad expansion, turning back the tide of immigration, purging their government of "white" Indian (the intermarried citizen) influence, and generally preserving the surviving old ways. The mixed bloods, perhaps tempted by the prospect of wealth and greater power and sensing the inevitability of the demise of the Chickasaw Nation, countered the National party's "pullback" program by making the Progressive party an agency for abetting the new order. Joined by intermarried whites (permitted by Chickasaw law to vote) and a few wealthy full bloods, the mixed-blood managers of the Progressive party developed a platform which advocated modernization of the Chickasaw Nation.

28 Muriel H. Wright, *A Guide to the Indian Tribes of Oklahoma*, 95.

This alignment was first tested in the election of 1886. William L. Byrd, a mixed blood dedicated to the full-blood viewpoint, was the National party's candidate for governor. William M. Guy was the Progressive party candidate. The election was so close as to be indecisive, and under Chickasaw law the legislature had to determine the victor. In the legislative canvass Guy won by a single-vote majority. Over National party protests Governor Guy completed negotiations with Santa Fe railway officials which led to the construction of that company's line through the Chickasaw Nation. The railroad issue intensified partisan feeling. Byrd again contested Guy in the 1888 election, and returns showed Guy the victor. National party leaders challenged the vote in certain pro-Guy precincts, the legislature investigated, rejected the ballots from the challenged precincts, and declared Byrd the victor. At that juncture, Sam Paul, head of the Chickasaw light horse police and a Guy supporter, marched his men on the capital and ordered the legislature to reconsider. That body retracted its verdict, Byrd and his supporters quietly departed Tishomingo, and Guy ostensibly became the accepted chief executive. But as soon as the light horse evacuated Tishomingo, the National party returned, took control of the government, and installed Byrd as governor. His was a reactionary administration which included disfranchisement of intermarried white citizens, the group he blamed for his defeat in 1886. Byrd's repressive policies provoked continuous turbulence which ended only with the demise of the Chickasaw Nation in 1906. Virulence and strife, deadly companions of each election, further weakened the nation and assured fulfillment of the federal government's divide-and-conquer strategy and the consummation of its goal to annihilate the Chickasaw Nation.[29]

[29] *Ibid.*, 93–94; An Act in Relation to United States Citizens, October 1, 1890, *Constitution and Laws of the Chickasaw Nation*, 270–71; and John B. Meserve, "Governor William Leander Byrd," *Chronicles of Oklahoma*, Vol. XII (December, 1934), 432–43.

CHAPTER THIRTEEN

DEATH OF A NATION

IN 1906 the Chickasaw Nation legally ended its existence as a semi-autonomous Indian republic, a sacrifice to national purpose. The federal government had determined to incorporate the land and people of Indian Territory into the American community, fusing the domains of the Chickasaws, Choctaws, Seminoles, Cherokees, and Creeks with Oklahoma Territory to form the emergent state of Oklahoma. Before this could be accomplished, the Indian governments had to be liquidated and the tribal estates, held in common ownership, had to be metamorphosed into the American land holding system of individual fee-simple ownership.

The federal government took a giant stride in this direction in 1893 when the Congress extended the provisions of the General Allotment Act to the Five Civilized Tribes. The statute provided for a federal commission to negotiate allotment agreements with the Chickasaws and other tribes of Indian Territory. This administrative body came to be known as the Dawes Commission, taking its name from the chairman, Senator Henry L. Dawes of Massachusetts. Meredith L. Kidd of Indiana and Archibald S. McKennon of Arkansas served with Dawes on the original commission. Following an organizational meeting in Washington on December 8, 1893, the Dawes Commission set out for Indian Territory. The commissioners met with tribal leaders at various towns, contacting Chickasaw officials at Fort Towson and Tishomingo. Dawes found the Indian spokesmen courteous but determined not to discuss the subject of allotment. In his first report to Congress Dawes stated that the "tribes largely ignored the overtures of the Commission or else refused to treat."[1]

Congressional determination to achieve a prompt solution to Indian Territory political and land problems was demonstrated by its adoption of several pertinent laws during 1895. As justification for these enactments Congress used the Dawes Commission reports and the observations of a congressional committee which investigated Indian Territory conditions during 1894. Both sources indicated official disgust and impatience with Indian leaders because of their lack of co-operation and their calculated determination not to discuss liquidation of tribal domains through allotment. Indian motives were varied. A principal consideration was the economic advantage derived from the communal land system by enterprising mixed bloods in each of the Indian nations. In the communal land system, through ancient custom and right, the mixed bloods were able to appropriate vast portions of the tribal estate for townsites, farms, and ranches. Allotment would drastically reduce the territory a mixed blood could utilize for personal profit. In the new order of allotment and private ownership, the land holdings of mixed bloods and full bloods would be equal. Dawes Commission members pointed out

> how completely the tribal governments have fallen under the control of the mixed bloods and adopted citizens and have been used by them to secure to the exclusive use and private gain of a few of their own number much of the tribal property in the land, and from other sources everything valuable and capable of producing profit. More than a third of the whole territory of one of the nations is exclusively appropriated and fenced in by barbed wire to the sole use of a few citizens for pasturage. . . . In short almost everything of tribal property in which every citizen Indian has of right an equal share has, if of any value, been appropriated to the use and gain of the few, while the real full blood has been left destitute and crowded out upon the mountains and unproductive land, to take care of himself as best he can.

The commission also lamented at the irregular status of non-Indians, especially the town dwellers, caused by the anachronistic application of curious tribal landholding customs to Indian Territory urban development. Its reports stated that Indian Territory towns were "without town government or town officers,

[1] *Report of the Commission to the Five Civilized Tribes for 1894*, 1–9.

town police, or police courts of any kind, and are unable to adopt or enforce any municipal ordinance or regulation. They cannot impose a tax for any municipal purpose." Each town was "merely a voluntary association of white residents with not only no power to govern their own organizations, but without a vote or voice in the election of the rulers, or the making of the laws under which they live." Implicit in the Dawes Commission reports was the appeal that Congress remedy the "inequities" suffered by full bloods and noncitizens by erasing certain ancient tribal customs, the sources of mixed-blood privilege, through legislation less permissive and more directive in character.[2]

An essential preliminary to allotment was the survey of Indian Territory tribal lands. In 1895, Congress appropriated $200,000 for this purpose. Eight survey parties, supervised by the director of the United States Geological Survey, Department of the Interior, began this task at once and completed the assignment in 1897. Also during 1895, Congress increased the authority of the Dawes Commission by directing it to proceed with the preparation of tribal rolls. Thus the commission had the power to designate those persons eligible for rights to land and other tribal property, Indians as well as whites and freedmen.[3]

Many tribal leaders feared that this delegation of additional authority to the Dawes Commission would lead to the wholesale enrollment of whites and Negroes. To thwart this grim prospect, they adopted a more conciliatory posture toward the Dawes Commission, indicating a willingness to discuss negotiation on allotment and other questions in return for assurances that they would have a voice in determining eligibility of those persons applying for inclusion on the tribal rolls. Choctaw officials, the first of the Five Civilized Tribes' leaders to indicate a willingness to discuss negotiation, invited the Dawes Commission to their nation. Since Chickasaw assent was required for any Choctaw agreement on land disposition, the commissioners urged Chickasaw leaders to join in the discussions. The commissioners claimed that they did in fact receive an invitation from the Chickasaw government to meet with tribal officials at Ardmore during July,

2 *Ibid.*, 1895, 55–57.
3 United States Geological Survey, *Nineteenth Annual Report*, Part I, 14–15.

1895. The commissioners were incensed that the governor and legislature "failed to appear, and only a few inter-married citizens greeted the commission." Piqued, the commissioners declared that "they will not come again to the Chickasaws, and that when the Chickasaws want anything they must hunt the commission."[4]

Despite Chickasaw intransigence, during December, 1896, the Choctaws signed an allotment agreement with the Dawes Commission which ceded the Choctaw-Chickasaw domains in trust to the United States. Federal officials were to assign allotments to Choctaw and Chickasaw citizens and administer the residue lands for the two tribes. A special Chickasaw delegation rushed to Washington to protest before Congress the Choctaws' unilateral negotiation, causing federal officials to withdraw from consideration the first allotment agreement negotiated by the Dawes Commission.[5]

This action by the Chickasaws deferred but by no means checked congressional determination to consummate national purpose in the Indian Territory. In 1897 Congress adopted a series of laws, to take effect in 1898, which severely reduced the autonomy of tribal governments and the jurisdiction of tribal courts. The most devastating enactment required that all acts of tribal legislatures be submitted for presidential approval. Between 1866 and 1897 only those tribal laws regulating freedmen and certain other matters had to be submitted for federal approval.[6]

Fearful that Congress next might require that they adopt and grant equal shares—including land—in the tribal estate to freedmen, who by 1897 nearly equaled the Indians in population, Chickasaw leaders reluctantly agreed to join Choctaw officials in negotiations with the Dawes Commission. At Atoka in the Choctaw Nation on April 23, 1897, Chickasaw and Choctaw representatives completed an allotment compact, the Atoka

---

[4] Fort Smith *Elevator*, July 31, 1896.

[5] Debo, *The Rise and Fall of the Choctaw Republic*, 258–59; and Report of the Chickasaw Commission, February 13, 1897, Chickasaw Nation Records, Oklahoma Historical Society.

[6] An Act Making Appropriations . . . and for other Purposes, March 4, 1897, *United States Statutes at Large*, XXX, 62–96.

Agreement, which provided that "all the lands within the Indian Territory belonging to the Choctaw and Chickasaw Indians shall be allotted to the members of said tribes so far as possible a fair and equal share thereof, considering the character and fertility of the soil and the location and value of the lands." Coal and asphalt lands were reserved from allotment for the benefit of the Choctaws and Chickasaws "exclusive of freedmen." The Chickasaw and Choctaw governments were to terminate on March 4, 1906, at which time Chickasaws and Choctaws were to become citizens of the United States. Freedmen and their descendants were each to receive a forty-acre allotment from the Chickasaw-Choctaw domains. All allotments were to be non-taxable as long as title remained with the original allottee, not to exceed twenty-one years.[7]

The Atoka Agreement was approved by both tribal governments, but the Chickasaws had the additional requirement of a national referendum on the question of allotment. Chickasaw voters rejected the Atoka Agreement. Thereupon Congress adopted the Curtis Act on June 28, 1898. This measure contained the Atoka Agreement and a proviso that it be resubmitted to Choctaw and Chickasaw voters. In many respects the Curtis Act closely approximated an organic act for the Indian Territory. It consolidated those laws which erased tribal autonomy and authorized the survey and platting of Indian Territory townsites and the sale of town lots. It made provision for the incorporation of towns and the creation of municipal governments including elections. Tribal trust funds were to be liquidated through per capita payments and all tribal governments were to terminate on March 4, 1906.[8]

As required by the Curtis Act, the Atoka Agreement was resubmitted to Choctaw and Chickasaw voters on August 24, 1898, and was approved by a combined majority of 798 votes. Pressure by Chickasaw and Choctaw leaders caused the Dawes Commission to allow two alterations in the Atoka Agreement. At South McAlester on September 5, 1899, an amendment was negotiated

---

[7] Atoka Agreement, April 23, 1897, in Kappler, *Laws and Treaties*, I, 646–56.
[8] An Act for the Protection of the People of the Indian Territory and for other Purposes, June 28, 1898, *United States Statutes at Large*, XXX, 495–519.

which provided that after October 31, 1899, no child born to any Chickasaw or Choctaw citizen or freedman, or a non-citizen who gained tribal citizenship by marriage, could be enrolled for allotment. The second amendment, called the Supplementary Agreement and negotiated in 1902, altered the 1899 amendment in that it provided for the enrollment of newborn Chickasaws. Freedmen claimed that this agreement applied to their offspring but the secretary of the interior ruled that Chickasaw freedmen were not a class of citizens of that nation within the meaning of the acts of Congress and that their children born after 1899 were not entitled to enrollment.[9]

The Dawes Commission staff proceeded with the preparation of tribal rolls for the Chickasaws, Choctaws, Creeks, Seminoles, and Cherokees as an essential preliminary to allotment in severalty. Having finally submitted to allotment, the Chickasaws were determined that only tribal citizens and bonafide Chickasaw freedmen would be enrolled. For this purpose Chickasaw leaders appointed a four-member commission, one from each of the Chickasaw counties, to work with the Dawes Commission staff. The Chickasaw Citizenship Commission evaluated the applications of the hordes of claimants, especially scrutinizing the credentials and claims of whites and freedmen, and challenging literally thousands of names entered on the Chickasaw rolls by the federal commissioners.[10]

Preparation of the Chickasaw freedmen roll provoked the greatest controversy between Chickasaw commissioners and Dawes Commission staff. The Chickasaws based their freedmen enrollment stand on the 1866 Reconstruction treaty which set the Chickasaw Nation's responsibility for those freedmen resident in their territory at the time of the Fort Smith Council, September, 1865. It was an established fact that the Chickasaw freedmen population at that time numbered no more than one thousand. This was confirmed by the 1866 treaty proviso by which the federal government appropriated from the Choctaws

[9] *Report of the Commission to the Five Civilized Tribes for 1899*, 9; Choctaw-Chickasaw Agreement, September 5, 1899, 56 Cong., 1 sess., *House Doc. No. 221*, 1–4; and *Report of the Commissioner to the Five Civilized Tribes for 1907*, 6.

[10] Report of the Chickasaw Citizenship Commission for 1899, Chickasaw Nation Records, Oklahoma Historical Society.

and Chickasaws their Leased District and paid them $300,000 for it, but held the sum in trust to be used to pay the expense of removing freedmen from the Choctaw and Chickasaw nations at a cost of $100 a Negro. Chickasaw commissioners claimed that federal officials, by setting the Leased District payment at $300,000, had acknowledged the total Choctaw and Chickasaw freedmen population at three thousand. Since the Chickasaw freedmen allocation was to be about $100,000, the Chickasaw commissioners held that this confirmed their freedmen population of one thousand and, plus natural increase, was the number entitled to enrollment. They pointed out that the federal government had not fulfilled its commitment to remove the freedmen and that the number of Negroes in the Chickasaw Nation, most of them immigrants, had drastically increased to the point that they outnumbered the Indians, making the Chickasaw Nation commonly referred to as "this African stronghold."[11]

In spite of vigilance and protest by the Chickasaw Citizenship Commission, the Dawes Commission staff peremptorily enrolled thousands of challenged freedmen and whites. The Choctaws were suffering a similar fate and, to protect tribal interests, Chickasaw and Choctaw leaders engaged the law firm of Mansfield, McMurry and Cornish to investigate the background of persons claiming enrollment rights. The Mansfield, McMurry and Cornish scrutiny confirmed convictions of tribal officials that the Dawes Commission staff had been unduly generous in its judgments on enrollment applications. Chickasaw and Choctaw officials appealed to Congress, and that body in 1902 created the Choctaw-Chickasaw Citizenship Court, a three-member federal tribunal, to render decisions on enrollment claims. Of 3,679 applications contested by Indian officials, the court allowed only 156 to be added to the Chickasaw and Choctaw rolls. Out of a total of 66,217 claimants, including freedmen, the Dawes Commission was permitted to enroll 35,638 to share in the combined Choctaw-Chickasaw domain, consisting of 11,660,952 acres, the Chickasaw portion embracing 4,707,904 acres. The Chickasaw rolls, completed on January 1, 1906, contained the names of 6,319 citizens—1,538 full bloods, 4,146 mixed bloods, and 635 inter-

11 Chickasaw Freedmen, 52 Cong., 1 sess., *Sen. Misc. Doc. No. 82*, 2.

married whites. The Chickasaw freedmen roll contained the names of 4,670 Negroes.[12]

The general survey of Indian Territory had been completed before 1900. Refinements of the general survey included platting of townsites which began on May 23, 1899. Each townsite was surveyed, platted, and appraised. Colbert, the first Chickasaw Nation town to be surveyed and platted, contained 129.74 acres and the appraised value of all lots was $5,175.75. Ardmore was the second Chickasaw Nation town to be surveyed, platted, and appraised. Proceeds from the sale of lots in each town were collected by federal officials and held in trust by the United States to be paid later to the Chickasaws on a per capita basis. While survey crews platted the Chickasaw Nation towns, appraisal teams evaluated the rural land to be allotted. Each forty-acre tract was examined and graded. Their classification of land showed a variance of from $6.50 an acre for natural open bottom land, cleared bottom land, and the best prairie land to twenty-five cents an acre for mountain land. The average value was $3.25 an acre which was used as a basis for assigning allotments, the amount of land allotted to each enrollee based on value an acre rather than total acreage. The average Chickasaw and Choctaw allotment contained 320 acres which included a 160-acre homestead. Each Negro on the Chickasaw and Choctaw freedman rolls received an allotment averaging 40 acres. This land division in the Chickasaw and Choctaw nations compared to the Seminole Nation where the allotment averaged 120 acres with a forty-acre homestead, the Seminole freedmen sharing equally with the Indians in size of allotment; the Creek Nation where the allotment averaged 160 acres with a forty-acre homestead, the Creek freedmen sharing equally with the Indians in size of allotment; and the Cherokee Nation where the allotment averaged 110 acres with a forty-acre homestead, and the Cherokee freedmen also sharing equally with the Indians in size of allotment.[13]

In the liquidation of the Chickasaw and Choctaw tribal estates,

[12] Chickasaw Freedmen, 60 Cong., 1 sess., *House Exec. Doc. No. 372*; Chickasaw Freedmen, 59 Cong., 1 sess., *House Doc. No. 20*, 385; and *Report of the Commissioner to the Five Civilized Tribes for 1909*, 7.

[13] "Notes and Document," *Chronicles of Oklahoma*, Vol. XXIV (Autumn, 1946), 360–62; and *Report of the Superintendent to the Five Civilized Tribes for 1915*, 9.

coal, asphalt, and timber lands were reserved from allotment as the common property of the two tribes. Several special tracts were reserved or sold for certain public purposes. In the Chickasaw Nation these included reservations of one acre each for twenty-three schools, one acre each for twenty-eight churches, and for thirty-three cemeteries tracts of from five to twenty acres each. One 640-acre tract near Sulphur, containing several mineral springs, was ceded to the United States for twenty dollars an acre and became Platt National Park.[14]

The Dawes Commission opened allotment offices at Atoka and Tishomingo on April 15, 1903, and began the assignment of land. By 1910 all but fifteen Chickasaw citizens and freedmen had received allotments. Chickasaw and Choctaw citizens and freedmen were permitted to select allotments in either the Choctaw or the Chickasaw nations. Federal officials supervised the sale of surplus Choctaw and Chickasaw lands, those not required for allotment purposes. As of 1912, 834,000 acres of this class of land had been sold for $5,655,501. The United States deducted the cost of advertising and other sale expenses, amounting to $32,771, and placed the balance in the joint Choctaw-Chickasaw account for per capita distribution.[15]

The governments of the Five Civilized Tribes were not to terminate until 1906, but the Curtis Act appropriated those few surviving prerogatives of tribal autonomy with the result that after 1898 the Chickasaw government was an empty shell. Every substantive function of tribal government passed from Indian to federal control. The Chickasaw constitution and laws no longer were operative, and tribal citizens were subject to administrative decrees and to the laws of Congress. Tribal officials, emasculated of their constitutional functions, had to stand idly by as federal agents collected tribal revenues, disbursed tribal funds, and moved cases from defunct tribal courts to federal courts. Even the Chickasaw Nation school system passed to federal control. United States agents set curricula and qualifications for teachers, directed the construction of new schools to accommodate the white and Negro children, and appointed teachers.

14 *Ibid.*, *1910*, 9.
15 *Ibid.*; and *Ibid.*, *1912*.

Until 1906, Chickasaw citizens went through the empty gesture of electing officials to staff the tribal government. Stripped of authority, the governor and other officials provided only moral leadership for the Chickasaws in this confused period of transition to the new order. They interceded for Indian citizens caught up in the transfer of cases from tribal to federal courts and watched the Dawes Commission staff assign allotments to insure that each Indian received his fair share of the tribal domain. And they joined Choctaw, Creek, Seminole, and Cherokee leaders to protest attempts by Congress to fuse Indian Territory and Oklahoma Territory to form the proposed state of Oklahoma. Chickasaw leaders were active in the unsuccessful separate statehood attempt for Indian Territory known as the Sequoyah Movement and authored a stream of resolutions to Congress which opposed "being included in Oklahoma or any state or territory except that now occupied by the Five Civilized Tribes."[16]

On November 16, 1907, Oklahoma, a fusion of Indian Territory and Oklahoma Territory, was admitted to the American Union as the forty-sixth state. Most citizens of the new state rejoiced and observed the event with enthusiastic celebration. But there was no joy among the Chickasaws—only grimness and melancholy—for this was the wake time of their nation. The Chickasaw Nation's death had been prolonged and painful. It had died a bit at a time. The ancient Chickasaw lifeways—the cement of their society—had provided identity, direction, and meaning for individual and group life and satisfying explanations for the mysteries of their natural universe. New ways and things, insinuated into Chickasaw society by the Europeans and Americans, had been displacing these lifeways for centuries. Tribal economics, religion, and societal structure were early casualties. That the genesis of ethnic erasure, detected by James Adair in the early eighteenth century, had been completed by the twentieth century was confirmed by John R. Swanton who lamented that "the ancient social organization" of the Chickasaws "is now so completely discarded" that "practically all the younger people know nothing about it,

---

[16] Chickasaw Resolution to Congress, October 17, 1905, Chickasaw Nation Records, Oklahoma Historical Society.

and even the older ones can furnish only fragmentary information on the subject."[17]

The two tenaciously surviving elements of Chickasaw culture which provided some integrating influence and certainly extended the Chickasaw Nation's longevity were tribal government, modified after removal, and the communal land system. By 1906 both had been extinguished. Adair's "beloved warriors" had been submerged into the common state and national community, occasionally thrusting forth into its arts, crafts, professions, and politics. Twentieth-century Chickasaws have come to occupy a dichotomous status in the new order—citizens of their state and nation, subject to state and federal law—but occasionally convened as Chickasaws by a federally appointed Chickasaw governor to share in per capita payments and discuss surviving tribal business growing out of treaties and litigation on land questions, to preserve some trace of the Chickasaw Nation through the tribal council and Chickasaw Tribal Protective Association, and perhaps nostalgically to contemplate their pristine origin and to search for the means to recover the devastating warrior power and primitive solace that only Ababinili can provide.

[17] Swanton, "Social and Religious Beliefs and Usages of the Chickasaw Indians," B.A.E. *44 Ann. Rept.*, 190.

SOURCES

I. Manuscripts

National Archives (Washington, D.C.)
Documents Relating to the Negotiation of Ratified and Unratified Treaties with the Various Tribes of Indians, 1801–69. Microcopy T–494
Letterbook of the Arkansas Trading House. Microcopy 142
Letters Received, Office of the Secretary of War, Indian Affairs, 1800–24. Microcopy 271
Letters Received, Office of Indian Affairs, 1824–81, Chickasaw Agency. Microcopy 234
Letters Received, Office of Indian Affairs, 1824–71, Southern Superintendency, 1857–71. Microcopy 234
Letters Sent, Secretary of War, Indian Affairs, 1800–24. Microcopy 15
Gilcrease Museum
Foreman Collection
Pitchlynn Collection
Miscellaneous Chickasaw Letters Collection
Mississippi State Archives
Governors' Records, Series A, III
Mississippi Provincial Archives, English Dominion
Mississippi Provincial Archives, French Dominion
Oklahoma Historical Society
Chickasaw Nation Records
Foreman Collection
Tennessee State Archives
Claybrooke Collection, Overton Papers
Coffee Collection

Miscellaneous Collections
Robertson Collection
Western History Collections, University of Oklahoma Library
Byrd Collection
Chickasaw Nation Collection
Documents Relating to the Five Civilized Tribes
Draper Collection
Frontier Wars Manuscripts (typescripts)
George R. Clark Manuscripts (typescripts)
Tecumseh Manuscripts (typescripts)
Guy Collection
Harris Collection
Johnston Collection
Moseley Collection
Overton Collection
Wolf Collection

II. GOVERNMENT DOCUMENTS AND PUBLICATIONS

American State Papers: Foreign Relations. Vol. I. Washington, 1832.
American State Papers: Indian Affairs. Vols. I and II. Washington, 1832–34.
Carter, Clarence E., comp. and ed. *Territorial Papers of the United States.* Washington, 1936–54.
The Territory of Alabama, 1817–1819. Vol. XVIII. 1952.
The Territory of Arkansas, 1819–1836. Vols. XIX, XX, and XXI. 1953–54.
The Territory of Louisiana-Missouri, 1803–1821. Vols. XIII, XIV, and XV. 1948–51.
The Territory of Mississippi, 1798–1817. Vols. V and VI. 1938.
The Territory of Orleans, 1803–1812. Vol. IX. 1940.
The Territory South of the Ohio River, 1790–1796. Vol. IV. 1936.
Correspondence on the Subject of Indians. Vol. II. Washington, 1835.
Final Report of the United States De Soto Expedition Commission, 76 Cong., 1 sess., *House Doc. No. 71,* 1939.
Journal of the Senate of the State of Mississippi. 13 sess. Jackson, 1830.
Kappler, Charles J., comp. and ed. *Indian Affairs: Laws and Treaties.* 3 vols. Washington, 1904.
Laws of the State of Alabama (1829–31).

Laws of the State of Mississippi (1817–30).

Report of the Commission to the Five Civilized Tribes, 1894–1905. Washington, 1894–1905.

Report of the Commissioner of Indian Affairs, 1836–1906. Washington, 1836–1906.

Report of the Commissioner to the Five Civilized Tribes, 1906–1918. Washington, 1906–18.

Report of the Superintendent for the Five Civilized Tribes, 1915–1920. Washington, 1915–20.

Report of the United States Indian Inspector for the Indian Territory, 1899–1907. Washington, 1899–1907.

Twelfth Census of the United States, Population, 1900. Vol. I, Pt. I. Washington, 1901.

United States Congress
27 Cong., 2 sess., *House Report No. 271.*
41 Cong., 2 sess., *Senate Doc. No. 36.*
45 Cong., 2 sess., *Senate Misc. Doc. No. 82; Senate Report No. 698.*
45 Cong., 3 sess., *Senate Report No. 744.*
46 Cong., 1 sess., *House Misc. Doc. No. 13; Senate Exec. Doc. No. 20.*
46 Cong., 2 sess., *House Report No. 755; Senate Misc. Doc. No. 41.*
50 Cong., 1 sess., *House Exec. Doc. No. 42.*
52 Cong., 1 sess., *Senate Misc. Doc. No. 82.*
53 Cong., 2 sess., *Senate Report No. 377.*
53 Cong., 3 sess., *Senate Misc. Doc. No. 24.*
54 Cong., 1 sess., *Senate Doc. No. 12; Senate Doc. No. 176; Senate Doc. No. 309.*
55 Cong., 1 sess., *Senate Doc. No. 157.*
55 Cong., 3 sess., *House Exec. Doc. No. 5.*
56 Cong., 1 sess., *House Doc. No. 221.*
59 Cong., 1 sess., *House Doc. No. 20; Senate Report No. 2516.*
60 Cong., 1 sess., *House Exec. Doc. No. 372.*

United States Court of Claims. *Chickasaw Nation v. United States.* XXII, 222–65.

United States Geological Survey. *Nineteenth Annual Report, 1897–98.* Pt. I. Washington, 1898.

United States Statutes at Large, I, III, IV, XVI, XXX.

War of Rebellion: A Compilation of the Official Records of the Union and Confederate Armies. Series I, Vols. III, XXXIV, XLVIII, LIII, Series IV, Vol. I. Washington, 1880–1900.

III. SPECIAL SOURCES

Constitution and Laws of the Chickasaw Nation. Parsons, Kansas, 1899.

Message of Honorable D. H. Johnston, Governor of the Chickasaw Nation, to the National Legislature at Tishomingo, Indian Territory, September 8, 1904. Tishomingo, 1904.

National Research Council, Division of Anthropology and Psychology. *Conference on Southern Prehistory.* Washington, 1932.

Public Dinner in honor of Chickasaw and Choctaw Treaties at Mr. Parker's Hotel in the city of Natchez, on the 10th Day of October, 1830. Natchez, 1830 (Pamphlet in Pitchlynn Collection, Gilcrease Museum Library).

WPA Historical Research Project. Source Material for Mississippi History: Pontotoc County. (1936–38), Vol. LVIII, Part I (Unpublished Manuscript).

Wright, Muriel H. Interview. Oklahoma City, Oklahoma, July 18, 1968.

IV. NEWSPAPERS AND PERIODICALS

Baptist Missionary Magazine, XXVI (1846).
Fort Smith *Elevator* (1896).
Fort Smith *Herald* (1851).
Latter Day Luminary (1818).
Little Rock *Arkansas Gazette* (1828–61).
Missionary Herald (1828–41).
Natchez *Courier* (1833).
Niles Register (1816–30).
Pontotoc *Chickasaw Union* (1837).
St. Louis *Commercial Bulletin* (1837).
Tishomingo *News* (1904).
Vandalia *Intelligencer* (1825).

V. THESES AND DISSERTATIONS

Brown, Loren N. "The Work of the Dawes Commission Among the Choctaw and Chickasaw Indians." Unpublished Ph.D. Dissertation, University of Oklahoma, 1937.

Buck, Carl R. "Economic Development of the Chickasaw Indians, 1865–1907." Unpublished M.A. Thesis, Oklahoma State University, 1940.

Davis, Caroline. "The History of the Schools and Educational Development in the Chickasaw Nation." Unpublished M.A. Thesis, University of Oklahoma, 1937.

Denison, Velma. "A Brief History of the Chickasaws in Oklahoma." Unpublished M.A. Thesis, George Peabody College, 1932.

Drain, Myrtle. "A History of the Education of the Choctaw and Chickasaw Indians." Unpublished M.A. Thesis, University of Oklahoma, 1928.

Draughon, Byrd L. "Christian Missions Among the Chickasaws." Unpublished M.A. Thesis, University of Oklahoma, 1946.

Jones, Onis G. "Chickasaw Governors and Their Administrations, 1856–1893." Unpublished M.A. Thesis, University of Oklahoma, 1935.

Moffitt, James W. "A History of Early Baptist Missions Among the Five Civilized Tribes." Unpublished Ph.D. Dissertation, University of Oklahoma, 1946.

O'Callaghan, Mary A. M. "The Indian Policy of Carondelet in Spanish Louisiana, 1792–1797." Unpublished Ph.D. Dissertation, University of California, 1941.

Spalding, Arminta Scott. "The Natchez Trace Parkway: A Study of Origins of an Interstate Federal Highway." Unpublished M.A. Thesis, Stephen F. Austin College, 1965.

Stewart, LeRoy E. "A History of the Chickasaws, 1830–1855." Unpublished M.A. Thesis, University of Oklahoma, 1938.

Ursula, Sister Mary. "The Catholic Church on the Oklahoma Frontier, 1824–1907." Unpublished Ph.D. Dissertation, St. Louis University, 1938.

Yarborough, James M. "The Transition of the Chickasaw Indians from an Organized Nation to a Part of a State." Unpublished M.A. Thesis, Oklahoma State University, 1936.

VI. Books

Abel, Annie H. *The American Indian as Slaveholder and Secessionist.* Cleveland, 1915.

———. *The American Indian as a Participant in the Civil War.* Cleveland, 1919.

————. *The American Indian Under Reconstruction*. Cleveland, 1925.

Adair, James. *The History of the American Indians*. Ed. with an introduction by Samuel C. Williams. Johnson City, Tennessee, 1930.

Alden, John R. *John Stuart and the Southern Colonial Frontier*. Ann Arbor, 1944.

Alvord, Clarence W., ed. *Kaskaskia Records, 1778–1790, Virginia Series, Collections of the Illinois State Historical Library*. Springfield, 1909.

————. *The Illinois Country, 1763–1818*. Chicago, 1922.

————, and Clarence E. Carter, eds. *The New Regime, 1765–1767, British Series, Collections of the Illinois State Historical Library*. Springfield, 1916.

Babcock, S. H., and J. Y. Bryce. *History of Methodism*. Oklahoma City, 1935.

Bartram, William. *Travels Through North and South Carolina, Georgia, East and West Florida, the Cherokee Country, the Extensive Territory of the Muscolgulges or Creek Confederacy and the Country of the Choctaws*. Philadelphia, 1791.

Bassett, John S. *Correspondence of Andrew Jackson*. Washington, 1927. Vols. I–VI.

Bearss, Ed, and Arrell M. Gibson. *Fort Smith: Little Gibraltar on the Arkansas*. Norman, 1969.

Benson, Henry C. *Life Among the Choctaw Indians*. Cincinnati, 1860.

Bossu, Jean-Bernard. *Travels in the Interior of North America, 1751–1762*. Trans. and ed. by Seymour Feiler. Norman, 1962.

Bourne, Edward G., ed. *Narratives of the Career of Hernando de Soto*. New York, 1922. Vols. I and II.

Caldwell, Norman W. *The French in the Mississippi Valley, 1740–1750*. Urbana, 1941.

Capers, Gerald M. *The Biography of a River Town: Memphis: Its Heroic Age*. Chapel Hill, 1939.

Caughey, John W. *Bernardo de Galvez in Louisiana, 1776–1783*. Berkeley, 1934.

————. *McGillivray of the Creeks*. Norman, 1938.

Chambers, Henry E. *Mississippi Valley Beginnings*. New York, 1922.

Charlevoix, P. F. X. de. *History and General Description of New France*. Trans. with notes by John G. Shea. Chicago, 1962. Vols. I–VI.

Claiborne, J. F. H. *Mississippi as a Province, Territory and State*. Jackson, Mississippi, 1880.

Clark, George Rogers. *George Rogers Clark Papers, 1781–1784*. Ed.

by James A. James. *Virginia Series, Collections of the Illinois State Historical Library.* Springfield, 1926.

Collot, Victor A. *Journey in North America.* Paris, 1836. Vols. I and II.

Conkling, Roscoe P., and Margaret B. *The Butterfield Overland Mail, 1857–1869.* Glendale, 1947. Vols. I–III.

Corry, John P. *Indian Affairs in Georgia, 1732–1756.* Philadelphia, 1936.

Cotterill, Robert S. *The Southern Indians: The Story of the Civilized Tribes Before Removal.* Norman, 1954.

Crane, Verner W. *The Southern Frontier, 1670–1732.* Philadelphia, 1929.

Creager, Charles E. *Father Murrow and His Ninety Busy Years.* Muskogee, Oklahoma, n.d.

Cushman, H. B. *History of the Choctaw, Chickasaw, and Natchez Indians.* Greenville, Texas, 1899.

Debo, Angie. *The Rise and Fall of the Choctaw Republic.* Norman, 1934.

Dixon, William H. *White Conquest.* London, 1876. Vols. I and II.

Du Pratz, Le Page. *The History of Louisiana.* London, 1763. Vols. I and II.

Fant, Mabel B. and John C. *History of Mississippi.* Oxford, Mississippi, 1920.

Fletcher, Alice C. *Indian Education and Civilization.* Washington, 1888.

Foreman, Grant. *The Five Civilized Tribes.* Norman, 1934.

———. *A History of Oklahoma.* Norman, 1942.

———. *Indian Removal.* Norman, 1932.

———. *Indians and Pioneers: The Story of the American Southwest Before 1830.* New Haven, 1930.

———. *Marcy and the Gold Seekers: The Journal of Captain R. B. Marcy, with an Account of the Gold Rush over the Southern Route.* Norman, 1939.

———. *Pioneer Days in the Early Southwest.* Cleveland, 1926.

French, Benjamin, ed. *Historical Collections of Louisiana.* New York, 1846. Vols. I–III.

———. *Historical Collections of Louisiana and Florida.* New York, 1875.

Gayarre, Charles. *History of Louisiana.* New Orleans, 1903. Vols. I–IV.

Gibson, Arrell M. *Oklahoma: A History of Five Centuries.* Norman, 1965.

Gideon, D. C. *History of Indian Territory.* New York, 1901.

Glisan, R. *A Journal of Army Life*. San Francisco, 1874.

Goode, W. H. *Outpost of Zion*. Cincinnati, 1863.

Greenleaf, Mary C. *Life and Letters of . . . a Missionary to the Chickasaw Indians*. Boston, 1858.

Gregg, Josiah. *Commerce of the Prairies*. Ed. by Max L. Moorhead. Norman, 1954.

Gross, Alexander. *History of the Methodist Episcopal Church, South*. New York, 1894.

Hamilton, Peter J. *Colonial Mobile*. Boston, 1897.

Hastain, E., comp. *Index to Choctaw-Chickasaw Deeds and Allotments*. Muskogee, 1908.

Hawkins, Benjamin. *Letters of Benjamin Hawkins, 1796–1806, Collections of the Georgia Historical Society*, IX. Savannah, 1916.

Henderson, Archibald. *The Conquest of the Old Southwest*. New York, 1920.

Hewatt, Alexander. *An Historical Account of the Rise and Progress of the Colonies of South Carolina and Georgia*. London, 1799. Vols. I and II.

Hill, Luther B. *A History of the State of Oklahoma*. Chicago, 1910.

Hitchcock, Ethan A. *A Traveler in Indian Territory: The Journal of Ethan Allen Hitchcock*. Ed. by Grant Foreman. Cedar Rapids, 1930.

––––. *Fifty Years in Camp and Field: A Diary of Major Ethan Allen Hitchcock*. Ed. by W. A. Croffut. New York, 1909.

Hodge, Frederick W., and Theodore H. Lewis, eds. *Spanish Explorers in the Southern United States*. New York, 1907.

Hodgson, Adam. *Letters from North America*. London, 1824. Vols. I and II.

Holmes, Jack D. L. *Gayoso: The Life of a Spanish Governor in the Mississippi Valley, 1789–1799*. Baton Rouge, 1965.

Houck, Louis. *The Spanish Regime in Missouri*. Chicago, 1909. Vols. I and II.

Howe, George. *History of the Presbyterian Church in South Carolina*. Charleston, 1870. Vols. I and II.

Hulbert, A. B. *The Paths of Inland Commerce*. New Haven, 1921.

Hulbert, H. S., and T. H. Ball. *The Creek War of 1813 and 1814*. Chicago, 1895.

Jacobs, Wilbur R. *Diplomacy and Indian Gifts*. Stanford, 1950.

––––., ed. *Indians of the Southern Colonial Frontier*. Columbia, South Carolina, 1945.

Jefferson, Thomas. *The Writings of Thomas Jefferson*. Ed. by Andrew A. Lipscomb. Washington, 1905. Vol. XVII.

———. *The Writings of Thomas Jefferson*. Ed. by H. A. Washington. Philadelphia, 1869–71.

Jennings, Marietta. *A Pioneer Merchant of St. Louis, 1810–1820*. New York, 1939.

Jewell, Horace. *History of Methodism in Arkansas*. Little Rock, 1892.

Johnson, Neil R. *The Chickasaw Rancher*. Ed. with an introduction by Arrell M. Gibson. Stillwater, 1961.

Johnson, Roy M. *Oklahoma History South of the Canadian*. Chicago, 1925. Vols. I–III.

Jones, Charles C. *Antiquities of the Southern Indians*. New York, 1873.

———. *History of Savannah, Georgia, from Its Settlement to the Close of the Eighteenth Century*. Syracuse, 1890.

———. *The History of Georgia*. Boston, 1883. Vol. I.

King, Grace E. *Jean Baptiste Le Moyne, Sieur de Bienville*. New York, 1893.

Kinnaird, Lawrence, ed. *Spain in the Mississippi Valley, 1765–1794. Annual Report for the American Historical Association for 1945*. Washington, 1949. Vols. I–III.

Lauber, Almon W. *Indian Slavery in Colonial Times Within the Present Limits of the United States*. New York, 1913.

Leftwich, Nina. *Two Hundred Years at Muscle Shoals*. Tuscumbia, Alabama, 1935.

Lowry, R., and W. H. McCardle. *A History of Mississippi*. Jackson, Mississippi, 1891.

Lowry, Woodbury. *The Spanish Settlement Within the Present Limits of the United States*. New York, 1911. Vols. I and II.

McCoy, Isaac. *Annual Register of Indian Affairs Within the Indian Territory*. Washington, 1838.

———. *History of Baptist Indian Missions*. Washington, 1840.

McCrady, Edward. *History of South Carolina Under the Royal Government, 1719–1776*. New York, 1901.

McDowell, W. L., ed. *Documents Relating to Indian Affairs*. Columbia, South Carolina, 1955.

———, ed. *Journals of the Commissioners of the Indian Trade*. Columbia, South Carolina, 1955.

McGee, G. B. *A History of Tennessee from 1663–1900*. New York, 1899.

McKenney, Thomas L. *Memoirs, Official and Personal*. New York, 1846.

———, and James Hall. *The Indian Tribes of North America*. Edinburgh, 1933. Vols. I–III.

Malone, James H. *The Chickasaw Nation*. Evanston, Illinois, 1922.

Margry, Pierre, ed. *Decouvertes et Etablissements des Francais, 1614–1754*. Paris, 1880. Vol. IV.

Maynard, Theodore. *De Soto and the Conquistadores*. New York, 1930.

Meserve, Charles F. *The Dawes Commission and the Five Civilized Tribes*. Philadelphia, 1896.

Mohr, Walter H. *Federal Indian Relations, 1774–1778*. Philadelphia, 1933.

Monette, John W. *History of the Discovery and Settlement of the Valley of the Mississippi*. New York, 1846. Vols. I and II.

Moore, H. H. *The Political Condition of the Indians and the Resources of the Indian Territory*. St. Louis, 1874.

Morrison, William B. *Military Posts and Camps in Oklahoma*. Oklahoma City, 1936.

Morse, Jedidiah. *A Report to the Secretary of War . . . on Indian Affairs*. New Haven, 1822.

Moseley, J. W., ed. *A Record of Missionary Meetings Held in the Chahta and Chikesha Nations and the Records of Tombigbee Presbytery from 1825 to 1838*. n.p., n.d.

Nasatir, Abraham P., ed. *Before Lewis and Clark*. St. Louis, 1952.

———. *Spanish War Vessels on the Mississippi, 1792–1796*. New Haven, 1968.

Nuttall, Thomas. *Journal of Travels into the Arkansas Territory During the Year 1819*. In *Early Western Travels (q.v.)*, Vol. XIII.

O'Beirne, Harry F., comp. *Leaders and Leading Men of the Indian Territory*. Chicago, 1891.

Ogg, Frederick A. *Opening of the Mississippi*. New York, 1904.

Ormsby, Waterman L. *The Butterfield Overland Mail*. Ed. by H. Wright and Josephine M. Bynum. San Marino, 1955.

Parkman, Francis. *La Salle and the Discovery of the Great West*. Boston, 1897. Vols. I and II.

———. *Pioneers of France in North America*. Boston, 1910.

Pease, Theodore Calvin, ed. *Illinois on the Eve of the Seven Years' War, 1747–1755*. Springfield, 1940.

Pickett, Albert J. *History of Alabama*. Charleston, 1851. Vc¹ and II.

Pound, Merritt B. *Benjamin Hawkins—Indian Agent*. Athe. , Georgia, 1951.

Rister, Carl C. *Baptist Missions Among the American Indians*. Atlanta, 1944.

Romans, Bernard. *A Concise Natural History of East and West Florida*. New York, 1775.

Rowland, Dunbar. *History of Mississippi*. Chicago, 1925. Vols. I and II.

———, ed. *Official Letterbooks of W. C. C. Claiborne, 1801–1816*. Madison, 1916. Vols. I and VI.

———, ed. *Mississippi Provincial Archives, English Dominion*. Nashville, 1911.

———, and Albert G. Sanders, eds. *Mississippi Provincial Archives, French Dominion*. Jackson, Mississippi, 1927–29. Vols. I–III.

Rowland, Eron. *Life, Letters and Papers of William Dunbar*. Jackson, Mississippi, 1930.

Royce, Charles C. *Indian Land Cessions in the United States*. Bureau of American Ethnology, *Eighteenth Annual Report*. Washington, 1899.

Schoolcraft, Henry R. *Historical and Statistical Information Respecting the History, Condition and Prospects of the Indian Tribes of the United States*. Philadelphia, 1851. Pt. I.

Serrano y Sanz, Manuel. *España y Los Indios Cherokis y Choctas en la Segunda Mitad del Siglo XVIII*. Sevilla, 1916.

Shaw, Helen L. *British Administration of the Southern Indians, 1756–1783*. Lancaster, Pennsylvania, 1931.

Shea, John G. *Discovery and Exploration of the Mississippi Valley*. Albany, 1903.

———. *History of the Catholic Missions Among the Indian Tribes of the United States, 1529–1854*. New York, 1854.

Skinner, Constance L. *Pioneers of the Old Southwest*. New Haven, 1919.

Stuart, James. *Three Years in North America*. Edinburgh, 1833. Vols. I and II.

Swanton, John R. *Early History of the Creek Indians and Their Neighbors*. Bureau of American Ethnology *Bulletin 73*. Washington, 1922.

———. *Indian Tribes of the Lower Mississippi Valley and Adjacent Coast of the Gulf of Mexico*. Bureau of American Ethnology *Bulletin 43*. Washington, 1911.

———. *Myths and Tales of the Southeastern Indians*. Bureau of American Ethnology *Bulletin 88*. Washington, 1929.

———. *The Indian Tribes of North America*. Bureau of American Ethnology *Bulletin 145*. Washington, 1952.

————. *The Indians of the Southeastern United States,* Bureau of American Ethnology *Bulletin 137.* Washington, 1946.

Thoburn, Joseph B., and Muriel H. Wright. *Oklahoma: A History of the State and Its People.* New York, 1929. Vols. I and II.

Thurston, G. P. *Antiquities of Tennessee.* Cincinnati, 1897.

Thwaites, Reuben Gold, ed. *Early Western Travels, 1748–1846* . . . . 32 vols. Cleveland, 1904–1907.

————., ed. *The Jesuit Relations and Allied Documents.* 73 vols. Cleveland, 1896–1901.

Tracy, Joseph. *History of the American Board of Commissioners for Foreign Missions.* Worcester, 1840.

Tuttle, Sarah. *Letters on the Chickasaw and Osage Missions.* Boston, 1831.

Walker, C. B. *The Mississippi Valley.* Burlington, Iowa, 1880.

Wallace, Joseph. *The History of Illinois and Louisiana Under the French Rule.* Cincinnati, 1893.

Weer, Paul. *Preliminary Notes on the Muskhogean Family.* Indianapolis, 1939.

Whitaker, Arthur P. *The Spanish-American Frontier, 1783–1795.* Boston, 1927.

Williams, Samuel C. *Beginnings of West Tennessee.* Johnson City, Tennessee, 1930.

————. *Early Travels in Tennessee Country.* Johnson City, Tennessee, 1928.

————. *History of the Lost State of Franklin.* New York, 1933.

Winfrey, Dorman H., ed. *The Indian Papers of Texas and the Southwest, 1825–1916.* Austin, 1966. I–V.

————. *Texas Indian Papers, 1825–1843.* Austin, 1959. Vols. I–III.

Winston, E. T. *Father Stuart and the Monroe Mission.* Meridian, Mississippi, 1827.

————. *Story of Pontotoc.* Pontotoc, Mississippi, 1931.

Wright, Muriel H. *A Guide to the Indian Tribes of Oklahoma.* Norman, 1951.

Wyeth, Walter N. *Isaac McCoy: Early Indian Missions, a Memorial.* Philadelphia, n.d.

Young, Mary E. *Redskins, Ruffleshirts, and Rednecks: Indian Allotments in Alabama and Mississippi, 1830–1860.* Norman, 1961.

VII. ARTICLES

Abel, Annie H. "The History of Events Resulting in Indian Consolidation West of the Mississippi," *Annual Report of the American Historical Association for 1906.* Washington, 1908.

Ashcraft, Allan C. "Confederate Indian Department Conditions in August, 1864," *Chronicles of Oklahoma*, Vol. XLI (Autumn, 1963), 270–85.

———. "Confederate Indian Territory Conditions in 1865," *Chronicles of Oklahoma*, Vol. XLII (Winter, 1964–65), 421–28.

———. "Confederate Indian Troop Conditions in 1864," *Chronicles of Oklahoma*, Vol. XLI (Winter, 1963–64), 442–49.

Balyeat, Frank A. "Early Chickasaw Schools," *Chronicles of Oklahoma*, Vol. XXXIV (Winter, 1956–57), 487–90.

Barry, Louise, ed. "With the First U.S. Cavalry in the Indian Country, 1859–1861," *Kansas Historical Quarterly*, Vol. XXIV (Autumn, 1958), 257–84.

"Bloomfield Academy and Its Founder," *Chronicles of Oklahoma*, Vol. II (December, 1924), 366–79.

Bond, Janet. "The Aboriginal Chickasaw Nation," *Chronicles of Oklahoma*, Vol. XV (December, 1937), 392–414.

Braden, Guy B. "The Colberts and the Chickasaw Nation," *Tennessee Historical Quarterly*, Vol. XVII (September, 1958), 222–49; (December, 1958), 318–35.

Brown, Loren N. "The Appraisal of the Lands of the Choctaws and Chickasaws by the Dawes Commission," *Chronicles of Oklahoma*, Vol. XXII (Summer, 1944), 177–91.

———. "The Choctaw-Chickasaw Court Citizens," *Chronicles of Oklahoma*, Vol. XVI (December, 1938), 425–43.

———. "The Dawes Commission," *Chronicles of Oklahoma*, Vol. IX (March, 1931), 71–105.

———. "The Establishment of the Dawes Commission for Indian Territory," *Chronicles of Oklahoma*, Vol. XVIII (June, 1940), 171–81.

Bryce, J. Y. "Beginnings of Methodism in Indian Territory," *Chronicles of Oklahoma*, Vol. VII (December, 1929), 475–86.

———. "Some Historical Items of Interest, Chickasaw Academy," *Chronicles of Oklahoma*, Vol. VII (December, 1929), 475–86.

———. "Some Notes of Interest Concerning Early Day Operations in Indian Territory by Methodist Episcopal Church South," *Chronicles of Oklahoma*, Vol. IV (September, 1926), 233–41.

Bullen, Rev. Joseph. "Excerpts from the Journal of Reverend Joseph Bullen, 1799 and 1800," ed. by Dawson A. Phelps, *Journal of Mississippi History*, Vol. XVII (October, 1955), 254–81.

Burris, George W. "Reminiscences of Old Stonewall," *Chronicles of Oklahoma*, Vol. XX (June, 1942), 152–58.

Caldwell, Norman W. "Chickasaw Threat to French Control of the Mississippi in the 1740's," *Chronicles of Oklahoma*, Vol. XVI (December, 1938), 465–92.

Campbell, T. N. "Medicine Plants Used by Choctaw, Chickasaw and Creek Indians in the Early Nineteenth Century," *Washington Academy of Sciences Journal*, Vol. XLI (September, 1951), 285–90.

Carr, S. J. "Bloomfield and Its Founder," *Chronicles of Oklahoma*, Vol. II (December, 1924), 364–79.

Cassal, Hilary. "Missionary Tour in the Chickasaw Nation and Western Indian Territory," *Chronicles of Oklahoma*, Vol. XXXIV (Winter, 1956–57), 397–416.

Chisholm, Johnnie B. "Harley Institute," *Chronicles of Oklahoma*, Vol. IV (June, 1926), 116–28.

Clark, William. "William Clark's Diary," ed. by Louise Barry, *Kansas Historical Quarterly*, Vol. XVI (May, 1948), 136–74.

Cooper, Douglas. "A Journal Kept by Douglas Cooper on an Expedition by a Company of Chickasaws in Quest of Comanche Indians," ed. by Grant Foreman, *Chronicles of Oklahoma*, Vol. V (December, 1927), 381–90.

Corbitt, D. C. "James Colbert and the Spanish Claims to the East Bank of the Mississippi." *Mississippi Valley Historical Review*, Vol. XXIV (March, 1938), 457–72.

———, and Roberta Corbitt. "Papers from the Spanish Archives Relating to Tennessee and the Old Southwest, 1783–1800," *East Tennessee Historical Society Publications*, (1937–40), 111–142, 312–16, 114–55, 62–93, and 100–117.

Cotterill, Robert S. "The Virginia-Chickasaw Treaty of 1783," *Journal of Southern History*, Vol. VIII (November, 1942), 483–96.

Crane, Verner W. "The Southern Frontier in Queen Anne's War," *American Historical Review*, Vol. XXIV (April, 1919), 379–95.

Davis, Caroline. "Education of the Chickasaws," *Chronicles of Oklahoma*, Vol. XV (December, 1937), 415–48.

Downes, Randolph C. "Cherokee-American Relations in the Upper Tennessee Valley, 1776–1791," *East Tennessee Historical Society Publications* (1936), 35–53.

Firebaugh, R. M. "Religious History of the Chickasaws," *Presbyterian Survey*, Vol. XL (December, 1949), 561–63.

Foreman, Carolyn T. "The Armstrongs of Indian Territory: Part I," *Chronicles of Oklahoma*, Vol. XXX (Autumn, 1952), 292–308.

———. "The Armstrongs of Indian Territory: Part II," *Chronicles of Oklahoma*, Vol. XXX (Winter, 1952), 420–53.

———. "Charity Hall," *Chronicles of Oklahoma*, Vol. XI (September, 1933), 912–26.

———. "Chickasaw Manual Labor Academy," *Chronicles of Oklahoma*, Vol. XXIII (Winter, 1945), 338–57.

———. "Education Among the Chickasaw Indians," *Chronicles of Oklahoma*, Vol. XV (June, 1937), 139–65.

———. "Mary C. Greenleaf at Wapanucka Female Manual Labor School," *Chronicles of Oklahoma*, Vol. XXIV (Spring, 1946), 26–39.

———. "Notes on the Chickasaw Light-Horsemen," *Chronicles of Oklahoma*, Vol. XXXIV (Winter, 1956), 484–85.

Foreman, Grant. "The California Overland Mail Route Through Oklahoma," *Chronicles of Oklahoma*, Vol. IX (September, 1931), 300–17.

———. "Early Post Offices in Oklahoma," *Chronicles of Oklahoma*, Vol. VI (March, 1928), 4–25.

Graebner, Norman A. "Cattle Ranching in Eastern Oklahoma," *Chronicles of Oklahoma*, Vol. XXI (September, 1943), 300–11.

———. "Pioneer Indian Agriculture in Oklahoma," *Chronicles of Oklahoma*, Vol. XXIII (Autumn, 1945), 232–48.

———. "The Public Land Policy of the Five Civilized Tribes," *Chronicles of Oklahoma*, Vol. XXIII (Summer, 1945), 107–18.

Halbert, H. S. "Shatola: Notes on a Chickasaw Town Name," *Proceedings of the Mississippi Valley Historical Association* (1914–15), 93–94.

Hamer, Philip M. "The British in Canada and the Southern Indians, 1790–1794," *East Tennessee Historical Society Publications* (1930), 107–34.

———. "Letters of Governor William Blount," *East Tennessee Historical Society Publications* (1932), 122–37.

———. "The Wataugans and the Cherokee Indians in 1776," *East Tennessee Historical Society Publications* (1931), 108–26.

Hiemstra, William L. "Choctaws and Chickasaws, 1845–1860." *Chronicles of Oklahoma*, Vol. XXVII (Spring, 1949), 33–40.

———. "Early Presbyterian Missions Among the Choctaw and Chickasaw." *Journal of Mississippi History*, Vol. X (January, 1948), 8–16.

———. "Presbyterian Missionaries and Mission Churches Among the Choctaw and Chickasaw Indians, 1832–1865." *Chronicles of Oklahoma*, Vol. XXVI (Winter, 1948), 459–67.

Holden, J. F. "The B. I. T.: The Story of an Adventure in Railroad

Building," *Chronicles of Oklahoma*, Vol. XI (March, 1933), 637–66.

Hood, Fred. "Twilight of the Confederacy in Indian Territory," *Chronicles of Oklahoma*, Vol. XLI (Winter, 1963), 425–41.

Howard, James H. "Some Chickasaw Fetishes," *Florida Anthropologist*, Vol. XII (March, 1959), 47–55.

James, Parthena L. "Reconstruction in the Chickasaw Nation: The Freedman Problem." *Chronicles of Oklahoma*, Vol. XLV (Spring, 1967), 44–57.

Jennings, Jessie. "Chickasaw and Earlier Indian Cultures of Northeast Mississippi," *Journal of Mississippi History*, Vol. III (July, 1941), 155–226.

Lewis, T. H. "Route of De Soto's Expedition from Taliepacana to Huhasene," *Publications of the Mississippi Historical Society*, Vol. VI (1902), 449–67.

Lien, Arnold J. "The Acquisition of Citizenship by the Native American Indians," *Washington University Studies*, Vol. XIII (October, 1925), 121–79.

Litton, Gaston L. "The Negotiations Leading to the Choctaw-Chickasaw Agreement, January, 1837," *Chronicles of Oklahoma*, Vol. XVIII (December, 1939), 417–27.

McCoy, Isaac. "Journal of Isaac McCoy for the Exploring Expedition of 1828," ed. by Lela Barnes, *Kansas Historical Quarterly*, Vol. V (1936), 227–77.

McDermott, John F., ed. "Isaac McCoy's Second Exploring Trip in 1828," *Kansas Historical Quarterly*, Vol. XIII (February, 1945), 400–62.

Malcolm, John. "Colbert Ferry on the Red River, Chickasaw Nation, Indian Territory, Recollections of John Malcolm," ed. by William B. Morrison, *Chronicles of Oklahoma*, Vol. XVI (September, 1938), 302–14.

Mashburn, Judge John H. "Chickasaw Courts, Reminiscences of Judge John H. Mashburn," ed. by Czarina C. Conlan, *Chronicles of Oklahoma*, Vol. V (December, 1927), 400–404.

Meserve, John B. "Governor Benjamin F. Overton and Governor Benjamin C. Burney," *Chronicles of Oklahoma*, Vol. XVI (June, 1938), 221–33.

———. "Governor Cyrus Harris," *Chronicles of Oklahoma*, Vol. XV (December, 1937), 373–86.

———. "Governor Daugherty (Winchester) Colbert," *Chronicles of Oklahoma*, Vol. XVIII (December, 1940), 348–56.

———. "Governor Jonas Wolf and Governor Palmer S. Mosely,"

Chronicles of Oklahoma, Vol. XVIII (September, 1940), 243–51.

———. "Governor Robert M. Harris," *Chronicles of Oklahoma*, Vol. XVII (December, 1939), 361–63.

———. "Governor William Leander Byrd," *Chronicles of Oklahoma*, Vol. XII (December, 1934), 432–43.

———. "Governor William M. Guy," *Chronicles of Oklahoma*, Vol. XIX (March, 1941), 10–13.

Morrison, William B. "Fort Washita," *Chronicles of Oklahoma*, Vol. V (June, 1927), 251–58.

Osborn, George C. "Relations with the Indians in West Florida During the Administration of Governor Peter Chester, 1770–1781," *Florida Historical Quarterly*, Vol. XXXI (April, 1953), 240–72.

Parsons, John, ed. "Letters on the Chickasaw Removal of 1837," *New York Historical Society Quarterly*, Vol. XXXVII (1953), 273–83.

Phelps, Dawson A. "The Chickasaw Agency," *Journal of Mississippi History*, Vol. XIV (April, 1952), 119–37.

———. "The Chickasaw Council House," *Journal of Mississippi History*, Vol. XIV (July, 1952), 170–76.

———. "The Chickasaw Mission," *Journal of Mississippi History*, Vol. XIII (October, 1951), 226–35.

———. "The Chickasaw, the English, and the French." *Tennessee Historical Quarterly*, Vol. XVI (June, 1957), 117–33.

———. "Stands and Travel Accommodations on the Natchez Trace," *Journal of Mississippi History*, Vol. XI (January, 1949), 1–54.

———. "Travel on the Natchez Trace," *Journal of Mississippi History*, Vol. XV (July, 1953), 157–63.

Rainwater, Percy L. "Indian Missions and Missionaries," *Journal of Mississippi History*, Vol. XXVIII (February, 1966), 15–39.

Roff, Joe T. "Early Days in the Chickasaw Nation," *Chronicles of Oklahoma*, Vol. XIII (June, 1935), 169–90.

Scroggs, William O. "Early Trade and Travel in the Lower Mississippi Valley," *Proceedings of the Mississippi Valley Historical Association*, Vol. II (1908), 235–56.

Shirk, George H. "Confederate Postal System in the Indian Territory," *Chronicles of Oklahoma*, Vol. XLI (Summer, 1963), 160–218.

———. "First Post Offices Within the Boundaries of Oklahoma," *Chronicles of Oklahoma*, Vol. XXVI (Summer, 1948), 179–244.

———. "The Place of Indian Territory in the Command Structure of the Civil War," *Chronicles of Oklahoma*, Vol. XLV (Winter, 1967), 464–71.

Siebert, Wilbur H. "The Loyalists in West Florida and the Natchez

District," *Proceedings of the Mississippi Valley Historical Association*, Vol. VIII (1914), 102–22.

Speck, Frank G. "Notes on Chickasaw Ethnology and Folk-Lore," *Journal of American Folk-Lore*, Vol. XX (January–March, 1907), 50–58.

———. "Some Outlines of Aboriginal Culture in the Southeastern United States," *American Anthropologist*, Vol. IX (April–June, 1907), 287–95.

Swanton, John R. "Aboriginal Culture of the Southeast," Bureau of American Ethnology *Forty-second Annual Report* (1928), 673–726.

———. "De Soto's Line of March from the Viewpoint of an Ethnologist," *Proceedings of the Mississippi Valley Historical Association*, Vol. V (1911), 147–57.

———. "Ethnological Problems of the Lower Mississippi Valley," *Proceedings of the Mississippi Valley Historical Association* (1908), 112–27.

———. "Social and Religious Beliefs and Usages of the Chickasaw Indians," Bureau of American Ethnology *Forty-fourth Annual Report* (1928), 169–273.

———. "Social Organization and Social Usages of the Creek Confederacy," Bureau of American Ethnology *Forty-second Annual Report* (1928), 23–472.

"Table of Land Values for Allotment of Lands in the Choctaw and Chickasaw Nations, 1902," *Chronicles of Oklahoma*, Vol. XXIV (Autumn, 1946), 360–62.

Thoburn, Joseph B. "Centennial of the Chickasaw Migration," *Chronicles of Oklahoma*, Vol. XV (December, 1937), 387–91.

Vann, R. P. "Reminiscences of Mr. R. P. Vann, East of Webbers Falls, Oklahoma," ed. by Grant Foreman, *Chronicles of Oklahoma*, Vol. XI (June, 1933), 138–44.

Warren, Harry. "Chickasaw Traditions, Customs, etc.," *Publications of the Mississippi Historical Society*, Vol. VIII (1904), 543–53.

———. "Missions, Missionaries, Frontier Characters and Schools," *Publications of the Mississippi Historical Society*, Vol. VIII (1904), 571–98.

———. "Some Chickasaw Chiefs and Prominent Men," *Publications of the Mississippi Historical Society*, Vol. VIII (1904), 555–70.

West, Elizabeth H. "The Indian Policy of Bernardo de Galvez," *Proceedings of the Mississippi Valley Historical Association* (1914), 95–122.

Williams, Robert L. "Hindman H. Burris, 1862–1940," *Chronicles of Oklahoma*, Vol. XX (June, 1942), 149–51.

Wright, J. B. "Ranching in the Choctaw and Chickasaw Nations," *Chronicles of Oklahoma*, Vol. XXXVII (Autumn, 1959), 294–99.

Wright, Muriel H. "American Indian Corn Dishes," *Chronicles of Oklahoma*, Vol. XXXVI (Summer, 1958), 155–66.

———. "Brief Outline of the Choctaw and Chickasaw Nations in Indian Territory, 1820 to 1860," *Chronicles of Oklahoma*, Vol. VII (December, 1929), 388–418.

———. "Colonel Cooper's Civil War Report on the Battle of Round Mountain," *Chronicles of Oklahoma*, Vol. XXXIX (Winter, 1961), 352–97.

———. "First Oklahoma Oil Was Produced in 1859," *Chronicles of Oklahoma*, Vol. IV (December, 1926), 322–28.

———. "General Douglas H. Cooper, C.S.A.," *Chronicles of Oklahoma*, Vol. XXXII (Summer, 1954), 142–84.

———. "The Great Seal of the Chickasaw Nation," *Chronicles of Oklahoma*, Vol. XXXIV (Winter, 1956), 388–91.

———. "Old Boggy Depot," *Chronicles of Oklahoma*, Vol. V (March, 1927), 4–17.

———. "Organization of Counties in the Choctaw and Chickasaw Nations," *Chronicles of Oklahoma*, Vol. VIII (September, 1930), 315–34.

———. "Review of Chickasaw Education Before the Civil War," *Chronicles of Oklahoma*, Vol. XXXIV (Winter, 1956), 486–87.

———. "Wapanucka Academy, Chickasaw Nation," *Chronicles of Oklahoma*, Vol. XII (December, 1934), 402–31.

Index

with France, 39, 42, 45; horses of, 42, 229; attempts of Spain and United States to negotiate with, 75; Virginia treaty with (1783), 76; treaty with Spain (1784), 77, 78; and Treaty of Hopewell (1786), 77, 78–79, 81, 91, 103; and 1801 treaty, 99–100, 103, 150–51; and 1816 treaty with United States, 100–101, 104, 139, 141; and 1818 treaty with United States, 100–103, 105; land cessions of, 103; agents of, 146, 154; and Treaty of Doaksville (1837), 158–59, 178, 192, 249, 254; and Franklin Treaty (1830), 172, 173; emigration of, 182–84, 187, 193, 216; removal of, 214; ancient society of, 216, 230, 238, 243; 1843 peace treaty with other tribes, 223; dwellings of, 231; Committee of Vigilance of, 247, 252; 1855 treaty with Choctaws, 254–55; courts of, 256; counties owned by, 256; treaties with Confederacy of, 261, 264, 272; national fund of, 261, 264, 297–98; legislature of, 271, 280, 289, 292, 294; Civil War peace treaties of, 273–76; Reconstruction treaties of (1866), 277–78, 290–91; governors of listed, 297–98; Progressive Party of, 298; National Party of, 299

Chickasaw Intelligencer: 231

Chickasaw Male Academy: 280

Chickasaw mixed bloods: 39, 64–65, 80, 106, 112, 116, 142, 146, 153, 158, 165, 168, 225, 232, 238, 245, 259, 287, 298, 301, 306

Chickasaw Old Fields: 6, 10, 63

Chickasaw Old Town: 149

Choctaw Academy and Mission: 109, 231

Choctaw and Chickasaw Mounted Rifles: 265

Choctaw-Chickasaw Baptist Association: 282

Choctaw-Chickasaw Citizenship Court: 306

Choctaw District: 217, 223, 231, 235

Choctaw Indians: 3, 35, 38, 40, 42, 44, 47, 49, 59, 66, 77, 79, 81, 86, 92, 97, 114, 156, 158, 162, 165, 167, 219, 225, 231, 233, 259, 262, 264, 270, 272, 274, 283, 285, 289, 294, 297, 300, 305, 309; mercenaries, 43; set-

tlements of, 184; constitution of, 242; council of, 242, 289

Choctaw Intelligencer: 231

Choctaw Nation: 38, 44, 92, 96, 217, 220, 240, 242, 249, 254, 258, 265, 267, 272, 279

Choctaw Telegraph: 231

Choctaw Trading House: 95

Chokkillisar, Chickasaw Nation: 96

Choquafaliah (Chickasaw district): 153

Chukafalaya: 6, 22

Chunkey (Chickasaw game): 18

Churches: 281

Chustenalah, Okla.: 267

Chusto Talasah, Okla.: 266

Cimarron River: 266

Civil War: 141, 260, 269, 283, 292

Clark, George Rogers: 72

Clark, Major S. N.: 291

Clark, William: 160, 162, 165

Clear Boggy River: 191, 235

Cocke, William: 93

Coffee, John: 102, 162, 165, 171, 175

Colbert, Benjamin Franklin: 226

Colbert, Carter: 275

Colbert, George: 96, 99, 150

Colbert, Holmes: 264, 275

Colbert, James: 72, 101, 150

Colbert, James Logan: 65

Colbert, Levi: 110, 142, 153, 161, 163, 166–67, 172, 174, 178, 217

Colbert, Pittman: 227, 245

Colbert, William: 98

Colbert, Winchester: 249, 258, 264, 268–69, 271, 273, 275, 280

Colbert family: 80, 87, 99, 142, 150, 159, 190, 225, 246, 250, 284, 307

Colbert Institute: 235

Colbert's Chickasaw Company: 73

Colbert's Ferry: 97, 101, 226

Coleraine, Ga.: 94

Columbus, Christopher: 264

Comanche Indians: 191, 220–21, 272, 297

Confederate States of America: 244, 259, 261, 264, 267, 276, 278–79; alliance with Indians of, 259, 262, 271; treaties of, 264; Army of, 264, 279; troops of, 265; War Department of, 268; agents of, 270; exiles of, 270; refugee depots of, 270; tribes allied with, 272–73

Confederation Congress: 77

Contractors: 193, 297

Index

French Colonial Office: 50, 53
French Company of the Indies: 47
French Lick: 76
French Party (Chickasaw Nation): 37, 42, 48, 70, 74–75, 80
Frisco Railroad: 284
Frontier taverns: 230
Full bloods: *see* Chickasaw full bloods

Gage, General Thomas: 71
Gaines, General Edmund P.: 148
Gaines, George P.: 162
Gaines' Trace: 148
Galvez, Bernardo de: 73
Gamble, James: 264
General Allotment Act: 300
General Conference of the Methodist Episcopal Church: 234
Georgia: 6, 53, 64, 82, 84, 91
Gleason, Anson: 114
Good Spring Baptist Church: 232
Grand River: 267
Great Britain: 56, 58, 73–74, 77, 82
Great Charleston-Chickasaw Trail: 148
Great Plains: 6
Guion, Isaac: 90
Gunn, James: 108, 140
Guy, Governor William M.: 298–99

Halwill Regiment: 52
Hargrove College: 282
Harney, General William S.: 273
Harper, Kenton: 224, 244
Harris, A. (sutler): 196
Harris, Governor Cyrus: 136, 257, 261, 271, 280, 297–98
Harris, Governor Robert M.: 298
Harrison and Glasgow Company: 193, 195
Hatsboro, Okla.: 225
Hawkins, Benjamin: 79, 103
Herron, General F. J.: 273
Hickeyubbee: 298
High Minko (Chickasaw principal chief): 18, 21
Hill, William: 93
Hinds, Thomas: 162, 165
Hitchcock, Major Ethan Allen: 196, 214, 219, 229, 242
Hogue, Rev. R. J.: 232
Holland, Rev. James: 111
Hopaye (Beloved Holy Men): 12–13, 17, 19
Hottuk Ishtohoollo (Chickasaw deity): 10

Hottuk Ookproose (Chickasaw deity): 10
Howell's Texas Battery: 268
Humphries, Rev. David: 110
Hunter, William: 265
Hunters: Chickasaw, 8, 25, 143

Iberville, Pierre Le Moyne d': 34, 38
Ibitoupa Indians: 64
Illinois country: 42, 47–48, 50, 54, 58, 62–63, 70
Imosaktca (Chickasaw moiety): 18–19
Indian captives: 40; *see also* Indian slaves
Indian Civilization Law: 109
Indian Mission Conference: 234
Indian Presbytery: 233
Indian Removal Act: 169
Indian slaves: 7, 28, 41, 43; traffic in, 40
Indian Territory: 189–90, 192, 194, 196, 215, 228, 232, 244, 259, 261–62, 265, 268–70, 272–73, 279, 283, 285, 294–95, 300–301, 303–304, 309
Indian Territory Methodist Conference: 281
Intcukwalipa (Chickasaw moiety): 18–19
Intemperance: 134
Intermarried whites: 307
International Councils: 296
Intertribal trade: 32
Intruders: 140, 154, 285, 292
Iroquois Indians: 48, 51
Ishehahtubby (Chickasaw leader): 223
Ishtehotopa (Chickasaw king): 174, 188, 245
Island Bayou: 232
Iyaganashas (Chickasaw religious being): 10, 14

Jackson, Andrew: 97, 99–100, 102, 104, 170, 172, 174
Jefferson, Thomas: 72, 94, 104
Johnston, Governor Douglas H.: 298
Johnstone, Governor George: 60, 66, 69, 107
Joliet-Marquette party: 33
Jones, Robert M.: 274

Kansas: 227, 229
Karmer Grenadier Regiment: 52
Kaskaskia, Illinois country: 51, 70
Kaskaskia Indians: 51
Keechi Indians: 223